"Kevin Chen has given us here a bold, fresh, groundbreaking study on how to understand the Pentateuch in the light of Jesus, Israel's promised Messiah. A nail in the coffin of Marcion's ghost! An important book worthy of serious engagement."
Timothy George, research professor at Beeson Divinity School of Samford University and general editor of the Reformation Commentary on Scripture

"Years ago I set out to understand the meaning of the Pentateuch as a follower of Jesus. After reading several commentaries on each of the books of the Pentateuch, I was disappointed to find precious little comment by scholars on the Messianic hope, suggesting to me that the Messiah had little if any place in the scholarly discussion of the grammatical-historical interpretation of the book. Dr. Chen's book represents a persuasive scholarly defense of Messianism as part and parcel of the literal meaning of the Pentateuch. I highly commend this book for laymen and scholars alike."
Seth D. Postell, academic dean, Israel College of the Bible, Netanya, Israel

"In this carefully researched work, Kevin Chen insightfully adapts and expands the methodology of John Sailhamer to illuminate the meaning of the Messianic vision of the Pentateuch. This widely engaging book contends that the network of Messianic prophecies found in the writings of Moses can be understood as a complex array or interrelated lenses designed and intended to project a coherent, sweeping vision of the Messiah at the center of their theological message. While wrestling with an array of complex hermeneutical issues associated with his approach, Chen thoughtfully contends that these intertextual relationships point to the presence of an authorially intended, unified Messianic theology in the Pentateuch. Offering perspective on matters of prophecy, typology, progressive revelation, and repetition, this volume offers readers much to consider with the hope of enabling biblical interpreters to read, understand, teach, and proclaim the Word of God in a more coherent and faithful manner."
David S. Dockery, president, Trinity International University/Trinity Evangelical Divinity School

"Evangelicals and other Christians often champion a 'Christ-centered' approach to the Old Testament, but there is no consensus on what this actually means. Building on the groundbreaking work of the late John Sailhamer, Kevin Chen offers a vision of the Pentateuch that grounds its messianic (Christ-centered) identity in the authorial intent of Moses and any subsequent (inspired) editors rather than in later (re-)interpretations by New Testament authors or later Christian theologians. The result is a messianic vision of the Pentateuch that is text-driven and spiritually compelling, and makes a needed contribution to the discussion about how the Old Testament ought to be interpreted. Even scholars who opt for a different approach will benefit from deep, open-minded engagement with the methodological questions Chen raises in this helpful book."
Nathan A. Finn, provost and dean of the university faculty at North Greenville University

"This wonderful book substantiates the claim that Moses wrote of Christ. It presents an abundance of textual and intertextual evidence from key passages including the major poetic sections of Genesis 49, Exodus 15, Numbers 23–24, and Deuteronomy 32–33. Kevin Chen demonstrates that the Pentateuch has been strategically composed to reflect and refract a radiant Messianic light into the rest of the Old Testament and the New Testament. I hope and pray this book is read widely and carefully."

Joshua G. Mathews, professor, Western Seminary, Portland, Oregon

"Stepping on the shoulders of his mentor John Sailhamer, Kevin Chen has charted his own course in showing the importance of the Messiah to the Pentateuch. Particularly clear is his reinforcement and solidification of Sailhamer's distinction between the Pentateuch and Sinai/Deuteronomic Law. The Pentateuch's message is Gospel, as it looks to the future salvation of the Messiah. While scholars will not always agree with Chen's conclusions, his writing is clear, insightful, stimulating, and well researched. Using apt illustrations, Chen challenges us to take a new look at old texts, and the results speak for themselves."

Stephen G. Dempster, professor of religious studies, Crandall University

The MESSIANIC VISION of the PENTATEUCH

KEVIN S. CHEN

An imprint of InterVarsity Press
Downers Grove, Illinois

InterVarsity Press
P.O. Box 1400, Downers Grove, IL 60515-1426
ivpress.com
email@ivpress.com

©2019 by Kevin S. Chen

All rights reserved. No part of this book may be reproduced in any form without written permission from InterVarsity Press.

InterVarsity Press® is the book-publishing division of InterVarsity Christian Fellowship/USA®, a movement of students and faculty active on campus at hundreds of universities, colleges, and schools of nursing in the United States of America, and a member movement of the International Fellowship of Evangelical Students. For information about local and regional activities, visit intervarsity.org.

All Scripture quotations, unless otherwise indicated, are the author's own translation.

Cover design and image composite: David Fassett
Cover images: Christ/cross sculpture: © filipe_lopes / iStock / Getty Images Plus
　　　　　　　statue of Moses: © Georgy Rozov / EyeEm / Getty Images
　　　　　　　wavy paper: © Colormos / DigitalVision / Getty Images
Interior design: Daniel van Loon
Interior images: Prism light rays © Nataniil / DigitalVision Vectors / Getty Images

ISBN 978-0-8308-5264-2 (print)
ISBN 978-0-8308-5797-5 (digital)

InterVarsity Press is committed to ecological stewardship and to the conservation of natural resources in all our operations. This book was printed using sustainably sourced paper.

Library of Congress Cataloging-in-Publication Data
Names: Chen, Kevin, 1979- author.
Title: The Messianic vision of the Pentateuch / Kevin S. Chen.
Description: Westmont : InterVarsity Press, 2019. | Includes
　 bibliographical references and index.
Identifiers: LCCN 2019036618 (print) | LCCN 2019036619 (ebook) | ISBN
　 9780830852642 (paperback) | ISBN 9780830857975 (ebook)
Subjects: LCSH: Bible. Pentateuch—Theology. | Jesus Christ.
Classification: LCC BS1225.6.M44 C44 2019 (print) | LCC BS1225.6.M44
　 (ebook) | DDC 222/.106—dc23
LC record available at https://lccn.loc.gov/2019036618
LC ebook record available at https://lccn.loc.gov/2019036619

| P | 25 | 24 | 23 | 22 | 21 | 20 | 19 | 18 | 17 | 16 | 15 | 14 | 13 | 12 | 11 | 10 | 9 | 8 | 7 | 6 | 5 | 4 | 3 | 2 | 1 |
| Y | 37 | 36 | 35 | 34 | 33 | 32 | 31 | 30 | 29 | 28 | 27 | 26 | 25 | 24 | 23 | 22 | 21 | 20 | 19 |

To my wife, Joyce

With great appreciation

for how our marriage parallels Genesis 24:58

CONTENTS

Preface	*ix*
Acknowledgments	*xi*
Abbreviations	*xiii*
Introduction	*1*
1 The Seed of the Woman	*35*
2 The Seed of Abraham in the Patriarchal Narratives	*67*
3 The Lion of Judah	*108*
4 Passover and the Song of the Sea	*145*
5 Shadows at Sinai	*169*
6 The Bronze Snake and Balaam's Oracles	*199*
7 The Prophet Like Moses	*224*
8 The Blessing of Judah	*247*
9 The Repeated Breaking of the Sinai/Deuteronomic Law	*270*
Conclusion	*287*
Bibliography	*291*
Author Index	*305*
Subject Index	*309*
Scripture Index	*317*

PREFACE

Although written without assuming all readers would notice, this book is an attempt to continue and extend the work of John H. Sailhamer. Thankfully, such a task falls not to one person or one book but to all who were influenced by him, especially those of us who are so privileged to be teaching or writing. Many of his former students have become fine teacher-scholars and are quite accomplished, even more so than I am. I am grateful to have studied with some of them and to have them as friends and conversation partners. As just one voice in a broader conversation, I consider it a tremendous honor that IVP Academic, which published Sailhamer's *magnum opus* ten years ago (*The Meaning of the Pentateuch*, 2009), has seen fit to publish a follow-up book written by someone still relatively early in his career (Lord willing). Part of the impetus for this book is that Sailhamer's two major works on the Pentateuch (the other being *The Pentateuch as Narrative*), while certainly emphasizing the centrality of the Messiah in the Pentateuch, necessarily also deal with other issues at length, especially the Sinai/Deuteronomic law. I felt that it would be helpful to produce a work that almost exclusively focuses on the Messiah in the Pentateuch and gives more extensive treatment of the Pentateuch's Messianic texts, including several that have not commonly been understood as such.

Familiarity with Sailhamer's work is not required to understand this book, but those who are familiar with it will quickly recognize that this book follows the general path that he trod, especially with respect to methodology and overall interpretation of the Pentateuch based on its structure and key poetic texts. At the same time, careful comparison would reveal that this book differs exegetically from his views at some key points (e.g., Gen 3:15) and goes significantly further at others (e.g.,

Gen 27:27-29; 49:8-12). As such, I do not expect that Sailhamer would have agreed with some of my conclusions. Of course, if it were my goal to follow him at every point, then this book would be unnecessary. That I have followed him at key places shows that I have often found his arguments convincing. At the same time, I have discovered other things in the Pentateuch that I believe fill out its Messianic vision even further. Sailhamer himself once remarked to me that he believed there was still much to be discovered in the Pentateuch. I hope I have discovered some of those things. Until that day when its Messianic vision is fully realized and the work of every person is tested by fire (1 Cor 3:13), it will be up to each reader to decide the extent to which I have faithfully set forth the Messianic vision of the Pentateuch.

ACKNOWLEDGMENTS

I would like to thank my former institution, Union University, for providing a semester-long sabbatical leave in 2017, during which I completed the first draft of the manuscript. My colleagues there in the School of Theology and Missions (and formerly Christian Studies), some of whom have moved on to other pursuits, have been a great encouragement. The collegial environment and its wonderful balance of Christian fellowship, excellent teaching, and quality scholarship have been formative during the past nine years. Southeastern Seminary was gracious to host me for two months of my sabbatical and allow me the full use of their library, which resulted in a highly productive time. Although he is no longer with us, my late doctoral adviser, Dr. John H. Sailhamer, deserves acknowledgment for the way his example, teaching, scholarship, and encouragement have shaped me. I would like to thank Jon Boyd and his team at IVP Academic for believing in this book and in me. Thank you to my parents for their constant encouragement. My brother Chris Chen and my friend Seth Postell have provided helpful feedback on portions of earlier versions of this book. Finally, I would like to thank my wife, Joyce, for her constant support, and I lovingly dedicate this book to her. I hope you find the Messianic vision of the Pentateuch as captivating as I do.

ABBREVIATIONS

ASV	American Standard Version
BDAG	Bauer, W., F. W. Danker, W. F. Arndt, and F. W. Gingrich. *Greek-English Lexicon of the New Testament and Other Early Christian Literature*. 3rd ed. Chicago, 1999
BDB	Brown, F., S. R. Driver, and C. A. Briggs. *A Hebrew and English Lexicon of the Old Testament*. Oxford, 1907
BibInt	*Biblical Interpretation*
BSac	*Bibliotheca Sacra*
BN	*Biblische Notizen*
CBQ	*Catholic Biblical Quarterly*
CSB	Christian Standard Bible
ESV	English Standard Version
ETL	*Ephemerides theologicae lovanienses*
GKC	*Gesenius' Hebrew Grammar*. Edited by E. Kautzsch. Translated by A. E. Cowley. 2nd. ed. Oxford, 1910
HALOT	Koehler, L., W. Baumgartner, and J. J. Stamm. *The Hebrew and Aramaic Lexicon of the Old Testament*. Translated and edited under the supervision of M. E. J. Richardson. 4 vols. Leiden, 1994–1999
Heb.	Hebrew
Hiph.	Hiphil
Hith.	Hithpael
JANES	*Journal of the Ancient Near Eastern Society*
JBL	*Journal of Biblical Literature*
JETS	*Journal of the Evangelical Theological Society*
JNES	*Journal of Near Eastern Studies*
JPS	Jewish Publication Society

JSOT	*Journal for the Study of the Old Testament*
KJV	King James Version
LA	*Liber annuus*
LS	*Louvain Studies*
LXX	Septuagint
MT	Masoretic Text
NASB	New American Standard Bible
NEB	New English Bible
Niph.	Niphal
NIV	New International Version
NKJV	New King James Version
NovT	*Novum Testamentum*
RSB	*Religious Studies Bulletin*
RSV	Revised Standard Version
SBJT	*Southern Baptist Journal of Theology*
SJOT	*Scandinavian Journal of the Old Testament*
TJT	*Toronto Journal of Theology*
TynBul	*Tyndale Bulletin*
VT	*Vetus Testamentum*
WTJ	*Westminster Theological Journal*
ZAW	*Zeitschrift für die alttestamentliche Wissenschaft*

INTRODUCTION

DID MOSES WRITE ABOUT JESUS?

"If you believed in Moses, you would believe in me; for he wrote about me" (Jn 5:46). Jesus made this bold statement after healing a paralyzed man and telling him to take up his mat and walk (Jn 5:5-8). However, since he did these things on the Sabbath, many from among the Jewish people were offended to the point of persecuting him (Jn 5:9-10, 16). In the face of such zeal for observing the laws of Moses, Jesus responded that reading Moses' writings (i.e., Genesis–Deuteronomy, or the "Pentateuch") should have persuaded them instead to believe in him as the Son of God and the Christ (see Jn 5:18; 20:31). Nevertheless, they rejected Jesus despite several reliable sources of testimony (Jn 5:32-38), including the Scriptures that they had so diligently studied (Jn 5:39-40).[1] Consequently, Jesus declared that they had actually failed to "believe [Moses'] writings" (Jn 5:47). This implies that, despite their study of this foundational text and devotion to Moses (Jn 5:45), they had both misunderstood the Pentateuch and misconstrued their relationship to the great prophet and lawgiver.[2] Their dedication to

---

[1] Also including John the Baptist (Jn 5:32-35), Jesus' works themselves (Jn 5:36), and God the Father (Jn 5:37-38).

[2] Rudolf Schnackenburg, *The Gospel According to St. John*, trans. Cecily Hastings et al. (New York: Crossroad, 1982), 2:129, calls Moses "a witness to Jesus through his writings." This is not only true for the passage about the "prophet like Moses" (Deut 18:15-18) because "the reference may be to all the writings of Moses (the Pentateuch), since γράμματα has this meaning elsewhere. . . . Those who were learned in the Scriptures (cf. 7:15) should, more than anyone, have been convinced through their study of them that Jesus was the Messiah promised by Moses." See also D. A. Carson, *The Gospel According to John*, Pillar New Testament Commentary (Grand Rapids: Eerdmans, 1991), 266, who is followed by Andreas Köstenberger, *John*, Baker Exegetical Commentary on the New Testament (Grand Rapids: Baker, 2004), 195. These two scholars agree that unbelieving Jews had misunderstood the Pentateuch but in the sense that they treated it as "an end in itself" rather than as pointing to Christ. Carson thinks that Deut 18:15 may be in view but that "it is perhaps more likely that this verse is referring to a certain *way* of reading the books of Moses." Köstenberger adds that the OT has a "prophetic orientation towards Jesus" and a "correspondence" to

Moses, though intensely passionate, was misguided because it was coupled with a rejection of the Messiah concerning whom he had written. In the context of avoiding unnecessary offense to Jewish people who were deeply committed to the laws of the Pentateuch, Acts 15:21 accordingly characterizes Jewish synagogues as traditionally "preaching [Moses]."[3] Though common both then and now, such a law-focused interpretation of the Pentateuch contrasts not only with Jesus but also Paul, who regularly preached the gospel from this same text (Acts 13:39; 26:22-23; 28:23) and from the other Old Testament Scriptures (Acts 17:2-3, 11).

Following another healing miracle by Jesus on the Sabbath, this time of a man born blind, the Pharisees concluded that he was not from God because he did not keep the Sabbath. The problem with their verdict, however, was that if Jesus were truly a "sinner," he could not have done such "signs" (Jn 9:16). God would not have listened to him, especially regarding this unprecedented healing miracle (Jn 9:31-33; 3:2). Nevertheless, the Pharisees' words to the man who could now see ("You are his disciple, but we are disciples of Moses"; Jn 9:28) show that they had driven a wedge between being a disciple of Moses and a disciple of Jesus. For them, it was impossible to be a faithful follower of Moses and a follower of Jesus simultaneously. The underlying reason for this was that they equated faithfulness to Moses and his writings with fastidious attention to keeping Pentateuchal laws, and Jesus, though himself a keeper of these laws, sometimes understood such "law keeping" very differently than they did (see Jn 7:23; Mt 12:3-12; Lk 14:5). In their minds, so sharp was the divide that they threatened expulsion from the synagogue for all who confessed Jesus as Messiah (Jn 9:22).[4]

Jesus' teaching. As it relates to the Messianic message of the Pentateuch, it is unclear whether their positions go as far as Schnackenburg's, which emphasizes Moses' "positive role" as a witness to Jesus (Schnackenburg, *John*, 1:277n217).

[3]See Darrell Bock, *Acts*, Baker Exegetical Commentary on the New Testament (Grand Rapids: Baker, 2007), 507; John Stott, *The Message of Acts*, The Bible Speaks Today (Downers Grove, IL: InterVarsity Press, 1994), 248; Craig S. Keener, *Acts: An Exegetical Commentary* (Grand Rapids: Baker, 2014), 3:2279.

[4]Bertold Klappert, "'Mose hat von mir geschrieben': Leitlinien einer Christologie im Kontext des Judentums Joh 5,39-47," in *Die Hebräische Bibel und ihre zweifache Nachgeschichte: Festschrift für Rolf Rendtorff zum 65. Geburstag*, ed. Erhard Blum et al. (Neukirchen-Vluyn: Neukirchener, 1990), 619-40, characterizes the Sabbath controversy as an "inner-Jewish conflict" (*innerjüdischen Konflikt*) concerning whether casuistic Sabbath tradition or love for fellow man has higher

Jesus' words in John 5:45-46, however, indicate that such a sharp distinction should not have been made. On the contrary, the expected response to a proper understanding of Moses' writings was actually faith in Jesus as the promised Messiah ("if you believed in Moses, you would believe in me").[5] Philip, one of Jesus' early disciples and a believing Jew, recognized this very truth when he told Nathanael, "We have found the one that Moses wrote about in the Law and the prophets wrote about as well" (Jn 1:45). Evidently, Philip experienced little of the cognitive dissonance and theological struggle that the unbelieving Jews did in reconciling Moses and Jesus (see Jn 9:16). Philip's words further imply that he already had Messianic expectations that had been formed by the Pentateuch and the prophets, even before he had met Jesus (Jn 1:43). As Wilhelm Vischer has said, "The Old Testament tells us *what* the Christ is; the New, *who* he is."[6] The particular difference between Philip and these Jews, then, had to do with rival interpretations of the Pentateuch.[7] Accordingly, Gentile outsiders in the book of Acts who observed similar theological debates

---

priority (623-24). His reference to the Jewish-Christian minority that had been expelled from the synagogue relates to this same conflict (639). Whereas he dates this conflict to the end of the first century (presumably based on the accepted date for the writing of the Gospel of John), those who hold to the historical accuracy of Scripture can affirm that this conflict took place even earlier during Jesus' earthly life.

[5]Klappert, "Mose hat von mir geschrieben," 634-36, emphasizes the "correspondence" (*Entsprechung*) between Moses and Jesus, which contrasts with the more familiar Law-Gospel "antithesis" (*Antithese*). For starters, Moses performed "signs" (אֹתוֹת, LXX σημεῖα) that led to a deliverance, and likewise Jesus' "signs" (σημεῖα) led to an eschatological deliverance. Furthermore, just as Moses' signs led to Israel believing "in the LORD and in Moses his servant" (Ex 14:31), so Jesus' signs were intended to give genuine knowledge of "you, the only true God and Jesus Christ whom you have sent" (Jn 17:3).

[6]Wilhelm Vischer, *The Witness of the Old Testament to Christ*, trans. A. B. Crabtree (London: Lutterworth, 1949), 1:7, emphasis original. Klappert, "Mose hat von mir geschrieben," 628, cites a slightly different form of this quote, instead referencing H. J. Iwand. Vischer continues, "He alone knows Jesus who recognizes Him as the Christ, and he alone knows what the Christ is who knows that He is Jesus."

[7]This is further demonstrated through the differing views on Jesus' identity expressed in Jn 7:40-42, both of which make reference to the OT. This led to a "division" (σχίσμα) among the crowd concerning Jesus (Jn 7:43; see Jn 9:16; 10:19). The Pharisees in turn despised the crowd's more positive appraisal of Jesus (Jn 7:31) and viewed them as those who "do not know the Law" (Jn 7:49). Commenting on Jesus' sweeping claim in Jn 5:39 that the Scriptures bear witness of him, Schnackenburg, *John*, 2:127, says that it "amounts to a brief statement of the Christian community's understanding of Scripture as opposed to the use of Scripture in Judaism. It reflects the controversy between Christianity and Judaism in the evangelist's own day [and for evangelicals, in Jesus'] and later. . . . This represents a high-point in the Christological interpretation of Scripture in primitive Christianity [and for evangelicals, by Jesus himself]."

repeatedly referred to them as "controversial questions" (ζητήματά) concerning Jewish law and religion (Acts 18:15; 23:29; 25:19-20; cf. 26:3).

There is no denying, of course, that Moses did give the Sinai (and Deuteronomic) law to Israel, a fact that Jesus himself acknowledged (Jn 7:19-23; 1:17). But the Pentateuch also describes Moses as having lifted up a serpent in the wilderness, which foreshadowed Jesus' saving death on the cross (Jn 3:14; see chap. 6 below). Moses also predicted the coming of a prophet like himself in the future (Deut 18:15-18), who some held to be the same person as the Messiah (Jn 6:14-15; see chap. 7 below). Thus the contentious issue regarding the interpretation of the Pentateuch back then and ever since is not whether the Pentateuch gives extensive attention to the Sinai/Deuteronomic law but how these laws relate to the important theme of the Messiah. Is the main point of the Pentateuch the giving of the Sinai/Deuteronomic law and the importance of keeping it, with Messianic passages playing a secondary role? Or is it the other way around? Or are these two themes equally important in a "both-and" sort of way? To put it differently, what does the Pentateuch as a unified literary whole really *mean*, especially with respect to the Sinai/Deuteronomic law and Messiah?[8] Does the author of the Pentateuch present one instead of the other as central to salvation, or does he set forth both equally? Arising from different interpretations of this foundational text, the aforementioned Jews who rejected Jesus emphasized a particular conception of "law keeping" (which was mixed with human traditions; see Mk 7:13), whereas Jesus and his disciples, who were also Jews, held the Messiah to be central to the Pentateuch, even as they upheld the laws but saw them as having a secondary role in the divine plan (e.g., Mt 19:8). Whichever center was chosen necessarily excluded the other, and the interactions between these two groups cited above have already shown that there was no "both-and" solution, no middle ground.[9] To believe in Jesus was to be put out of the synagogue (Jn 9:22, 35-38).

---

[8]See John Sailhamer, *The Meaning of the Pentateuch: Revelation, Composition, and Interpretation* (Downers Grove, IL: InterVarsity Press, 2009); James Todd III, *Sinai and the Saints: Reading Old Covenant Laws for the New Covenant Community* (Downers Grove, IL: InterVarsity Press, 2017), 82-85.
[9]The book of Galatians is also a strong argument against a "both-and" view of the Sinai/Deuteronomic law and Christ.

The natural question that arises for readers of Scripture is how Jesus and the disciples understood the Pentateuch to center on the Messiah. Is not far more attention given to the laws? Even the casual reader comes away from the Pentateuch with a strong impression of the number of laws (613 according to the traditional count) and the importance of keeping them. At first glance, it is hard to conceive of the primary purpose of the Pentateuch as being anything other than keeping the Sinai/Deuteronomic law. However, there is more to the picture. For starters, Jesus, who was certainly aware of the Pentateuch's repeated charges to keep its laws, pointed out that "none of you keeps the Law" (Jn 7:19),[10] which was true not only for those whom Jesus was addressing but for the human race generally (Is 24:5-6; Rom 3:9, 19-20; 11:32). The issue then is not simply the importance of God's laws, but the reality of our inevitable failure to observe them. As is well-known, there are serious consequences for breaking divine laws, including curse and death (Deut 27:26; Ezek 18:20). Since both disobedience and divine wrath are certain, zeal for law-keeping and even our best efforts, by themselves, are a dead end (see Rom 10:2) because they never result in actual, perfect law keeping. Even the sacrificial system itself was apparently unable to turn away divine wrath in certain situations (Ex 32:10-14; Num 14:12, 29; 15:30; 25:11; 1 Sam 3:14; Ps 51:16-17 [MT vv. 18-19]). Taking a different angle on this theological controversy, Jesus also perceptively linked the objections of those who did not believe in him to a greater desire for glory from men than from God (Jn 5:41-44; 11:47-48; 12:42-43; see Rom 2:23; 3:27).

Messianic Prophecy in the Pentateuch as Light Through a Prism

A more thorough treatment of this theological debate must directly deal with the role of the Messiah in the Pentateuch. Along these lines, the purpose of this book is to argue that the Pentateuch itself sets forth an authorially intended, coherent portrait of the Messiah as the center of its theological message. "Authorially intended" refers to both the human author's intent and the divine author's intent, which are held to be one and

---

[10]This will be developed in further detail in chap. 9. Jesus' knowledge of the sinfulness of unbelieving Jews accords with his earlier claim that Moses would accuse them before the Father (Jn 5:45).

the same. While not unprecedented, such a view is uncommon and sometimes unheard of among contemporary readers of the Bible, who often recognize a few Messianic prophecies in the Pentateuch but usually do not see them as part of its central message. Instead, the Pentateuch is taken as a book primarily promoting the Sinai/Deuteronomic law that merely contains a few scattered Messianic prophecies. In other words, the Messiah is in the Pentateuch but on the periphery at best, not the center.

In response, the metaphor of light passing through a prism can be used to illustrate and explain this phenomenon. Indeed, Messianic prophecies in the Pentateuch are not presented to readers all at once, as if they were directly viewing the "white light" that enters a prism (from the left-hand side in figure 1).[11] Instead, these prophecies are scattered, or "dispersed," just as a prism disperses light into its component wavelengths, including the rainbow of colors of the visible spectrum.

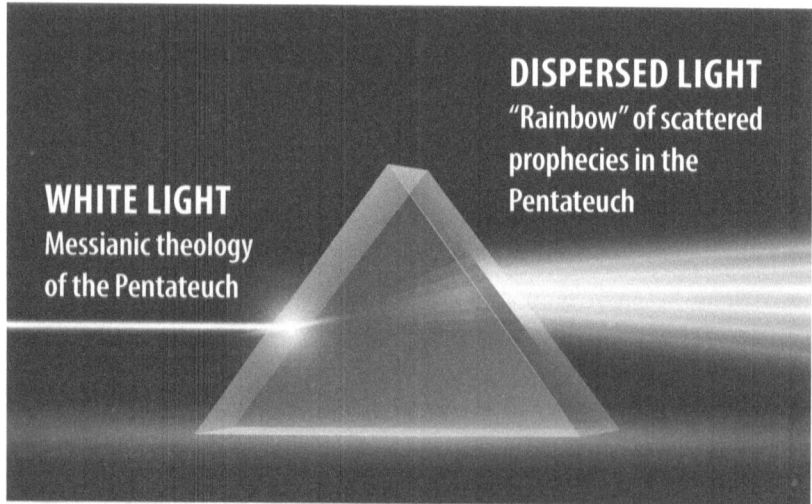

Figure 1. Messianic prophecy as light through a prism

---

[11]"White light" is composed of light from the entire spectrum. The fact that white light passing through a prism disperses not only into visible light (i.e., colors) but also invisible light (such as infrared and ultraviolet) fits with the fact that the Pentateuch does not capture the *full* glory of the Messiah, which would be impossible (Ex 34). For a human being to behold this directly and fully would be like looking directly into the sun, which scientists tell us radiates intense white light.

At the same time, each prophecy, wherever it is found in the Pentateuch, also contributes to the fuller vision of the Messiah that emerges when it is appropriately related to the others and to the Pentateuch as a whole. It is as though readers are being occasionally shown one color after another, accompanied by clues in the text that these colors should be recombined in their mind's eye into a larger picture. These clues typically consist of repeated words and themes but may also include wordplay,[12] similar syntax, or the use of the same literary genre. The more these repetitions converge in two (or more) passages, the more likely the author intends for the reader to relate them and interpret them "intertextually."[13] Although used differently by various scholars, the term *intertextuality* (and its cognates) in the present work concerns, in the words of de Beaugrande and Dressler, "the ways in which the production and reception of a given text depends upon the participants' knowledge of other texts."[14]

To develop the metaphor from the field of optics further, each Messianic prophecy can be treated as a "lens" that combines and focuses select Messianic "wavelengths" or "colors" (i.e., themes). The analogy of

---

[12] For recent treatments of this topic, see Isaac Kalimi, *Metathesis in the Hebrew Bible: Wordplay as a Literary and Exegetical Device* (Peabody, MA: Hendrickson, 2018); Gary Rendsburg, *How the Bible Is Written* (Peabody, MA: Hendrickson, 2019), 358-410. Wordplay can be used by authors to link texts with similar words.

[13] For discussion of criteria for determining the probability of an intentional relationship between two or more texts, see Richard Hays, *Echoes of Scripture in the Letters of Paul* (New Haven, CT: Yale University Press, 1989), 29-33; Benjamin Sommer, "Exegesis, Allusion, and Intertextuality in the Hebrew Bible: A Response to Lyle Eslinger," *VT* 46 (1996): 483-87; Jeffery M. Leonard, "Identifying Inner-Biblical Allusions: Psalm 78 as a Test Case," *JBL* 127 (2008): 241-65.

[14] Robert de Beaugrande and Wolfgang Dressler, *Introduction to Text Linguistics* (New York: Longman, 1981), 182. Likewise they explain that intertextuality "concerns the factors which make the utilization of one text dependent upon knowledge of one or more previously encountered texts" (10). There is certainly controversy over the use of the term *intertextuality*, with some arguing that this term should not be used by biblical scholars in combination with authorial intention because of its different usage by others. See Russell Meeks, "Intertextuality, Inner-Biblical Exegesis, and Inner-Biblical Allusion: The Ethics of a Methodology," *Biblica* 95 (2014): 280-91. Nevertheless, we do not see sufficient reason to abandon the term so long as it is clearly defined and used accordingly. Though defining intertextuality more broadly as including non-textual things such as artifacts and ruins, Peter Leithart, *Deep Exegesis: The Mystery of Reading Scripture* (Waco, TX: Baylor University Press, 2009), 117-18, rightly notes that a competent interpreter "brings knowledge of earlier portions of the text he is interpreting, as well as knowledge of other texts, and these also shed light on the particular text he is studying." If he is right that "every great writer, and many lesser ones, knew of other works in that tradition and wrote against the background of that tradition," then intentional intertextuality should be expected within the OT.

a lens is not being used here of something that the human eye looks through but instead of something that focuses incident light rays (see figure 2). The themes present in a particular Messianic prophecy are never the full "spectrum" but always a subset of the whole and are often selected in relation to the preceding narrative context of the particular passage. Each Messianic prophecy or "lens" is thus uniquely designed and has a unique "output." The number of themes present in a particular Messianic prophecy varies from one prophecy to another. Naturally, the longer prophecies will tend to combine more "colors" than the shorter ones.

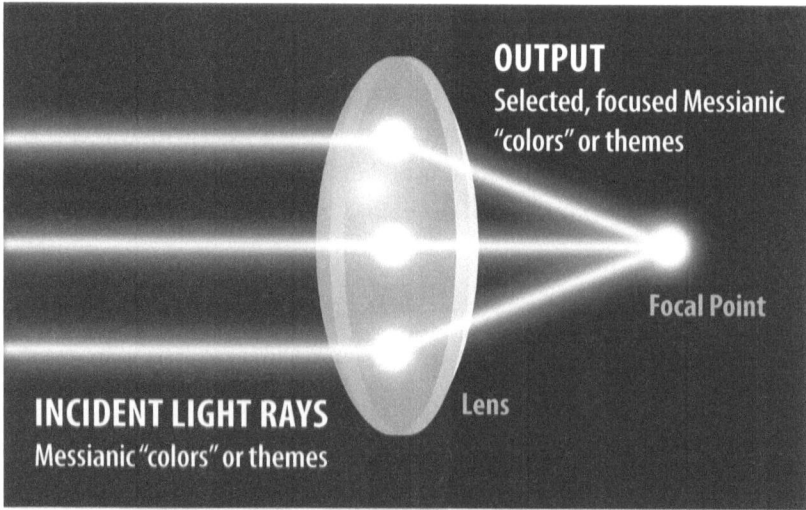

Figure 2. Messianic lens and focal point

Furthermore, such light that passes through one lens, such as Genesis 3:15 (the "seed of the woman" prophecy), is often picked up by another lens that appears later in the Pentateuch, such as Genesis 12:3 ("in you will all the families of the earth be blessed"; note "seed" in v. 7). Notably, the later passage in this case (Gen 12:3) does not contain all the themes of the earlier one (Gen 3:15), but only select ones. In figure 3, note that not all the light from the first lens is passed on to the second lens. This serves to illustrate the general phenomenon that later Messianic prophecies often only take up select portions of earlier ones.

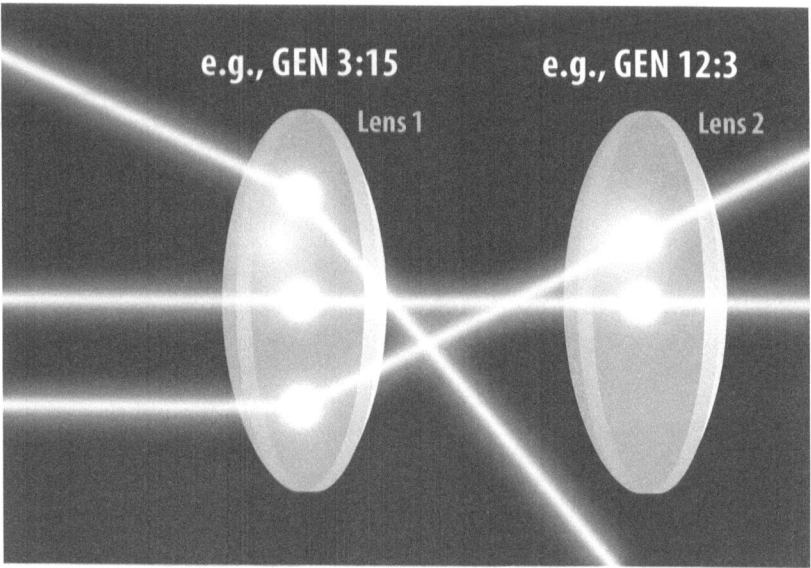

Figure 3. Portions of Messianic "light" passing through multiple prophecies

Although the preceding example involved the referencing of only one earlier passage, some Messianic prophecies reference multiple earlier passages. This becomes increasingly likely for prophecies that appear later in the Pentateuch, since there are a greater number of earlier prophecies available from which to draw. For example, Numbers 24:9 cites both Genesis 27:29 and Genesis 49:9 (see chap. 6 below). To add to the complexity, Genesis 27:29 and Genesis 49:9 are related to one another, as well as to Genesis 3:15 and Genesis 12:3 (see figure 4; see also chaps. 1–3 below). Thus Messianic prophecies in the Pentateuch, though indeed "dispersed," are linked to one another in intricate and fascinating ways. While each of these passages, considered in isolation, already radiate uniquely beautiful light, together they synergistically project a panoramic picture that captures far more than their piecemeal sum. The unique light from each passage both directly contributes to this wide-angle picture and is passed on to other passages, and this positive-feedback cycle repeats. This network of Messianic prophecies can be thought of as a complex array of interrelated lenses that the author of the Pentateuch has carefully designed in order to project for his readers a coherent, sweeping vision of the Messiah. These intricate intertextual relationships thus provide important evidence for the presence of an authorially intended, unified Messianic theology in the Pentateuch.[15]

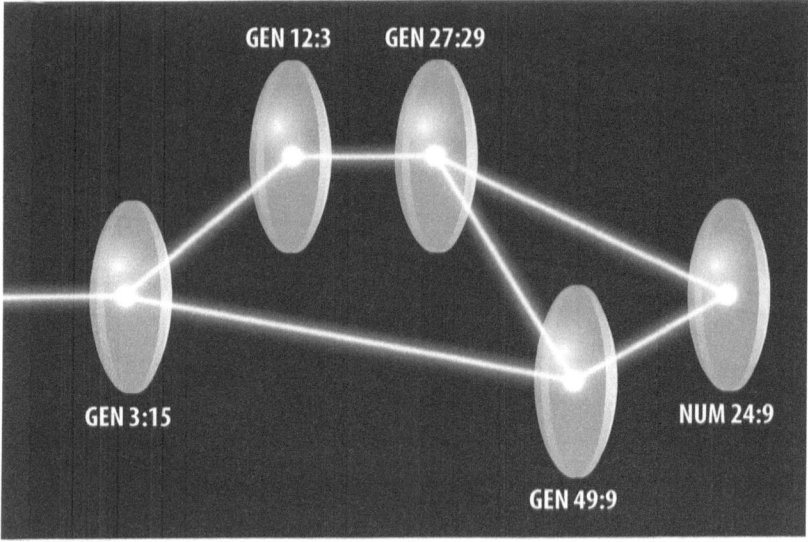

Figure 4. Network of Messianic prophecies

Intentional Foreshadowing as "Reflection"

In addition to direct prophecy, the Pentateuch also contains authorially intended foreshadowing of the Messiah. Such passages, including the one about Jacob's "ladder" in Genesis 28:10-22 (see chap. 2 below), are not prophecies per se but display intentional "reflections" of the Messiah. To continue the optical analogy, these passages can be thought of as "mirrors," though not the modern "plane" (i.e., planar) mirrors that are common in

---

[15]Franz Delitzsch, *Messianic Prophecies in Historical Succession*, trans. Samuel I. Curtiss (Edinburgh: T&T Clark, 1891), 21, likewise observed that "the idea of the God-man is first announced in single rays of light." However, he also believed that the Messiah "does not yet stand in the centre of Old Testament faith." This is because for Delitzsch Messianic passages are "like isolated points without connecting lines" (10). Indeed, "Christological development, which goes through the Old Testament, is like a path of light, which consists of rays of light proceeding from single points of light [such as Moses, David, Isaiah]" (11). Keeping with his historical model, Delitzsch referred to this christological development as "the gradual rising of light." While recognizing that Messianic passages are indeed dispersed, the conviction of the present work is that intertextuality provides the "connecting lines" that Delitzsch thought were absent. As such, this network of passages is linked to the overall compositional strategy of the Pentateuch.

homes and cars. Such flat mirrors reflect essentially all the visible light that strikes them. The image that we see in these kinds of mirrors is comparable to a photograph. In the Bible, the closest things to photographs of the Messiah are the four Gospels, with their direct narrative accounts of Jesus' life. But intentional foreshadowing of the Messiah in the Pentateuch is not like a photograph but instead like a reflection from a pool of water, which is a kind of natural mirror.

Although under certain circumstances water can be a serviceable mirror (cf. Jas 1:23), as in photographs of nature scenes reflected off a clear lake, the image it reflects depends on how still the surface is, the viewing angle, the lighting, and even its makeup.[16] The assessment of the French impressionist Claude Monet as "the painter of water *par excellence*" is a helpful analogy, for in his paintings water "takes on an infinite variety of appearances according to the condition of the atmosphere, the type of bed over which it flows, or the silt that it carries along. It can be clear, opaque, calm, agitated, fast-flowing, or sleepy, depending on the temporary conditions observed by the artist."[17] As such, reflections from water are not usually as sharp as those from modern plane mirrors. The sharpness depends especially on the nature and magnitude of any disturbance (e.g., ripples) on the surface of the water. Furthermore, the intensity of the reflection will also not be as strong as one from a modern plane mirror since water reflects less of the incident light. In this respect, water resembles ancient mirrors, which reflected only "through a glass, darkly" (1 Cor 13:12 KJV). Thus an image reflected from water is dimmer and its "edges" blurrier.

By analogy, intentional foreshadowing is comparatively indirect in relation to Messianic prophecy. Generally speaking, everything in a Messianic prophecy directly concerns the Messiah, whereas a passage with intentional foreshadowing also has elements that are not about the Messiah. This is expected because the latter also often serves the purpose of developing an ongoing narrative storyline. Although Messianic prophecies are also part of this storyline, their frequent expression in poetic

---

[16]Pure water, for instance, reflects differently than sea water. The term used to quantify reflectivity is *albedo*.

[17]Charles Stuckey, ed., *Monet: A Retrospective* (New York: Hugh Lauter Levin Associates, 1985), 67, emphasis original.

form serves as a pause in the progress of the narrative. To return to the example of Genesis 28:10-22 and Jacob's "ladder," this passage both develops the narrative of Jacob's flight from Esau while at the same time containing elements of intentional foreshadowing of the Messiah. Readers of Scripture should not assume that everything in this passage intentionally foreshadows the Messiah. Rather, they must carefully determine on an exegetical basis which elements the author seems to be setting forth as relating to the Messiah. Each passage with such intentional foreshadowing will have to be analyzed in its own right, as though the surface of each reflecting pool has its own unique disturbance profile along with its own lighting and angle. Correspondingly, passages with intentional foreshadowing of the Messiah vary in their emphasis, intensity, and perspective. In some cases, a Messianic prophecy can even simultaneously employ intentional foreshadowing (see chaps. 1, 3, and 7 below).

In theory, mirrors can be designed such that they mimic these varied surfaces of water. They can be curved to match the particular pattern of ripples and their reflectivity can be matched to the reflectivity of a given body of water. Like the "lenses" of Messianic prophecy described above, a passage containing authorially intended foreshadowing of the Messiah includes only select Messianic themes, again usually ones that relate to the literary context. In other words, each "mirror" gives an important, though incomplete, angle on what the coming king will be like. Intertextual evidence drawn from the Pentateuch itself suggests that these mirrors are interconnected with the lenses of direct prophecy and are intended by the author to contribute to the overall portrait of the Messiah projected by the Pentateuch as a whole.

Holding Tightly to the Human Author's Intent

The preceding has emphasized that there is an *authorially intended* Messianic vision of the Pentateuch that consists of an interrelated network of authorially intended, direct Messianic prophecy and authorially intended foreshadowing. Here as elsewhere, authorial intent refers to that of the human author, which is viewed as being identical to the divine intent of Scripture (2 Pet 1:20-21). This position, which will be defended in detail below, distinguishes the present approach from the more popular typological approach to seeing Christ in the Old Testament.[18] While there is some overlap in method and results, typology instead emphasizes patterns and correspondences between people, events, and institutions (e.g., elements of the sacrificial system) in salvation history as recorded in the Bible, especially between such "things" in the Old Testament and Christ. David L. Baker defines a "type" as "a biblical event, person or institution which serves as an example or pattern for other events, persons or institutions."[19] For example, a practitioner of typology might observe parallels between Abraham's command to sacrifice Isaac (Gen 22:1-18) and the actual sacrifice of Jesus on the cross, concluding that Isaac is a "type" (τύπος, "pattern" or "example") of Christ. Such language is indeed used in Romans 5:14 of Adam as a "pattern" (τύπος) of Christ and in 1 Corinthians 10:1-6 of Israel's failures in the wilderness as "examples" (τύποι) for believers, especially those in Corinth.

Whether or not τύπος is used in a technical sense in these passages,[20] what should be clear is that typology is "primarily a method of *historical* interpretation, based on the continuity of God's purpose throughout the history of his covenant. It seeks to demonstrate the correspondence between the various stages in the fulfilment of that purpose."[21] As an interpretation of (historical) events, typology seeks historical analogies among *referents* of the biblical text (e.g., events, persons, institutions). As such, Baker distinguishes typology both from prophecy (which is verbal and prospective, rather than historical and retrospective) and even more importantly from exegesis of the biblical text, which seeks the ideal of an objective (and often rich) meaning of the text by grammatical-historical

---

[18]For a brief historical survey of this method, see Stanley Gundry, "Typology as a Means of Interpretation: Past and Present," *JETS* 12 (1969): 233-40. For classic, full-length treatments, see Patrick Fairbairn, *The Typology of Scripture* (Philadelphia: Daniels and Smith, 1852); Leonhard Goppelt, *Typos: The Typological Interpretation of the Old Testament in the New*, trans. Donald Madvig (Grand Rapids: Eerdmans, 1982). Also, R. M. Davidson, "Typological Structures in the Old and New Testaments" (ThD diss., Andrews University, 1981). For a summary of more recent views and additional bibliography, see W. Edward Glenny, "Typology: A Summary of the Present Evangelical Discussion," *JETS* 40 (1997): 627-38.

[19]David L. Baker, *Two Testaments, One Bible: The Theological Relationship Between the Old and New Testaments*, 3rd ed. (Downers Grove, IL: InterVarsity Press, 2010), 180.

[20]Baker, *Two Testaments*, 175n9, argues against this.

[21]G. W. H. Lampe, "Typological Exegesis," *Theology* 56 (1953): 202, emphasis original.

analysis and discovers textual (rather than historical) analogies.²² Leonhard Goppelt remarks accordingly, "Only historical facts—persons, actions, events, and institutions—are material for typological interpretation; words and narratives can be utilized only insofar as they deal with such matters."²³

Although typological patterns are suggestive and noteworthy, the important distinction is that this book approaches them in a different way. The present purpose is not to discover historical analogies but textual ones that can be shown to be part of an author's compositional strategy. Accordingly, rather than drawing comparisons between things in the Pentateuch and Christ regardless of whether the author of the Pentateuch intended them as such, authorial intent is treated as essential, a sine qua non. Without it, it is impossible to speak a Messianic vision of the Pentateuch itself.²⁴ The key issue is not simply the similarities between specific things in the Pentateuch and Christ but how the author intended for specific passages in the Pentateuch to be understood by even his earliest readers.²⁵ This is because no matter how many "types" of Christ might be found, they are not necessarily intended by the author of the Pentateuch,²⁶ much less related to one another in a grand Messianic vision that he casts for his readers. In fact, the existence of a type does not require that such foreshadowing be intended by the author. Our emphasis on the author's intent

---

²²Baker, *Two Testaments*, 181.

²³Goppelt, *Typos*, 17-18. Davidson, "Typological Structures," 407, tries to have it both ways: "Typology in these hermeneutical passages is not only a theology of history but an interpretation of Scriptural passages, not only an interpretation of persons, events, and institutions *per se* but an interpretation of these realities *as recorded in Scripture*" (emphasis original). Nevertheless, his recognition that typology is "a theology of history" shows that it cannot be simply equated with exegesis.

²⁴The same basic problem remains even when it is granted that some OT prophets understood bits and pieces of eschatological salvation; e.g., Lampe, "Typological Exegesis," 202, "To some extent, indeed, the form of the pattern [of the biblical record of God's acts] was already perceptible to the prophets of the Old Testament, even though they could see but a small portion of the whole."

²⁵Fairbairn, *Typology of Scripture*, 40, does describe types as "designed" and "pre-ordained" by God to correspond to the gospel, but to say that God in his infinite wisdom intended, say, the Passover lamb to foreshadow of the death of the Messiah should not be confused with the human author of the Pentateuch self-consciously intending the same through the compositional strategy of his book.

²⁶E. Earle Ellis, foreword to Goppelt, *Typos*, xv, "While it can be plausibly argued that the OT writers themselves had in view a future significance of the things they were relating, this is not necessary for the argument that such a significance was placed in them by God as the NT claims."

goes hand-in-hand with our high value of exegesis that seeks to discover this intent.²⁷

A typological approach, for example, allows for seeing the "seed of the woman" as a type of Christ while at the same time remaining noncommittal regarding whether Genesis 3:15 is actually a direct Messianic prophecy and thus intended by the author to be understood as such.²⁸ Another representative example is reading the Servant Songs in Isaiah "not . . . as direct predictions of Jesus, but the vision of the righteous Servant, even if it was referred by the prophet to the faithful remnant of Israel, [which] was completely realized only when the Servant's role was enacted and fulfilled by our Lord, who personified the Remnant."²⁹ Although there can be genuine reasons for doubting whether this or that passage is indeed a Messianic prophecy, sometimes this is compounded with a general reticence regarding such prophecies across the board.³⁰ But to adopt an overall

---

²⁷We have in mind the distinction made by Johann August Ernesti, *Institutio interpretis Novi Testamenti*, 5th ed. (Leipzig: Libraria Weidmannia, 1809), 32, who pointed out that some interpretations may be "true doctrinally, but not grammatically and exegetically" (*verae dogmaticae, sed non grammaticae et ἐξηγητικῶς*). We recognize that the term *exegesis* is sometimes used differently to describe a particular interpretive approach (e.g., theological exegesis, patristic exegesis, medieval exegesis, Jewish exegesis) regardless of its effectiveness in discovering the author's intent. For a recent defense of the author's intent as it relates to the NT use of the OT, see Abner Chou, *The Hermeneutics of the Biblical Writers: Learning to Interpret Scripture from the Prophets and Apostles* (Grand Rapids: Kregel, 2018), 26-30.

²⁸For example, note the measured comment on Gen 3:15 by Graeme Goldsworthy, *According to Plan: The Unfolding Revelation of God in the Bible* (Downers Grove, IL: InterVarsity Press, 2002), 106: "The enmity between the snake's offspring and the woman's offspring foreshadows the conflict between Christ and Satan. The New Testament gives only the briefest support for this in the reference to God crushing Satan under the feet of Christians (Rom 16:20). It is possible that God's Son being born of a woman also recalls this prediction (Gal 4:4)." For him Gen 3:15 foreshadows Christ and Satan but not necessarily in a way intended by the author of the Pentateuch. What Goldsworthy does not consider here are certain grammatical issues related to the word *seed* and how the meaning of this passage is further unfolded in the Pentateuch itself by the author. In view of these considerations (see chaps. 1–3 below), there are good reasons to see this author as intending a direct Messianic prophecy in Gen 3:15, while at the same time using suspense to pique the interest of readers, who will discover more about this "seed" as they continue to read.

²⁹Lampe, "Typological Exegesis," 203.

³⁰For representative examples, see the helpful survey in Michael Rydelnik, *The Messianic Hope: Is the Hebrew Bible Really Messianic?* (Nashville: Broadman and Holman, 2010), 1-7. A little more than forty years prior, Raymond Brown, "The Problems of 'Sensus Plenior,'" *ETL* 43 (1967): 467, observed that "in general there is a tendency to distrust emphasis on the OT *prediction* of Christ. The relation between the two Testaments is seen more in terms of typology (W. Eichrodt, G. von Rad) or in terms of promise/fulfillment running through salvation history (W. Zimmerli, C. Westermann)." It appears that not much has changed. For critical scholars, this is a natural

posture of "maybe" to the Old Testament's direct testimony of Christ seems a far cry from Paul's declaration that "all God's promises are 'yes' in him," not "yes and no" (2 Cor 1:19-20).[31] With typology, "yes and no" situations easily arise because what matters most are similarities between Christ and various things in the Old Testament. In such a framework, it is possible to cite many types in the Pentateuch that "point to" Christ while at the same time believing that the authorially intended message of the Pentateuch itself is primarily the Sinai/Deuteronomic law and its importance.

As it relates to a Messianic vision in the Pentateuch itself, the problem with such an approach is that if, for example, Genesis 3:15 is not intended by the author as a Messianic prophecy, then it cannot be part of an authorially intended Messianic vision that the Pentateuch sets forth. The same holds true for every supposed Messianic prophecy in the Pentateuch. Likewise, if Jacob's ladder in Genesis 28:10-22 merely foreshadows Christ but not in a way intended by the author himself, then it is not part of a carefully crafted Messianic vision in the Pentateuch either. "Seeing Christ" in these passages would not be based on "exegesis" (discovering the

---

consequence of rejecting the possibility of predictive prophecy. Brown remarks, "To the critical exegete it was apparent that Isaiah did not know about Jesus" (460). In seeming agreement, Brown, speaking for himself, states, "there is no real evidence that the Hebrew prophets fully or partially foresaw the distant future" (461). Walter Kaiser, in his review of *The Lord's Anointed: Interpretation of Old Testament Messianic Texts*, ed. Philip Satterthwaite, Richard Hess, and Gordon Wenham (Grand Rapids: Baker, 1995) in *JETS* 42 (1999), 101-2, sees the tendency toward "a much too cautious and minimalistic approach" in some of the articles as traceable all the way back to the work of Anthony Collins, who, in *A Discourse of the Grounds and Reasons of the Christian Religion* (London, 1724), 40, sees the citation of OT passages in the NT as "apply'd in a secondary, or typical, or mystical, or allegorical, or enigmatical sense, that is, in a sense different from the obvious and literal sense, which they bear in the Old Testament." He even calls the idea that Isaiah the prophet had the virgin birth "literally and primarily in view ... a very great *absurdity*" (42, emphasis original). For additional comment on Collins's work and its influence, see Hans Frei, *The Eclipse of Biblical Narrative: A Study in Eighteenth and Nineteenth Century Hermeneutics* (New Haven, CT: Yale University Press, 1974), 66-70; and Iain Provan, "The Messiah in the Books of Kings," in *The Lord's Anointed*, 68-69. Fairbairn, *Typology of Scripture*, 26, remarks that the beginning of the eighteenth century was a low point in the life of the church and its writings. Vibrant faith and sound doctrine were in decline, and a "worldly philosophizing spirit ... softened down, if it did not entirely renounce, all that was peculiar in the gospel. Under the influence of such a spirit, Christ was not allowed to maintain in his proper place in the New Testament, and how much less, then, in the Old?"

[31]Some "promises" are fulfilled within the OT itself (e.g., 1 Kings 2:27; 16:34). Paul evidently did not mean these "promises" which were already historically fulfilled and not directly related to the coming of the Messiah. For an extended discussion of "promise" in the OT and the NT, see Sailhamer, *Meaning of the Pentateuch*, 419-38.

inherent meaning of the text) but "eisegesis" (reading meaning into the text).[32] When it comes to the theology of the Pentateuch itself, it is crucial whether foreshadowing is authorially intended or not, and for that matter, whether a prophecy is specifically and exclusively Messianic or open to multiple fulfillments.[33] A well-informed belief in an intricately designed Messianic vision in the Pentateuch can rely neither on mere correspondences that could be interpreted as accidental, nor on vague prophecies. Thus, there is a logical priority that is given to exegesis of the author's intent in the present work that is not given in typological approaches. With this priority comes a focus on the text of Scripture wherein the author's intent is best discerned. In contrast, typology, which does not hold to the author's intent in the same way, at best attempts to treat both the biblical text and the historical events it describes, since it relies on the overarching chronological framework of salvation history.[34]

One way for those who advocate typology to address the methodological challenge of whether or not types are authorially intended is to posit a difference between the human author's intent and the divine author's intent in Scripture. For example, the author of the Pentateuch may

---

[32]As a representative example of this terminology, see Grant Osborne, *The Hermeneutical Spiral: A Comprehensive Introduction to Biblical Interpretation*, 2nd ed. (Downers Grove, IL: InterVarsity Press, 2006), 57.

[33]E.g., Gregory Beale, *The Temple and the Church's Mission* (Downers Grove, IL: InterVarsity Press, 2004), characterizes the promise that David's "son" will build a temple as "fulfilled only partially by Solomon" (109), since it found "final fulfilment" or "long-range fulfilment" in Christ's resurrection (234-35). For a helpful survey of views of this general nature, see Rydelnik, *Messianic Hope*, 16-18, 23-24.

[34]See Geerhardus Vos, *Biblical Theology* (Edinburgh: Banner of Truth, 1948), 6-7, "We must place act-revelation by the side of word-revelation." This is because for him the subject matter of biblical theology is the "History of Special Revelation" (v), rather than exegesis of the books of the Bible themselves with a view toward their interrelationship. His broader concept of revelation plays a major factor in his approach. In his "The Idea of Biblical Theology as a Science and as a Theological Discipline," in *Redemptive History and Biblical Interpretation: The Shorter Writings of Geerhardus Vos*, ed. Richard Gaffin (Phillipsburg, NJ: P&R, 1980), 6, he even asserts, "Compared with revelation proper, the formation of the Scriptures appears as a means to an end." On reliance on the overarching chronological framework of salvation history, see Gundry, "Typology as a Means of Interpretation: Past and Present," 234, who favors an understanding of typology as "a means to express the Biblical understanding of history." Graeme Goldsworthy, *Gospel-Centered Hermeneutics: Foundations and Principles of Evangelical Biblical Interpretation* (Downers Grove, IL: InterVarsity Press, 2006), 247, refers to "typology as a method of salvation history hermeneutics. Typology seems to be a fairly natural corollary to salvation history." But as Vischer, *Witness of the Old Testament*, 18, points out, it is one thing to say that Jesus is the Christ as defined by the OT and another to say that he is the climax of salvation history.

not have meant Isaac to be a type of Christ in Genesis 22, but the striking similarities to the death of Christ on the cross suggest that this type was divinely intended over and above the original intention of the human author. The New Testament plays a major role in this approach and can be used as support, for example, in seeing Israel as a type of Christ (Mt 2:15) and water from the rock likewise (1 Cor 10:4), even though the human authors of the respective Old Testament texts cited most likely did not have the Messiah in mind. This line of reasoning is often also applied to prophecy, such that the prophet Isaiah had in mind the birth of an "Immanuel" during his day and was not thinking of the virgin birth (Is 7:14), but God took Isaiah's words to a new level in the birth of Christ (Mt 1:22-23). When applied to typology, the human intent and the divine intent can be said not to conflict, but the divine intent includes and goes beyond the human intent without violating it (i.e., sensus plenior).[35]

Although frequently adopted, there are several problems with such an approach.[36] By distinguishing the divine author's intent from the human author's intent, the fundamental starting point and objective basis for hermeneutics becomes muddled, and more subjectivity is introduced into

---

[35] See Raymond Brown, *The 'Sensus Plenior' of Sacred Scripture* (Baltimore: St. Mary's, 1955), 92-93. He is careful to point out that, "whether or not the human author fully intended it," sensus plenior "exists in the words of the text" and is "latent in the text." As such, it is distinct from "the typical sense which is primarily a sense of 'things' written about in the text." Instead, it "presupposes the literal sense of the passage and is a development of that literal sense." But this clear distinction between sensus plenior and the typical sense has not always been maintained by others, as Brown's historical survey of sensus plenior repeatedly shows in his "The History and Development of the Theory of a Sensus Plenior," *CBQ* 15 (1953): 141-62, esp. 145-46, 151-56. As another example, Gundry, "Typology as a Means of Interpretation: Past and Present," 237, essentially links typology "as a species of predictive prophecy" to sensus plenior: "Though the Old Testament writers may have been unaware of these things, still God in His inspiration of them intended this result." See also Raymond Brown, "The 'Sensus Plenior' in the Last Ten Years," *CBQ* 25 (1963): 262-85. He reaffirms that, "In principle all proponents of the SP agree that the SP and the typical sense are two different senses because the SP deals on the plane of the abstract values of language and the typical sense with concrete realities of person, thing, and event" (269). Brown again characterizes sensus plenior as a meaning "which by the normal rules of exegesis would not have been within [the human author's] clear awareness or intention but which by other criteria we can determine as having been intended by God."

[36] As Brown himself acknowledged in "The Problems of 'Sensus Plenior,'" *ETL* 43 (1967): 460-69. See also Kevin Duffy, "The 'Sensus Plenior' of Scripture: A Debate and Its Aftermath," *LS* 38 (2014): 228-45, who calls this approach "incoherent" because "the *sensus plenior* of a text is, and is not, located in the original meaning of a text.... Of all the inadequacies we have seen, this incoherence is the most fundamental. Ancient texts cannot be read like this" (244).

the interpretive process.[37] For standard hermeneutical approaches that rightly focus on the intent of the human author,[38] this confuses the task and goal of interpretation. If the divine intent can go beyond the human intent, how does the reader know when this happens? Only when there is warrant from the New Testament, or can it happen more generally?[39] Either way, is there a legitimate hermeneutical basis for it? In such cases, what is the relative importance of each intent, and why? From a hermeneutical standpoint, there is no systematic way of distinguishing between the human intent and the divine intent, or, equivalently, of ascertaining the divine intent that goes beyond the meaning of the words of the human author. This is because sound hermeneutical methodology for any text is geared toward determining the human author's intent. As the work of dual authorship, Scripture is a special case, but Christians have generally affirmed that the human author's intent is the same as the divine author's intent (2 Pet 1:20-21), with those who practice typological hermeneutics making an exception for types. The former explains why citations of the Old Testament in the New are sometimes attributed to a human author (Mt 3:3; Rom 11:9) and other times to the divine author (Heb 3:7; 10:15) without ever implying any difference in meaning, status, or authority as God's Word.

Related to this, human authors of the Old Testament are often viewed as though they did not or could not know much about the Messiah, based on statements such as are found in Ephesians 3:3-5 that the "mystery of

---

[37] The phrase "more subjectivity" acknowledges that there is inherent subjectivity that comes from the interpreter's perspective, even as he seeks the objective (and rich) goal of the author's intent.

[38] E.g., E. D. Hirsch, *Validity in Interpretation* (New Haven, CT: Yale University Press, 1967).

[39] Assuming that sensus plenior is already present in an OT text at the time it was written and recognizing that the citation of the OT in the NT is not systematic and, in a sense, ad hoc, it would seem that sensus plenior would be expected in at least some OT texts not cited in the NT. Similarly, if sensus plenior exists in OT texts, there seems to be no inherent reason why it cannot also exist in NT texts. Gabriel's explanation of Jeremiah's "seventy years" (Dan 9:2; Jer 25:11-12; 29:10) as "seventy weeks" (Dan 9:21-27) is not quite suitable as an example of sensus plenior because there are indications in Jeremiah itself (and elsewhere in the OT) that the restoration involves more than merely a physical return of some Israelites to the land (which took place about seventy calendar years later under Cyrus). For example, the wholehearted seeking of the Lord described in Jer 29:13 is linked to eschatological salvation and the new covenant (Deut 4:29-30; Jer 31:31-34), which did not take place during the Persian period. Granting that Gabriel probably did provide some supernatural insight into the future (Dan 9:25-27), it is likely that the "seventy years" (and the number seventy itself) had figurative potential all along.

Christ" has only recently been made known (see also Rom 16:25; Col 1:26). It can then be argued that their prophecies about the Messiah were unintentional at times, analogous to Caiaphas' unwitting statement about the benefits of Jesus' death in John 11:49-52. However, "the mystery of Christ" need not be interpreted in this way,[40] and Kaiser argues on the basis of 1 Peter 1:10-12 that Old Testament prophetic authors did know that they were writing about the coming Messiah, including his sufferings and subsequent glorification, even if they did not know exactly when he would come.[41] If Isaiah 53 is taken as a direct Messianic prophecy, it would seem that the prophet knew that the Messiah would suffer and then be exalted. If this prophet knew such things, then other prophets likely knew as well. Other passages in the New Testament confirm that these human authors were not unwittingly communicating about the Messiah in their writings (Jn 1:45; 5:46; Acts 2:30-31). Unlike the unbelieving Caiaphas who spoke more truthfully than he realized (Jn 11:51),[42] these godly believers looked forward greatly to the Messianic age (Lk 10:23-24; 1 Pet 1:10-12), as did some others in Jesus' day such as Simeon (Lk 2:25-26), Anna (Lk 2:36-38), the disciples (Jn 1:45), and Joseph of Arimathea (Lk 23:50-51).

A hermeneutical approach that holds tightly to the human author's intent also better explains the debates that Jesus and Paul had with others about the meaning of the Old Testament (e.g., Lk 20:27-44; Acts 17:1-4, 17; 18:4, 19; 19:8-9). Just before explaining "from Moses and from all the prophets . . . in all the Scriptures the things concerning himself" while on the road to Emmaus, Jesus rebuked the two discouraged disciples for their foolishness and slowness "to believe in all that the prophets have spoken" (Lk 24:25-27).

---

[40]Significantly, the "mystery" in all three passages is linked to the inclusion of Gentiles in the people of God (Rom 16:26; Eph 3:6; Col 1:27). But this truth is revealed in the OT (e.g., Deut 32:43; Is 19:25; 49:6), which suggests that this "mystery" actually was known to the few faithful prophets. This is consistent with Paul's own reference to its hiddenness from "the sons of men" (Eph 3:5), a reference to humanity generally, but its revelation to himself (Eph 3:3), holy apostles and (OT?) prophets (Eph 3:5), and the "saints" (Col 1:26). The emphasis on its revelation in the present age may concern the actual inclusion of Gentiles in large number in the church, in fulfillment of OT prophecies.

[41]Walter Kaiser, "The Single Intent of Scripture," in *The Right Doctrine from the Wrong Texts?*, ed. Gregory Beale (Grand Rapids: Baker, 1994), 56-57. See also his *The Uses of the Old Testament in the New* (repr., Eugene, OR: Wipf and Stock, 1985), 18-21.

[42]Kaiser, "Single Intent," 59-61. Though also invoking progressive revelation and sometimes coming to different conclusions, see the argument for the prophets' extensive knowledge in Chou, *Hermeneutics of Biblical Writers*, 95-105.

From Jesus' perspective, they should have understood from the Old Testament itself that the Messiah would suffer, die, and rise from the dead. Although he presumably could have confronted them for not believing *his* words that predicted the same (e.g., Lk 9:22), instead he held them responsible for not believing what the Old Testament had already said.[43] Even more to the point, Paul testified to King Agrippa that these same essential elements of the gospel were "nothing but what the prophets and Moses said would happen" (Acts 26:22-23). In other words, the gospel preached by Paul and fulfilled in Christ did not in any way go beyond what the Old Testament had predicted beforehand.[44] In both of these examples, Jesus and Paul assume that the Old Testament can be read and understood on its own terms by nonscholars as declaring the good news of the Messiah and the new covenant. Moreover, they nowhere suggest that a new hermeneutical method is needed, which would have undercut the force of their arguments.

The issue, then, was and is the exegesis of the Old Testament on its own terms since it was the only Bible of Jesus and the earliest church.[45] A typological approach does not work as well under these constraints because it is more focused on correspondences and parallels between the testaments than the authorial intent of respective biblical books. As such, typological arguments are more easily rejected by those who hold fast to the meaning of the Old Testament itself because such arguments appear to be more of an illegitimate Christian "appropriation" of the Old Testament than a fair-minded exegesis of it.[46] Furthermore, the New

---

[43] Lk 24:44 and Jn 2:22 imply that these two are in harmony.

[44] Vischer, *Witness of the Old Testament*, 11, "In their preaching of Jesus the Messiah the apostles in no way desire to declare anything else than that which is written in the Old Testament."

[45] Contra Richard Gaffin in *Biblical Hermeneutics: Five Views*, ed. Stanley Porter and Beth Stovell, (Downers Grove, IL: InterVarsity Press, 2012), 101, who characterizes such an approach as "illegitimate, as well as redemptive-historically (and canonically) anachronistic. To seek to interpret the various Old Testament documents for themselves apart from the vantage point of the New exposes one ultimately to misinterpreting them." Despite Gaffin's seemingly confused assertion that "the Old Testament is to be read in light of the New . . . because Jesus and the New Testament writers read it this way," this is not what Jesus and Paul did since the NT had not yet been written, and they did not misinterpret the OT. Gaffin seems to have driven a wedge between exegesis of the OT and the gospel, which is unnecessary. If Jesus and NT authors were right about the OT, then we have no need to fear interpreting the OT on its own terms because its message is in complete harmony with the gospel and the NT.

[46] Klappert, "Mose hat von mir geschrieben," 629, refers to "the problem of this Gentile-Christian appropriation" of the Old Testament before citing a warning from Bonhoeffer not to think in terms of the NT too quickly. Klappert also believes that Bonhoeffer came "in his later phase

Testament had not yet been written in Jesus' and Paul's day, thus excluding the most important source of authority for typology. Typological arguments are harder to make in terms of the Old Testament alone. As a more subjective and complicated interpretive method,[47] typology is also more vulnerable to charges of mishandling the text, the very thing that Paul denied. On the contrary, careful study of (Old Testament) Scripture is repeatedly commended in the New Testament (Acts 17:11; 2 Tim 2:15; 2 Pet 3:16). Although typology may be attractive to Christians because it offers a Christocentric view of Scripture while sidestepping exegetical controversies over whether certain Old Testament passages were originally intended as Messianic, an approach that more highly values the meaning of the Old Testament on its own terms has more potential because it can argue for the inherently Christocentric nature of the Old Testament on more solid and more widely accepted hermeneutical ground.[48] For the same reason, such an approach has advantages over Richard Hays' "figural interpretation" of the Old Testament, which has similarities to typology and is described by Hays as "reading backwards [i.e., from the life, death, and resurrection of Jesus]," "christological," metaphorical, distinct from predictive prophecy and the intent of Old Testament authors, "necessarily retrospective rather than prospective," "revisionary," and an "extraordinary hermeneutical revolution."[49]

---

more and more to the realization that the Old Testament does not belong to Christ, but Christ belongs to the Old Testament" (628). Although not all would say it in this way, see Goppelt's characterization of typology and its implied view of the OT in *Typos*, 202, "The OT is not the inspired letter to the extent that it is for Judaism. It is a witness to redemptive history, to a provisional and inadequate salvation, and a prophecy that points beyond these things."

[47]Note the following statements in Goppelt, *Typos*: "The NT does not regard [typology] as a formal hermeneutical technique" (200); its "results ... are primarily statements about NT salvation, not statements about the OT" (200); "typology begins and ends with present salvation. NT typology is not trying to find the meaning of some OT story or institution" (201); "NT typology does not have a closed system of detailed interpretations or any appropriate rules for their discovery. Typology is not a hermeneutical method with specific rules of interpretation. It is a spiritual approach that looks forward to the consummation of salvation and recognizes the individual types of that consummation in redemptive history" (202).

[48]Also, it is more consistent methodologically because the same exegetical method is applied throughout Scripture. In contrast, typology requires a merger of common exegetical method with typological method.

[49]Richard Hays, *Echoes of Scripture in the Gospels* (Waco, TX: Baylor University Press, 2016), 2-4. He has self-consciously borrowed the term *figural* from Erich Auerbach, *Mimesis*, trans. Willard Trask (Princeton, NJ: Princeton University Press, 1953), 16, 48-49, 73-76, 555. Auerbach in turn has adapted it from the Latin *figura*, especially as used by the church fathers. See his "Figura,"

INTRODUCTION

Klappert points out that the Gospel of John itself is early evidence that there was a Jewish-Christian hermeneutic that was derived from the Old Testament itself, was well versed in Jewish tradition, and performed a Messianic, christological exegesis of Scripture.[50] He distinguishes this hermeneutic from the Gentile-Christian "appropriation" of the Old Testament that began later in the second century A.D. The bottom line is that if a Messianic exegesis of the Old Testament can be legitimately set forth, the fruit will be powerful evidence for the truthfulness of Scripture and the gospel of Jesus Christ. In this case, both the New Testament and the Old Testament can be unreservedly regarded as "equally Christian Scripture"[51] (rather than elevating the New Testament over the Old Testament), such that "the two Testaments, breathing the same spirit, point to each other."[52]

THE PENTATEUCH AS A SINGLE BOOK AND COMPOSITION

Since we are searching for an authorially intended Messianic theology in the Pentateuch, a necessary initial step is to determine whether the

---

in *Scenes from the Drama of European Literature* (New York: Meridian, 1959), 11-76. Auerbach traces figural interpretation all the way back to Paul, who by it "intended to strip the Old Testament of its normative character and show that it is merely a shadow of things to come," "subordinated [figural interpretation] to the basic Pauline theme of grace versus law, faith versus works," and no longer treated the OT as "a book of the law and history of Israel and became from beginning to end a promise and prefiguration of Christ, in which there is no definitive, but only a prophetic meaning which has not been fulfilled" (50-51). Auerbach thus conceives of figural interpretation to be quite radical. He also dichotomizes between the legal-historical aspects of the OT and its prophetic aspects, the latter which for some reason are not considered "normative," inductively derived from the OT, or "definitive." As Hays notes in *Echoes of Scripture in the Gospels*, 367n4, Hans Frei also picked up on this term and discusses it at length in *The Eclipse of Biblical Narrative*. That Hays's approach contrasts with ours is evident through his belief that "it would be an unwarranted hermeneutical presumption to read the Law and the Prophets as deliberately *predicting* events in the life of Jesus" (348, emphasis original). Accordingly, he believes that the OT has "unexpected foreshadowing," which contrasts with our belief in intentional foreshadowing. See also Christopher Seitz, *Prophecy and Hermeneutics: Toward a New Introduction to the Prophets* (Grand Rapids: Baker, 2007), 7-10, 99, who also uses "figural" interpretation and downplays authorial intention because of later canonical shaping, context, and form.

[50]Klappert, "Mose hat von mir geschrieben," 628. He believes that this hermeneutic has been largely lost by the church in its history. Nevertheless, for him this hermeneutic is "exemplary" (*vorbildlich*).

[51]Baker, *Two Testaments*, 87.

[52]Vischer, *Witness of the Old Testament*, 7. He similarly says that the OT and NT "stand facing each other like the two sections of an antiphonal choir looking towards a central point [i.e., Jesus the Christ]" (25).

Pentateuch is five books (Genesis, Exodus, Leviticus, Numbers, and Deuteronomy) or one. Though not necessarily an exciting question in and of itself, how it is decided will greatly impact the exegesis and theology of the Pentateuch. If the Pentateuch is five books, then each book should be studied for its own theology of the Messiah, or relative lack thereof (e.g., Leviticus). The interpreter would then attempt to unify these five separate visions. If they are not easily integrated, then it may be difficult even to speak of a single Messianic vision of the Pentateuch. On the other hand, if the Pentateuch is one book, then the interpreter can search for a Messianic vision of the Pentateuch as a whole. Rather than seeking out the Messianic theologies of five books and then attempting to merge them, this instead involves an integrated view of the theology of the Pentateuch from the outset. A unified literary work would be more likely to yield a unified Messianic theology of some kind. The following chapters will provide evidence for this.

The testimony of Scripture itself strongly suggests that the Pentateuch is a single book, not five books. Significantly, later passages refer to "the book" written by Moses but never his "books" (e.g., 2 Chron 25:4; Neh 8:1).[53] Whether referring to what we now call the book of Exodus (Mk 12:26) or the book of Deuteronomy (Neh 13:1; see Deut 23:3), they simply refer to "the book of Moses." Likewise, in Matthew 22:36-40 Jesus cites the Great Commandment (Deut 6:5) and the command to love one's neighbor (Lev 19:18) as though they are both part of the same literary work, "the Law" (Mt 22:36; as distinct from "the Prophets" in Mt 22:40). This provides good reason to view Genesis through Deuteronomy not as five books but as a literary unity that bears an all-encompassing authorial design. Lengthy though it is, readers therefore ought to directly inquire after its overarching theology for its Messianic vision.

To speak of the Pentateuch in this way is to treat it as a "composition," which is a unified literary work that is written and organized purposefully

---

[53]See the helpful chart in Y. C. Wong, *Creation, Covenant, and Restoration: An Introduction to the Major Theological Themes of the Torah* [Chinese] (Hong Kong: Tien Dao, 2000), 23-24. It is true that Jn 5:47 refers to Moses' "writings" (γράμμασιν), but the singular "writing" is generally not used of a literary work. BDAG says that this holds true even for single copies. For engagement with critical issues related to the "book" of Moses in Ezra-Nehemiah, see H. G. M. Williamson, *Ezra, Nehemiah*, Word Biblical Commentary (Waco, TX: Word, 1985), xxxvii-xix, 385.

such that it bears a coherent message from its author.[54] The Pentateuch is not a mere collection of stories, laws, poems, and genealogies that have been gathered together haphazardly. Rather, every passage in the Pentateuch has a meaningful connection not only to its immediate context but also to the Pentateuch as a whole. This means that sometimes a passage in another part of the Pentateuch, even one that is separated by many chapters, can be the author's way of shedding light on the passage under consideration. The author's particular way of expressing his message through his composition (e.g., repetition, themes, structure, intertextuality) can correspondingly be called a "compositional strategy."[55] There are good reasons for viewing biblical books in general as compositions in this sense. For example, John 20:30-31 explains that the purpose of the Gospel of John is for readers to "believe that Jesus is the Christ, the Son of God." Likewise, Luke 1:1-4 states that the Gospel of Luke was written carefully to give "certainty" to Theophilus concerning the gospel that he had learned. Furthermore, the New Testament epistles self-evidently bear a message from their respective authors to their readers. To be sure, sometimes the author, such as Paul, has several different topics that he addresses rapid fire in certain sections (e.g., 1 Cor 5–7) but even so, an epistle as a whole still has unifying, major themes (e.g., "law" and gospel in Galatians). Similarly, the Pentateuch as a book bears an overarching message from its author. This message includes the various messages of individual passages, such as Abram's obedience to the Lord's call (Gen 12:1-4), while at the same time going even further and ultimately consisting of a greater, overall message that relates to how all these pieces fit together compositionally.

In keeping with the uniform testimony of Scripture (e.g., Deut 31:24-26; Josh 1:7-8), we hold that the author of the Pentateuch was Moses, and the message of Pentateuch is Moses' own message.[56] Since Moses was a prophet, a unique prophet no less (Num 12:6-8; Deut 34:10), readers should expect

---

[54]See Georg Fohrer, *Exegese des Alten Testaments* (Heidelberg: Quelle und Meyer, 1973), 136-43. For a summary of this and other relevant literature, see my *Eschatological Sanctuary in Exodus 15:17 and Related Texts* (New York: Lang, 2013), 31-33. Although a compositional approach can also be a canonical approach, we have deliberately avoided using "canonical" to avoid confusion with the different approaches of Childs and Sanders.

[55]Sailhamer, *Meaning of the Pentateuch*, 11

[56]We leave as an open question the extent to which Moses used sources. At least some use of sources is hard to dispute (e.g., "the Book of the Wars of the LORD" in Num 21:14).

that his message is a prophetic message. Thus, the Messianic vision of the Pentateuch argued for in this book is Moses' own vision. This holds true even though there is probably a small percentage of the Pentateuch that Moses was not directly responsible for, such as the passage concerning his death in Deuteronomy 34. Presumably, a later prophet is responsible for this passage (and possibly others) but was all the while under the guidance of the Holy Spirit (2 Tim 3:16; 2 Pet 1:20-21) such that Moses' original message was preserved and in some cases accentuated (e.g., Deut 34; see chap. 7 below). In support of this nuanced view of the Mosaic authorship of the Pentateuch, long after this prophetic hand brought the Pentateuch into its final form (or *Endgestalt*), Jesus still said that Moses wrote about him in his writings, but his opponents had not believed these same writings (Jn 5:46-47; cf. Jn 1:45). Jesus thus assumes the Mosaic authorship of the Pentateuch (whether in its original or final form) and the preservation of Moses' original message in the final form of the Pentateuch.

The idea that Moses and other authors of the Old Testament could not have known (or known much) about the Messiah has already been partially addressed above. Rather than assuming *a priori* what biblical authors could or could not have known and then allowing that assumption to influence our exegesis of their writings, it is better not to assume anything about what they knew and simply to take them at their (written) word. Vischer urges us to "read the Old Testament as it stands, in the best sense of the word naïvely; not as those who know before they read what they will find there."[57] Regarding the question of what biblical authors knew, it is safe to conclude that what they intended by their writings, they also knew. Other than that, there is little evidence that shows what they did or did not know. Likewise, neither should the beliefs of Second Temple Judaism be uncritically privileged as a reliable guide to the meaning of the Old Testament. Strictly speaking, both assumptions about biblical authors' knowledge and how their work has been interpreted over the ages (as valuable as this history can be, it is still *reader*-oriented) are distinct from exegesis that seeks the intended meaning of these authors communicated through their writings. If Moses himself actually knew much about the Messiah as shown

---

[57] Vischer, *Witness of the Old Testament*, 30.

through the sweeping Messianic vision that he set forth in the Pentateuch, then it was also possible, though not necessarily common, for the Pentateuch's earliest readers to come to the same understanding. On the other hand, one would expect that later prophetic authors of other Old Testament books not only read the Pentateuch but also understood its true meaning (Josh 1:7-8; Ps 1:2; Jer 8:8; Mal 4:4).

The Pentateuch as Instruction
Rather Than Mere Law or Historical Record

The Pentateuch is more commonly referred to in Scripture as "the Law of Moses" or simply, "the Law" (e.g., Mal 4:4; Lk 24:44; Rom 3:21).[58] At first glance, this presents a significant obstacle to the possibility of a Messianic vision occupying the center of its authorially intended message. If the Pentateuch is repeatedly called "the Law" by the Scriptures, then how can law not be the focus of its compositional strategy? The answer lies in the meaning of the Hebrew word *torah* that has been traditionally translated in these contexts as "law." As is widely acknowledged, *torah* is better understood to mean "instruction" in a broader sense.[59] For example, Proverbs 1:8 speaks of a mother's *torah* or parental instruction. Likewise, Psalm 78 begins with a call to heed the psalmist's *torah* (Ps 78:1), which consists of lessons drawn from stories about past generations of Israelites. Neither of these examples give any hint of the legal context that the English word *law* implies. To be sure, *torah* can be used in legal contexts, and in such cases should be understood and translated as "law" (e.g., Ex 12:49; Lev 6:9), but the point is that the word itself does not always mean "law" or imply a legal context.

As it relates to the Pentateuch, one important implication is that this book should not automatically be viewed as "law," even though Scripture so frequently refers to it as "the Law" or "the Law of Moses"! Instead, the Pentateuch should be viewed as "instruction" in a broad sense. The common references to the Pentateuch in Scripture do not specify *a priori* what kind of instruction it contains, only that it is a book of instruction of some kind.

---

[58]It is true that "the Law" can also refer to the OT as a whole, as it does in Rom 3:19. The preceding OT citations in Rom 3:10-18 come from various OT books, mostly from the Psalms.
[59]See HALOT, BDB.

Determining the precise nature of this instruction requires further study of the compositional strategy of the Pentateuch. Though counterintuitive and perhaps even wearisome, readers of Scripture must therefore constantly remind themselves that "the Law of Moses" should really be thought of as "the instruction of Moses," despite the traditional, entrenched English translation of this phrase.[60] Accordingly, this work only uses "the Law" to refer to the Pentateuch when citing a biblical passage that translates *torah* (or its Greek translation *nomos*) in this way. Otherwise, it will be referred to as the Pentateuch and its laws usually as "Sinai/Deuteronomic law." This latter phrase is shorthand for the laws in the Pentateuch, the vast majority of which were given at Sinai and then expounded on in much of Deuteronomy. There will also be occasions when "Sinai law" is used because the laws in Deuteronomy are not in view. Relatedly, the Hebrew word *torah* will never be used to refer to the Sinai/Deuteronomic law.

This distinction between the Pentateuch and its laws, both of which are referred to in English translations as "the Law," is essential not only for understanding the Pentateuch but also for biblical theology, especially in the Pauline epistles. Whereas Paul uses *nomos* in still more ways—e.g., the law of the conscience (Rom 2:15), the entire Old Testament (Rom 3:19), marriage law (Rom 7:1-2)—a distinction between his use of *nomos* as referring to the Pentateuch and as referring to the Sinai/Deuteronomic law can be detected. For example, the "law" that came 430 years after Abraham is not the Pentateuch but the Sinai law, "ordained through angels by the hand of a mediator" (Gal 3:17, 19; see Ex 12:40; Deut 33:2-4; Acts 7:53; Heb 2:2). That Paul believed the Pentateuch teaches the gospel is clear from his citation of Genesis 15:6 with reference to Abraham's justification by faith in Galatians 3:6 and his follow-up citation of Genesis 18:18 as having "preached the gospel beforehand to Abraham" (Gal 3:8). Therefore, when Paul says that "the law is not of faith" (Gal 3:12), he is not referring to the Pentateuch but to the Sinai/Deuteronomic law. In fact, Schmitt has shown that the Pentateuch has a "faith theme" (*Glaubensthematik*) (Gen 15:6; Ex 4:31; 14:31; 19:9; Num 14:11; 20:12).[61] For Paul, the close

---

[60] See KJV and the translations of Tyndale and Wycliffe that came before it.
[61] Hans-Christoph Schmitt, "Redaktion des Pentateuch im Geiste der Prophetie," *VT* 32 (1982): 170-89.

relationship between the Sinai law and Deuteronomic law is evident through his successive quotations of Deuteronomy 27:26, Leviticus 18:5, and Deuteronomy 21:23 in Galatians 3:10, 12-13, with no indication of any difference in subject matter.

The distinction between the Pentateuch's message of faith and the system of the Sinai/Deuteronomic law is also found in Romans. The "righteousness of God" is manifested "apart from the law" (i.e., Sinai/Deuteronomic), but borne witness to by "the Law [i.e., the Pentateuch] and the Prophets" (Rom 3:21). Paul's extended discussion of Abraham as an example of justification by faith in Romans 4 immediately follows his claim that his preaching of the gospel "upholds the Law" (i.e., the Pentateuch, or perhaps the OT; Rom 3:31). On the other hand, when using covetousness as an example of how "the law" reveals sin (Rom 7:7), he was referring to the Tenth Commandment, which is part of the Sinai/Deuteronomic law. It is this law that has "snuck in" secondarily (Rom 5:20). Thus, for Paul the Pentateuch teaches the new covenant of the Messiah, whereas the Sinai/Deuteronomic law, if taken in isolation from the holistic *torah*/instruction of Moses (i.e., the Pentateuch), can lead to a mistaken reliance on "works of the law" (Rom 3:20; Gal 3:10).

Another important implication of understanding the Pentateuch as a book of instruction is that it is more than just an accurate historical record of ancient history. It certainly is that and does provide accurate accounts of creation, the patriarchs, Israel's experiences in Egypt and in the wilderness, and so forth, but it also does more. In particular, it bears a prophetic message from God (2 Pet 1:20-21). Accurate historical accounts by themselves do not necessarily do this. Stated differently, the Pentateuch as a whole not only records accurate history but also bears a coherent message. To be sure, its message is intertwined with the history it records, but its purpose is certainly not limited to accurately recording the past. This distinct prophetic message is observed especially in key predictive passages. Thus the Pentateuch's message and theology are not reducible to the historical facts it records. As a point of comparison, the Gospel of John likewise contains accurate historical accounts, but the book as a whole was written for the purpose of encouraging faith in Jesus as the Christ, the Son of God (Jn 20:30-31). Its author did not simply collect everything that he could find about the life and ministry of Jesus but carefully chose what to include and exclude for the purpose of his book (Jn 21:25). The Pentateuch should likewise be understood as having selective, accurate historical accounts that have been carefully woven together into a unified literary work so as to communicate a message of "instruction" from the author.

Understanding the author's message in a biblical book is best achieved by focusing on the book itself and its contents for its compositional strategy, rather than trying to reconstruct the historical events it describes, despite the increasing availability of material from archaeology and modern historical research.[62] These things have value in understanding the historical circumstances themselves and in apologetics, but the author's intent must still be discerned by focusing on what the author himself wrote.[63] Historical reconstruction beyond the biblical record is important and has its appropriate place, but it should never be confused with understanding the message of a biblical book. Whereas the former attempts to generate as complete a picture of a historical situation as possible, the latter seeks to understand history as it has already been interpreted in the biblical text by the biblical author under the guidance of the Holy Spirit. A believer's primary goal in reading Scripture is an accurate, dynamic understanding of this inspired text (2 Tim 3:16), rather than a comprehensive knowledge of the historical events described in the Bible, as might be sought by a professional historian.

The Structure of the Pentateuch and Its Importance

If the Pentateuch as a whole bears a coherent message and if we are to focus on the text itself to discern the author's intent, where is the reader to begin? Certainly, the fundamental steps would be to read it (Deut 17:18-20), discuss it (Deut 6:7), and meditate on it (Josh 1:8). Another important step,

---

[62]See the treatment of "text" and "event" in John Sailhamer, *Introduction to Old Testament Theology: A Canonical Approach* (Grand Rapids: Zondervan, 1995), 36-85.

[63]See Sailhamer, *Meaning of the Pentateuch*, 104, where he likens filling in historical details left out of the biblical text to painting historical details into the shadows of one of Rembrandt's paintings. His point is that the shadows are purposeful and communicate "Rembrandt's focus." Similarly, Auerbach, *Mimesis*, points out that, especially when contrasted with Homer, biblical narrative details "only so much of the phenomena as is necessary for the purpose of the narrative, all else [is] left in obscurity; the decisive points of the narrative alone are emphasized, what lies between is nonexistent" (11; see also 23).

especially with such a lengthy book, would be to determine how it is organized. Like a table of contents in modern books, understanding the structure of the Pentateuch can help readers see how the author organized his work and provide an important first step in understanding the whole book. Stated differently, the structure of a book can be a key part of its compositional strategy. For modern readers of the Pentateuch, perhaps the most natural way of understanding the structure of the Pentateuch is to simply divide it into the five sections that modern Bibles do: Genesis, Exodus, Leviticus, Numbers, and Deuteronomy. Direct, textual evidence for such a division goes as far back as the great Greek biblical codices of the fourth and fifth century AD,[64] with even earlier references to the same in Josephus and Philo.[65] However, as was pointed out above, the New Testament never refers to "Genesis," or any of the other four "books," as such. In other words, there is no inherent reason why the structure of the Pentateuch as designed by its author centuries before actually corresponds to this fivefold division. In fact, many believe that the present fivefold division of the Pentateuch was influenced by practical limitations on scroll length. This required its division into smaller portions, which was done in a standardized fashion at an early stage.[66]

In any case, the most reliable way to determine the structure of biblical books, which do not come with tables of contents, is to look for repeating literary patterns in the books themselves. For example, scholars have long observed the structural function of lengthy teaching discourses in the book of Matthew.[67] Each of these five discourses is punctuated by a concluding statement (Mt 7:28; 11:1; 13:53; 19:1; 26:1). In contrast to a table of contents which stands apart from the body of the book, these structuring elements are part of the flow of the book itself. As such, they have the

---

[64]Codices Sinaiticus, Alexandrinus, and Vaticanus. Although most of the Pentateuch is missing from Codex Sinaiticus, a few pages that do remain attest to a fivefold division through reference to "Leviticus," "Numbers," or "Deuteronomy" at the top of respective pages.
[65]Josephus, *Against Apion* 1.8; Philo, *On Abraham* 1.1. For further discussion, see Kenneth Mathews, *Genesis 1–11:26*, New American Commentary (Nashville: Broadman and Holman, 1996), 42.
[66]Matthews, *Genesis 1–11:26*, 42.
[67]Though there is discussion of whether it is primary or secondary to the structure of Matthew. See Craig Blomberg, *Matthew*, New American Commentary (Nashville: Broadman and Holman, 1992), 22-23; Donald Hagner, *Matthew 1–13*, Word Biblical Commentary (Dallas: Word, 1993), li; R. T. France, *The Gospel of Matthew*, New International Commentary on the New Testament (Grand Rapids: Eerdmans, 2007), 2-5, 8-10.

potential not only to provide organization but also to communicate key ideas. In the case of Matthew, they bring a clear emphasis on the content of Jesus' teaching. Similarly, Sailhamer has shown that the disparate material in the Pentateuch follows a recognizable pattern of narrative, poetry, and epilogue.[68] This cycle repeats four times (see figure 5).

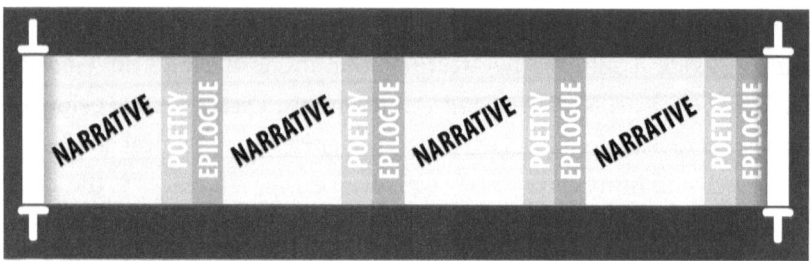

Figure 5. Structure of the Pentateuch

Of particular importance in this overall design are the four sections of poetry (Gen 49:2-27; Ex 15:1-18; Num 23:7-10, 18-24; 24:3-9, 15-24; Deut 32:1-43; 33:2-29), which are the longest in the Pentateuch. Sailhamer has further noted that three of them bear the remarkable similarities of the appearance of the phrase "in the last days" (Gen 49:1; Num 24:14; Deut 31:29), a main human character of the preceding narrative calling others together to listen, and the giving of a Messianic prophecy (Gen 49:8-12; Num 24:7-9, 17-19; Deut 33:7). The other poem (Ex 15:1-18) also involves a main human character leading others (in song), and it is closely linked to the other three poems. These passages will be analyzed in more detail in the subsequent chapters, but for the present purposes the key point is that through these poems the coming of the Messiah is intertwined with the structure of the Pentateuch and hence its overall compositional strategy.

By themselves, these four major poetic sections provide a significant piece of evidence that the coming of the Messiah is central to the composition of the Pentateuch and its theological message. Although Messianic prophecies are much shorter and less frequent than listings of laws, they

---

[68]John Sailhamer, *The Pentateuch as Narrative: A Biblical-Theological Commentary* (Grand Rapids: Zondervan, 1992), 34-37.

are given at crucial junctures (or "seams") throughout the Pentateuch. In contrast, the Sinai Law begins only in Exodus 20. Moreover, the change in literary form from narrative to poetry should pique readers' interest and encourage them to pay even closer attention.[69] The same literary device is also used in the Messianic prophecies of Genesis 3:15 and Genesis 27:27-29, which appear in shorter poems.

"My Lord and My God!"

Following the death of Jesus, the disciples were so distraught that they doubted reports of his resurrection, even though he had repeatedly told them about it. Perhaps the most famous example of this was "doubting Thomas," who declared that he would not believe unless he saw the nail marks on Jesus' body and touched his wounds (Jn 20:25). Remarkably, eight days later Jesus appeared again to the disciples, this time with Thomas present, and the disciple was indeed invited to touch Jesus' wounded body (Jn 20:26-27). At this, his doubt disappeared, as he exclaimed, "My Lord and my God!" (Jn 20:28).

In a broad sense, Thomas's doubt concerning the resurrection of Jesus parallels many Christians' doubt concerning the centrality of the Messiah in the Old Testament, especially the Pentateuch. Perhaps we are so used to equating the Pentateuch with the Sinai/Deuteronomic law that we don't expect much else. It may also be that sometimes we don't even know what to look for amidst the many laws, genealogies, and historical narratives. My conviction is that the Messiah really is there in the Pentateuch, and my experience is that seeing him in these texts as the ancient author intended leads to the same declaration of wonder and worship as Thomas's "My Lord and my God!" I hope that this book will help you see for yourself that the Bible is a work of genius, beauty, and glory, surpassing even the greatest masterpieces humanity has ever produced, and as such is itself a powerful testimony to the triune God and the gospel of Jesus Christ proclaimed on its pages.

> Uncover my eyes so that I may see wonders from your law. (Ps 119:18)

> Then he opened their mind to understand the Scriptures. (Lk 24:45)

---

[69] See James W. Watts, *Psalm and Story: Inset Poems in Hebrew Narrative*, JSOT Supplement Series (Sheffield: JSOT Press, 1992).

1

THE SEED OF THE WOMAN

The prophecy concerning the "seed of the woman" in Genesis 3:15 is the first Messianic prophecy in the Pentateuch, and hence in the Bible. Though brief, it sets forth critical parameters in the overall Messianic vision of the Pentateuch. Since it draws on the preceding narrative of Genesis 1–2, it is best understood in relation to this context. In this way, Genesis 3:15 will be seen as not only a direct prophecy of the Messiah but also one that selectively alludes to Adam as intentionally foreshadowing a coming king and priest. It is both a "lens" and a "mirror."

Adam as King and Priest

Genesis 1 recounts God's creation of the heavens and the earth (Gen 1:1) and his activities over the course of six days (Gen 1:3-31).[1] The culmination of these activities was day six (Gen 1:24-31), as indicated by the greater attention it receives and its unique connection to the divine evaluation, "it was very good" (Gen 1:31). The importance of day six is also related to the creation of humans (Heb. אָדָם, 'adam). Made in the image of God and created male and female, they were commanded by God to rule over all the animals of the sea, sky, and land (Gen 1:26-28). They were also instructed to reproduce and "fill the earth and subdue it" (Gen 1:28). For food, God gave them seed-bearing plants and fruit trees (Gen 1:29).

The bringing forth of plants and animals on previous days (Gen 1:11-12, 20-22, 24-25) is thus related to the rule and sustenance of humankind. Although not exhaustive of the purpose of these other created things,

---

[1] It is beyond the scope of the present discussion to enter into the complex debates about the age of the earth and how this passage can be reconciled with modern scientific views on the origin of life and of the universe. Our focus is necessarily on the creation of humankind, especially as it relates to Gen 3:15.

Genesis 1 thus implies that they came to be for the sake of humans. In turn, the sky (Gen 1:6-8), seas, and land (Gen 1:9-10) were necessary to provide a habitat for these various living things. Even the appointment of the sun and moon "to separate between the day and the night" and to mark "appointed times," "days," and "years" (Gen 1:14) was for the benefit of humankind, which alone has the capacity to keep track of such things. Suggestively, the "rule" of the two great lights (Gen 1:16, 18) broadly parallels the rule of humankind in Genesis 1:26-28, as will be discussed further at the end of the chapter. In any case, what emerges from Genesis 1 is a picture of God's special creation of humankind in his likeness and his purpose that they fill the earth and rule over it.

The high-level account of the creation of humankind in Genesis 1:26-27 is made specific in Genesis 2:7 with a close-up view of how "the Lord God formed the man [הָאָדָם] from the dust of the ground." The name of this first man, correspondingly, was "Adam" (Gen 2:20). There is thus a complex wordplay on the Hebrew word 'adam in the opening chapters of Genesis. It is used of humankind corporately (Gen 1:26; 5:1-2), an individual human (Gen 2:7, 8, 15), and as a name for this first man (Gen 5:3-5). The literary effect is to present Adam as both a historical figure and a representative of humankind, who is especially responsible to fulfill God's command to rule as a sort of king and to multiply (Gen 1:26-28).

Adam was subsequently placed in the Garden of Eden (Gen 2:15), where he received the command not to eat from the tree of the knowledge of good and evil (Gen 2:16-17), named animals, and was given his wife as a helper (Gen 2:18-25). Scholars such as T. Desmond Alexander and Gordon Wenham have pointed out the many parallels between the Garden of Eden and the tabernacle, which include the Lord "walking about" in their midst (Gen 3:8; Lev 26:12), their entrance from the east and being guarded by cherubim (Gen 3:24; Ex 25:18-22; 26:1, 31; Num 3:38), the resemblance of the lampstand to the tree of life (Gen 2:9; 3:22; Ex 25:31-35), the presence of gold and onyx (Gen 2:11-12; Ex 25:7, 11, 17; 28:9), and the use of the same two Hebrew verbs (שָׁמַר, עָבַד) to describe Adam's tasks in the garden and the Levites' in the tabernacle (Gen 2:15; Num 3:7-8; 8:26).[2] These extensive

---

[2] T. Desmond Alexander, *From Paradise to the Promised Land*, 3rd ed. (Grand Rapids: Baker, 2012), 123-24. Gordon Wenham, "Sanctuary Symbolism in the Garden of Eden Story," in *Proceedings of*

intertextual linkages within the Pentateuch itself cast the Garden of Eden as a prototypical sanctuary and Adam as a sort of prototypical Levite or priest.[3] This ministerial role, however, does not involve an altar or sacrifices.

It is noteworthy that the tabernacle seems to more closely resemble the Garden of Eden in its post-Fall state than its original state. This is because the representations of cherubim guarding the mercy seat and embroidered on the veil and the curtains of the tabernacle parallel the real cherubim who guard the way back to the tree of life *after* the sin of Adam and Eve (Gen 3:24). Before their disobedience, the first couple had free access to the tree of life (Gen 2:9, 15). Thus, the tabernacle and its representations of cherubim serve as a reminder of this first sin and its consequences, as well as an implicit reminder of the innumerable sins committed by the sons of Adam since then. The restricted access to the Holy of Holies corresponds to the restricted access to the tree of life after the Fall, and both of these realities indicate that fellowship with God, among other things, has been broken (Heb 9:8). The provisionary nature of the tabernacle is also implied through its being based on a "pattern" (Ex 25:9, 40). Accordingly, the tabernacle did not have real cherubim, only representations of them.

Nevertheless, the Garden of Eden in its original state still has many parallels to the tabernacle, and its casting as a prototypical sanctuary still stands. As it relates to Adam, he is thus presented as not only a historical figure and representative of the human race who was to fill the earth with his offspring and rule, but also as a kind of priest who ministered in a pristine garden sanctuary and who had free access to the tree of life. Thus, when Genesis 1 and Genesis 2 are read together (as they should be), the

---

the Ninth World Congress of Jewish Studies, Division A: The Period of the Bible (Jerusalem: World Union of Jewish Studies, 1986), 19-25. Since Wenham is interested in parallels to the tabernacle or the temple, he also notes the connection between the Edenic river and the ones in Ps 46:5 and Ezek 47:1-12. The portable tabernacle, perhaps naturally, is not linked to a river. It did have a bronze basin for washing that had water in it (Ex 30:18). The closest thing to a river associated with the tabernacle was the "many waters" that flowed from the rock in Num 20:11. Ps 78:16, 20 refers to these waters as "streams" and "rivers" (cf. Ps 78:15; 74:15; 105:41).
[3]See the helpful analysis and interaction with relevant literature in Seth Postell, *Adam as Israel: Genesis 1–3 as the Introduction to the Torah and Tanakh* (Eugene, OR: Wipf and Stock, 2011), 111-14. Also, Gregory Beale, *The Temple and the Church's Mission* (Downers Grove, IL: InterVarsity Press, 2004), 66-76; John Sailhamer, *The Pentateuch as Narrative: A Biblical-Theological Commentary* (Grand Rapids: Zondervan, 1992), 100-101.

combined effect is that Adam is presented as a sort of priest-king, ministering and reigning in prototypical garden-like temple.[4]

THE SEED OF THE WOMAN

Despite the privileges given to Adam and Eve in the Garden of Eden, they were deceived by the serpent into eating the forbidden fruit (Gen 3:1-7). Whereas on the one hand Eve was motivated by hunger and the pleasant appearance of the fruit, she was also attracted to the tree of the knowledge of good and evil because it was "desirable for gaining wisdom" (Gen 3:6). This emphasis on wisdom accords with both the name of the tree itself and the serpent's last words to Eve, "you will be like God [or, 'gods'], knowing good and evil" (Gen 3:5). The language of "knowing good and evil" also appears in Deuteronomy 1:39 with reference to children who characteristically lack such knowledge because of their youth. This suggests that Adam and Eve forsook a childlike faith in the Lord in favor of their physical desires and pride.[5] While seeking wisdom in fear of the Lord is commendable (Prov 1:7), they erred by seeking it apart from the Lord, who alone possesses complete wisdom (Prov 2:6).[6]

Adam and Eve's pursuit of wisdom was thus a failure. What Eve "saw" (רָאָה) to be "good" (טוֹב) in Genesis 3:6 actually brought trouble, pain, and death (Gen 3:16-19). Evidently, human perception that something is "good" may be incomplete or even flawed, unlike God's (Gen 1:4, 10, etc.). In trying to become "wise" apart from the Lord, they instead "became fools" (Rom 1:22). While Eve was not necessarily wrong about the fruit being good for food and pleasing to the eye, there were also many other beautiful, delicious fruits in the Garden that were not forbidden by the Lord (Gen 2:9, 16). In Adam and Eve was fulfilled the proverb, "There is a way that seems upright before a man, but its end is the ways of death" (Prov 14:12;

---

[4] See Wenham, "Sanctuary Symbolism," 21, where he suggests that Adam was an "archetypal Levite" and had a "quasi-priestly role." Such a figure becomes explicit in Gen 14 with Melchizedek.
[5] Wenham, *Genesis 1–15*, Word Biblical Commentary (Waco, TX: Word, 1987), 75. Postell, *Adam as Israel*, 116, further points out that the words תַּאֲוָה and חָמַד in Gen 3:6 link this sin to the sin of coveting forbidden in the tenth commandment (Ex 20:17; Deut 5:21). To this may be added that their desire to be "like God" violated the first commandment (Ex 20:3; Deut 5:7). These allusions to the Decalogue resemble an inclusio that casts Adam and Eve as breaking the whole Sinai/Deuteronomic law.
[6] See Wenham, *Genesis 1–15*, 63-64. For more on wisdom, see the discussion of Bezalel in chap. 5 below.

16:25). Thus, when the Lord God remarked that "the man has become like one of us, knowing good and evil" (Gen 3:22), it is best understood as an ironic reference to their pride and human-centered attempt at gaining wisdom. By acting according to their own thoughts of what was good, they had implicitly placed themselves above God.

After confronting Adam and Eve about their sin (Gen 3:8-13), the Lord pronounced judgment on the guilty parties, beginning with the serpent (Gen 3:14-15). This creature was to be more cursed than any other land animal and was sentenced to crawl on its belly.[7] After predicting that "enmity" (אֵיבָה) between the woman and the serpent would continue between their respective "seed" (זֶרַע), the judgment of the serpent reaches its climax with a prophecy that the woman's "seed" will crush the serpent's head, though the serpent will crush this seed's heel also (Gen 3:15). Sometimes referred to as the prophecy of the "seed of the woman" or the *protoevangelium* ("first gospel"), this verse has been interpreted from ancient times as predicting the final defeat of the serpent by this "seed."[8]

The crucial interpretive issue is whether this passage is indeed a direct prophecy of the Messiah. Though he related Genesis 3:15 to Christ and Satan via "anagogy," Calvin famously remarked, "I interpret this simply to mean that there should always be the hostile strife between the human race and serpents, which is now apparent; for, by a secret feeling of nature, man abhors them."[9] Calvin's interpretation resembles Rashi's before him, who interpreted Genesis 3:15 as only concerning conflict between humans

---

[7]This humiliation will continue forever and is linked to eschatological salvation, as shown by Is 65:25 and Mic 7:17. Lev 11:41-44 associates the serpent with other creatures that swarm or teem on the earth (שׁרץ, רמשׂ). Both verbs can also be used of creatures that swarm in water (Gen 1:20-21; Lev 11:46).
[8]See Irenaeus, *Against Heresies* 5.21.1; Justin Martyr, *Dialogue with Trypho* 100; see R. A. Martin, "The Earliest Messianic Interpretation of Gen 3:15," *JBL* 84 (1965): 425-27, who argues that the LXX is the earliest Messianic interpretation of this verse.
[9]John Calvin, *Commentaries on the First Book of Moses called Genesis*, Calvin's Commentaries, trans. John King (Grand Rapids: Baker, 2003), 167. Calvin's connection of Gen 3:15 to the defeat of Satan only by "anagogy" is defined by the editor in a footnote "a raising on high, especially elevation of the mind above earthly things to abstract speculations (in ecclesiastical writings), to the contemplation of the sublime truths and mysteries of Holy Scripture" (168). That Calvin uses "anagogy" as distinct from the literal sense: "There is, indeed, no ambiguity in the *words* here used by Moses; but I do not agree with others respecting their *meaning*; for other interpreters take the seed for *Christ*, without controversy" (170). For more on anagogy, see Henri de Lubac, *Medieval Exegesis: The Four Senses of Scripture*, trans. E. M. Macierowski (Grand Rapids: Eerdmans, 2000), 2:179-81. For more on Calvin's reading of Gen 3:15, see Hans Frei, *The Eclipse*

and snakes, with the striking of the heel being fatal ("You will not stand upright and you will bite him on the heel, and even from there you will kill him").[10] Rashi's interpretation leaves no clear winner in the struggle. Rashi and Calvin raise multiple issues here that will be dealt with below, but as for the serpent, it is no ordinary creature. It talks, knows about and twists God's earlier command (Gen 2:16-17; 3:1-4), and will live for many generations before being crushed ("he will crush you [not: 'your offspring']"). The serpent is thus better understood as an animal that was empowered and filled by Satan. Other passages confirm that Satan is closely identified with *this* serpent (Is 27:1; Rev 12:9) but not necessarily with serpents in general in the natural world. Whereas the serpent in Eden was probably a natural, physical serpent, Satan is essentially a spiritual being who can also take different forms—for example, falling like lightning (Lk 10:18), entering Judas (Lk 22:3), or appearing as an angel of light (2 Cor 11:14).

Seth Postell has further pointed out the divine verdict on Cain for murdering Abel (Gen 4:11), "cursed are you [אָרוּר אַתָּה] from the ground," casts him as the seed of the serpent, who received a similar verdict, "cursed are you [אָרוּר אַתָּה] more than every beast" (Gen 3:14), for tempting Adam and Eve unto their death (Gen 3:19).[11] Postell also observes that "cursed [אָרוּר] be Canaan, a servant of servants will he be to his brothers" in Genesis 9:25 relatedly casts Canaan as part of the serpent's seed while the subsequent blessing of Shem in Genesis 9:26-27 suggests the ultimate victory of the seed of the woman from Shem's line, which becomes even clearer when this seed is connected to Genesis 49:8-12 (see chap. 3 below).

Such an interpretation of the seed of the serpent as referring not to snakes in the natural world but to those who follow the deceitful, usurping, murderous way of Satan is confirmed by Scripture broadly. This "seed" includes both demons (2 Pet 2:4; Jude 6; Rev 12:9) and wicked human beings. Outside of Genesis 1–11, the Pentateuch likewise confirms that evil

---

of Biblical Narrative: A Study in Eighteenth and Nineteenth Century Hermeneutics (New Haven, CT: Yale University Press, 1974), 25-27.

[10]A. J. Rosenberg, *Genesis: A New English Translation/Translation of Text, Rashi, and Other Commentaries* (New York: Judaica, 1993), 1:57. Rashi's arguments still hold weight for those who might read Gen 3 as having mythological elements.

[11]Seth Postell, "Genesis 3:15: The Promised Seed," in *The Moody Handbook of Messianic Prophecy: Studies and Expositions of the Messiah in the Old Testament*, ed. Michael Rydelnik and Edwin Blum (Chicago: Moody Publishers, 2019) 244-45, 247.

humans are part of the serpent's seed. Numbers 24:17 is a Messianic prophecy that alludes to Genesis 3:15 through the common theme of crushing the head of an enemy, but the enemy here is a human enemy, Moab (see chap. 6 below). The effect is to link hostile Moab (and in this context Edom) with the serpent and his seed. Deuteronomy 32:31-33 generalizes this for all such human "enemies." Psalm 58:3-4 correspondingly characterizes the wicked generally as going astray from birth, deceitful, having the "venom of a serpent," and being "like a deaf adder that has stopped up its ear." Psalm 140:3 describes evil and violent men likewise, "They make their tongue sharp like a serpent's; the poison of a viper is under their lips." Even more obvious examples are John the Baptist and Jesus calling the Pharisees "offspring of vipers" (γεννήματα ἐχιδνῶν, Mt 3:7; 12:34; 23:33; Lk 3:7).

A related major difficulty in Genesis 3:15 is determining the precise referent of the "seed" of the woman. The Hebrew word translated "seed" or "offspring" (זֶרַע) is grammatically singular but can have either a singular or plural referent, much like the English words that typically are used to translate it. When used of human offspring (contra Gen 1:11-12), it can refer to an individual descendant (i.e., one "seed" or "offspring"), or it can refer to a person's descendants generally (i.e., "seed" or "offspring" considered collectively).[12] It can function as a collective noun (such as "family" or "clergy") but strictly speaking should not be classified as a collective noun because it does not always refer to a group. Still, the usage of the word allows for the possibility that it is the offspring of the woman collectively who will defeat the serpent.[13] However, the explicit

---

[12]A few even attempt to avoid this either-or. Derek Kidner, *Genesis*, Tyndale Old Testament Commentaries (Downers Grove, IL: InterVarsity Press, 1967), 75-76, thinks that the woman's seed, "like the seed of Abraham, is both collective (cf. Rom. 16:20), and, in the crucial struggle, individual (cf. Gal. 3:16), since Jesus as the last Adam summed up mankind in himself." Similar is James Hamilton, "The Skull Crushing Seed of the Woman: Inner-Biblical Interpretation of Genesis 3:15," *SBJT* 10 (2006): 30-54, who further defines the collective seed as those "who hope for the victory of their seed" (31) and "who trust God" (43). But in view of the grammatical considerations below, the only way for a both-and is for "her seed" to be collective, but then it would not be the referent of "he" because "he" must refer only to an individual. In that case, the pronoun *he* would not have a proper referent in the preceding context. This is not the way pronouns function typically, nor does it cohere with Messianic passages that use the word *seed*.

[13]Calvin, *Genesis*, 170, was certain of this, "for who will concede that a *collective* noun is understood of one man *only*? Further, as the perpetuity of the contest is noted, so victory is promised to the human race through a continual succession of ages. I explain therefore, the *seed* to mean

use of the singular independent personal pronoun to refer to this seed ("He [הוּא] will crush your head") suggests that an individual seed is in view. In contrast, both Isaiah 61:9 and Isaiah 65:23 use *seed* (זֶרַע) collectively in combination with a plural independent personal pronoun, *they* (הֵם and הֵמָּה, respectively): "For they [הֵם] are seed [זֶרַע] that the Lord has blessed" (Is 61:9), and, "For they [הֵמָּה] are seed [זֶרַע] blessed by the LORD" (Is 65:23).

The use of a singular independent personal pronoun to refer to an individual "seed" is paralleled by other passages (Gen 15:3-4; 21:13; 2 Sam 7:12-14; 1 Chron 17:11-13), and the use of a plural independent personal pronoun to refer to a collective "seed" is paralleled by Isaiah 57:3-4 (which twice uses the independent plural pronoun *you*). The only potential exception to the apparent rule of a singular independent personal pronoun being used to refer to an individual seed and a plural independent personal pronoun to refer to a plural (collective) seed is Isaiah 41:8, but even this is explainable based on the singular *you* primarily referring to *Israel* rather than to *seed* later in the verse ("You [sg.] are Israel my servant, Jacob whom I have chosen, the seed [זֶרַע] of Abraham my friend"). Also, "Israel" is consistently treated as grammatically singular here and in the surrounding context ("You [sg.] are Israel, my servant [sg.], Jacob, whom I have chosen you [sg.]"; see Is 41:9-10; 42:19; 43:1-7; 44:1-3).[14] In combination with so many nouns in apposition to one another in this verse (e.g., Israel, servant, Jacob), the use of the singular independent personal pronoun in Isaiah 41:8 does not only relate to *seed* and is not necessarily an exception to the rule. After all, "Israel" can be referred to as "the seed of Abraham." Even so, excluding Isaiah 41:8 and Genesis 3:15, the other seven parallel passages just cited use independent personal pronouns whose grammatical number (i.e., singular or plural) corresponds to whether the referent of *seed* is

---

the posterity of the woman generally." Many contemporary scholars also take this view, including Wenham, *Genesis 1-15*, 81, who believes that a Messianic reading is justifiable only as sensus plenior, not as part of the authorially intended, literal sense. But, as pointed out already, *seed* only functions like a collective noun sometimes, not all the time, as these scholars believe.

[14]Israel can thus be referred to with a singular independent personal pronoun (see also Num 22:3). This does not affect grammatical issues related to *seed*, however, since in such contexts Israel is a collective noun, whereas *seed* can refer to either a singular or a group (see *beast* [בְּהֵמָה] in Neh 2:12; Eccles 3:18; *tree* in Gen 1:11-12; 2:17).

singular or plural (see table 1.1 below).[15] In other words, a singular independent personal pronoun is used to refer to an individual seed, not to a collective seed. While a thorough grammatical analysis of *seed* also requires treatment of its usage as the subject of singular and plural verbs and its usage with adjectives, participles, and pronominal suffixes,[16] the present considerations concerning its usage as the referent of an independent personal pronoun strongly favor interpreting the woman's seed in Genesis 3:15 as an individual.

Broader contextual considerations in the Pentateuch and the Old Testament provide significant support for this. Several of the above passages

Passage with *seed* and independent personal pronoun with same referent	Independent personal pronoun	Referent	Do the grammatical numbers match?
Gen 3:15	he	to be determined	to be determined
Gen 15:3-4	he	singular	yes
Gen 21:13	he	singular	yes
2 Sam 7:12-14	he (v. 13) he (v. 14)	singular (both)	yes
Is 41:8	you (sg.)	Plural	no, but the singular pronoun you is more directly referring to "Israel, my servant, Jacob whom I have chosen"
Is 57:3-4	you (pl., v. 3) you (pl., v. 4)	plural (both)	yes
Is 61:9	they	plural	yes
Is 65:23	they	plural	yes
1 Chron 17:11-13	he (v. 12) he (v. 13)	singular (both)	yes

Table 1.1. The use of *seed* with independent personal pronouns

[15]For this research, every passage with *seed* and an independent personal pronoun within a one-verse radius was collected, sifted for false positives, and analyzed. Lev 11:37-38 was not included because it concerns plant seed(s), which is typically collective (except 1 Sam 8:15 and perhaps Jer 2:21) and is accompanied by only singular grammatical elements (see Deut 14:22), including independent personal pronouns and pronominal suffixes (see Lev 26:16; 27:30).

[16]See chap. 2 below, which will discuss Jack Collins, "A Syntactical Note (Genesis 3:15): Is the Woman's Seed Singular or Plural?," *TynBul* 48, no. 1 (1997): 139-48. In a footnote he calls Is 41:8 "not a true exception" because "in the fancy of the author the patriarch is ideally present" (143). Neither Collins's article nor John Walton's critique of it in *Genesis*, NIV Application Commentary (Grand Rapids: Zondervan, 2001), 225 (including n. 3), isolate the subset of data concerning independent personal pronouns.

not only use the same singular pronoun *he* (הוּא) to refer to an individual seed but also concern related content and suggest an intentional intertextual connection to Genesis 3:15. The promise of a seed was later passed to Abram (Gen 12:7), who was not only promised numerous offspring (Gen 12:2) but also a seed who would become his heir (Gen 15:3-4). The individual referent of this seed is strongly suggested through its juxtaposition with another individual, Eliezer of Damascus (Gen 15:2; note הוּא is used of him), who will otherwise become the heir (for discussion of the switch to a plural *seed* in Gen 15:5, see chap. 2 below). As in Genesis 3:15, this "seed" is referred to by the Lord in direct speech using the singular pronoun *he* (הוּא):

> And Abram said, "Behold you have not given a seed [זֶרַע] to me, and behold, the son of my house will be my heir." And behold, the word of the Lord came to him saying, "This one will not be your heir but one who will go out from your loins [אֲשֶׁר יֵצֵא מִמֵּעֶיךָ; i.e., a seed], he [הוּא] will be your heir." (Gen 15:3-4)

In a striking use of the same language of a "seed . . . who will go out from your loins," David was likewise promised an heir (2 Sam 7:12).[17] That this "seed" is an individual, and a royal one at that, is evident through his building a temple and sitting on David's throne forever (2 Sam 7:13). The same singular pronoun is used by the Lord in direct speech to refer to him twice in 2 Samuel 7:12-14:

> I will establish your seed [זֶרַע] after you, who will go out from your loins [אֲשֶׁר יֵצֵא מִמֵּעֶיךָ], and I will establish his [sg.] kingdom. He [הוּא] will build a house for my name, and I will establish the throne of his [sg.] kingdom forever. I will be a father to him [sg.], and he [הוּא] will be a son to me.

The double use of the pronoun "he" here parallels its two uses in Genesis 3:15 and Genesis 15:4 combined. Similar arguments apply to the parallel passage in 1 Chronicles 17:11-13, which substitutes "seed . . . who will be from your sons" (אֲשֶׁר יִהְיֶה מִבָּנֶיךָ, 1 Chron 17:11) for "seed . . . who will go out from your loins" (2 Sam 7:12). The singular referent for seed is even clearer in 1 Chronicles 17:11 through its distinction from David's sons in general, his collective "seed" as it were. The Lord likewise refers to this

---

[17]These are the only two places in the OT that use this phrase.

individual royal heir twice with the singular pronoun *he* (1 Chron 17:12-13). Genesis 15:3-4, 2 Samuel 7:12-14, and 1 Chronicles 17:11-13 are further related to one another through being linked to a prophetic "vision" (Gen 15:1; 2 Sam 7:17; 1 Chron 17:15) received by Abram and David, respectively. The many lexical, syntactic, and thematic connections between these passages, along with still more commonalities between the Abrahamic and Davidic covenants such as a great name (Gen 12:2; 2 Sam 7:9), nationhood (Gen 12:2; 2 Sam 7:10), land (Gen 12:7; 2 Sam 7:10), worldwide blessing (Gen 12:3; Ps 72:17), kingship (Gen 27:29; 2 Sam 7:12-16), and eternality (Gen 17:7; 2 Sam 23:5) suggest that the two covenants along with the original promise of Genesis 3:15 are fulfilled by the same Abrahamic, Davidic, and Messianic seed, just as Matthew 1:1 implies. Even the statement about Ishmael in Genesis 21:13 ("He is your seed") is related to who will become Abraham's heir (Gen 21:10-12; 22:17).

Though the word *seed* is absent, the same pronoun *he* also appears twice in a divine oracle in a related context in Zechariah 6:13, "And he [הוּא] will build the temple of the LORD, and he [הוּא] will bear majesty." Here the individual is not only a temple-building king but clearly a Messianic priest-king. Isaiah 53 likewise concerns a highly exalted, and hence royal, priestly figure (Is 52:13, 15; see Is 6:1), who is referenced with the same pronoun *he* five times (Is 53:4, 5, 7, 11, 12). Isaiah 53 and Zechariah 6 not only bring us full circle back to the depiction of Adam as a priest-king but also, together with Genesis 15:3-4 and 2 Samuel 7:12-14, link the promise of a seed in Genesis 3:15 even more strongly to an individual Messianic figure.[18] Additionally, it is as though the Lord's own words in direct speech, sometimes mediated through a prophet, strategically use the pronoun *he* to refer to this "seed" in these various passages in order to direct readers to pay close attention to this individual promised seed. Relatedly, the second masculine singular pronoun *you* (אַתָּה) appears in such key Messianic passages as Genesis 49:8 (יְהוּדָה אַתָּה "You are Judah"; see chap. 3), Psalm 2:7 (בְּנִי אַתָּה "You are my son"), and Psalm 110:4 (אַתָּה־כֹהֵן לְעוֹלָם "You are a priest forever").

At first glance, it may seem that the content of Genesis 15:3-4 itself can only be distantly related to such a hope. However, the Hebrew verb for "to

---

[18]The phrase "heels of your Messiah" in Ps 89:52 also links this seed to an individual royal figure.

be an heir" used in Genesis 15:4 (יָרַשׁ) can also mean to "possess" and is used of a "seed" possessing the gate of his "enemies" (Gen 22:17) and of "those who hate him" (Gen 24:60). As such, the broader use of this word in the Pentateuch links the individual "seed" who will be Abram's heir in Genesis 15:4 to an individual "seed" who will defeat his enemies and possess their gates in Genesis 22:17; 24:60.[19] Moreover, the mention of "enemies" (אֹיְבָיו) in Genesis 22:17 ties this network of passages back to the "enmity" (אֵיבָה) between the woman and the serpent in Genesis 3:15. This enmity had been "set" (שִׁית) by the Lord himself, but he declares in similar language in Ps 110:1, "I will set [שִׁית] your enemies [אֹיֵב] as a footstool." Thus, according to the purpose of God, the enmity ends when the Messiah reigns in fullness. By repeating several terms from Genesis 3:15, Eve's naming of Seth in Genesis 4:25 ("God has set [שִׁית] for me another seed [זֶרַע] in place of Abel, for Cain killed him"; also אִשָּׁה "woman") seems both to link Cain's fratricide to the problem of "enmity" and the promise of the seed of the woman to God graciously "setting" (i.e., providing) an individual seed.[20]

Using a cognate noun of the verb "to be an heir," Numbers 24:18 foretells that the Messiah's "enemies" (אֹיְבָיו), represented by Moab and Edom, will be his "possession" or "inheritance" (יְרֵשָׁה). Furthermore, the word "Seir" (שֵׂעִיר; referring to the land of Edom) in Num 24:18 plays on "gate" (שַׁעַר) in Gen 22:17 (and 24:60) such that their respective clauses strikingly play off of one another ("and may your seed *possess the gate of his enemies*" [וְיִרַשׁ זַרְעֲךָ אֵת שַׁעַר אֹיְבָיו] and "*Seir, his enemies*, will be a *possession*" [יִהְיָה יְרֵשָׁה שֵׂעִיר אֹיְבָיו]).[21] The context of Num 24:18 implies that this possession will take place "in the last days" (Num 24:14). The eschatological "possession"

---

[19]For an argument in favor of a singular referent for "seed" in Gen 22:17; 24:60, see T. Desmond Alexander, "Further Observations on the Term 'Seed' in Genesis," *TynBul* 48, no. 2 (1997): 364-68. See the more thorough discussion of these passages in chap. 2 below. These two passages show that the identity of Abram's heir should not be simply equated with Isaac (Gen 21:10), even though it is appropriate to mention him in this connection just as Abram himself is described as an heir to the promises (Gen 15:8).

[20]Postell, "Genesis 3:15."

[21]The association between "Seir" (שֵׂעִיר) and "gate" (שַׁעַר) is even stronger when it is remembered that vowel letters, such as are found in "Seir," were not always consistently used. See Ernst Würthwein, *The Text of the Old Testament*, trans. Erroll Rhodes, 2nd ed. (Grand Rapids: Eerdmans, 1995), 21-22; Isaac Kalimi, *Metathesis in the Hebrew Bible: Wordplay as a Literary and Exegetical Device* (Peabody, MA: Hendrickson, 2018), 12.

of Edom is likewise the major theme of Obadiah 15-21. Micah 1:15 relatedly predicts that the Lord will bring "the possessor" or "the heir" (הַיֹּרֵשׁ). In Isaiah 65:9, the Lord promises to bring out a "seed" from Jacob related to the coming of a "possessor" (יוֹרֵשׁ) from Judah (see Gen 49:8-12; Num 24:17). Using different words, Psalm 2:8 declares that the nations will be the Messiah's "inheritance" (נַחֲלָה) and the ends of the earth his "possession" (אֲחֻזָּה). Thus the Pentateuch and other Old Testament passages link the seed of the woman in Genesis 3:15 to a royal individual who will climactically defeat his enemies and inherit all that is promised in the Abrahamic covenant (Gen 15:3-4).

A corporate understanding of the "seed of the woman," whether referring to the human race in general, Israel, or the righteous, does not fit the reality of humanity as a whole being helplessly mired in sin (Gen 6:5; 8:21; Deut 31:21) and subject to a divine death sentence (Gen 5:5-29; Ps 90:3, 7-9). Whereas the serpent's initial victory was also a victory for sin and death (see Gen 3:19, 22; 4:7), neither the human race, Israel, nor the righteous in and of themselves show any signs whatsoever of being able to conquer any of these three foes. Rather, the Lord himself will slay the serpent (Is 27:1), put away sin (Mic 7:19; Ps 103:12), and vanquish death (Is 25:1; Hos 13:14). Moreover, there is nothing in the Old Testament that links any of these groups to being struck on the heel by the serpent while simultaneously defeating him. Even if Romans 16:20 is considered, it is still the Lord who crushes Satan under the feet of his people. A close parallel is that of faithless Israel being fatally bitten by snakes in Numbers 21:4-9, which only reinforces their need to be saved by the Lord from the same three enemies (Deut 8:15; Jer 8:17; see chap. 6 below).

Another specific problem with interpreting the "seed of the woman" corporately as referring to humanity in general is that it leads to a misunderstanding of the conflict between the serpent's seed and her seed (Gen 3:15). If the woman's seed refers to humanity generally, then the serpent's seed cannot also include humanity generally and is most naturally equated with demons only, who have followed Satan. The parties in conflict then would be Eve and the human race on one side, and Satan and demons on the other. But the idea that the conflict predicted in Genesis 3:15 is primarily between humans and demons does not square with the aforementioned passages in

Scripture that liken wicked human beings to serpents. Such passages show that the wicked are part of the serpent's seed.[22]

Some might suggest in response that the wicked are part of the serpent's seed but Israel or the righteous are part of the woman's. But neither Israel nor the righteous are inherently any better than the wicked, as suggested by Paul's application of Psalm 140:3 ("They make their tongue sharp like a serpent's; the poison of a viper is under their lips") in Romans 3:13 to all people, including Jews and Greeks (Rom 3:9-20). In the same context (Rom 3:10-12), Paul also cites Psalm 14:1-3, which emphatically states, "There is none righteous, not one . . . there is no one doing good, not even one." This truth is confirmed in the Pentateuch itself in the Jacob narrative and as such would have been comprehensible even to its earliest (Israelite) readers. The circumstances of Jacob's birth (i.e., grasping Esau's heel, which parallels the serpent striking a heel in Gen 3:15 if both acts are imagined as silhouettes, and the alternate name Edom seen as a wordplay on Adam), his birth name (Jacob means "he grasps the heel" or "he supplants"), and his deceptiveness in his early years cast the younger Jacob in the mold of the serpent. It is only through the Lord's faithfulness to his covenant with Abraham and his grace that Jacob becomes Israel (Gen 28:13-15; 32:24-30). Not only had his name been changed but so had his character through a genuine knowledge of the Lord (Gen 30:33; 31:38-42; 32:9-12; 33:10-11). The transformation of the nation of Israel's namesake and forefather from resembling a serpent to confessing that God had been his shepherd all his life (Gen 48:15) shows paradigmatically that both the Israelites themselves and the righteous are not exempt from the same wicked tendencies of humanity generally. Neither group in and of itself can hope to crush the head of the serpent, since their subjection to sin and death shows that they too have been defeated by him. Other passages are especially clear about the Israelites' inability to save themselves. Joseph's brothers ("the sons of Israel" in Gen 42:5) were guilty of the capital offense of kidnapping their brother and selling him as a slave (Gen 37:27-28; 40:15; Deut 24:7). A comparison of Isaiah 1:4 and Isaiah 14:20 reveals that Israel, as "the seed of evildoers," was not essentially different

---

[22]T. Desmond Alexander, "Messianic Ideology in the Book of Genesis," in *The Lord's Anointed: Interpretation of Old Testament Messianic Texts*, ed. Philip Satterthwaite, Richard Hess, and Gordon Wenham (Grand Rapids: Baker, 1995), 24, 31.

from Babylon. In fact, Ezekiel 3:5-7; 5:6-7 even characterizes Israel as worse than the nations. Israel was just as needy of the Lord's grace as their forefather Jacob (Is 59:5; Jer 9:4 [MT v. 3]; Hos 12:1-3 [MT vv. 2-4]).

The preceding passages repeatedly link all unredeemed human beings collectively to the serpent's seed. Related to the seed of the woman, this contradicts taking this seed as her posterity collectively, whether referring to the entire human race or even Israel or the righteous. It would be incoherent to understand the woman's seed as human beings generally, who are wicked, while at the same time taking the serpent's seed as including not only demons but also wicked human beings. Since Israel (including their namesake) and the righteous suffer from the same wicked tendencies as everyone else, all human beings in the present fallen world apart from the salvation of the Lord are in a broad sense part of the serpent's seed because of their wickedness (Jn 8:44; Eph 2:1-3; 2 Cor 4:4), even though paradoxically they are still made in the image of God (Gen 1:26-27; see Acts 17:28). Interpreting the seed of the woman as the human race also conflates the seed of the woman with the "sons of Adam" (Gen 11:5), who are all subject to sin and death (Ps 14:2; 53:2; 89:47; 90:2).

Equating the woman's seed simply with Israel or the righteous is appealing because it fits with the development of the theme of seed in the Pentateuch that narrows it to this specific line (Gen 12:7; 24:60; 28:13-14), often related to conflict with the wicked (e.g., Abel in Gen 4:1-12; Israel in Ex 1:7-14). But this specific line cannot simply represent the righteous (in contrast with the wicked seed of the serpent) because of the mixed character of not only Jacob (and the nation of Israel) but also key figures such as Noah (Gen 9:20-21) and Abraham (Gen 12:11-13; 16:1-4; 20:2). Nevertheless, there is another way to explain this feature of the Pentateuch. Although this narrowing does at points relate to Israel's role in the Abrahamic covenant (e.g., Gen 15:13-16) and the Lord's faithfulness to this covenant, at other points and with respect to Genesis 3:15 it relates to the Messiah coming from Israel's line to save both his own nation and all the nations of the world (Is 49:5-6).[23] In order for this to happen (Num 22:12; 24:17), it

---

[23]We do not hold that the Messiah is a spiritual "Israel" as some argue on the basis of Is 49:3. The "and now" of Is 49:5 can be taken as a sharp transition from the preceding context, as in Is 43:1; 44:1; 47:8; 48:16.

was necessary at least for Israel to be preserved, which naturally included foretastes of eschatological victory (e.g., the exodus). However, Israel's limited victories over enemies never achieved final victory. Thus the conflict in Genesis 3:15 makes the most sense if it concerns an individual seed of the woman, the serpent, and all who follow the serpent, be they demons or humans. Incidentally, if Jacob is taken as a paradigm, then the righteous people of God are not innately righteous but delivered out of a former life of following in the serpent's pattern (Jn 5:24; Col 1:13). This resembles Abram being called out of "Ur of the Chaldeans" (Gen 15:7), that is, Babel/Babylon (Gen 11:9; Is 13:19). Just as Abraham would become "father of a multitude of nations" (Gen 17:4-5), so Jacob would become a "congregation of peoples" (Gen 28:3; 48:4; 49:10). If the preceding arguments hold, then Israel and the righteous are not the focus of Genesis 3:15, even though they are aligned with the seed of the woman and share in his conflict with the serpent and its seed.[24] They can also be linked to the conflict between the serpent and Eve because she is "the mother of all living" (Gen 3:20).

There are thus good reasons for understanding Genesis 3:15 as the first direct prophecy of the Messiah in the Pentateuch and the Old Testament. As such, it selectively combines important Messianic themes, such as enmity with the serpent, the promise of seed, the key role of a woman, the crushing of the serpent's head, and the crushing of his own heel. To these may be added other themes in the preceding context that are intentionally linked to Genesis 3:15. In any case, to use the optical metaphor, this verse is a "lens" that deliberately focuses select Messianic wavelengths from the overall spectrum.

---

[24]It is understandable why Hamilton ("Skull Crushing Seed," 33) takes the seed as including the people of God because it explains conflicts such as those between Cain and Abel, Isaac and Ishmael, Israel and Egypt, and Esther and Haman. Like us, he believes that the seed of the serpent is best understood as the enemies of God and his people. But in his focus on "the theme of the head crushing seed of the woman in the Bible" (31), he does not give enough weight to grammatical considerations that strongly suggest that the "he" in Gen 3:15 refers only to an individual. If this is true, then Eve's "seed" most likely also refers to an individual, in keeping with standard pronoun usage. Though Hamilton references Collins and Alexander, he ends up emphasizing the "ambiguity between the one and the many" here and elsewhere in the OT (32-33). As a result, he conflates Jael's defeat of Sisera and David's defeat of Goliath with the Messianic fulfillment of "he will crush your head" (35). These two passages, however, are better treated as reminders and foretastes of the fulfillment of Gen 3:15, since, among other things, neither involves the victor being struck on the heel.

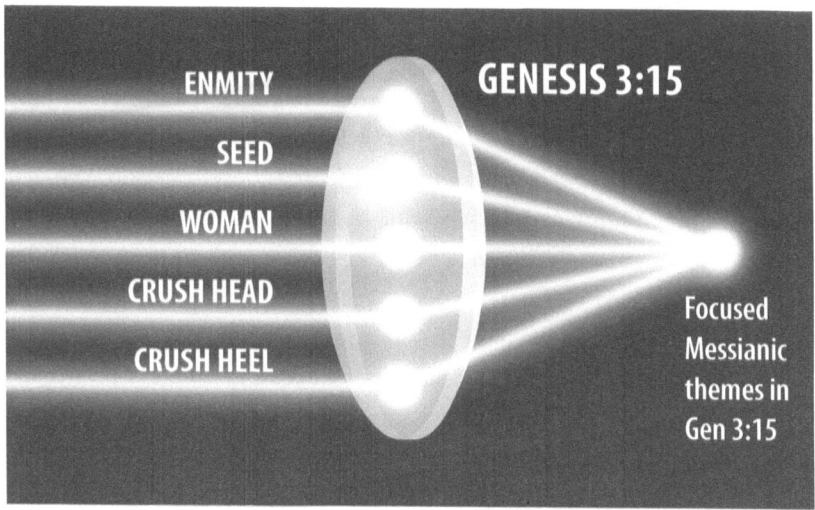

Figure 1.1. The lens of Genesis 3:15

Each of these five themes deserves consideration. Since enmity and seed were already treated above, the discussion turns now to the other three, beginning with the key role of a woman. As has long been observed, the promise of salvation focuses especially on Eve. The Lord referred to the future deliverer as her seed, rather than Adam's. Eve was the one who had been deceived by the serpent (Gen 3:1-6, 13), but she would have the last laugh when one of her offspring defeated him. Such themes are reiterated in the blessing of Rebekah, which predicted that "your seed will possess the gate of his enemies" (Gen 24:60). The relationship of this verse to Genesis 3:15 has already been discussed above. Thus Rebekah's imminent marriage to Isaac implies that the "seed of the woman" prophecy as well as related promises to Abraham will be fulfilled through her (and incidentally, not through humanity generally). In the process, the crucial role of women in the Lord's redemptive plan is foregrounded again.[25]

One of the best examples of a woman's victory over an enemy is in Judges 4–5, where Deborah and Jael led Israel in triumph over Sisera and his army. Although Barak and his men fought in the battle, Judges 4:8-9 makes clear that the glory of victory would not be his, "for the LORD will

---

[25]Such an emphasis is also found in Ex 2:1-10 surrounding the preservation of baby Moses' life through his mother, his sister, and Pharaoh's daughter.

sell Sisera into the hand of a woman." Sure enough, using a cunning that recalls the serpent's (Gen 3:1), Jael drove a tent peg through the temple of Sisera as he slept in her tent (Judg 4:17-21). The themes of cunning and the crushing of the head of the enemy provide strong evidence that this passage should be viewed as intentionally related to Genesis 3:15. While it cannot be the fulfillment of Genesis 3:15 because Jael, a woman, cannot be the "he" who crushes the enemy's head, it provides an arresting reminder of this prophecy and a foretaste of its victorious fulfillment. Such a relationship between these two passages is reinforced by the poetic recounting of this victory in Judges 5:25-27, which uses words and themes in common with both Genesis 3:15 (a woman and crushing the "head" [רֹאשׁ] of an enemy) and Genesis 49:8-12 ("milk" [חָלָב], "between [his or her] feet" [מִבֵּין רַגְלָיו, בֵּין רַגְלֶיהָ], "stoop down" [כָּרַע], "lie down" [רָבַץ, שָׁכַב]). The latter passage is itself a prophecy that specifies among other things that the Messiah will come from Judah (see chap. 3 below).

Like Eve and Rebekah, Ruth is also highlighted for bearing a seed in relation to the Lord's saving plan (Ruth 4:12).[26] Her comparison to Judah's wife Tamar befits not only her status as a righteous outsider and the Levirate nature of her marriage to Boaz (see Gen 38:1-26; Deut 25:5-10) but also links her to the fulfillment of the Messianic prophecy given to Judah in Genesis 49:8-12. Just as Tamar had married into the Judah's house and became part of the Messiah's line, so did Ruth (see Ruth 4:17-21). Through the son she bore, Ruth was considered someone who "built" the nation of Israel, much like Rachel and Leah had centuries ago (Ruth 4:11). The combination of "seed" and "building" language in Ruth 4:11-12 relates to the "building up" of the nation (through royal descendants), while at the same time tying into the Lord's promise to her great-grandson David three generations later that the Lord would build a house for David and that David's "seed" would build a house for the Lord (2 Sam 7:11-13; 1 Chron 17:10-12). It is fitting to connect these texts to still other Old Testament passages that speak of the Lord building Jerusalem and Zion (Ps 51:18; 102:16; 127:1; 147:2; Jer 24:6; 31:28).

As pointed out above, Zechariah 6:13 predicts that the Messiah will build the eschatological temple of the Lord, and Eve, Rebekah, and Ruth

---

[26]Both Rebekah and Ruth are called "young woman" (Gen 24:16, 28, 55, 57; Ruth 2:5-6; 4:12).

are especially highlighted as being part of his ancestral line. The book of Ruth is in the third and last section of the Hebrew Bible known as the Writings, as is the book of Esther. These two books remind readers of the crucial role of women in the salvation plan of God, which was set forth at the outset in Genesis 3:15.[27] The seed of a *woman* will ultimately be victorious over the serpent. Although there is not space here to enter into the longstanding debate over Isaiah 7:14, suffice it to say that the birth of Immanuel from a "virgin" (עַלְמָה) certainly fits with this broader theme.[28]

The climax of Genesis 3:15 involves the twin themes of the seed crushing the head of the serpent and the serpent crushing his heel. The former describes the final defeat of the serpent and suggests the similar defeat of sin (which he uses successfully to tempt) and death (which ensues as divine punishment for sin).[29] That the crushing of a head refers to final victory is supported not only by the aforementioned Judges 4–5 but also by passages such as Psalm 74:13 ("you broke the heads of Leviathan"), Psalm 110:6 ("he crushes the head"), and Habakkuk 3:13 ("you crush the head from the house of wickedness"), the last of which seems to play on an alternate meaning of "head" (רֹאשׁ) as "leader" or "chief," which is left open in the Hebrew text of Genesis 3:15 (הוּא יְשׁוּפְךָ רֹאשׁ, lit., "He will crush you [on?] the head").[30] Whereas the subject in both Psalm 74:13 and Habakkuk 3:13 is the Lord, Numbers 24:17 predicts that the Messiah will do the same thing to the "foreheads" (פֵּאָה) of Moab and all the sons of Seth, two groups representative not only of Israel's enemies but also of the serpent's "seed" (Num 24:18). The subject in Psalm 110:6 is probably also the Messiah, and its phrase "he crushes the head" (מָחַץ רֹאשׁ) draws simultaneously on Genesis 3:15 (רֹאשׁ "head") and Numbers 24:8, 17 (מָחַץ "crush") while linking these two passages together in an eschatological context. Reinforced by Psalm 110:6, Numbers 24:17-18 thus provides evidence from within the Pentateuch itself for a Messianic interpretation of Genesis 3:15,

---

[27]Stephen Dempster, *Dominion and Dynasty* (Downers Grove, IL: InterVarsity Press, 2003), 39, 223.
[28]The use of the same term related to Rebekah in Gen 24:43 further strengthens this connection.
[29]Wenham, *Genesis 1-15*, 80, asserts, "the serpent symbolizes sin, death, and the power of evil."
[30]Citing Gen 3:15; 37:21; Deut 22:26; 33:11; 2 Sam 3:27; Jer 2:16; and Ps 3:8, GKC §117ll classifies this construction as a subcategory of the double accusative, in which "the second accusative sometimes more closely determines the nearer object by indicating the part or member specially affected by the action." But even such a specification of what is struck in Gen 3:15 does not exclude the possibility of wordplay.

and Psalm 74:13 and Habakkuk 3:13 hint at his close relationship with the Lord himself, since both achieve eschatological victory by crushing enemy heads. Such considerations can be easily related to the Lord's promise to the Messiah in Ps 110:1 to "set your enemies as a footstool,"[31] especially since Psalm 110:6, borrowing language from both Genesis 3:15 and Numbers 24:17, describes the Messiah's victory with the phrase, "he crushes the head" (מָחַץ רֹאשׁ). The common themes of a defeated enemy and the heel or feet of the victor further suggest that the seed crushes the serpent's head by stomping on it (see Ps 91:13; Is 63:3), a victory in which the Lord's people will share (Is 26:6; Mic 5:8; Rom 16:20; see Deut 33:29).

More mysterious at first glance is the precise meaning of the serpent striking the heel of the seed. At the very least, this means that the seed will be injured by the serpent even as he defeats him. But what kind of injury might this be? Since there are not very many ways in which a snake can harm a person, the most natural way to understand this injury is as snakebite.[32] Although it is common knowledge that such bites are not necessarily poisonous, the broader context of the Pentateuch suggests that the reader is supposed to understand the seed of the woman as suffering a poisonous snakebite, even a fatal one. This is because an important parallel passage in the Pentateuch references fatal snakebites. Numbers 21:4-6 describes Israel grumbling again and being bitten by "fiery serpents" so that "many people from Israel died." This passage has additional words and themes in common with Genesis 3:15 that suggest an intentional intertextual relationship (see chap. 6 below). Genesis 49:17 seems to support the casting of snakebites as at least poisonous. It likens Dan to a "serpent" (נָחָשׁ) that bites the "heels" (pl. of עָקֵב) of a horse, resulting in its rider falling backward. For a powerful war horse to react so suddenly and forcefully to a snakebite, presumably by rearing up on its hind legs, if not falling backward itself, suggests that this bite was at least poisonous. In any case, the similarity of language and imagery to Genesis 3:15 of a snake injuring a heel evidently led to a recollection of this earlier passage in the following verse (Gen 49:18) through a prayer regarding the salvation it promised ("I wait for your salvation, O LORD"). Using different vocabulary for

---

[31]Ps 8:6 similarly says that the Lord has "put all things under his feet."
[32]As Rashi does. He also believes that the bite is fatal and relates Gen 3:15 to Gen 49:17.

snakes, Deuteronomy 32:33 accordingly refers to the "venom of serpents" (חֲמַת תַּנִּינִם) and "poison [head?] of cobras" (רֹאשׁ פְּתָנִים; see Deut 32:24). In view of this additional evidence from the Pentateuch itself, the serpent striking the heel of the seed in Genesis 3:15 most likely refers to a poisonous, even fatal, snakebite.[33]

Thus the seed of the woman will not merely be injured by the serpent but will be killed by him. In other words, Genesis 3:15, when understood in the broader compositional context of the Pentateuch, predicts that the seed's victory will come at the cost of his own suffering and death. The ancient conflict between Eve and the serpent will be brought to a climactic end in this way through a self-sacrificing hero, the Messiah. Although his death makes Genesis 3:15 anticlimactic, the subsequent unfolding of the Pentateuch's Messianic vision will reveal that death is not the end for this seed (see chap. 3 below). Nevertheless, Genesis 3:15 sets forth important boundaries for the whole spectrum of the Pentateuch's Messianic vision. By presenting him as a fatally wounded champion, it has already taken a bold first step in unfolding the grand vision that will ultimately encompass both his salvation of humanity and his own death.

Intentional Foreshadowing of the Messiah

Whereas the preceding section focused on a direct, exclusively Messianic fulfillment of Genesis 3:15 and its significance as such, this section shows that this text also simultaneously draws on the preceding narrative to portray Adam, especially before the Fall, as intentionally foreshadowing the Messiah. The clearest indication of this is the relationship between the command that Adam rule the animals (Gen 1:26-28; 2:19-20) and the serpent's successful temptation of him and Eve (Gen 3:1-6). In short, the eating of the fruit of the tree of knowledge of good and evil was not only rebellion against the Lord's direct command in Genesis 2:17 but also a failure to properly rule all the animals of the earth. Genesis 3:1 explicitly includes the serpent in this group, describing it as "more cunning than all of the animals of the field which the Lord God made." For its crime, it was

---

[33] Also, Job 20:16 accordingly refers to the lethal venom of a snake. Ps 58:4; 140:3; and Prov 23:32 refer to poisonous snakebites without clear evidence in the immediate context whether such bites are also fatal.

accordingly "cursed more than every beast and every living thing of the field" (Gen 3:14).[34] By obeying the serpent instead of subduing it (Gen 1:28), Adam effectively subverted the authority that the Lord intended for him to have over all creatures of the earth.

With this recent failure still fresh in the reader's mind, Genesis 3:15 predicts that a seed of the woman will crush the serpent's head. Properly understood in its context, this verse is saying that the rule that Adam was supposed to exercise over all the animals but failed to (Gen 3:1-6) will be realized by the Messiah, who will subdue the unruliest of them.[35] Genesis 3:15 foretells the coming of the Messiah in such a way that it deliberately alludes to Adam and the rule intended for him as the representative head of the human race. In this way, the author of the Pentateuch self-consciously presents Adam in Genesis 1–3 as intentionally foreshadowing the Messiah and his perfect rule. Thus, when Roman 5:14 refers to Adam as a "type" (τύπος) of Christ, such patterning is already discoverable from an exegesis of Genesis 1–3 itself.[36] For the purposes of his argument in Romans 5:12-21, Paul did not highlight the rule that was intended for Adam but instead his failure as a representative of the human race and the subsequent "reign" of death and sin (Rom 5:14, 17, 21). To be sure, the latter implicitly recalls Adam's failure to reign and dovetails with the "reign" of grace and of believers through Jesus Christ (Rom 5:17, 21). The overall correspondence of thought to Genesis 3:15 in its original context is unmistakable.

As already pointed out above, the rule that human beings were commanded to exercise in Genesis 1:26-28 is intertwined with the rule that the

---

[34] Ephrem the Syrian (4th century AD) sees this judgment as fitting "because you deceived those who rule over all beasts." He thus implicitly recognizes the present point we are making that Adam's sin was a failure to rule the animals. See Andrew Louth, ed., *Genesis 1–11*, Ancient Christian Commentary on Scripture (Downers Grove, IL: InterVarsity Press, 2001), 89.

[35] Calvin, *Genesis*, 171, passingly references "one stronger than he [i.e., Satan] has descended from heaven, who will subdue him." It is important to remember that Calvin arrives at this idea differently than we do, since he interprets the seed collectively, i.e., "the posterity of the woman generally" (170). But, he reasons, "we must necessarily come to one head, that we may find to whom the victory belongs. So Paul, from the seed of Abraham, leads us to Christ. . . . Wherefore, the sense will be (in my judgment) that the human race, which Satan was endeavouring to oppress, would at length be victorious." While it is true that Christ wins the victory over Satan for believers as our representative, this view still does not account for the use of the singular pronoun *he* in Genesis 3:15 and its implication that the seed of the woman is singular.

[36] A similar argument applies to 1 Cor 15:21-22, 45-49, which focuses on Adam and Jesus as respective heads of the human race.

first and representative human, Adam, was supposed to exercise in the Garden of Eden, an archetypal sanctuary. His exile from this perfect place in which he was supposed to live forever in fellowship with the Lord parallels the promise of land to Abraham and later to the nation of Israel, who themselves will face the problem of exile (Deut 4:25-27; 30:1).[37] In view of this broader theme in the Pentateuch, it stands to reason that the seed in Genesis 3:15 will lead the Lord's people back to this pristine place (at least in essence) from which he will take on both the royal and priestly roles originally given to Adam.

A more direct reason to see priestly overtones in the Messianic prophecy of Genesis 3:15 is that the Pentateuch characterizes the serpent as an unclean animal (Lev 11:41-43). The Lord's judgment of this creature in Genesis 3:14 includes the statement, "you will travel on your belly" (גָּחוֹן), and Leviticus 11:42 declares that "everything that travels on its belly" (כֹּל הוֹלֵךְ עַל־גָּחוֹן) is "detestable" (שֶׁקֶץ). These are the only two places in the Pentateuch and the Old Testament where this word for "belly" appears. Also noting common themes of eating, clean/unclean, and divine commandment(s), Nobuyoshi Kiuchi sees "Genesis 3 as the background of Leviticus 11" and even argues that an implicit criteria for a clean or unclean animal is its resemblance to the serpent hinted at in Leviticus 11:42.[38] Whether or not the latter is true, the broader compositional context of the Pentateuch still implies that, in addition to disobeying the prohibition against the forbidden fruit and failing to properly rule the animals (Gen 1:26-28; 2:17), Adam had also made himself "detestable" and "unclean" by listening to the serpent (Lev 11:43) and had defiled the garden sanctuary.[39] Priests would later be charged with making a distinction "between the unclean and the clean" (Lev 10:10), something that Adam clearly failed to do. This priestly charge is linked to the extensive instructions concerning cleanness and uncleanness in the subsequent context in Leviticus 11–15, which Kiuchi also sees as having "the fall of Gen. 3 as its

---

[37] For more on the parallels between the Garden of Eden and the Promised Land, see John Sailhamer, *Genesis Unbound* (repr., Eugene, OR: Wipf and Stock, 1996).

[38] Nobuyoshi Kiuchi, *Leviticus*, Apollos Old Testament Commentary (Downers Grove, IL: InterVarsity Press, 2007), 204-7. Beale, *Temple and the Church's Mission*, 69-70, calls the serpent an "unclean creature" and "foul serpent."

[39] Postell, *Adam as Israel*, 113, 129.

immediate literary and ideological background."[40] He notes that the order of addressees in Genesis 3:14-19 (serpent, woman, man) matches the order in Leviticus 11–13: "everything that travels on its belly" (Lev 11:42), "a woman" who has given birth (Lev 12:2), and "a man" (Lev 13:2). Sailhamer further points out that the casting out of Adam and Eve from the Garden parallels the exclusion of the unclean leper in Leviticus 13:46.[41] Moreover, the exposure of Adam's nakedness (Gen 3:7-11) contrasts with what was later prescribed for priests (Ex 28:42). His shame about his nakedness also suggests the reality of his uncleanness (see Ezek 16:61-63; 20:43; 36:31). Such considerations reinforce the priestly overtones of Genesis 2 and tie them to the promise of salvation in Genesis 3:15.

The important implication is that the seed of the woman will not only defeat the serpent but will thus also decisively remove uncleanness from creation by destroying its source, the ultimate unclean animal. Cleansing, of course, is one of the primary duties of a priest (e.g., Lev 13:6, 13). The purification effected by the seed of the woman, however, evidently will not involve the shed blood of a sacrificial animal but his own blood flowing from his heel. He himself will die a sacrificial death. As was true for the striking of the head of the enemy (see above discussion of Num 24:17; Ps 74:13; Hab 3:13), both the Messiah and the Lord himself are credited equally for this eschatological cleansing (see Deut 32:43; Is 52:15; Ezek 16:63; 36:25). In any case, the bottom line is that when the serpent is recognized not only as one of the animals but as an *unclean* animal, the seed of the woman is then recognized as being both a king who rules all the animals and a priest who removes uncleanness through sacrificing his own life.

As seen above, other Old Testament prophecies such as Zechariah 6:13 also predict that the Messiah will be a priest-king ("And he will bear majesty and will sit and rule on his throne, and he will be a priest on his throne"). To this passage may also be added Psalm 110:4, which says to the king seated at the right hand of the Lord that "You are a priest forever, in the order of Melchizedek." If the preceding argument is valid for Genesis 3:15 employing intentional foreshadowing to present the Messiah as a priest-king, then these later passages are not innovations but are

---

[40]Kiuchi, *Leviticus*, 225.
[41]Sailhamer, *Pentateuch as Narrative*, 110. See also Postell, *Adam as Israel*, 124, 129.

wholly within bounds of the authorially intended meaning of the Pentateuch. A similar argument can be made for Psalm 8, which receives a Messianic interpretation in Hebrews 2:6-9. If the seed of the woman in Genesis 3:15 is being presented by the author of the Pentateuch as the ruler over all creation that Adam failed to be, then it is conceivable that Psalm 8:4-8 picks up on an intended Messianic meaning of Genesis 1–3, rather than only indirectly relating to the Messiah while focusing on its meaning for humans generally. In fact, there is actually little reason to think that Adam's descendants generally will fulfill the command to rule any better than he did, as some interpretations of Psalm 8 assume.[42] If anything, such rule became more difficult with the curse on the ground (Gen 3:17-19), the reign of death and sin (Gen 3:19; 4:7; 5:5-27; 6:5; 8:21), and animals' subsequent fear of humankind (Gen 9:2). The reality of continued hostility from the serpent and his offspring also implies that humanity's intended rule will not be realized for a while. Indeed, it is the seed of the woman who will bring an end to this conflict by fulfilling the original command to rule. Psalm 8 confirms this with its emphasis on an individual "son of Adam" (Ps 8:4) who will be crowned with "glory and honor" (Ps 8:5) and will rule over all creation (Ps 8:6-8).[43] Hebrews 2:6-9 can then be seen as being in full accord with both Psalm 8 and Genesis 1–3.

The preceding considerations show that Genesis 3:15, in addition to being a direct prophecy, simultaneously employs intentional foreshadowing to cast a vision of the Messiah. On the one hand, as direct prophecy it explains that the seed of the woman will defeat the serpent at great cost to himself. On the other hand, its relationship to the preceding context, especially those parts that concern Adam, implies that this seed will fulfill the command to rule that Adam had failed to and be a priest who will decisively deal with uncleanness. It is important to distinguish this

---

[42]E.g., Peter C. Craigie and Marvin E. Tate, *Psalms 1-50,* 2nd ed., Word Biblical Commentary (Nashville: Thomas Nelson, 2004), 107-9; H. J. Kraus, *Psalms 1-59,* trans. Hilton C. Oswald (Minneapolis: Fortress, 1993), 183; James L. Mays, *Psalms,* Interpretation (Louisville: Knox, 1994), 65-69.

[43]If psalms are intentionally interrelated in the Book of Psalms as a whole (as we believe), then the appearance of the same terminology in Messianic contexts elsewhere in the Psalter (Ps 21:6; 45:2-4; 110:1) further supports the Messianic interpretation of Ps 8. See David C. Mitchell, *The Message of the Psalter: An Eschatological Programme in the Book of Psalms,* JSOT Supplement Series, ed. David J. A. Clines and Philip R. Davies (Sheffield: Sheffield Academic, 1997).

exegetical result from the mere drawing of correspondences between Adam and Christ without regard to the authorial intent of Genesis 1–3 and the Pentateuch itself. Of course, not everything that concerns Adam in Genesis 1–3 intentionally foreshadows the Messiah. Obviously, his eating of the forbidden fruit does not directly correspond to anything that the Messiah will do (see Mt 4:3-4). Indeed, this act amounts to Adam being defeated by the serpent, an ordering which will be reversed climactically by the seed of the woman. Instead, Adam's failure intentionally foreshadows the later failure of Israel, as Postell has shown.[44]

To return to the optical analogy, Genesis 3:15 thus acts like both a "lens" that combines select Messianic "wavelengths" (or themes) and a "mirror" that reflects select attributes of the coming king. Appropriately, the unique wavelengths and reflected elements projected by this text are integrally related to the preceding narrative context (Gen 1–3). As a "mirror," Genesis 3:15 is not like a typical plane mirror that we are accustomed to in our homes and cars, but rather like a surface of water that has unique ripples, lighting, and angle with respect to the object it reflects. It does not reflect everything about the Messiah but only select elements in a unique configuration. Compared to those elements communicated via direct prophecy, those communicated via the "reflections" of intentional foreshadowing are relatively indirect. There is still light that comes from the latter, but it is dimmer. This is why the kingly and especially the priestly implications of Genesis 3:15 are not as obvious at first glance and only emerge when the direct prophecy is investigated in closer relationship to the preceding context and the context of the Pentateuch as a whole. As pointed out above, the "edges" of such reflections are usually blurry, which requires the interpreter to carefully (i.e., exegetically) determine the extent of intentional foreshadowing employed.

Suffice it to say that Messianic prophecy can be very "dense"—that is, it can say a lot with just a few words. On one level, this should not be

---

[44]See Postell, *Adam as Israel*. The correspondences between Adam, Israel, and the Messiah illustrate the problem with referring to Adam as a "type" without regard to authorial intention. Is Adam a type of Christ, or of Israel, or both? As if this were not confusing enough, is Israel in turn a type of Christ? The issue is not that of the clear parallels between the various entities but that of potentially reductionistic views of Adam, which result from focusing too much on Adam the person rather than the biblical text and the varied points it makes related to Adam. The reality is that Gen 1–3 intentionally casts Adam in some respects as foreshadowing Christ and in others as foreshadowing the failure of Israel at Mount Sinai.

surprising since many such prophecies, including Genesis 3:15, are expressed via poetry, which by nature of its terseness and frequent use of figurative language is generally denser than narrative. If the four Gospels provide the closest thing to a "photograph" of the Messiah through their direct narrative accounts of Jesus' life and ministry, then Genesis 3:15 and other Messianic prophecies expressed through poetry by comparison provide a more figurative, though no less true, depiction. While recognizing the limitations of this analogy, we suggest that the Gospel narratives are to these poetic prophecies as a photo of the night sky is to van Gogh's classic painting *Starry Night*.[45] Readers of the Bible get to enjoy the beauty of both kinds of depictions, one more like a photograph and the other more figurative. Elizabeth Drew, author of multiple books on English poetry and literature, captures the difference well,

> The basic difference between words used in poetry and in prose is the amount of activity they transmit.... The greater the poet the more value he will wring from his medium: music, meaning, memory; simplicity and ornament; image and idea; dramatic force and lyrical intensity; direct statement and oblique suggestion; color, light, power—all are distilled from his words.[46]

This holds true for poetry in the Old Testament especially because biblical Hebrew as a language is concisely expressed and hence well-suited for poetic expression.[47] Accordingly, a poetic line often consists of only three or four Hebrew words. When this literary form is used to communicate Messianic prophecy, there is thus a good chance that it bears a high concentration of Messianic content. Furthermore, as seen above through the Hebrew word *'adam* (אָדָם, referring to humanity, an individual man, or the name of the first man), biblical Hebrew is rich with wordplay, and Hebrew poetry often employs this literary device to great effect. Furthermore, biblical authors can use the related literary devices of double entendre and

---

[45] In a letter to his sister Willemien, Vincent van Gogh wrote, "One can speak poetry just by arranging colours well, just as one can say comforting things in music." See the Van Gogh Letters Project, "To Willemien van Gogh Arles, on or about Monday, 12 November 1888," Letter 720, accessed December 2017, www.vangoghletters.org/vg/letters/let720/letter.html.

[46] Elizabeth Drew, *Poetry: A Modern Guide to its Understanding and Enjoyment* (New York: Dell, 1959), 74.

[47] See Tremper Longman III and Raymond B. Dillard, *An Introduction to the Old Testament*, 2nd ed. (Grand Rapids: Zondervan, 2006), 26-27; W. G. E. Watson, *Classical Hebrew Poetry: A Guide to Its Techniques* (Sheffield: JSOT Press, 1986), 251.

polysemy in still other ways,[48] as evidenced by the various significances of the serpent (as empowered and filled by Satan, but at the same time as one of the animals—and an unclean one at that). In the case of Genesis 3:15, a high level of information is communicated not only through the terse and figurative language inherent to its poetic form but also through additional connotations drawn from its relationship to the preceding narrative context and other parts of the Pentateuch.[49]

This explains in part how the coming of the Messiah can play such a large role in the intended message of the Pentateuch, even though he receives comparatively far less attention than other topics, such as the giving of the Sinai/Deuteronomic law and the overarching narrative itself. The casual reader may unwittingly gloss over Messianic prophecies that are actually loaded with intended meaning and conclude that the Messiah is at most peripheral to the message of the Pentateuch. This would be a mistake, however, because Messianic prophecies, especially those in poetic form, are meant to be pondered slowly and mined for the depths of their intended meaning. Just as the tiny nucleus of an atom bears a tremendous amount of energy, so even a brief Messianic prophecy is packed with important content. As will be further shown in the subsequent chapters, these prophecies are even related to one another intertextually in an intricate network that synergistically projects a sweeping vision of the Messiah.

The "Building" of Eve and the "Rule" of the Great Lights

The preceding has argued that the use of Adam to intentionally foreshadow the Messiah in Genesis 3:15 includes his kingly and priestly roles and excludes his eating of the forbidden fruit and the subsequent consequences.

---

[48]See the work of Gary Rendsburg, including "Janus Parallelism in Gen 49:26," *JBL* 99 (1980): 291-93; "Double Polysemy in Gen 49:6 and Job 3:6," *CBQ* 44 (1982): 48-51; "Double Polysemy in Proverbs 31:19," in *Humanism, Culture, and Language in the Near East: Studies in Honor of Georg Krotkoff*, ed. A. Afsaruddin and A. H. Mathias Zahniser (Winona Lake, IN: Eisenbrauns, 1997), 267-74; "Word Play in Biblical Hebrew: An Eclectic Collection," in *Puns and Pundits: Word Play in the Bible and in Near Eastern Literature*, ed. S. B. Noegel (Bethesda, MD: CDL Press, 2000), 137-62. Although one may not always agree with his conclusions, Rendsburg's insightful work in this area nevertheless clearly shows the use of polysemy as a literary device in the OT.

[49]In support of this, Wenham, *Genesis 1-15*, 80, comments on Gen 3:15, "If elsewhere in the narrative we have double-entendre and symbolic language, it would be strange for it to disappear here, so that the serpent is just a snake and not an anti-God symbol."

It might be asked whether anything else in Genesis 1–3, especially the pre-Fall portion in Genesis 1–2, might also intentionally foreshadow the Messiah. One suggestive passage is the formation of Eve while Adam slept (Gen 2:21-22). While there are no clear ties to Genesis 3:15 (unlike the themes of royalty and priesthood), the language and themes do link to many other important passages in the Pentateuch and the Old Testament. For example, a "deep sleep" (תַּרְדֵּמָה) also fell on Abram (Gen 15:12) immediately prior to the Lord's formal institution of the Abrahamic covenant (Gen 15:13-21).[50] Later, this same covenant was the focus of Jacob's dream at Bethel (Gen 28:12-22), which took place after he had "lain down" to sleep (Gen 28:11). Joseph, in turn, also had revelatory dreams, presumably while sleeping (Gen 37:6-10). His dreams are also closely related to the direct prophecy about the Messiah in Genesis 49:8-9. The Pentateuch itself thus links Adam's sleep directly to the Abrahamic covenant and secondarily to the rule of the Messiah, though not through Genesis 3:15.[51] This should not be troublesome because there is no inherent reason why all the Messianic light in Genesis 1–3 without exception must pass through the lens of Genesis 3:15.

Furthermore, the "building" (בָּנָה) of Eve from Adam's "rib" or "side" (צֵלָע; Gen 2:21-22) parallels the building of the tabernacle, especially its "sides" (צֶלַע; Ex 26:20, 26-27, 35; 36:25, 31-32).[52] Genesis 2 thus not only has parallels to the tabernacle through its description of the Garden of Eden but also through the "building" of Eve. Both Solomon's temple and the eschatological temple in Ezekiel also have such "sides" (1 Kings 6:5;

---

[50] Gen 2:21 and Gen 15:12 are the only two places in the Pentateuch where this word appears. It is used in unrelated contexts elsewhere in the OT (1 Sam 26:12; Job 4:13; 33:15; Prov 19:15; Is 29:10).

[51] A link to Gen 3:15 could be the relationship between sleep and death (Ps 13:3; cf. Ps 3:5; 4:8) and in turn the Messiah's death through a fatal snakebite.

[52] Victor Hamilton, *The Book of Genesis: Chapters 1-17*, New International Commentary on the Old Testament (Grand Rapids: Eerdmans, 1990), 178-79; Nahum Sarna, *Genesis*, JPS Torah Commentary (Philadelphia: JPS, 1989), 22. As seen in Ruth 4:11, women are not only "built" but themselves are "builders" of the nation. Likewise, the church is built by God (Mt 16:18; Eph 2:20-22; 1 Pet 2:5) while at the same time exhorted to build itself up (1 Cor 14:12; 1 Thess 5:11). The word translated "side" uses the same three consonants as the verb meaning "to limp." This verb is used in Gen 32:31 (MT v. 32) of Jacob limping after his encounter at Peniel. As a distant echo of Gen 2:21-22, his limping (צלע) from a nighttime injury may suggest that the removal of Adam's rib (צלע) while he slept connects with the theme of suffering. This extraction presumably involved the opening up of Adam's flesh, which the Lord subsequently "closed up" when he was finished (Gen 2:21).

Ezek 41:5-11). Conversely, the bride in Song of Songs is praised for her beauty in terms of a majestic building, "Your neck is like the tower of David, built [בָּנוּי] with rows of stone" (Song 4:4). She is also "lovely like Jerusalem" (Song 6:4). The eschatological temple, in turn, is inextricably linked to eschatological Zion and eschatological Israel, which is not only "built" by the Lord (Ps 102:16; 147:2; Jer 31:4, 28) but is also his bride (Is 62:4-5; Hos 2:19-20). Prophetic passages thus closely link and even blur the distinction between the eschatological temple and the Lord's eschatological people, thus further connecting the themes of building a sanctuary and "building" a bride in the Pentateuch. Though more evidence may be necessary to call this demonstrably intentional, the creation of Eve to be Adam's wife thus does suggestively foreshadow the formal institution of the Abrahamic covenant and the building of the tabernacle, the temple, and the eschatological temple. The Abrahamic covenant is also linked directly to Genesis 3:15, especially through the theme of "seed" (Gen 12:7; 15:3, 5), and, as pointed out already, the eschatological temple will be built by the Messiah (Zech 6:12-13).

Another suggestive thread in Genesis 1–2 that is not obviously tied to Genesis 3:15 is that the rule of the sun and moon broadly parallels the rule of man (Gen 1:16-18, 26-28), as noted above. The sun, moon, and human beings are the only created things that exercise dominion in Genesis 1. In both cases, dominion is not given to an individual entity but to a plurality. This is clear with the sun and moon (Gen 1:16-18), implied through reference to human beings as "male and female" (Gen 1:27), and confirmed for the latter through plural verb forms for "let them rule" (Gen 1:26) and "subdue it and rule" (Gen 1:28). Furthermore, the noun used for the rule of the sun and moon in Genesis 1:16 (מֶמְשָׁלָה) is typically used elsewhere in the Old Testament of human rule (e.g., 1 Kings 9:19 and 2 Chron 8:6; 2 Kings 20:13 and Is 39:2; Jer 34:1) or divine rule (Ps 103:22; 114:2; 145:13). Its appearance in Genesis 1:16 and similarly in Psalm 136:8-9 are the exceptions. Likewise, the verb in Genesis 1:18 (מָשַׁל) is typically used of human rule (Gen 3:16; 4:7; 37:8; Ezek 19:14) or divine rule (Judg 8:23; 1 Chron 29:12; 2 Chron 20:6). The broader use of these two related terms thus provides another reason to associate the "rule" of the sun and moon with the rule of humans. The noun מֶמְשָׁלָה is even used of Messianic rule in Micah 4:8 and the verb מָשַׁל likewise in Psalm 8:6, Micah 5:2, and Zechariah 6:13.

As such, there is at least a thematic connection between the rule of the sun and moon and the rule of human beings, including the realization of the latter rule through the seed of the woman in Genesis 3:15. The use of the same terminology for the rule of the sun and moon elsewhere in the Old Testament for the rule of a human being or God further strengthens this connection. Granted, there is a qualitative difference between these two kinds of rule in that the former "rules" merely by giving "light upon the earth" from an exalted location (Gen 1:15, 17), not by exercising personal rule. Nevertheless, these various strands are drawn together in several Messianic texts that compare the rule of the Messiah to the "rule" of the sun. For example, 2 Samuel 23:3-4 compares the ideal Messianic ruler to "the light of morning, when the sun rises." Likewise, Isaiah 9:2 describes the coming of the Messianic king as the coming of a "great light" (אוֹר גָּדוֹל) upon those in darkness (see Is 60:1-3). The sun and moon in Genesis 1:16 had been similarly called "the two great lights" (שְׁנֵי הַמְּאֹרֹת הַגְּדֹלִים), with the sun being the "greater light" of the two (הַמָּאוֹר הַגָּדֹל). Isaiah 42:6; 49:6 reinforces the Messianic connection further by referring to the Messiah as a "light to the nations" (אוֹר גּוֹיִם). Along these lines, Malachi 4:2 associates the eschatological "day of the LORD" with the rising of the "sun of righteousness . . . with healing in its wings" for those who fear the Lord's name.

Thus, although the connecting line between rule of the great lights in Genesis 1:16-18 and the rule of the seed of the woman in Genesis 3:15 may seem faint, several later Old Testament passages clearly link the rule of the Messiah to the rule of the sun. It is plausible that the authors of these passages did so on the basis of studying of Genesis 1-3. From early on, meditation on the Pentateuch had been commended by the Lord himself (Deut 17:18-20; Josh 1:8). If later biblical authors were not only guided by the Holy Spirit but were also diligent students of the Pentateuch, then they have provided in their own writings inspired interpretations of Genesis 1-3, which is itself inspired (2 Tim 3:16). Despite the use of different terms for human rule in Genesis 1:26, 28 (רָדָה, כָּבַשׁ), it could have been that the thematic link between the great lights and the seed of the woman in Genesis 1-3 itself, along with their being the only created things to have this privilege, led later biblical authors to explicitly link them in their own writings. But these authors would not have been limited to Genesis 1–3, which is only a small part of a larger composition, the Pentateuch. Convergence of the same themes is found in Joseph's second dream (Gen 37:9), where the sun and moon are mentioned in connection with his future rule. The sun and moon bowing down to him even suggests that Joseph's and especially the Messiah's rule (Gen 49:8; see chap. 3) are even greater than those of the sun and moon. Toward the end of the Pentateuch, the verb used for the Lord "rising" from Seir (Deut 33:2) is one that typically refers to the rising of the sun (זרח; see Is 60:1; Mal 4:2). It is as though the Lord's rule is also compared to the sunrise. Just as both the Lord and the Messiah are described in different passages as crushing the head of the enemy and securing eschatological purification, the likening of the Lord's reign and the Messiah's reign to the sunrise is yet another hint at their close relationship.

Conclusion

The prophecy concerning the seed of the woman in Genesis 3:15 is a direct Messianic prophecy and the first one in the Bible. As such, it boldly sets forth key parameters in the Messianic vision of the Pentateuch. In particular, Genesis 3:15 predicts the coming of a man who will defeat the serpent at the cost of his own life, thus securing final victory over humanity's ancient enemy as their ideal representative. Based on the context of Genesis 1–3 and the broader context of the Pentateuch, this prophecy also implies that this seed will realize the kingly and priestly roles that Adam had failed to. The seed will rule and subdue the unruliest creature of them all and decisively remove uncleanness from creation. Although brief, the brilliant and multifaceted light emitted from Genesis 3:15 ought to attract the reader's close attention amidst the ongoing narrative storyline. Rightly appreciated, its dense, highly concentrated Messianic content shows where the Pentateuch's center of gravity lies. Salvation will come through the seed of the woman, not through the Sinai/Deuteronomic law which will be given later. Subsequent Messianic prophecies in the Pentateuch are likewise weighty with similar effect, as the following chapters will show.

2

THE SEED OF ABRAHAM IN THE PATRIARCHAL NARRATIVES

From Cain to Babel

The prophecy of an individual seed who will defeat the serpent, rule the earth, and banish uncleanness was not quickly fulfilled, as the subsequent narrative reveals (Gen 4–11). In stark contrast to the promise of a male offspring who will kill the snake and win the victory over evil for humanity, Cain killed his own brother, the godly Abel, out of jealousy (Gen 4:3-8). The sin of murder was repeated in Cain's line through Lamech (Gen 4:23-24), the seventh generation from Adam. Rather than humankind ruling as they were intended to (Gen 1:26, 28; 3:15), sin and death ruled over them (Gen 4:7; "and he died," Gen 5:5, 8, etc.; Rom 5:14, 17, 21). The faithful few included Enoch, also the seventh generation from Adam, and Noah, both of whom "walked with God" (Gen 5:22, 24; 6:9; cf. Gen 17:1).[1]

Sadly, God's original command that humankind "multiply" (רָבָה) and "fill [מָלֵא] the earth" (Gen 1:28), though being carried out in a sense in the days of Noah (Gen 6:1), had also resulted in the increase (רַבָּה) of humanity's wickedness (Gen 6:5) such that "the earth was filled [מָלֵא] with violence" (Gen 6:11, 13; see Gen 4:23-24). The creation that previously was "very good" (טוֹב מְאֹד) had been corrupted by human beings (Gen 6:11-12), whose hearts were "only evil [רַע] all the time" (Gen 6:5; 8:21). Earlier, the Lord brought "pain" (עָצַב, עִצָּבוֹן) on Adam and Eve as part of the just punishment for their sin (Gen 3:16-17), and now his own heart was "in

---

[1] Adam, in contrast, hid in the trees when God was "walking" in the garden (Gen 3:8). The use of Hith. הָלַךְ in all these passages implies that Adam was not "walking with God."

pain" (Hith. עָצַב) over the wickedness of humanity (Gen 6:6). If the traditional interpretation of "the sons of God" is correct, then the line of Seth also had been compromised (Gen 6:1-2), and Noah, though a righteous man, became drunk and naked in a way that recalls Adam's failure (Gen 9:20-25).[2] The flood had not changed the evil bent of the human heart (Gen 6:5; 8:21), as further confirmed through the wicked act of Ham (Gen 9:22-25; cf. Deut 31:21). Several chapters later, the "sons of Adam" again united against God at the Tower of Babel, where they attempted to "make a name" for themselves lest they "scatter across the face of the whole earth" (Gen 11:4-5). This act of pride and rebellion (see Gen 1:28; 9:1) was frustrated by the Lord who confused their language and scattered them anyway (Gen 11:6-9).

Nevertheless, there are indications in Genesis 4–11 amidst the gloomy realities of human sin and divine judgment that the Lord remained determined to bless humanity. The hope that Noah would bring comfort and relief from humanity's "painful toil" (עִצָּבוֹן) on a cursed land (Gen 5:29) was ultimately fulfilled through Noah's sacrifice (Gen 8:20-22) and the Lord's everlasting covenant with him (Gen 9:9-17). This covenant included protection for "all flesh" (כָּל־בָּשָׂר) from being destroyed by such a flood again (Gen 9:11, 15, 17). The ark had saved Noah's family and representative animals of every kind (Gen 7:13-16). Because there had been so much water, this floating instrument of salvation "was exalted above the earth" (Gen 7:17) including "every high mountain" (Gen 7:19), which suggestively resembles the eschatological Mount Zion in Isaiah 2:2. As he had at the beginning with Adam, the Lord "blessed" Noah's family and commanded that they "be fruitful and multiply and fill the earth" (Gen 9:1; see Gen 9:7; 1:28). There is however no repetition of the command to rule the animals, only the implication that this rule will become more difficult because of the animals' newfound fear of humans (Gen 9:2). As noted above, sin had by no means been eradicated, and the eternal salvation

---

[2] Noah was "a man of the ground" (אִישׁ הָאֲדָמָה; Gen 9:20); Adam was formed of dust "from the ground" (מִן־הָאֲדָמָה; Gen 2:7). Noah "planted a vineyard" (וַיִּטַּע כָּרֶם; Gen 9:20); the Lord God planted a garden (וַיִּטַּע יְהוָה אֱלֹהִים גַּן; Gen 2:8). Noah's sin involved drinking wine (Gen 9:21); Adam's sin involved eating fruit (Gen 3:6). Both sins resulted in "nakedness" (Gen 3:7, 10-11; 9:21-23), the appropriate covering of that nakedness (Gen 3:21; 9:23), and curse (Gen 3:14, 17; 9:25).

achieved by the seed of the woman in fulfillment of Genesis 3:15 was still yet to come.

BLESSING TO ALL THE FAMILIES OF THE LAND THROUGH ABRAM

Against the dark backdrop of sin and divine wrath in Genesis 1–11, and especially the rebellion at Babel (or Babylon),[3] God called Abram to leave his homeland for a new land (Gen 12:1-3). As Genesis 15:7 makes plain, the patriarch was not called out of Haran (Gen 11:31-32) but out of Ur of the Chaldeans (Gen 11:28; Neh 9:7). In other words, he was called out of Babylon (see Is 13:19; Jer 25:12) and hence from among the "sons of Adam" (Gen 11:5). The juxtaposition of Babel/Babylon and Abram is reinforced through the highlighting of Shem and the theme of "name" in the preceding context.[4] Shem and "name" are linked via wordplay because the Hebrew word for "name" (שֵׁם) is the same word as the proper noun Shem. Of Noah's three sons, it is Shem through whom the promised blessing will come (Gen 9:26-27), and his genealogy is not only mentioned twice (Gen 10:21-31; 11:10-32) but frames the Tower of Babel passage (Gen 11:1-9). Unlike the builders who wanted to make a "name" for themselves (Gen 11:4), the Lord himself promised to make great the "name" of Abram, Shem's descendant (Gen 12:2), a promise which is repeated to David (2 Sam 7:9).

Despite the intrusion of sin and death, the Lord's saving plan to "bless" humanity persisted (Gen 9:1) and would be fulfilled through Abram. The related Hebrew words for "bless" and "blessing" appear a total of five times in Genesis 12:2-3, thus answering the comparable repetition of words for "curse" in the preceding chapters (Gen 3:14, 17; 4:11; 5:29; 8:21; 9:25). The original blessing at creation (Gen 1:22, 28; 5:2), though disrupted by sin, would indeed be spread to "all the families of the earth" (Gen 12:3). Suggestively, the animals that had been spared from the flood with Noah exited the ark "by their families" (Gen 8:19), perhaps giving a picture of the eternal salvation for a "remnant" of humanity through Abram. More to the point, the "families" of the earth that need divine blessing are listed

---

[3]These two English words are translations of the same Hebrew word בָּבֶל. See Gen 10:10; 11:9; 2 Kings 17:24; Is 13:1.

[4]Likewise, Israel/Jerusalem and Babylon are juxtaposed in Is 13–14 (see Is 14:1-4) and Rev 17–21.

in the genealogy in Genesis 10 (see Gen 10:5, 18, 20, 31-32). But not every individual will be blessed, as Genesis 12:3 implies. It is only those who "bless" Abram who will be blessed. The one who "curses" him will indeed be cursed. Evidently, there will be some from every "family" who choose the former. There is thus a clear division of human beings into two groups—those who bless Abram and are blessed, and those who curse him and are cursed (see Gen 27:29). The related reference to his "seed" who will possess the land (Gen 12:7) further implies that these covenant promises will not find their fulfillment in Abram himself but in his offspring.

The themes of divine blessing on humanity through an individual, their division into two groups, and a "seed" that receives land recall the prophecy of the seed of the woman in Genesis 3:15 and its context in Genesis 1–3. Earlier, the Lord's purpose to bless humanity (Gen 1:28) had been disrupted by Adam and Eve's sin, but Genesis 3:15 promised an individual "seed" who will defeat the serpent, rule as Adam should have, and banish uncleanness forever. Such things would seem to concern blessing for "all the families of the land" (Gen 12:3). That Abram's seed will be given the land (Gen 12:7) contrasts with Adam's exile from the Garden (Gen 3:22-24). Indeed, other passages imply that the Messiah will be a Moses-like figure who will lead a "second exodus" of the Lord's people back to the land (Deut 18:15-19; 34:10-12; Ezek 37:22-24; Hos 1:11). The conflict between the seed of the woman and the seed of the serpent also parallels that between those who bless Abram (and hence align themselves with him) and those who curse him.

The many connections between Genesis 3:15 and Genesis 12:1-3 imply that the latter passage is intentionally related to the former and represents a major step forward in the execution of the Lord's salvation plan expressed earlier in the Garden of Eden.[5] The reader of the Pentateuch now

---

[5] Though again viewing the seed of the woman as sometimes singular and sometimes plural, which is consistent with his article referenced in the previous chapter, see James Hamilton, "The Seed of the Woman and the Blessing of Abraham," *TynBul* 58 (2007): 260-62, 266n37, 268. As a result of our view that the seed of the woman is singular only, our position sees a direct correspondence between the Messianic prophecy of Gen 3:15 and the Messianic elements of the promises to Abraham. In contrast, Hamilton, while still arguing for continuity but seeing some ambiguity surrounding the seed of the woman in Gen 3:15 (which allows him to call Abel a "seed of the woman"), focuses on the Abrahamic blessings as a response to the curses of Gen 3 and "an allusion" in Num 24:17 back to Gen 3:15 (257, 265-66).

knows that the seed of the woman will come through Abram's line. It is as though Genesis 12:1-3, 7 has picked up some of the light that passed through the "lens" of Genesis 3:15, in particular the themes of salvation for humanity, enmity between two groups, and seed. This is not to say, however, that Genesis 12:1-3, 7 picks up all the light from Genesis 3:15. It certainly does not—the key role of a woman, the Messiah's defeat of the serpent, and the Messiah's being struck on the heel are all absent. Conversely, Genesis 12:1-3 also contains some elements that are not in Genesis 3:15 or its context, such as the promise of a great name and becoming a great nation (Gen 12:2). The indirect reference to the future nation of Israel shows that Genesis 12:1-3 should not be thought of exclusively in Messianic terms. Indeed, the implicit inclusion of Israel in this passage raises important questions regarding which elements of Genesis 12:1-3 concern Israel and which ones concern the Messiah. Will blessing come to all the families of the earth through Israel generally, or through the Messiah specifically? Does "I will bless those who bless you, and the one who curses you I will curse" apply unconditionally to Israel or only to the Messiah? The answers to these questions are not yet clear at this point in the Pentateuch, but they will be resolved by subsequent passages (e.g., Gen 27:29; Num 24:9). Nevertheless, despite its mixed character, Genesis 12:1-3 can still be broadly considered as a "lens" that focuses Messianic light, some of which is picked up from Genesis 3:15.

THE SEED OF ABRAHAM: INDIVIDUAL OR PLURAL?

In addition to the questions just posed, there is the related question of whether Abram's "seed" in Genesis 12:7 is singular or plural. Unlike in Genesis 3:15, the referent of seed cannot be determined based on grammatical considerations. In fact, in view of Abram becoming a "great nation" in Genesis 12:2, some have taken his "seed" in Genesis 12:7 and elsewhere as always referring to Israel. The promise of land here would then only concern Israel. To be sure, there are clear examples in which Abram's "seed" does have a plural referent and is naturally equated with Israel (Gen 13:16; 15:5, 13; 17:7-12; 22:17a). However, there are other examples in which Abram's seed refers to an individual male descendant, not his offspring generally. As shown in the previous chapter, the use of *seed* to refer to an individual can be determined with high probability if used along with a singular independent personal pronoun (e.g., *he*), as is the case in Genesis 3:15 and Genesis 15:3-4. Conversely, plural independent personal pronouns (e.g., *they*) are used when "seed" is used collectively (Is 61:9; 65:23). Although this rule is decisive for these passages, there are many other important appearances of the word *seed* in the patriarchal narratives without an independent personal pronoun, such as Genesis 12:7. As was the case in Genesis 3:15, whether or not these uses of *seed* refer to an individual or a group can make a major difference in interpretation, especially in relation to the Messianic vision of the Pentateuch.

In order to treat these other uses of *seed*, it is necessary to further analyze its function as the subject of singular and plural verbs, its usage with adjectives and participles, and its use as the referent of pronominal suffixes. For starters, Jack Collins notes that when *seed* refers to an individual, "it appears with singular verb inflections, adjectives, and pronouns."[6] This is not surprising because *seed* is always *grammatically* singular and seems to be used with plural verbs, adjectives, and pronouns only if its referent is plural. The problem is that when *seed* does have a plural referent, it can be the subject of either a singular verb (Gen 13:16; 16:10; Is 14:20; Ps 102:28 [MT v. 29]) or a plural verb (Ex 32:13). Thus, while *seed* as the subject of a plural verb implies a collective seed, *seed* as the subject of a singular verb is inconclusive.[7] Likewise, *seed* with a singular adjective or participle is inconclusive because *seed* with plural referent actually takes singular adjectives and participles (Ps 37:25, 112:2; Job 5:25; 21:8).

Despite these ambiguities, Collins observes, "When *zeraʿ* [*seed*] denotes 'posterity' [i.e., plural referent] the pronouns (independent pronouns, object pronouns, and suffixes) are always plural."[8] Among other examples,

---

[6]Jack Collins, "A Syntactical Note (Genesis 3:15): Is the Woman's Seed Singular or Plural?," *TynBul* 48, no. 1 (1997): 144. He cites Gen 4:25 as an example of a singular (attributive) adjective modifying an individual seed (i.e., Seth). Although the treatment in the previous chapter highlighted singular independent personal pronouns, Gen 15:3-4 and 2 Sam 7:13-14 also use singular verbs and singular pronominal suffixes along with a singular seed.

[7]See discussion of a possible exception to this ambiguity in Is 54:3 below.

[8]Collins, "Syntactical Note," 143. In a footnote, he cites only Is 48:19 as being "more difficult," while suggesting that the singular pronominal suffix "his" in "his name" refers to Jacob in the preceding context (see Is 48:1, 9, 12). He points out that taking the singular "his" as referring to the collective seed is "harsh in view of the intervening plural" (i.e., "descendants"). Regarding Is 41:8, see discussion in chap. 1 above. Another possibly problematic passage that we found in our own

he cites Genesis 17:9, "You will keep my covenant, you and your seed [וְזַרְעֲךָ] after you, for their [pl.] generations." The point is that Abraham's collective seed is referred to with a plural pronominal suffix (*their*). In other words, even though (singular) verbs, adjectives, and participles used with *seed* do not clearly indicate whether *seed* has a singular or plural referent, independent personal pronouns (as demonstrated in chap. 1) and pronominal suffixes do. To illustrate these different grammatical elements at play, consider Genesis 15:13, "Your seed will be [sg. verb] sojourners in a land not theirs [pl.], and they will serve [pl. verb] them, and they will afflict them [pl.]." This verse uses *seed* collectively and refers to Israel's enslavement in Egypt. In keeping with Collins's observations, this collective seed is the subject of both a singular verb (יִהְיֶה, "will be") and a plural verb (וַעֲבָדוּם, "and they will serve them") in this passage.[9] Despite this flexibility with respect to verbs, both relevant pronominal suffixes are plural ("not theirs"; "they will afflict *them* [pl.]"), in keeping with the rule. Other passages with plural pronominal suffixes referring to a collective seed include Genesis 17:7-8; 48:11-12; Exodus 30:21; Deuteronomy 10:15; 2 Kings 17:20; Nehemiah 9:2; Psalm 106:27; Jeremiah 23:8; 30:10; 31:27-28; 33:26; 46:27; and Ezekiel 20:5.

Collins's observations regarding the usage of *seed* not only with independent personal pronouns but also pronominal suffixes suggest that there

---

comprehensive analysis of *seed* is Deut 4:37, in which a singular pronominal suffix ("he brought you [sg.] out") is naturally taken to refer to the collective seed of the patriarchs ("their seed"). The LXX somewhat smooths out this problem in its rendering, "he chose their seed with them, you [pl.]," while still retaining the singular in "he brought you [sg.] out." The problem is absent in the Old Latin and Syriac, both of which use a plural ("he brought you [pl.] out"). A parallel passage in Deut 10:15 likewise uses a plural *you*. Nevertheless, the alternation between singular and plural *you* in Deut 4:37 and Deut 10:15 could be another example of similar alternation throughout Deuteronomy, referred to by scholars as *Numeruswechsel* (see Deut 12). Also see John Sailhamer's apparent use of the same rule that Collins derives but for Jer 4:2 in *The Meaning of the Pentateuch: Revelation, Composition, and Interpretation* (Downers Grove, IL: InterVarsity Press, 2009), 483-84. He cites GKC §135p: "plural suffixes refer to collective singulars." Contra John Walton, *Genesis*, NIV Application Commentary (Grand Rapids: Zondervan, 2001), 225 (including n. 3), who claims that *seed* is a "collective noun that typically takes singular pronouns in its place" and that most of Collins's examples involve "situations where the text is speaking of several people's posterities, thus demanding a plural [e.g., Gen 9:9]." But Walton has contradicted GKC without providing evidence (GKC §135p lists Gen 15:13; Num 16:3; 1 Sam 2:8; Zeph 2:7) and neglected unambiguous examples that support Collins's point.

[9]The Hebrew noun translated "sojourners" is also singular here, even though it does have a plural form (Ex 22:21). The reason for the singular may be to maintain consistency with the following singular grammatical elements in the clause.

may be additional passages besides Genesis 15:3-4 in which the seed of Abraham has a singular referent. Alexander cites Genesis 22:17b and Genesis 24:60.[10] These passages both use a singular pronominal suffix to refer to Abraham's seed, which following Collins's rule implies that the seed is an individual: "And may your seed possess the gate of *his* [sg.] enemies" (Gen 22:17b); "And may your seed possess the gate of *his* [sg.] haters" (Gen 24:60). Alexander is careful to distinguish the seed in Genesis 22:17a, which is plural ("I will certainly multiply your seed like the stars of the heavens"), from the seed in Gen 22:17b, which is singular.[11] He points out that the verb in Genesis 22:17b ("and may [he] possess") disrupts the syntax and pattern of verbs forms used in Genesis 22:17a ("I will bless" and "I will multiply"), further opening the door for a change in referent for *seed*.[12]

Although John Walton calls Alexander's argument "special pleading,"[13] the rapid, subtle switch from a plural referent to a singular referent is paralleled in Genesis 15:3-5 (Gen 15:3-4, singular; Gen 15:5, plural; also perhaps Gen 26:4-5). Isaiah 54:3 may also be an example of such a switch. Although it has been shown above that the use of a singular or plural verb is inconclusive, Isaiah 54:3 uses singular and plural verbs with the same "seed" as subject, "Your seed will possess [וְיִרַשׁ sg.] nations, and desolate cities they [i.e., "your seed"] will cause to be inhabited [יוֹשִׁיבוּ pl.]." Whereas the second part of this statement must take *seed* collectively because it uses a plural verb, the first part uses words and themes found in other Messianic prophecies (Gen 22:17b-18; 24:60; Ps 2:8) and is probably treating *seed* as singular. The alternative is to take a collective seed also as the subject of "Your seed will possess the nations," with the singular verb used for stylistic variation but without semantic difference and in a somewhat

---

[10]T. Desmond Alexander, "Further Observations on the Term 'Seed' in Genesis," *TynBul* 48, no. 2 (1997): 364-68.

[11]Alexander, "Further Observations," 366.

[12]Gen 22:17a uses two *yiqtol* verbs, and *yiqtol* is commonly followed by perfect + waw consecutive (*weqatal*). Although this is indeed how the LXX has read וְיִרַשׁ in Gen 22:17b (the consonantal text being the same), the MT has read it as a jussive. The MT reading is more likely because it agrees with the parallel וְיִירַשׁ in Gen 24:60, which is unambiguously a jussive. See Alviero Niccacci, "A Neglected Point of Hebrew Syntax: YIQTOL and Position in the Sentence," *LA* 37 (1987): 7-19.

[13]Walton, *Genesis*, 225n3.

confusing manner. Though the referent of *seed* does not change in Genesis 24:60, the verse itself mentions both offspring generally ("our sister, become thousands of ten thousands!") and an individual descendant. Including Genesis 15:3-4, there are thus three passages in which Abraham's "seed" refers to an individual. The strong link to the individual seed in Genesis 3:15 implies that these passages are also direct Messianic prophecies and should be treated as "lenses."

Furthermore, Genesis 15:3-4, Genesis 22:17b, and Genesis 24:60 each focus on an individual seed who "possesses" (יָרַשׁ) something, whether the Abrahamic inheritance or enemy gates. The importance of the theme of possession is also shown through its presence in the surrounding context of each passage. Flanked by Genesis 22:17b and Genesis 24:60, Genesis 23 concerns Abraham purchasing a burial plot from the Hittites and hence relates to the broader theme of his possession of the land (see אֲחֻזָּה, Gen 23:4, 9, 20; מִקְנָה, Gen 23:18). As such, it is a foretaste of the realization of the promise first given in Genesis 12:7.[14] One day "all the land of Canaan" will be his "everlasting possession" (אֲחֻזָּה, Gen 17:8).[15] The related verb קָנָה ("to acquire or purchase"; see Gen 25:10; 33:19) is correspondingly found in the context immediately preceding Genesis 15:3-4 after Abram defeated several kings in battle (Gen 14:19, 22). Indeed, to be Abram's heir (Gen 15:3-4) ought to encompass all the covenant promises made to him, including those concerning both enemies (Gen 12:3; 22:17b; 24:60) and land (Gen 12:7). The thematic convergence of an individual seed and his "possession" of an inheritance, his enemies, and land in these passages and their contexts further strengthen the connection to the Messianic seed of the woman, the "heir of all things" (Heb 1:2), who will fulfill the promise of Genesis 3:15. The victorious "seed" in Genesis 24:60 even recalls the "seed of a woman" (Gen 3:15) because Rebekah is the one being addressed.

---

[14] For a parallel in the Jacob story, see Gen 33:18-20, where he bought a piece of land near Shechem. After some struggle with the Philistines, Isaac eventually had space "to be fruitful in the land" and to enjoy wells at Rehoboth and Beersheba (Gen 26:22-33). Nevertheless, the Pentateuch makes clear that all three patriarchs merely "sojourned" in the land (Gen 17:8; 26:3; 28:4; 35:27; 37:1; 47:9).

[15] Gen 26:3-4 suggestively refers to "all these lands" that will be given to Isaac and his "seed." The use of the plural ("lands") leaves open the possibility that Abraham was indeed "heir of the world" (Rom 4:13), not merely Canaan.

Such considerations shed light back on Genesis 12:1-7. It was noted above that, taken in isolation, the Lord's promises to bless those who bless you and curse the one who curses you, to bless "all the families of the earth" (Gen 12:3), and to give land to Abram's seed (Gen 12:7) could be taken as applying first and foremost to Israel. Indeed, there are numerous passages in which the promise of land is given to Israel (e.g., Gen 15:13-21; Ex 32:13; Josh 1:2-4). But as has just been shown, the passages above also tie "possession," including that of land, to an individual Messianic seed of Abraham (see Is 8:8). Thus, sometimes Abraham's "seed" refers to an individual and sometimes to a group, depending on the passage. Related to the land, Israel will ultimately be exiled from it, but the Messiah will bring them back to dwell in the land permanently (Jer 23:5-6; Hos 1:11; 3:5). Another open issue in Genesis 12:1-7 concerns the promise of worldwide blessing (Gen 12:3). But since Genesis 22:17b concerns an individual Messianic seed, the blessing for "all the nations of the earth" through "your seed" in Genesis 22:18 also proceeds from the same individual seed (see Gen 18:18; 26:4). Sailhamer points out that Jeremiah 4:2 ("nations will be blessed in him") appears to be interpretively citing Genesis 22:18 ("all the nations of the earth will be blessed in your seed"), having replaced "in your seed" with the unambiguously singular "in him."[16] All of this in turn suggests that the aforementioned blessing for "all the families of the earth" in Genesis 12:3 is actually fulfilled through the Messiah, not through Israel in and of themselves (or Abraham himself). Israel had only "given birth to wind" and had not brought about "salvation" (Is 26:18; 49:4). Likewise, the promise to bless those who bless you and curse the one who curses you (Gen 12:3), though sometimes related to Israel (Num 22:6, 12; 23:7-11, 20; see Ex 23:22), is ultimately focused by other Pentateuchal passages on the Messianic king (Gen 27:29; Num 24:9). Even the promise to become a "great nation" in Genesis 12:2 needs to be understood in relation to other passages, which reveal that Abraham would not only become such a nation but a "father of many nations" (Gen 17:4-6; see Gen 28:3). This suggests that he was never intended to be Israel's forefather only and that his "fatherhood"

---

[16]Sailhamer, *Meaning of the Pentateuch*, 481-89.

would not be limited to his biological progeny. Also, even though Israel did multiply and become a mighty nation (Ex 1:7-9; Num 22:3-6; Deut 26:5; 1 Kings 3:8), their exile reversed this (Deut 28:62; Is 1:9), and the permanent and hence actual fulfillment of becoming a great nation depends on the eschatological reign of the Messiah (Hos 1:10–2:1; 3:5; see Is 54:1-3).

These considerations support taking Genesis 12:1-3, 7 as a "lens," despite its mixed character and ambiguity when examined in isolation. As shown already, Genesis 15:3-4, Genesis 22:17b-18, and Genesis 24:60 are direct Messianic prophecies. The relationship of these four lenses to Genesis 3:15 and to one another is illustrated schematically in figure 2.1, where the labeled connecting lines show the Messianic themes that are passed from one prophecy to another.

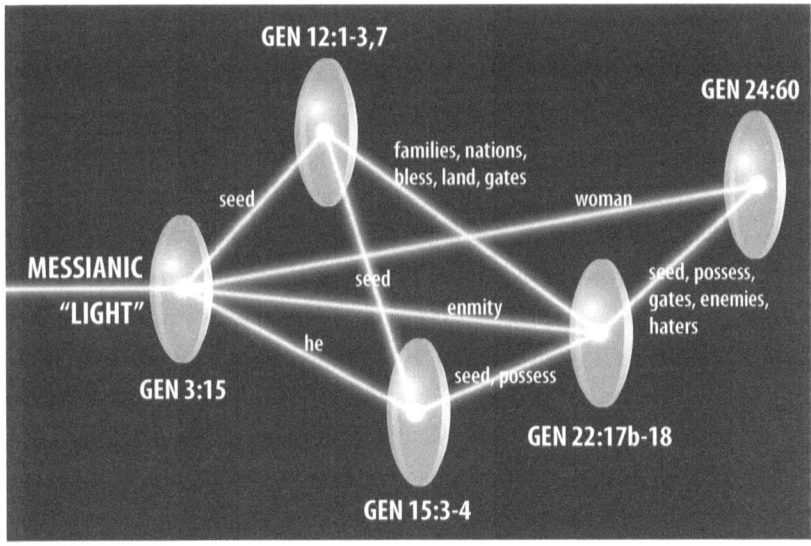

Figure 2.1. Intricate relationship among five Messianic prophecies in Genesis

The intricate relationship among these five passages illustrates the complex nature of Messianic prophecy in the composition of the Pentateuch. Significantly, the latter four passages all depend on Genesis 3:15, but none of them mention the serpent nor the Messiah's suffering. To be sure, other passages (Gen 49:8-12; Num 24:7-9) will reference his death and even his resurrection. Nevertheless, the dependence of the present four passages on Genesis 3:15 reinforces the foundational role of this prophecy in the Messianic vision of the Pentateuch. At the same time, the contents of the latter four passages are not limited to that of Genesis 3:15. Genesis 12:1-7 also draws on themes of blessing and land from Genesis 1–3, and the Hebrew verb translated "to possess" in Genesis 15:3-4; 22:17b-18; 24:60, though thematically related to themes of Eden, land, and exile in Genesis 1–3, is absent from those chapters. Indeed, its appearances in Genesis 15:3-4 are its first ones in the Pentateuch. Messianic prophecies are thus interwoven with one another and with the Pentateuch as a whole. They contain select words and themes that relate both to their various literary contexts and to other such prophecies elsewhere in the Pentateuch. As more of them are identified and examined, especially in relationship to one another, the Messianic vision of the Pentateuch is further unveiled with increasing clarity and glory.

Melchizedek: Mere Type or Intentional Foreshadowing?

Before proceeding to the next Messianic prophecy in the patriarchal narratives (Gen 27:27-29), it is fitting to consider the Melchizedek narrative in Genesis 14:18-20 and the sacrifice of Isaac in Genesis 22:1-19, both of which are often considered to be "types" of Christ. We begin with the former. Although appearing in only one other passage in the Old Testament (Ps 110:4), Melchizedek is related extensively to Christ in Hebrews 7. The author of Hebrews points out that this enigmatic figure served as both king and priest, blessed Abraham, received a tithe from him, was both a "king of righteousness" and a "king of peace," and was (presented as?) "without father, without mother, without genealogy, neither having a beginning of days nor an end of life, but like the Son of God he remains a priest forever" (Heb 7:1-3). There is no question that there are striking parallels between Melchizedek and Christ. However, the important issue related to the Messianic vision of the Pentateuch is not simply the parallels themselves, as suggestive as they are, but what evidence there might be in the Pentateuch itself that its author intended Melchizedek to foreshadow the Messiah. The role of Melchizedek in the compositional strategy of the Pentateuch has not often been sought out, but Joshua Mathews has helpfully pursued this.[17] The thesis of his work is that "there is a textually recognizable and demonstrably distinct priestly-succession—an order of Melchizedek—intended in the composition of the Pentateuch and continuing throughout the OT canon (Tanak)." As one of two "corollary subpoints," he also explores "the role that Melchizedek plays in the overall eschatological and messianic message throughout the Pentateuch and the Tanak as a whole."[18] His thesis, especially this corollary, is directly relevant to our present task, and select elements of his analysis are given below.

Melchizedek suddenly appears in Genesis 14:18-20 in the context of Abram's rescue of Lot following a battle between two groups of kings. Incidentally, Genesis 14 contains the first uses of the common Hebrew word for "king" (מֶלֶךְ) in the Pentateuch.[19] One group of five kings is headlined by the kings of Sodom and Gomorrah (Gen 14:2, 8, 10, 11) and the other group of four kings by Kedorlaomer, king of Elam, against whom the former group had rebelled (Gen 14:4, 5, 9). One of these four kings was a certain Amraphel king of Shinar, who is curiously listed first in Genesis 14:1. Mathews points out that the fronting of this king of "Shinar" is an intentional link to the Tower of Babel, which was built in the "land of Shinar" (Gen 11:2).[20] He cites as another link between Genesis 11:1-9 and Genesis 14 the mention of "bitumen" (Gen 11:3; 14:10). Shinar is also mentioned in the Table of Nations in Genesis 10, where it was the site of Nimrod's kingdom, which included Babel/Babylon (Gen 10:10). Many of the other locations referenced in Genesis 14:1-2 are also found in Genesis 10 (Elam, Gen 10:22; Sodom, Gomorrah, Admah, Zeboiim, Gen 10:19). Even "Goiim" (גּוֹיִם) or "nations," the dominion of Tidal (Gen 14:1), is a play on the word *nation* (גּוֹי; Gen 10:5, 20, 31-32).

---

[17]Joshua G. Mathews, *Melchizedek's Alternative Priestly Order: A Compositional Analysis of Genesis 14:18-20 and Its Echoes Throughout the Tanak*, Bulletin for Biblical Research Supplements (Winona Lake, IN: Eisenbrauns, 2013). See also Alan Kam-Yau Chan, *Melchizedek Passages in the Bible: A Case Study for Inner-Biblical and Inter-Biblical Interpretation* (Berlin: De Gruyter, 2016).
[18]Mathews, *Melchizedek's Alternative Priestly Order*, 2-3.
[19]This is not to say that it is the first appearance of the *theme* of kingship/kingdom. Using different language, humankind was intended to "rule" (רָדָה; Gen 1:26, 28). The semantically related מָשַׁל is used of the "rule" of the sun and moon (Gen 1:16, 18), the man's "rule" over his wife (Gen 3:16), and Cain's need to "rule" over sin (Gen 4:7). Nimrod also had a "kingdom" (מַמְלָכָה; Gen 10:10).
[20]Mathews, *Melchizedek's Alternative Priestly Order*, 56-57.

Thus most of the key players in Genesis 10–12 and Genesis 14 are essentially the same: the nations (including Babylon) and Abram. As was already discussed, Genesis 10–12 has a global scope and contrasts Abram with Babel/Babylon and the "sons of Adam" (Gen 10:10; 11:5, 9). He was called out from among them to be part of the line from which the promised seed of the woman would come and bring blessing to all (Gen 3:15; 12:1-3). Genesis 14 likewise contrasts Abram with the fallen human race through his defeat of Kedolaomer's alliance of kings (Gen 14:14-17), whose dominion included Shinar/Babylon and Goiim/nations. This alliance had recently defeated the other five kings (Gen 14:8-11). The implication is that Abram, with the Lord's help (Gen 14:20), has become greater than these nine kings and is on his way to becoming the "great nation" that the Lord promised (Gen 12:2). Mathews also suggests that Abram's pursuit of his enemies to Dan, often used to mark the northern boundary of Israel (Judg 20:1; 1 Sam 3:20; 1 Kings 4:25), and even further to Hobah, north of Damascus (Gen 14:14-15), fulfills the Lord's recent command to "walk throughout the length and breadth of the land, for I will give it to you" (Gen 13:17).[21] Since the Lord had relatedly promised Abram "all the land that you see" in every direction (Gen 13:15), his pursuit of Kedorlaomer to these distant places may also serve to activate this promise by extending the boundaries of the land that he will ultimately receive (see Josh 1:3-4). In any case, the preceding considerations show that Genesis 14 is closely tied to Genesis 10–13 and to the Lord's covenant promises to Abram, especially as they concern greatness and land.

The greatest human character in Genesis 14, however, is not Abram but Melchizedek, king of Salem and priest of God Most High, who both "blessed" Abram and received a "tithe" from him (Gen 14:18-20). Previously, it was the Lord who had blessed Abram (Gen 12:2), and the next tithe mentioned in the Pentateuch is promised to the Lord by Jacob (Gen 28:22). These similarities not only imply that Melchizedek is greater than Abram (Heb 7:4-7) but indirectly associate the priest-king with the Lord himself. Nevertheless, Melchizedek's statement, "blessed be God

---

[21] Mathews, *Melchizedek's Alternative Priestly Order*, 54-55.

Most High" (Gen 14:20), maintains a distinction between him and the Lord while at the same time casting him as a mediator between the Lord and Abram. Standing between the two, this priest blessed both parties in turn (Gen 14:19-20). Priestly bestowal of blessings is also found in Exodus 18:10, Leviticus 9:22-23, and Numbers 6:23-27.[22]

Just as the first use of the common Hebrew word for "king" (מֶלֶךְ) appears in Genesis 14, so does the first tithe and the first use of the common Hebrew word for "priest" (כֹּהֵן; Gen 14:18, 20). Melchizedek is thus the first explicit "priest-king" in the Pentateuch. He is greater than the other nine kings not only because he is greater than Abram who defeated them but also because he alone is both priest and king. As the tenth king mentioned, Melchizedek also parallels other important figures who are tenth in a list (Noah as the tenth from Adam, Gen 5:1-32; Abram as the tenth from Shem, Gen 11:11-26; David as the tenth from Perez, Ruth 4:18-21; see Dan 7:7-8).[23] Melchizedek is thus a "king of kings" of sorts, who fittingly meets Abram at "the Valley of the King" (Gen 14:17). The tithe "of everything" (Gen 14:20) that he received consisted of the wealth of the nations (Gen 14:16; Is 60:5, 11; Hag 2:7; Heb 7:4). Mathews points out that the spoils of war "would have included the spoils of the eastern armies [i.e., led by Kedorlaomer] as well as those of the other peoples they defeated on their way to engage the five-king alliance (vv. 5-7)."[24] Thus, the kings of the earth may fight over who owes what to whom, as suggested by Genesis 14:4, but in the end everything that they have belongs to the Lord (Gen 14:19) and a tenth of it will be paid to Melchizedek. Abram himself had benefited from Melchizedek's mediatorial priestly ministry and fittingly paid this tithe. This ministry included not only blessing but also "bread and wine" (Gen 14:18), which relates to the theme of food in the context (Gen 14:11, "and they

---

[22]Regarding Ex 18:10, that Jethro is a "priest" is clear from Ex 18:1. The terms *sojourner* (גֵּר) in Ex 18:3 and *Eliezer* (אֱלִיעֶזֶר) in Ex 18:4 are also important in Gen 15:2, 13.

[23]See Gennady Pshenichny, "Abraham in the Canonical Hebrew Bible: A Study of the Abrahamic Narrative of Genesis with a View Toward the Reading of That Text by the Later Canonical Authors" (Ph.D. diss., Southeastern Baptist Theological Seminary, 2007), 15-16, 84-85. The number ten also appears notably elsewhere (e.g. the ten plagues of Egypt, the Ten Commandments).

[24]Mathews, *Melchizedek's Alternative Priestly Order*, 60. One wonders whether the tithe also included a portion of "all" (כֹּל) of Abram's own possessions as well (see Gen 12:5, 20; 13:1-2), which included some of Egypt's possessions (Gen 12:16). See Gordon Wenham, *Genesis 1-15*, Word Biblical Commentary (Waco, TX: Word, 1987), 317.

took . . . all their food [כָּל־אָכְלָם] and left"; Gen 14:24, "what the young men have eaten [אָכְלוּ] . . . let them take their share").

Although Melchizedek is the first (and only) person in the Pentateuch to be *called* both "king" and "priest," he is not the first to be characterized as such. Adam, as discussed in the previous chapter, is also cast by the Pentateuch as king and priest in the Garden of Eden (Gen 1:26-28; 2:15), even though these offices are not explicitly attributed to him. More significantly, the seed of the woman in Genesis 3:15 is also cast as the ideal king and priest, since by crushing the serpent's head he both exercises dominion over the unruliest animal and destroys the source of all uncleanness (see chap. 1 above). His sudden appearance in the storyline as one whose glory far outshines all other human characters in the context parallels Melchizedek's sudden appearance and outshining of Abram and the nine kings in Genesis 14:18-20. Although Joseph was *almost* a priest-king as second-in-command to the king of Egypt (Gen 41:40-44) and as married to the daughter of a priest (Gen 41:45, 50; 46:20), and although Israel was supposed to be a "kingdom of priests" (Ex 19:6), what is apparent is that the two exemplary priest-kings in the Pentateuch are the seed of the woman and Melchizedek. The author of the Pentateuch first presents the perfect priest-king in Genesis 3:15 via prophecy, and then in Genesis 14:18-20 he describes Abram's encounter with a priest-king who resembles the one to come in many respects.[25]

The meaning of Melchizedek's name ("king of righteousness"; Heb 7:2) and his rule over "Salem" (a wordplay on *shalom*, "peace") strengthen his association with the Messianic priest-king, whose names include "prince of peace" (Is 9:6; see Mic 5:5), "righteous one" (Is 53:11), and "the LORD our righteousness" (Jer 23:6). Rather than being fanciful, to follow the author of Hebrews in emphasizing the meaning of Melchizedek's name and the double meaning of his role as "king of Salem/peace" is in accord with frequent wordplay in the preceding context.[26] Most of these wordplays are on personal names ("Eve," Gen 3:20; "Cain," Gen 4:1; "Seth," Gen 4:25; "Noah," Gen 5:29), though a few concern place ("Babel,"

---

[25]Melchizedek obviously does not match the seed of the woman in every respect. For example, he does not crush the head of the serpent nor is he struck on the heel by it.

[26]See Richard Hess, *Studies in the Personal Names of Genesis 1–11* (Winona Lake, IN: Eisenbrauns, 2009).

Gen 11:9) or role/status ("woman," Gen 2:23). Most of them are explained in the text, but some are implicit (e.g., *'adam*, meaning "Adam/man/humanity"; "Eden," meaning "delight"; "Abel," meaning "breath"). Indeed, Melchizedek, true to his implicit role as a "king of peace," was not involved with the battles of Genesis 14 and brings only blessing and food. His implicit identity as a "king of righteousness" contrasts with David, who freely confessed that he and his house did not and would not provide righteous rule (2 Sam 23:3-5; see KJV, NKJV), apart from the Messiah.[27] On the other hand, Melchizedek's rule over Salem, or Jerusalem, links him to the house of David and implicitly the eternal kingdom promised in the Davidic covenant (2 Sam 7:13, 16).[28] David and his line, however, were of the tribe of Judah and were not priests (Mt 12:3-4; Heb 7:14). But in Psalm 110, David foresees that one of his own descendants (his "Lord") will be both king and priest in the order of Melchizedek in Zion (Ps 110:4; Zech 6:13). "Zion" (Ps 110:2) is the site of the reign of the Lord's "Messiah" in Psalm 2:6 and is paralleled with "Salem" in Psalm 76:2.[29] In view of the separation of kingly and priestly offices in Israel into different tribes (Judah and Levi; see Deut 17:18), the coming of one who is both king and priest is exceptional. Such a person's glory not only far surpasses all of Israel's kings and priests but fulfills the prophecy of Genesis 3:15 as well as the Abrahamic and Davidic covenants,[30] and matches the profile of the priest-king Melchizedek.

In addition to the links to Genesis 10–13, Mathews shows that there are also extensive connections between Genesis 14 and Genesis 15 that

---

[27]After describing the blessings of a righteous ruler in 2 Sam 23:3-4, David declares, "But my house is not so with God" (כִּי־לֹא־כֵן בֵּיתִי עִם־אֵל; 2 Sam 23:5). Most modern English translations turn this statement into a rhetorical question that reverses its meaning, "For is not my house so [i.e., righteous] with God?" But in the absence of the typical interrogative-heh (הַ) that marks these kinds of questions, it is better to take this sentence at face-value as an indicative, especially since it fits with the failures of David and his house described at length in the preceding chapters (2 Sam 11–20).

[28]On Salem/Jerusalem, see BDB, HALOT.

[29]The LXX/Vulgate also read Gen 33:18 (וַיָּבֹא יַעֲקֹב שָׁלֵם עִיר שְׁכָם) as, "And Jacob came to Salem, the city of the Shechemites." Modern English translations instead read, "And Jacob came safely to the city of Shechem." This fits with his wish to return "in peace" (בְשָׁלוֹם) in Gen 28:21. At the same time, in the very next verse (Gen 28:22), he promised a tithe, which recalls Gen 14:20.

[30]For further discussion, see Werner Schatz, *Genesis 14: Eine Untersuchung* (Bern: Lang, 1972), 274-75, 279-80. A brief response to Schatz can be found in Mathews, *Melchizedek's Alternative Priestly Order*, 120-21.

reinforce the connection between Melchizedek and the Abrahamic covenant.[31] He includes the phrase "after these things" in Genesis 15:1 that links Genesis 14 and Genesis 15, the use of מָגֵן in Genesis 14:20 ("delivered") and Genesis 15:1 ("shield"),[32] and language of "possession" (רְכוּשׁ, Gen 14:11-12, 16, 21-23; 15:14; see also the wordplay in Gen 15:1 using שָׂכָר, "reward"; /מִקְנֶה קָנָה, Gen 14:19, 22). Possession language and themes have already been well-established in the preceding context (Gen 12:5, 16; 13:1-2, 6). Even more importantly, this theme and its corresponding language is tied to the Messianic prophecies in Genesis 15:3-4; 22:17b; 24:60 through the verb יָרַשׁ ("to possess"), as discussed above. To put these pieces together, the Lord, as "possessor of heaven and earth" (Gen 14:19), not only handed over possessions and enemies into Abram's hand (Gen 14:16, 20) but will do so in fullness for his Messianic seed (Gen 15:3-4; 22:17b; 24:60).

There are still other connections between Genesis 14 and Genesis 15 that relate the former to the Abrahamic covenant and his seed, such as "Damascus"/"son of Meshek" (Gen 14:15; 15:2), "house" (Gen 14:14; 15:2-3), and the numerical value of "Eliezer" as 318 (Gen 14:14; 15:2). Mathews insightfully observes, "In these three instances, Abraham's suggested replacement for the seed [Eliezer of Damascus, 'the son of my house'] is compositionally connected with an element of the remarkable victory God achieved for Abram in chapter 14."[33] That is, Abram, with only 318 men from his "house," pursued his enemies as far as Damascus (Gen 14:14-15). This surprising connection is meant to "remind the reader [of Gen 15:1-3] of Yahweh's miraculous protection and victory in the immediately prior narrative [i.e., Gen 14:14-16] . . . [such that] Yahweh would also prove miraculously faithful to his promise of a seed for Abram."[34] Abram's doubt concerning a "seed" to be his "heir" in Genesis 15:2-3 leads directly to this promise of the same in the next verse. If Genesis 15:2-4 concerns an individual seed/heir, even the Messiah, as argued previously, then the miraculous provision suggested relates not

---

[31]Mathews, *Melchizedek's Alternative Priestly Order*, 61-70.

[32]Mathews, *Melchizedek's Alternative Priestly Order*, 61, "The deliverance of Abram's foes into his hand, for which Melchizedek blessed God Most High, is thus connected to Yahweh's word of exhortation to Abram in chapter 15."

[33]Mathews, *Melchizedek's Alternative Priestly Order*, 67.

[34]Mathews, *Melchizedek's Alternative Priestly Order*, 67-68.

only to Isaac but to this eschatological seed/heir. When Abram believes the Lord's promise, the crediting of his faith as "righteousness" (צְדָקָה; Gen 15:6) provides yet another link to Genesis 14, this time to the meaning of Melchizedek's name, "king of righteousness."[35] It is as though Abram's faith in the Lord's miraculous covenant provision and his faith climactically being counted as "righteousness" are intertwined with the exalted person of Melchizedek, "the king of righteousness" (see Jer 23:6), and the blessing that he brings.

Although more could be said, the preceding discussion shows that Genesis 14, and Melchizedek in particular, is compositionally related to the Abrahamic narrative and especially the Abrahamic covenant in Genesis 15, including its Messianic aspects. This is evident through the repetition of words and themes, such as those surrounding blessing, possession, and enemies. As shown above, the global scope and significance of Abram's call in Genesis 12:1-3 is repeated in his battle with the kings and subsequent interaction with Melchizedek, who receives a tithe from Abram consisting of the wealth of the nations (Gen 14:20). The Lord's blessing of Abram in Genesis 12:2-3 is paralleled by Melchizedek's blessing of Abram in Genesis 14:19. While it is true that the Lord himself subsequently "blessed" Abram (Gen 24:1, 35), on this occasion he blessed him through Melchizedek, a mediator between Abram and the Lord. Just as Melchizedek was the means of blessing for Abram in Genesis 14:18-20, so the seed of Genesis 15:3-4 will be the means of blessing for the whole earth (Gen 22:16-18), including Abram himself. As great as Abram was for having defeated kings and receiving promises of a great name and a great nation, Melchizedek was thus far greater than the patriarch. As a glorious priest-king characterized by righteousness and peace (Is 9:6; Jer 23:6), Melchizedek is compositionally related to the seed of the woman, who will be the ideal priest-king. The first to be called a priest and the first king of Salem/Jerusalem thus matches the last priest and last king in Zion (Ps 110), who is predicted in Genesis 3:15. The fulfillment of the Davidic covenant unto worldwide blessing is even presented in terms of partaking of "bread" and "wine" in Isaiah 55:1-5. Some readers may still want more evidence,

---

[35] Mathews, *Melchizedek's Alternative Priestly Order*, 71.

but even so, the preceding considerations suggest that Melchizedek, albeit faintly perhaps, intentionally foreshadows the Messiah.

The Sacrifice of Isaac

The (near-)sacrifice of Isaac in Genesis 22:1-19 has also long been considered a "type" of Christ. Despite lacking explicit support from the New Testament, readers of Scripture have recognized the correspondence between the command to Abraham to sacrifice his beloved son Isaac (Gen 22:2) and the actual sacrifice of the Son of God on the cross. Isaac's obedience to his father, especially carrying "wood" (Gen 22:6-8; see Jn 19:17), further supports this.[36] In a different way, Gerard Van Groningen has argued that "Isaac, as a person, typologically demonstrated messianic qualities," but "his being placed on and bound to the altar is not to be considered typologically messianic" because he was not actually sacrificed.[37] Instead, it is the slain ram that is the type of Christ's substitutionary death.[38] Regardless of how one construes the typology, the parallels between Genesis 22 and Jesus' sacrifice on the cross are striking. Nevertheless, the key issue relating to the Messianic vision of the Pentateuch once again is not the mere presence of these parallels, as noteworthy as they are, but whether there is any textual evidence in the Pentateuch itself suggesting that Genesis 22 is intended by the author to be linked to this overarching vision.

At the very least, Genesis 22:17b-18 is a direct Messianic prophecy as argued above and as such provides one such link. Not only will the Lord

---

[36]For additional parallels, see Jean Danielou, *From Shadows to Reality: Studies in the Biblical Typology of the Fathers* (London: Burns and Oates, 1960), 120. He also surveys the interpretation of Gen 22 in post-biblical Jewish literature, the NT, and especially the church fathers, including the typological readings of Irenaeus, Tertullian, Augustine, Athanasius, Gregory of Nyssa, and Chrysostom (115-30). For further discussion, see Leopold Sabourin, "Isaac and Jesus in the Targums and in the New Testament," *RSB* 1, no. 2 (Mar 1981): 37-45; Ed Noort and Eibert Tigchelaar, eds., *The Sacrifice of Isaac: The Aqedah (Genesis 22) and Its Interpretations* (Leiden: Brill, 2002); Devorah Schoenfeld, *Isaac on Jewish and Christian Altars: Polemics and Exegesis in Rashi and the Glossa Ordinaria* (Fordham: New York, 2013).

[37]Gerard Van Groningen, *Messianic Revelation in the Old Testament* (Grand Rapids: Baker, 1990), 145. He cites "persistent difficulties" with taking the binding of Isaac as a type of the substitutionary death of Christ (144; see 12, 56-72 for an explanation of his overall approach). Also objecting to Isaac as a type of Christ is Stanley Walters, "Wood, Sand, and Stars: Structure and Theology in Gn 22:1-19," *TJT* 3, no. 2 (1987): 325-27.

[38]For an alternative synthesis of these different typological issues, see the discussion in Danielou, *From Shadows to Reality*, 125-26.

multiply Abraham's descendants (Gen 22:17a), but one of them will "possess the gate of his enemies" (Gen 22:17b) and bring blessing to "all the nations of the earth" (Gen 22:18). That this seed is not Isaac is implied through the similar things said about his and Rebekah's seed (Gen 24:60; 26:4-5; cf. Gen 17:19), not to mention his not fitting the profile of Genesis 3:15. The reference to the seed's "enemies" (pl.) in Genesis 22:17b and "haters" in Genesis 24:60 relates not only to his battle with the serpent but also the "enmity" between him and the serpent's seed. Both types of conflict are directly predicted in Genesis 3:15. A singular enemy and a group of enemies parallel "the one [sg.] who curses you" in Genesis 12:3 and "the ones [pl.] who curse you" in Genesis 27:29. But what was spoken to Abraham in Genesis 22:17b-18 does not transparently relate the preceding narrative and the command to sacrifice Isaac to a broader Messianic theology in the Pentateuch. To discern this, Genesis 22:1-19 itself must be examined more closely.

In an insightful article, Stanley Walters points out the concentric structure of Genesis 22:2-12 ("your son, your only one," Gen 22:2, 12; "the place his God had mentioned to him," Gen 22:3, 9; "the two of them went along together," Gen 22:6, 8; "my son," Gen 22:7, 8), which not only highlights the theme of sonship but "draws particular attention to the dialogue which stands at its centre or waist: Isaac's only words in the story and Abraham's reply."[39] This exchange consists of Isaac's question, "Behold, the fire and the knife, but where is the lamb [הַשֶּׂה] for the burnt offering?" and Abraham's answer, "God will provide [or "see"; רָאָה] for himself the lamb [הַשֶּׂה] for the burnt offering." It is as though Abraham already knows and believes in the forthcoming divine provision.[40] Even though the concentric pattern in Genesis 22:2-12 does not encompass the whole passage, which continues to Genesis 22:19, the theme of the Lord's provision of a lamb does extend to the substitutionary sacrifice of a "ram" (אַיִל; Gen 22:13) and the naming of the site for posterity "the Lord will provide" (Gen 22:14; note the future orientation), which in turn connects back to the challenges to the continuance of Abraham's "seed" and the fulfillment of the Lord's related covenant promises (Gen 22:15-18).

---

[39]Walters, "Wood, Sand, and Stars," 311-12.
[40]Gordon Wenham, *Genesis 16–50*, Word Biblical Commentary (Dallas: Word, 1994), 109, favors "a positive reading [of Abraham's response to Isaac], i.e., as an expression of hope, a prophecy, or a prayer, though to Isaac it may have sounded like an evasion."

Moreover, the promised provision, Walters observes, contrasts with Abraham's earlier offering of a ram in Genesis 15:9, such that "Abraham had brought a ram to YHWH, now YHWH will bring one to Abraham."[41] The connection between Genesis 22 and the sacrificial system instituted at Mount Sinai is further strengthened through the parallel use of a ram as a "burnt offering" (עֹלָה) for both the ordination of priests and the Day of Atonement (Ex 29:18; Lev 8:18-21; 9:2; 16:3, 5),[42] as well as the abundant use of additional terminology in Genesis 22 associated with this system.[43] Significantly, Walters also points out that, "In the sacrificial economy, the animal being offered to God must be brought by the worshipper."[44] Taking the ram as representative of "the entire apparatus of offerings burnt and otherwise," he concludes that Genesis 22 implies that "the cult is God's own provision.... As the ram was God's gift to himself, made because Abraham was unable to give it, so also the entire cult is God's gift to himself."[45]

Despite Walters's many insights, there is an alternative to his conclusion regarding the provision of the ram. Rather than taking it as communicating the divine provision of the entire cult, it can instead be interpreted as a purposeful contrast to the sacrificial system instituted at Mount Sinai. It was, after all, an animal provided and chosen by the Lord, not Abraham the worshiper. Furthermore, the sacrifice of the ram is inextricably linked to the sacrifice of a human being (Isaac), something forbidden under the Sinai law (Lev 20:2-5). The many links between Genesis 22:1-19 and the sacrificial system are thus better understood as serving ultimately to contrast the two rather than to show their continuity. The sacrifice of Isaac and the Lord's provision of a ram stand outside of this system rather than fully harmonizing with it.

---

[41] Walters, "Wood, Sand, and Stars," 309.

[42] Walters, "Wood, Sand, and Stars," 309, points out the common theme of the Lord's "appearing" (Gen 22:14; Lev 9:4; 16:2).

[43] Walters, "Wood, Sand, and Stars," 317. E.g., "offer up" (עֹלָה), "mountain" (הַר), "wood" (עֵץ), "place" (מָקוֹם), "fire" (אֵשׁ), "altar" (מִזְבֵּחַ), "arrange" (עָרַךְ), "slaughter" (שָׁחַט). The related phrases, "one of the mountains that I will tell you" (Gen 22:2) and "the place which God said to him" (Gen 22:3, 9), parallel thematically and syntactically the phrase, "the place which the LORD your God will choose" (Deut 12:5, 11, 21; 14:24-25; 16:6; 17:8; 26:2).

[44] Walters, "Wood, Sand, and Stars," 318.

[45] Walters, "Wood, Sand, and Stars," 318-19. He seems to be partially motivated by Jewish-Christian unity (see especially 326-27).

Genesis 22:1-19, however, is continuous with Genesis 3:15.[46] As argued previously, the seed of the woman will die from a fatal snakebite, and now, Isaac, *a* seed in the lineage of *the* seed (see Gen 22:17b; Gen 24:60), faced certain death. In both cases, the death was ordained by the Lord and had cultic significance. Isaac was to be a burnt offering, and the seed of the woman would destroy uncleanness by crushing the head of the unclean serpent. Each death would also be violent, one by knife and the other by snakebite. The reference to Isaac as a "son" ten times in Genesis 22:1-19 matches the reference to the individual seed of the woman as "he" in Genesis 3:15, which implies that he too is a son. As a particularly beloved and precious son (Gen 22:2, 12, 16), Isaac is compositionally linked not only to favored sons in the subsequent narrative (e.g., Jacob, Joseph, Judah) but also to the mention of a precious firstborn son in Zechariah 12:10, a Messianic prophecy (Jn 19:37). Thus the common ethical question of how God could command human (child) sacrifice in Genesis 22:1-19 should not be viewed in isolation. To be sure, it was only a test for Abraham (Gen 22:1) and is explicitly forbidden elsewhere (Lev 20:2-5), but the seed of the woman, the most precious son of all (Mt 3:17), will indeed die as a sacrifice as foretold by Genesis 3:15. While it would probably be going too far to call the Messiah's death a "human sacrifice," some broader parallels remain. Genesis 22:1-19 gives a reminder and foretaste of his climactic death, as well as insight into it.

The relationship between Genesis 3:15 and Genesis 22:1-19 is thus related to what has been called "narrative patterning." Iain Provan explains,

> one of the things that is striking about biblical storytelling is its use of narrative patterning. The biblical story is quite self-consciously told in such a way that events and characters in the later chapters recall events and characters in the earlier chapters, by way of comparison and contrast. We are thus invited to read the various chapters of the story together in order to gain a fuller understanding of what is being said overall.[47]

---

[46] Some have already made the connection between the seed in Gen 3:15 and Gen 22:17b-18, e.g., Alexander, "Further Observations," 367-68; and Jared M. August, "The Messianic Hope of Genesis: The 'Protoevangelium' and Patriarchal Promises," *Themelios* 42, no. 1 (2017): 58-62, who adds that both passages also share the common theme of universal blessing.

[47] Iain Provan, "The Messiah in the Books of Kings," in *The Lord's Anointed: Interpretation of Old Testament Messianic Texts*, ed. Philip Satterthwaite, Richard Hess, and Gordon Wenham (Grand

Note that for Provan the phenomenon of narrative patterning is not accidental but intended by the author, who has "quite self-consciously told [the story] in such a way." Strictly speaking, Genesis 3:15 and Genesis 22:1-19 do not involve a contextually later narrative passage being patterned after an earlier narrative passage but rather a later narrative patterned after a brief but important poem. Since in this case the earlier passage is a Messianic prophecy (Gen 3:15), the patterning in Genesis 22:1-19 takes on Messianic significance. It is as though the brilliant light being focused through the lens of Genesis 3:15 is being reflected off the mirror of Genesis 22:1-19. The near death of Abraham's other son, Ishmael, in Genesis 21:12-21 is also part of this broader patterning, as it prepares the way narratively in the preceding context for a climax in Genesis 22:1-19.[48] A close connection between these two passages is also implied by the phrase "after these things" at the outset of the latter passage (Gen 22:1; cf. Gen 15:1). The narrative of Genesis 22:1-19, in turn, will serve as a pattern for a later narrative passage concerning the Passover in Exodus 12 (see chap. 4 below). In both passages, there is a "lamb" (שֶׂה; twice in Gen 22:7-8; five times in Ex 12:3-5) that dies as a substitute for a son (Gen 22:13; Ex 12:12-13, 29; cf. Gen 44:33).

If Genesis 22:1-19 is indeed purposefully patterned by the author after Genesis 3:15 (while still being a historically accurate record), then Genesis 22:1-19 should be thought of as intentionally foreshadowing the death of the Messiah. It is important to note that such a conclusion is not drawn simply by pointing out correspondences between Genesis 22:1-19

Rapids: Baker, 1995), 74. John Sailhamer, *The Pentateuch as Narrative: A Biblical-Theological Commentary* (Grand Rapids: Zondervan, 1992), 37-44, calls this phenomenon "narrative typology." Link and Emerson use the terminology "typological writing" as opposed to "typological reading." See Peter Link and Matthew Emerson, "Searching for the Second Adam: Typological Connections between Adam, Joseph, Mordecai, and Daniel," *SBJT* 21 (2017): 125-26.

[48]Though the Abrahamic covenant would not be fulfilled through Ishmael's line (Gen 21:10-12; see Gen 15:3-4), the Lord had also "blessed" him and promised both to "make him fruitful and multiply him greatly" and "to make him into a great nation" (Gen 17:20; see Gen 21:13, 18). Lexical parallels between Gen 21:10-21 and Gen 22:1-19 include "son" (throughout), "to be an heir" (Gen 21:10; 22:17), "youth" (נַעַר; Gen 21:12, 17-20; 22:5, 12), "seed" (Gen 21:12-13; 22:17-18), "to wake up early" (Gen 21:14; 22:3), "angel of God/the Lord called to [Hagar/Abraham] from heaven" (Gen 21:17; 22:11, 15), and lifting or opening "eyes" to "see" life-saving divine provision (Gen 21:19; 22:13). Thematic and stylistic parallels include the death of Abraham's son, obeying a voice (Gen 21:12; 22:2-3, 18), taking and carrying provisions for a journey (Gen 21:14; 22:3, 6), a bush or thicket (Gen 21:15; 22:13), and avoidance of using the names of the two sons. The name Ishmael is not used at all in Gen 21:10-21, and Isaac's name is absent from Gen 22:10-19.

and relevant New Testament passages. Though suggestive, these relationships do not provide any evidence that the author of the Pentateuch intended Genesis 22:1-19 to be understood in that way. Rather, the conclusion is based on the likelihood that Genesis 22:1-19 is intentionally patterned after Genesis 3:15, itself a direct Messianic prophecy. Remarkably, this patterning involves both Isaac and the divinely provided "lamb" intentionally foreshadowing the Messiah in their respective ways.[49]

Thus, the Messianic prophecy in Genesis 22:17b-18 not only links up with other Messianic prophecies elsewhere in the Pentateuch but fits with the immediate context in Genesis 22:1-19. All the covenant promises concerning Abraham's seed had been endangered by death (according to the command of the Lord himself!) and along with them the prophecy of the seed of the woman (see Gen 3:15; 21:12). However, Abraham's obedience ultimately resulted in the reaffirmation of these promises (Gen 22:16-18), including the ones that specifically pertain to the Messiah (Gen 22:17b-18). Although some see a tension between divine blessing resulting from Abraham's obedience here ("because you have done this thing," Gen 22:16) but from the Lord himself elsewhere (e.g., Gen 12:1-3),[50] the attribution of such high value to the giving up of a precious son to death squares with the implied merits of the death of the seed of the woman in Genesis 3:15. Incidentally, by giving up his son whom he "loved" (Gen 22:2), it is as though Abraham, by faith (Gen 22:8), has kept the Great Commandment to "love the LORD your God with all your heart and with all your soul and with all your strength" (Deut 6:4; see Gen 18:19; 26:5).

---

[49] For more on the latter, see the discussion of Judah in chap. 3 and the Passover in chap. 4 below, both of which will deal with the theme of substitution.

[50] R. W. L. Moberly, "The Earliest Commentary on the Akedah," *VT* 38 (1988): 303, points out that in this text the blessings are a reward for his obedience (Gen 22:18; see Gen 18:19; 26:4-5). As such, there is an apparent tension with the doctrine of justification by faith. For interaction with Moberly, see Wenham, *Genesis 16–50*, 112, "This is analogous to the assumptions underlying intercessory prayer. Here, too, faithful human response to God is taken up and incorporated within the purposes and activity of God." Regarding the doctrine of justification by faith, Moberly's observations do not indicate a genuine tension once it is recognized that Abraham's obedience was the fruit of his faith. The Abrahamic promises are still unconditional at their core, since the Lord takes it upon himself to fulfill them, but he does so in such a way that their conditions are fulfilled, first and foremost by himself and also by his transformed followers. The same general principle holds true for the Davidic covenant (see 2 Sam 7:12-16).

Regarding the Lord's swearing an oath on himself (Gen 22:16), Gordon Wenham points out, "This is the first and only oath in the patriarchal stories, though it is frequently harked back to (24:7; 26:3; 50:24; Exod 13:5; often in Deuteronomy)."[51] Notably, these retrospective passages most often refer to the promise of land (Ex 13:11; 33:1; Deut 1:8; 6:10), even though the land is not explicit in Genesis 22:16-18. This suggests that the oath applies to the entire Abrahamic covenant (which itself was instituted through a solemn ceremony), even those that are not directly stated in this passage. Both Genesis 24:7 and Genesis 26:3 treat the original promise of land in Genesis 12:7 ("to your seed I will give this land") as being under the purview of the oath in Genesis 22:16-18. The solemnity of the oath is reinforced through the phrase "the oracle of the LORD" (Gen 22:16), which appears only once elsewhere in the Pentateuch in Numbers 14:28 in the context of an oath that an entire generation of Israelites will die in the desert ("as I live"; see Num 32:10; Deut 1:34).[52] The seriousness of the Lord's words in this other context gives further insight into his firm commitment to the Abrahamic covenant and the seed of the woman prophecy that is intertwined with it.

The high drama of Genesis 22:1-19 thus concludes with the strongest affirmation by the Lord that the Messianic seed will come as promised. The promises will be fulfilled in spite of and through death (Gen 3:15). At this point in the narrative, Abraham has been through many trials, but the command to sacrifice Isaac is, according to Umberto Cassuto, "the final

---

[51]Wenham, *Genesis 16–50*, 111. Given the close relationship between the recently preceding passage about Ishmael in Gen 21:12-21 and Gen 22:1-19, it should not be surprising that the passage concerning Abraham and Abimelech in Gen 21:22-34 is also strategically linked to Gen 22:1-19. The verb *to swear* occurs three times in Gen 21:23-24, 31, along with the related words *seven* (Gen 21:28-30) and *Beersheba* (Gen 21:14, 31-33; note its reappearance in Gen 22:19). There is even the word *covenant* in Gen 21:27, 32 (see Gen 26:28; 31:44), which has an implicit tie to Gen 22:16-18 (see Gen 15:18). Thus, in addition to being an essential part of the ongoing narrative, Gen 21 also provides strategic thematic and lexical preparation for Gen 22:1-19.

[52]Moberly, "Earliest Commentary," 308, notes that the two phrases, "upon myself I swear" and "oracle of the LORD," are "unparalleled in Genesis but are common in prophetic literature." To make the point even stronger, this combination of phrases is unparalleled in the Pentateuch. Though not using both phrases at the same time, in the Pentateuch the Lord also swears that the earth will be filled with his glory (Num 14:21), Moses will not enter the Promised Land (Deut 4:21), Israel will be raised up as a holy people for himself (Deut 28:9; see Deut 28:12), and the Lord's enemies will be avenged (Deut 32:40-42).

and severest ordeal."[53] Nevertheless, the passing of this climactic "test" (Gen 22:1) results in "the last and most sublime promise."[54] Indeed, Genesis 22:16-18 consist of "the most sublime blessings and the most comprehensive assurances, which sum up all that had been promised him previously,"[55] especially, in our view, those specifically concerning the seed himself in Genesis 22:17b-18. Abraham's being "childless" (עֲרִירִי, Gen 15:2; see Lev 20:20-21; Rom 4:19) was thus overcome multiple times, and likewise Sarah's being "barren" (עֲקָרָה, Gen 11:30; see Is 54:1), the latter possibly associated via wordplay with Isaac being "bound" (עָקַד, Gen 22:9). These things are integrally linked to the Lord's original plan to "bless" (Gen 1:28; 12:2-3) and how this plan is fulfilled against all odds. Abraham saw these realities "from afar" (Gen 22:4; Heb 11:13), but we, "upon whom the end of the ages has come" (1 Cor 10:11), need not do so.[56]

A Lens and a Mirror: Isaac's Blessing and Jacob's "Ladder"

The last passages in the patriarchal narratives that concern the Messiah are Genesis 27:27-29 and Genesis 28:10-22. It will be argued below that the first passage is a Messianic prophecy (a "lens") and the second an instance of intentional foreshadowing of the Messiah (a "mirror"). Both passages are found in the Jacob narrative. The Lord's covenant promises to Abraham and Sarah (Gen 17:19) had been passed down to Isaac and Rebekah (Gen 21:12; 24:60) and are now in the complicated process of being passed down to Jacob. This process involved a divine oracle given to Rebekah while still pregnant with Jacob and Esau (Gen 25:22-23) and Jacob's

---

[53] Umberto Cassuto, *A Commentary on the Book of Genesis, Part II: From Noah to Abraham. Genesis 6:9–11:32*, trans. Israel Abrahams (Jerusalem: Magnes, 1964), 294. Starting with Gen 12:1-7 and ending with Gen 22, he counts ten such tests (294-96). The instruction to "go" to a "land" that the Lord would tell him in Gen 22:2 recapitulates Abraham's first trial to "go" to a "land" that the Lord "will show you" (Gen 12:1). For more on the structure of the Abrahamic narrative, including a helpful summary of literature, see Pshenichny, "Abraham in the Canonical Hebrew Bible," 14-17.
[54] Cassuto, *Commentary on the Book of Genesis, Part II*, 294.
[55] Cassuto, *Commentary on the Book of Genesis, Part II*, 296.
[56] Heb 11:13 ("not receiving the promises but seeing them from afar [πόρρωθεν]") suggests an allusion, albeit with a different word in the LXX (μακρόθεν; though see the use of πόρρωθεν to translate מֵרָחֹק in Is 43:6; 49:21; Jer 23:23), to מֵרָחֹק in Gen 22:4 such that it has both a spatial and temporal nuance. The latter is attested in 2 Sam 7:19/1 Chron 17:17; 2 Kings 19:25/Is 37:26; Is 22:11 (see Ezek 12:27).

manipulative acquisition of Esau's birthright as firstborn (Gen 25:29-34). These things came to a head when Jacob deceived his father Isaac with his mother Rebekah's help and stole Esau's blessing in Genesis 27:1-29.

After a long and suspenseful sequence, Isaac finally blessed Jacob in Genesis 27:27-29. Far from seeing this as primarily concerning family relations and an aged father blessing a son, the alert reader recognizes that the blessing is not merely from Isaac but from the Lord (Gen 27:27: "like the scent of the field which the LORD has blessed"). Indeed, the extensive use of the words *bless* and *blessing* in this chapter (Gen 27:4, 7, 10, 12, 19, etc.) pick up on the Lord's blessing of Adam (Gen 1:28; 5:2), Noah (Gen 9:1), Abraham (Gen 12:2-3; 22:17-18; 24:1), and Isaac (Gen 25:11; 26:3-4, 12, 14). Thus, Isaac's blessing of Jacob in Genesis 27:27-29 continues the Lord's plan of blessing that began at creation, continued with Noah, and came into sharper focus with the Abrahamic covenant.

Although these blessings have both their individual and corporate aspects, especially related to "seed," the blessing in Genesis 27:27-29 emphasizes the individual aspect. Grammatical singulars relating to Jacob are used throughout ("my son"; "which the LORD has blessed [it/him]"; "may God give to you [sg.]"). Furthermore, the promise of rule over his brothers and the nations better fits an individual than a group. Although kings will come from Abraham (Gen 17:6, 16), several passages discussed above lead the reader of the Pentateuch to expect an individual, eschatological king from Abraham's line (Gen 3:15; 15:3-4; 22:17b-18; Gen 24:60).

Isaac's smelling (רִיחַ) of Jacob's pleasant "scent" (רֵיחַ) in connection with the Abrahamic covenant (Gen 27:27) recalls the Lord's smelling (רִיחַ) of the "pleasing aroma" (רֵיחַ נִיחֹחַ) of Noah's sacrifice after the flood (Gen 8:20-22) and the subsequent Noahic covenant (Gen 9:9-17). But whereas the "pleasing aroma" in Genesis 8:20-21 came from burnt offerings of clean animals, parallel to sacrifices offered under the Sinai law (e.g., Ex 29:18, 41-42; Lev 1:9, 13; 2:2), here the pleasing smell comes from Jacob himself ("the scent of my son") and his clothes ("the scent of his clothes"). The compositional association of Jacob and his clothes with acceptable animal sacrifice is highly suggestive in view of the implied death of the seed of the woman by snakebite in Genesis 3:15 and the related (near-)sacrifice of Isaac in Genesis 22:1-19. Clothes will also play an important role in the Joseph narrative, especially the Messianic prophecy in Genesis 49:8-12 (see chap. 3 below). Also compositionally linked to earlier passages is Jacob's enjoyment of the fruitfulness of the earth (Gen 27:28), which relates to both Edenic abundance and the Abrahamic promise of land.[57] The "dew of heaven" not only waters the land but also signifies divine favor (Deut 33:13, 28; Ps 133:3).

The promise of rule over "peoples" and "nations" as well as his "brothers" and "mother's sons" (Gen 27:29) is difficult to understand in isolation. Wenham demurs, "The precise meaning of the prayer/prediction, 'May peoples serve you and nations bow down before you,' is less clear."[58] Victor Hamilton does not directly explain its meaning either.[59] To complicate matters further, the reference to "brothers" and "mother's sons" (pl.) does not fit with the reality that Jacob only had one brother, Esau. Even though Jacob's relatives from Laban's family are also his "brothers" (Gen 29:4, 15; 31:46), they are certainly not his "mother's sons." To explain this, Hamilton suggests that "'brothers'/'mother's sons' may be poetic craft."[60] Wenham again demurs, saying that "Jacob will be honored by Esau and any other brothers he may have,"[61] the latter phrase perhaps a tacit acknowledgment of the interpretive problem concerning Jacob's brother(s). In an ironic reversal, Jacob even "bowed down to the ground seven times" to Esau in Genesis 32:3. However, these problems of interpretation vanish when this statement is related to the broader compositional strategy and recognized as being fulfilled by one of Jacob's descendants rather than directly by Jacob himself (see Gen 37:5-10; 48:12; 49:8). This is implied by the Lord's affirmation in the next chapter that the Abrahamic covenant has been passed down to Jacob and his "seed" (Gen 28:13-14). Jacob only had one brother from the same mother and never ruled the nations, but his seed will have many brothers and will rule the world. Like his forefathers Abraham and Isaac, Jacob received the promises but awaited their fulfillment (Heb 11:8-21).

---

[57]See C. F. Keil and Franz Delitzsch, *Commentary on the Old Testament: The Pentateuch* (Peabody, MA: Hendrickson, 1996), 177.
[58]Wenham, *Genesis 16–50*, 209.
[59]Victor Hamilton, *The Book of Genesis: Chapters 18–50*, New International Commentary on the Old Testament (Grand Rapids: Eerdmans, 1995), 222.
[60]Hamilton, *Book of Genesis 18-50*, 222.
[61]Wenham, *Genesis 16–50*, 210.

Once a broad enough context is allowed to illumine Genesis 27:29, it becomes increasingly evident that the promised rule over "brothers" and "nations" will be fulfilled by the Messianic king. Although Joseph came close to fulfilling this after being put in charge in Egypt (Gen 37:5-10; 41:41, 57; 42:6-9), he was all the while still under the authority of Pharaoh (Gen 41:40, 43). Furthermore, Genesis 49:8-12 re-presents the Joseph narrative in terms of an eschatological king from the line of Judah (see chap. 3 below). During "the last days" (Gen 49:1), his "brothers" and "father's sons" will praise him and "bow down" to him (Gen 49:8). In the context of the Joseph narrative, these two groups are easily identified as all of Joseph's brothers (who came from different mothers but the same father), who are in turn even called the "tribes of Israel" before the fact (Gen 49:16, 28). The parallel to the "brothers" and "mother's sons" in Genesis 27:29, along with the difficulty of identifying these groups otherwise, suggests that Israelites are also in view here well.

Closer investigation of the paired acts of serving (עָבַד) and bowing down (הִשְׁתַּחֲוָה) in Genesis 27:29 yields further insight. The use of these two verbs together typically relates to worship, especially of idols. This usage is consistent in the Pentateuch (Deut 4:19; 8:19; 11:16; 17:3; 29:25; 30:17) and in the rest of the Old Testament (e.g., 1 Kings 9:6, 9; 16:31; Jer 8:2; 13:10).[62] For example, in the first part of the Ten Commandments after prohibiting other gods or making a carved image (Ex 20:3-4), the Lord continues, "You shall not bow down [הִשְׁתַּחֲוָה] to them, and you shall not serve [עָבַד] them" (Ex 20:5; Deut 5:7-9; 8:19). This is what the nations do (Ex 23:23-24; Josh 23:7) and what Israel eventually does after failing to drive them out of the land and subsequently intermarrying with them (Judg 2:11-13,19). Israel will also worship idols when scattered among the nations (Deut 4:27-28). But Isaac's prophetic blessing in Genesis 27:29 casts a strikingly different vision. Ultimately, both Israel and the nations will worship

---

[62] According to our analysis, with only the exceptions discussed below, every time these two verbs appear together in the same verse, they concern the worship of idols. To be sure, each verb is used separately to express the worship of the Lord (e.g., *serve* in Ex 23:25; Deut 6:13 and *bow down* in Ps 95:6; 97:7), and in Ps 22:29-30 they appear in consecutive verses for the same. Nevertheless, it should be noted that each verb by itself, or even the combination of the noun *servant* with the verb *bow down*, does not necessarily imply worship; e.g., "serve" (Gen 14:4) and a "servant" who "bows down" (Gen 24:52).

("serve" and "bow down to") a king from the line of Abraham, Isaac, and Jacob.[63] Psalm 72, a psalm of Solomon, confirms this and further implies that this king was not David or Solomon, "May all kings bow down [הִשְׁתַּחֲוָה] to him, and all nations serve [עָבַד] him!" (Ps 72:11). It is in him that all nations will be blessed (Ps 72:17; Gen 22:18). In the compositional strategy of the Pentateuch, the worship of this human king (Gen 27:29; see Is 49:7; 52:13) evidently does not violate the prohibitions against idolatry in the Ten Commandments (Ex 20:3-5; see Lev 25:55), which assumes that all are to serve and bow down to the Lord (Ps 22:29-30). In other words, the fulfillment of the Abrahamic covenant is a Messianic king who is both human and God, even the Lord himself.

The last line of Genesis 27:29, "Cursed are those who curse you, and blessed are those who bless you," picks up on the similar statement to Abraham in Genesis 12:3 ("I will bless those who bless you and the one who curses you I will curse"). This is not only another indication that the Abrahamic blessings are being passed down to Jacob but focuses the fulfillment of this particular promise in Genesis 12:3 on an individual Israelite king, not the nation of Israel corporately. In the context of Genesis 27:27-29, the one who blesses the divinely appointed ruler of the world will be blessed, and the one who curses him will be cursed. Subsequent Messianic prophecies in the Pentateuch (Gen 49:8-10; Num 24:9) pick up light from the lens of Genesis 27:27-29 and further clarify that the king in view here is indeed the Messianic king.

A few more observations concerning the relationship of Genesis 27:27-29 to the Abrahamic covenant are in order. First, although many passages concerning the Abrahamic covenant focus on Abraham's collective seed (Israel), this text only secondarily mentions Israel ("brothers" in Gen 27:29) in relation to an individual descendant of Jacob ruling over them. Such a focus on Israel's eschatological king and a secondary reference to Israel is

---

[63]See Hippolytus in Mark Sheridan, ed., *Genesis 12–50*, Ancient Christian Commentary on Scripture (Downers Grove, IL: InterVarsity Press, 2002), 175, "And also the words 'Let peoples serve you, and princes bow down to you' have been accomplished now. Whom else do the faithful peoples serve and the princes of the church worship but Christ, in whose name they also receive their salvation? . . . nobody adored Jacob, nor did he become lord of his brother Esau; on the contrary, he ran away from him in a fright and was the first to adore him, for seven times. Therefore the words of Isaac have been accomplished in the Savior. . . . That is why Isaac says, 'Cursed be everyone who curses you, and blessed be everyone who blesses you.'"

also attested in Numbers 24:17-19, 2 Samuel 7:8-16, and Isaiah 49:5-6. At the same time, Jacob will later be renamed Israel (Gen 32:28) and still represents the future nation in some sense (e.g., Is 40:27). Indeed, his exaltation over Esau befits his Messianic seed's rule over Edom (Num 24:17-18), which in some passages is a wordplay on "humankind" (*'adam*; see Is 34:1-5; 63:1-6; Amos 9:12; Obad 1:15-21).

Second, oftentimes when the nations are mentioned in passages concerning the Abrahamic covenant, it is said that they will be blessed by Abraham and his seed (Gen 18:18; 26:4). It was argued above that Genesis 22:17b-18 even says that they will experience this blessing through his individual, Messianic seed. But what else can be said about *how* the nations will be blessed through the Messiah? The nations also appear in the blessing of Genesis 27:29, but as worshiping an Israelite king. If those who "serve" and "bow down" to the king in the first part of this verse are also those who "bless" him and are "blessed" in the last line of this verse, then blessing comes to the nations through the king's worldwide rule and their worship of him. This is exactly what Psalm 72 implies (see especially Ps 72:11, 17). The logic is thus consistent: there will be those who bless and worship this royal seed from every nation, and in this way all the nations will be blessed through him (Gen 12:3; 27:29; 28:14).

Third, Isaac's address of Jacob as "my son" (Gen 27:27) picks up on the important theme of sonship in the Abrahamic covenant. As pointed out above, the individual seed in Genesis 3:15 is male ("he") and hence a son (Is 9:6), and Genesis 22:1-19 refers to Isaac as a "son" ten times and climactically reiterates the promise of "seed" (Gen 22:16-18). Chan observes that seed and son appear together in Genesis 15:3 and remarks that because the promise of seed had not yet been fulfilled, "someone else's 'son' . . . would become his heir [i.e., Eliezer, 'the son of my house']."[64] If Genesis 3:15, Genesis 15:3-4, and Genesis 22:1-19 are intertextually related, as argued above, then the latter two passages not only link seed and son but do so with Messianic implications (Gen 3:15). Incidentally, the linkage of seed to a son in these passages also accords with an individual referent of seed. Although *seed* does not appear in Genesis 27:27-29, this suggests that the

---

[64]Chan, *Melchizedek Passages*, 67-68.

title "my son" (Gen 27:27) should not be passed over too quickly as only relating to Jacob. In further support of this, it has already been argued above that Isaac's blessing in these verses would not be fulfilled by Jacob but by one of his descendants. This suggests that his individual seed, who will please his father, enjoy the fruitfulness of the earth, and rule the world, will also bear the title, "my son." This title is reused in Genesis 49:9 (see chap. 3 below). Together, these two texts provide direct support from the Pentateuch itself for "my son" as a title for the Messiah.

References to a Davidic king as a "son" of God in later Scripture, such as 2 Samuel 7:14, Psalm 2:7, and Matthew 2:15, are sometimes interpreted in terms of such a status being ascribed to kings in the Ancient Near East or references to Israel as the Lord's "son" (Ex 4:22-23; Deut 1:31).[65] But as it relates to this title, Israel is a compositional foil in the Pentateuch for the Messiah, analogous to the use of "my servant" in the book of Isaiah (e.g., Israel in Is 49:3-4; Messiah in Is 52:13). Hence, 2 Samuel 7:14 ("he shall be a son to me") and especially Psalm 2:7 ("You are my son") are more appropriately interpreted in light of Genesis 27:27 and Genesis 49:9.[66] Such a special status aligns with the divinity implied of him in Genesis 27:29.

Jacob's theft of the blessing, which was his second major act of deception (Gen 27:36), aroused such anger in Esau that he wanted to kill him (Gen 27:41).[67] But Rebekah, who seemed to find out about everything (Gen 27:5-10), heard of this and urged Jacob to flee to her brother Laban's house in Haran (Gen 27:41-45). Using the legitimate reason of Jacob needing a wife from their own people (Gen 27:46; 26:34-35), she was able

---

[65] P. Kyle McCarter, Jr., *II Samuel: A New Translation with Introduction, Notes, and Commentary*, Anchor Bible (Garden City, NY: Doubleday, 1984), 207; Peter Craigie and Marvin Tate, *Psalms 1–50*, 2nd ed., Word Biblical Commentary (Nashville: Nelson, 2004), 67. This also comes out in discussion of Mt 2:15, "Out of Egypt I called my son." See David Turner, *Matthew*, Baker Exegetical Commentary on the New Testament (Grand Rapids: Baker, 2008), 91; Donald Hagner, *Matthew 1–13*, Word Biblical Commentary (Dallas: Word, 1993), 36.

[66] For a discussion of Gen 49:8-12 and Ps 2, see Paul Lai, "Jacob's Blessing on Judah (Genesis 49:8-12) within the Hebrew Old Testament: A Study of In-textual, Inner-textual, and Inter-textual Interpretation" (Ph.D. diss., Trinity Evangelical Divinity School, 1993), 319-22. Though focusing on Israel as "son," see Jon Levenson, *The Death and Resurrection of the Beloved Son* (New Haven, CT: Yale University Press, 1993), 67, "The story of the humiliation and exaltation of the beloved son reverberates throughout the Bible because it is the story of the people about whom and to whom it is told. It is the story of Israel the beloved son, the first-born of God."

[67] Gen 33:11 suggests that this blessing was ultimately meant to be shared, not stolen for one's own personal gain.

to secure the support of Isaac, who instructed him to go to Laban's house to find a wife and affirmed that the Abrahamic blessings had been passed down to him (Gen 28:1-4). These two are of course related, since Jacob needed a wife in order to be "fruitful" and "multiply" and have "seed" who will "possess" land (Gen 28:3-4). Naturally, Jacob obeyed his father in this instance (Gen 28:5, 10) and left home.

This leads to Jacob's encounter with the Lord in a dream at Bethel (Gen 28:10-22). He "came upon" (פָּגַע) a "place" (מָקוֹם) where he "spent the night" (לִין; Gen 28:11). Taking one of the "stones" (אֶבֶן) from that "place" (Gen 28:11), he fell asleep and "dreamed" (חָלַם; Gen 28:12). The "ladder" (סֻלָּם) that he saw linking heaven and earth and with angels ascending and descending on it (Gen 28:12) is famously referenced by Jesus during a conversation with Nathanael (Jn 1:47-51). In response to Nathanael's amazement over Jesus' knowledge of him (Jn 1:47-49), Jesus replied that he would see even "greater things than these" (Jn 1:50), such as "heaven opened, and the angels of God ascending and descending on the Son of Man" (Jn 1:51). Scholars have debated the nature of this citation over the centuries, with interpretations ranging from Jacob seeing a vision of Christ on earth to Jesus merely alluding to Jacob's ladder as illustrative of his superiority to prior revelatory acts.[68] Rather than entering into this particular debate directly, the analysis below will show that there is exegetical warrant for Jesus' apparent reference to himself as Jacob's ladder in John 1:51. The argument will involve the complex intertextual relationship of four passages: Genesis 11:1-9, Genesis 28:10-22, Genesis 37:5-10, and Genesis 49:8-12.

A comparison of the Tower of Babel (Gen 11:1-9) and Jacob's ladder (Gen 28:10-22) reveals some important similarities. First, both had to do with reaching the heavens. The builders of the "city and tower" (עִיר וּמִגְדָּל) in Genesis 11:4 intended that "its head/top will be in the heavens"

---

[68]See Ambrose in *John 1–10*, Ancient Christian Commentary on Scripture, ed. Joel C. Elowsky (Downers Grove, IL: InterVarsity Press, 2007), 87, "This means he foresaw Christ on earth." For a survey of ancient Jewish interpretations, see James Kugel, *The Ladder of Jacob* (Princeton, NJ: Princeton University Press, 2006), 9-35. Andreas Köstenberger, "John," in *Commentary on the New Testament Use of Old Testament*, ed. Gregory Beale and D. A. Carson (Grand Rapids: Baker, 2007), 429-30, calls this "an allusion to the story of Jacob in Gen. 28 . . . [Jesus] will be the place of much greater divine revelation than that given at previous occasions (cf. Heb. 1:1-3). . . . Jesus is the 'new Bethel,' the place where God is revealed, where heaven and earth, God and humanity meet."

(רֹאשׁוֹ בַשָּׁמַיִם), and Genesis 28:12 says of the "ladder" (סֻלָּם) that "its head/top was reaching to the heavens" (רֹאשׁוֹ מַגִּיעַ הַשָּׁמָיְמָה). Both contexts also involve "stone" (אֶבֶן; Gen 11:3; 28:11, 18, 22) and a worldwide scope ("all the earth," Gen 11:1; "the sons of men," Gen 11:5; "west, east, north, south . . . all the families of the land," Gen 28:14). Yitzhak Peleg also points out that both passages involve action on the "vertical and horizontal axes," as expressed through the verbs *ascend* (Gen 28:12), *descend* (Gen 11:5, 7; 28:12), *scatter* (Gen 11:4, 8-9), and *break forth* (Gen 28:14).[69]

While these similarities encourage the reader to relate these two passages, their differences ultimately lead to a contrast between the Tower of Babel and Jacob's ladder. Yair Zakovitch has investigated the general phenomenon in the Old Testament in which a later narrative "inverts the storyline of the original narrative."[70] This relates to and can be seen as a subcategory of Provan's "narrative patterning" discussed above. The key difference between the Tower of Babel and Jacob's ladder involves the final fate of each endeavor. The former was a failure, having been thwarted by God through the confusion of language (Gen 11:6-8), whereas the latter actually bridged heaven and earth such that angels traversed it (Gen 28:12). The success and failure of each was determined by the initiative and motivation behind them. The "sons of Adam" were rebelling against the Lord's command to fill the earth and were seeking their own glory (Gen 1:28; 11:4), but the "ladder" that Jacob dreamed about was of divine origin. Accordingly, the Lord's subsequent words and Jacob's response focus on the greatness of God (Gen 28:15-22). Even the stones in each passage are different. Whereas the stone that Jacob used as a pillow and later set up as a memorial at "Bethel" (בֵּית־אֵל) was an ordinary one (Gen 28:10, 18, 22), the stone used by the builders of "Babel" (בָּבֶל) was the product of strenuous human effort (Gen 11:3). Thus, as Peleg remarks, "The beginning of the Bethel ritual site is a mirror-image of the beginning of Babylon."[71] Citing

---

[69]Yitzhak Peleg, *Going Up and Going Down: A Key to Interpreting Jacob's Dream (Gen 28:10–22)*, trans. Betty Rozen (London: Bloomsbury, 2015), 259. He also cites Jacob's travels in Gen 28:15, 20-21 as an example of action on the horizontal plane.

[70]Yair Zakovitch, "Through the Looking Glass: Reflections/Inversions of Genesis Stories in the Bible," *BibInt* 1 (1993): 139. In describing this as "a strategy used by narrators to aid the reader," it is clear that Zakovitch sees this literary device as authorially intended.

[71]Peleg, *Going Up and Going Down*, 262.

Zakovitch in agreement, Peleg adds, "The gate of heaven is Bethel, not in Babylon."[72] Like Genesis 12 and Genesis 14, Genesis 28:10-22 also relates to Babel/Babylon.

With the intertextual relationship between Genesis 11:1-9 and Genesis 28:10-22 established, we turn to Genesis 37:5-10 and Genesis 49:8-12. The intertextual relationship between these latter two passages themselves will be explained in detail in chapter three below. Briefly, Joseph's dreams of rule, especially of his "brothers" who "bow down" to him (Gen 37:5-10), are not only fulfilled in his own life (Gen 42:6-9) but are recast in Genesis 49:8-12 as part of the vision of the Messiah, to whom his "father's sons" will likewise "bow down." Thus Genesis 37:5-10 and Genesis 49:8-12 are linked to one another and to the Messianic vision of the Pentateuch. If Genesis 28:10-22 can be linked compositionally to Genesis 37:5-10 and Genesis 49:8-12, then there is indeed an exegetical basis for Jesus' comparison of himself to Jacob's ladder in John 1:51, since Genesis 49:8-12 is a direct Messianic prophecy.

The language of "brothers" who "bow down" in Genesis 37:5-10 and Genesis 49:8 immediately recalls Genesis 27:29, in which Jacob himself received the promise that his "brothers" would "bow down" to him. But unlike Genesis 27:29 and Genesis 49:8 which also include the nations, Joseph's dreams only directly concern his brothers and, in his second dream, his parents also. Nevertheless, there are several additional links between Genesis 27–28 and Genesis 37. One lexical connection between Genesis 28:10-22 and Genesis 37:5-10 is the verb *dream* (חָלַם; Gen 28:12; 37:5-6, 9, 10); another is the verb *stand* (נָצַב; Gen 28:12; 37:7). To relate this to the narrative plotline, Jacob had been given a blessing of rule over "brothers" and nations (Gen 27:29) and dreamed about a ladder that had been "stood up" between heaven and earth (Gen 28:12), and now his son Joseph also had a dream about rule over his "brothers" (Gen 37:5-8), which involved his sheaf arising (קוּם) and "standing up" (נָצַב). The narrative itself suggests that Jacob himself linked his dream at Bethel to Joseph's dreams.[73] Although Jacob initially rebuked his son concerning his second dream and

---

[72]Peleg, *Going Up and Going Down*, 263, citing Yair Zakovitch, *Through the Looking Glass: Reflection Stories in the Bible* [Hebrew] (Tel Aviv: Hakibbutz Hameuhad, 1995), 60-61. We confess that we are unable to read Modern Hebrew and must rely on Peleg's citation here.

[73]Jacob also had a dream related to his acquisition of Laban's flocks in Gen 31:10-11. Incidentally, the dream also references Bethel and the pillar Jacob anointed there (Gen 31:13).

its implication that his parents would bow down to him (Gen 37:10), Jacob ultimately "kept the matter in mind" (Gen 37:11). After all, he had a dream years ago that he knew was from God, so how could a father so quickly dismiss the dreams of his favorite son, which, even though they were offensive, had similarities to his own dream and blessing? This suggests that Jacob henceforth would wait and see if Joseph's dreams were from God, and if so, how they might relate to the blessing and dream that Jacob himself had received as a younger man in Genesis 27:29 and Genesis 28:12, respectively.

Having established the compositional relationship among these four passages, an important theme can be detected: exaltation. This theme is expressed in a few different ways but most noticeably through the verbs *arise* (קוּם), *stand up* (נָצַב), and *ascend* (עָלָה). Although Genesis 11:1-9 uses none of these verbs, it does concern a "tower . . . whose top/head will be in the heavens" and a "name" (Gen 11:4). What is exalted in this passage is human effort, human pride, and the "city and tower" itself (Gen 11:4-5). In Genesis 28:12, a "ladder" is made to "stand [נָצַב] toward the earth and its head/top was reaching the heavens." In contrast with the Tower of Babel, this ladder does effectively bridge heaven and earth and as such is honorable. In Genesis 37:7, Joseph's sheaf "arose" (קוּם) and was "stood up" (נָצַב) and honored by his brothers' sheaves. In Genesis 49:8-12, Judah has "ascended" (עָלָה) and is praised and bowed down to by his brothers (Gen 49:8-9; 28:12). The "peoples" obey him also (Gen 49:10). The theme of exaltation in these four passages is depicted in figure 2.2.

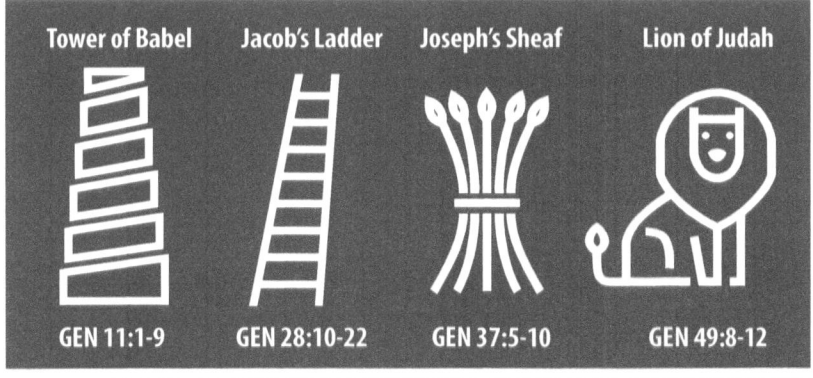

Figure 2.2. The theme of exaltation in four Genesis passages

The textual features represented in figure 2.2 can be further analyzed. Although all four passages involve exaltation of someone or something, the nature of the exaltation varies. Clearly, the exaltation of humanity surrounding the Tower of Babel is short-lived and ultimately in vain. It is sharply contrasted with the exaltation of the Lord and the ladder in Genesis 28:10-22. Joseph's exaltation over his brothers and parents, though part of the divine plan, will be ultimately overshadowed by the eschatological exaltation of the Lion of Judah over his brothers and the nations in Genesis 49:8-12. The two passages that involve an idealized exaltation are thus Genesis 28:10-22 and Genesis 49:8-12, which show evidence of being linked intertextually via Genesis 37:5-10 and suggest a close relationship between the ladder and the Lion of Judah. These relationships appear to be part of a broader compositional strategy of the Pentateuch that relates Genesis 28:10-22 to all three other passages through common words and themes. Such considerations lend exegetical credence to Jesus' application of Jacob's ladder to himself in John 1:51.

Additional considerations concerning the memorial "stone" and the "ladder" further support this. As pointed out above, the ordinary "stone" that had been Jacob's pillow (Gen 28:11) is set up as a memorial (Gen 28:18). Jacob's attribution of extraordinary value to something originally thought to be ordinary parallels his changed view of the "place" where he had slept, "How awesome is this place! This is none other than the house of God, and this is the gate of heaven" (Gen 28:17; Is 53:2). The "gate [שַׁעַר] of heaven" contrasts with the enemy "gate" in Genesis 22:17b and Genesis 24:60. Jacob's setting up the stone as a "pillar" (מַצֵּבָה) which shares the same root as the verb *stand* (נָצַב) and his pouring "oil on its head/top [רֹאשׁ]" (Gen 28:18, 22; 35:14) further suggests that the stone has been set up specifically to memorialize the ladder that "stood" and whose "head/top" touches the heavens (Gen 28:12). Reflecting back on this in Genesis 31:13, "the God of Bethel" reminds Jacob that he "anointed [מָשַׁח] a pillar [מַצֵּבָה] there." This pillar is the first thing in the Pentateuch to have oil "poured" (יָצַק) on it and to be "anointed" (מָשַׁח). "Oil" (שֶׁמֶן) was part of Isaac's blessing of Jacob (Gen 27:28, "the fatness [or oils] of the earth"), which relates to rule (Gen 27:29) and is commonly poured on the "head" of priests (Ex 29:7; Lev 8:12; 21:10) or kings (1 Sam 10:1; 2 Kings 9:3, 6). Most of these same verses also use the verb *anoint* (Ex 29:7; Lev 8:12; 1 Sam 10:1; 2 Kings 9:3, 6).

This suggests that the "stone" Jacob set up is linked both to the ladder as a miniature memorial of it and to priests and kings who are similarly anointed on their head. Priestly and kingly overtones relate to the ladder as an exalted form of mediation between heaven and earth. Such overtones suggest a thematic link to the exemplary priest-kings in Genesis 3:15 and Genesis 14:18-20, the seed of the woman and Melchizedek. Jacob, who is promised "oil" (Gen 27:28), is instead anointing something else in Genesis 28:18, just as Abraham's greatness in Genesis 14 gives way to Melchizedek's. Cornelius Houtman rejects the connection between the pillar and the ladder, seeing "more reason to suppose a relation of the massebah [i.e., pillar], the *standing* stone (vv. 16-18), to Yahweh, *standing* by Jacob [v. 13]."[74] The Lord is indeed called the "stone of Israel" (Gen 49:24) who has shepherded Jacob throughout his life (Gen 48:15).[75] While we prefer to read Genesis 28:13 as the Lord standing above the ladder ("and behold, the LORD was standing above it"),[76] the more important point is that choosing between relating the pillar to the ladder *or* to the Lord is a false dichotomy. Genesis 27:29 has already implied that the Messiah is divine through his being worshiped by Israel and the nations. As a result, he can be closely related to the ladder, the pillar, and the Lord, all of which "stand."

Before concluding this section, additional comment on the Hebrew word translated "ladder" (סֻלָּם, *sullam*) is in order. This word appears only here in the whole Old Testament and is hence difficult to define precisely. In the context of Genesis 28:12, not much more can be said about this *sullam* other than that it is something that links heaven and earth and can be traversed by angels. Thus, it has been understood as a ladder, a temple tower, a stair-like entrance to a tower, a ziggurat, or a staircase. Houtman believes that *sullam* is derived from the same root (סלל, *sll*) as *mesillah* (מְסִלָּה; Is 57:14; 62:10) and *maslul* (מַסְלוּל; Is 35:8), both of which mean "highway" or "track," and concludes that some kind of way or path is

---

[74]Cornelius Houtman, "What Did Jacob See in His Dream at Bethel? Some Remarks on Genesis XXVIII 10–22," *VT* 27 (1977): 343, emphasis original.

[75]The word *stone* also appears in the Jacob narrative in connection with the "large stone" that he moved from the well (Gen 29:2-10; see Is 33:2).

[76]See Peleg, *Going Up and Going Down*, 68-70.

meant.⁷⁷ Peleg further observes, "In most instances, particularly in the Prophets, the *sll* root appears in connection with the return to Zion, a possibly oblique reference to the return from exile to the land were God abides."⁷⁸ Even if *sullam* is not derived from the same root and only linked by wordplay, it provides a possible source (among others) for Jesus' statement, "I am the way" (Jn 14:6). While affirming the validity of Houtman's observations and conclusion, it is difficult to entirely avoid any association of *sullam* with a tower because of its height and compositional contrast with the "tower" (מִגְדָּל) at Babel (Gen 11:4-5), which presumably was also supposed to be ascended and descended by humankind. Furthermore, later Old Testament passages also refer to the Lord as a "tower" (מִגְדָּל) using this same word (Ps 61:3; Prov 18:10). The difficulty of *sullam*, if intentional, may even be an authorially intended means of causing the reader to slow down and pay greater attention to this word.⁷⁹

Conclusion

This chapter has shown that the patriarchal narratives make a significant contribution to the Messianic vision of the Pentateuch, which began to

---

⁷⁷Houtman, "What Did Jacob See?," 337-38, 340.
⁷⁸Peleg, *Going Up and Going Down*, 252.
⁷⁹See Michael Riffaterre, *Semiotics of Poetry* (Bloomington, IN: Indiana University Press, 1978), 2, who characterizes an "ungrammaticality" as effected by "a deviant grammar or lexicon." For example, the poetic line "false treasures in empty wardrobes" is a contradiction in one sense, but its purpose is to emphasize emptiness and disillusionment" (3-4). Not all ungrammaticalities involve contradiction. Using another example involving multiple related ungrammaticalities, he describes their effect, "The ungrammaticalities spotted at the mimetic level [i.e., relating to information conveyed by the text] are eventually integrated into another system. As the reader perceives what they have in common, as he becomes aware that this common trait forms them into a new paradigm, and that this paradigm alters the meaning of the poem, the new function of the ungrammaticalities changes their nature, and now they signify as components of a different network of relationships" (4). Accordingly, he describes two stages of reading, "heuristic," "where the first interpretation takes place," and "retroactive," which involves "a second interpretation, for the truly *hermeneutic* reading" (5). The latter involves not only the perception of ungrammaticalities but the integration of these "stumbling blocks" as key elements into the correct interpretation of the poem. He writes, "the obstacle that threatens meaning when seen in isolation at first reading is also the guideline to semiosis, the key to significance in the higher system, where the reader perceives it as part of a complex network" (6). It is possible to acknowledge Riffaterre's insights and generalizing them for narrative and intertextuality in the OT without following him, for example, on his de-emphasis on the author—e.g., "The literary phenomenon, however, is a dialectic between text and reader" (1). For an application to biblical studies, see Cynthia Edenburg, "How (Not) to Murder a King: Variations on a Theme in 1 Sam 24; 26," *SJOT* 12 (1998): 68-69. In our view, Riffaterre's basic ideas aptly describe what is being communicated especially in Gen 3:15 and Gen 49:8-12 (see chap. 3 below).

unfold in Genesis 3:15. That prophecy foretold a seed of the woman who will defeat the serpent at the cost of his own life and who will have both kingly and priestly characteristics. This promise of a seed is strategically linked to the seed of Abraham. Even though Abraham's seed sometimes refers demonstrably to a collective, grammatical and intertextual considerations strongly suggest that sometimes his seed refers specifically to an individual (Gen 15:3-4; 22:17b-18; 24:60), the same Messianic seed of Genesis 3:15. These three direct Messianic prophecies in the Abrahamic narrative characterize the coming seed as an heir to all the Abrahamic promises, including land, possessions, and enemies. Interwoven with these same three prophecies, evidence from the biblical text itself suggests that the priest-king of Salem, Melchizedek (Gen 14:18-20) intentionally foreshadows the eschatological priest-king of Genesis 3:15, and that the sacrifice of Isaac and the substitution of a ram (Gen 22:1-19) are intended to provide an illustration of the death of the seed/son as foretold in Genesis 3:15. As the narrative progresses, the covenant promises are passed down to Isaac and then to Jacob, who receives a blessing from his father that will be fulfilled by the Messiah. The scent of this "son" and his clothes will please his father just like the scent of Noah's sacrifice pleased the Lord. The Messiah will also enjoy the fruitfulness of the land and will rule and even be worshiped by Israel and the nations, which suggests his divinity. Those who bless him will be blessed, and those who curse him will be cursed. Jacob's "ladder" not only picks up on the Abrahamic promises generally but is compositionally linked to the Tower of Babel (Gen 11:1-9), Joseph's dreams (Gen 37:5-10), and the Messianic prophecy of the Lion of Judah (Gen 49:8-12). So far, the intricate network of Messianic passages in the Pentateuch consists of five prophecies/lenses (Gen 3:15; 15:3-4; 22:17b-18; 24:60; 27:27-29) and five instances of intentional foreshadowing/mirrors (Adam via Gen 3:15; the sun in Gen 1:16-18; Melchizedek in Gen 14:18-20; the sacrifice of Isaac/ram in Gen 22:1-19; and Jacob's ladder in Gen 28:10-22). The clarity and fullness of the Messianic vision of the Pentateuch will only increase in the subsequent chapters.

3

THE LION OF JUDAH

One of the highlights of Messianic prophecy in the Pentateuch is Genesis 49:8-12, which centers on a king from the line of Judah who will rule Israel and the nations "in the last days" (Gen 49:1). It is the longest continuous Messianic prophecy in the Pentateuch, and as such focuses many wavelengths, or themes, in the spectrum of the Messianic vision of the Pentateuch. As is the case for the Messianic prophecies already considered (Gen 3:15; 15:3-4; 22:17b-18; 24:60; 27:27-29), its content relates both to its immediate narrative context and to other Messianic prophecies in the Pentateuch. Genesis 49:8-12 is also a hotly contested passage, with many disputing that it is indeed a Messianic prophecy. Some would take this passage as referring only to David (and possibly Solomon also), or to David and Jesus as multiple fulfillments. The discussion below will argue that Genesis 49:8-12 is an exclusively Messianic prophecy and will explain its contents, which include, remarkably, his resurrection from the dead.

THE BLESSING OF JACOB AND "IN THE LAST DAYS"

As John Sailhamer has pointed out, the blessing of Jacob in Genesis 49:1-27 is one of the four major poetic sections in the Pentateuch and as such plays an important role in its structure and compositional strategy.[1] Although critical scholars treat this passage as a late insertion to the Joseph narrative and sometimes virtually ignore it in studies of Genesis 37–50, a compositional approach to the Pentateuch treats every passage as integral to the whole work, especially Genesis 49:1-27.[2] To review, the

---

[1] John Sailhamer, *The Pentateuch as Narrative: A Biblical-Theological Commentary* (Grand Rapids: Zondervan, 1992), 35.
[2] Some who consider it a late insertion grant the possible antiquity of the poem itself; e.g., Hermann Gunkel, *Genesis*, trans. Mark Biddle (Macon, GA: Mercer, 1997), 453, "The poem, itself

overall structure of the Pentateuch consists of a repeating sequence of a lengthy narrative section, a major poetic section, and a brief narrative epilogue. This sequence repeats four times. Hence, it has four major poetic sections, called such because they are much longer than other poetic sections in the Pentateuch (e.g., Gen 3:14-19). Genesis 49:1-27 is the first major poetic section in this series; the second is Exodus 15:1-18; the third consists of the four medium-length poems in Numbers 23:7-10, 18-24; 24:3-9, 15-24; and the fourth and longest is Deuteronomy 32:1-43; 33:2-29. In the first, third, and fourth of these (i.e., all except Ex 15:1-18), "the central narrative figure (Jacob, Balaam, Moses) calls an audience together (imperative: Gen 49:1; Nu 24:14; Dt 31:28) and proclaims (cohortative: Gen 49:1; Nu 24:14; Dt 31:28) what will happen (Gen 49:1; Nu 24:14; Dt 31:29) in 'the end of days' (Gen 49:1; Nu 24:14; Dt 31:29)."[3] Although Exodus 15:1-18 also involves the central narrative figure (Moses) leading an audience (Israel) with a cohortative (Ex 15:1), the other three major poetic sections in particular are thus not only similar in genre (i.e., poetry) and relative length but also have even more lexical, syntactical, and thematic similarities. Sailhamer relates these seminal findings to Messianic prophecies in each of these three poems (Gen 49:8-12; Num 24:7-9, 17-19; Deut 33:7), which demonstrate the centrality of the Messiah to the composition of the Pentateuch as a whole.

One of the key issues in this argument is the precise meaning of the Hebrew phrase *be'akherit hayyamim* (בְּאַחֲרִית הַיָּמִים), translated by Sailhamer here as "in the end of days" (see KJV, ASV, JPS, NKJV) but by

---

very old, was, however, only inserted into the patriarchal legends at a late date.... In fact, it seems to have belonged first to the book of J." Jürgen Ebach, *Genesis 37-50*, Herders Theologischer Kommentar zum Alten Testament (Freiburg: Herder, 2007), 574, traces Gen 49 to a "priestly adaptation of the Joseph story." Relatedly, Franziska Ede, *Die Josefsgeschichte* (Berlin: De Gruyter, 2016), 445, "In OT research, a relative consensus dominates concerning the priestly origin of vv. 1a,28-33," which frame the blessing itself in Gen 49:1-27. For examples of those who virtually ignore it, see Lothar Ruppert, *Die Josephserzählung der Genesis* (Munich: Kösel-Verlag, 1965), 162, comments that Gen 49:1-28 "is doubtless of a later date" and proceeds to pass it over, "Therefore the 'Blessing' is not considered in the following." See also Donald Redford, *A Study of the Biblical Story of Joseph*, Supplements to Vetus Testamentum (Leiden: Brill, 1970), 25, "The content of the blessing suggests Canaan, and undoubtedly stems from a different tradition to that of the Joseph Story." Redford only passingly refers to specific portions of the blessing in footnotes.

[3]Sailhamer, *Pentateuch as Narrative*, 36.

most other more recent English translations as "in [the] days to come" (see RSV, NAS, NIV, ESV, CSB). The underlying interpretive issue is whether Jacob's blessing merely concerns the generic future ("in the days to come") or the eschatological future specifically ("in the end of days" or "in the last/latter days"). As it relates to Genesis 49:8-12, what is at stake is whether the Messiah, who comes "in the last days" (see Heb 1:2), is specifically in view or not. For if Jacob was only speaking of the future generally, this allows for the possibility that Genesis 49:8-12 refers to David and perhaps Solomon, both of whom also reigned powerfully.

Before discussing more detailed issues concerning the meaning and translation of this controversial phrase,[4] it should be noted that the nine English translations cited above consistently translate the same phrase as "in the last/latter/end of days" elsewhere in the Old Testament, with just a few exceptions, as table 3.1 shows. Evidently, the English translation of this phrase is far more consistent in these other ten Old Testament instances than in the four found in the Pentateuch. This has already been shown for Genesis 49:1, and it also holds true for Numbers 24:14, Deuteronomy 4:30, and Deuteronomy 31:29.

This brief analysis reveals that outside the Pentateuch *be'akherit hayyamim* (בְּאַחֲרִית הַיָּמִים) is almost always translated "in the last/latter/end of days." Within the Pentateuch, it is usually translated as "in the latter/end of days" in Numbers 24:14 and Deuteronomy 4:30. But it is only translated that way about half the time in the other two Pentateuchal passages, Genesis 49:1 and Deuteronomy 31:29. The KJV, ASV, JPS, and NKJV always translate the phrase eschatologically. The RSV, NAS, and ESV usually do, with two exceptions in the Pentateuch (Gen 49:1 and either Num 24:14 or Deut 31:29). The CSB never translates it eschatologically in the Pentateuch but usually does elsewhere (except Jer 23:30 and 30:24), and the NIV usually translates it noneschatologically across the Old Testament, except in Isaiah 2:2, Hosea 3:5, and Micah 4:1.

---

[4] E.g., W. Staerk, "Der Gebrauch der Wendung באחרית הימים im at. Kanon," *ZAW* 11 (1891): 247-53; E. Lipinski, "באחרית הימים dans les textes préexiliques," *VT* 20 (1970): 445-50; see also the more recent survey and bibliography in William Tooman, *Gog of Magog: Reuse of Scripture and Compositional Technique in Ezekiel 38–39* (Tübingen: Mohr Siebeck, 2011), 94-97.

	KJV	ASV	JPS	RSV	NAS	NKJV	NIV	ESV	CSB
Gen 49:1	"in the last days"	"in the latter days"	"in the end of days"	"in days to come"	"in the days to come"	"in the last days"	"in days to come"	"in days to come"	"in the days to come"
Num 24:14	"in the latter days"	"in the latter days"	"in the end of days"	"in the latter days"	"in the days to come"	"in the latter days"	"in days to come"	"in the latter days"	"in the future"
Deut 4:30	"in the latter days"	"in the latter days"	"in the end of days"	"in the latter days"	"in the latter days"	"in the latter days"	"in later days"	"in the latter days"	"in the future"
Deut 31:29	"in the latter days"	"in the latter days"	"in the end of days"	"in days to come"	"in the latter days"	"in the latter days"	"in days to come"	"in days to come"	"in the future"
Is 2:2	"in the last days"	"in the latter days"	"in the end of days"	"in the latter days"	"in the last days"	"in the latter days"	"in the last days"	"in the latter days"	"in the last days"
Jer 23:20	"in the latter days"	"in the latter days"	"in the end of days"	"in the latter days"	"in the last days"	"in the latter days"	"in days to come"	"in the latter days"	"in time to come"
Jer 30:24	"in the latter days"	"in the latter days"	"in the end of days"	"in the latter days"	"in the latter days"	"in the latter days"	"in days to come"	"in the latter days"	"in time to come"
Jer 48:47	"in the latter days"	"in the latter days"	"in the end of days"	"in the latter days"	"in the latter days"	"in the latter days"	"in days to come"	"in the latter days"	"in the last days"
Jer 49:39	"in the latter days"	"in the latter days"	"in the end of days"	"in the latter days"	"in the last days"	"in the latter days"	"in days to come"	"in the latter days"	"in the last days"
Ezek 38:16	"in the latter days"	"in the latter days"	"in the end of days"	"in the latter days"	"in the last days"	"in the latter days"	"in days to come"	"in the latter days"	"in the last days"
Dan 2:28	"in the latter days"	"in the latter days"	"in the end of days"	"in the latter days"	"in the latter days"	"in the latter days"	"in days to come"	"in the latter days"	"in the last days"
Dan 10:14	"in the latter days"	"in the latter days"	"in the end of days"	"in the latter days"	"in the latter days"	"in the latter days"	"in the future"	"in the latter days"	"in the last days"
Hos 3:5	"in the latter days"	"in the latter days"	"in the end of days"	"in the latter days"	"in the last days"	"in the latter days"	"in the last days"	"in the latter days"	"in the last days"
Mic 4:1	"in the last days"	"in the latter days"	"in the end of days"	"in the latter days"	"in the last days"	"in the latter days"	"in the last days"	"in the latter days"	"in the last days"

Table 3.1. Translation of *be'akherit hayyamim*

The obvious inconsistency in English translations is reflective of an ongoing controversy over predictive prophecy, the authorship of the Pentateuch, and the extent and nature of Old Testament authors' knowledge of a "Messiah" and eschatology.⁵ For example, if Moses wrote the Pentateuch and is responsible for this phrase, could he have known about the eschatological reign of the Messiah? If not, then *be'akherit hayyamim* cannot mean "in the last days." To make the point even stronger for inerrantists, could Jacob who originally spoke these words have known about the eschatological reign of the Messiah? The same logic applies. On the other hand, those who deny the Mosaic authorship of the Pentateuch (and usually also the possibility of predictive prophecy) have argued, for example, that the phrase is eschatological but added by a much later hand during a time in which there was a Messianic and eschatological consciousness (i.e., the post-exilic period),⁶ or that an earlier (non-Mosaic) hand who lived before such a consciousness arose is responsible for the phrase but did not mean anything eschatological by it.⁷ Neither of these latter two options are ideal for many theologically conservative Christians.

Though not typically used in isolation from linguistic arguments, the problem with the general mode of argumentation sketched out above, whether it springs from a theologically conservative or theologically liberal perspective, is that it is not rooted deeply enough in the usage of the phrase *be'akherit hayyamim* itself and of its constituent words. Instead, it is based primarily on conjecture about how much the author of the phrase knew or did not know, which then drives the precise determination of the meaning of the phrase. But just as the most reliable method for determining the meaning of a word is through examining its usage in as many contexts as possible, so the most reliable method for determining the meaning of a

---

⁵For the controversy over predictive prophecy, see, e.g., Gunkel, *Genesis*, 450, who says of Gen 49:1-28a, "They are descriptions of the author's present [circumstances] in the mouth of the partriarch, *vaticinia ex eventu* [prophecies after the event] by prophets." For the controversy over knowledge of a "Messiah" and eschatology, see, e.g., Sigmund Mowinckel, *He That Cometh*, trans. G. W. Anderson (New York: Abingdon, 1954), who argues that Israel's concepts of Messiah and eschatology arose in the post-exilic period: "In *later* [emphasis mine] Judaism the term 'Messiah' denotes an eschatological figure. He belongs to 'the last time'; his advent lies in the future. To use the word 'Messiah' is to imply eschatology, the last things. It is, therefore, a misuse of the words 'Messiah' and 'Messianic' to apply them, for instance, to those ideas which were associated in Israel or in the ancient east with kings who were actually reigning [i.e., before exile], even if, as we shall see, these ideas were expressed in exalted and mythical terms" (1).
⁶W. Staerk, "Der Gebrauch der Wendung באחרית הימים im at. Kanon," 247-53; Gunkel, *Genesis*, 454.
⁷E. Lipinski, "באחרית הימים dans les textes préexiliques," 445-50.

phrase is examining the usage of the phrase and its constituent words in as many contexts as possible. Since the preposition *be* (בְּ), meaning "in" in this phrase, and the word *hayyamim* (הַיָּמִים), meaning "the days," are well understood and not in dispute, the deciding factors will be the respective meanings of the phrase itself and of the word *'akherit* (אַחֲרִית).

Of the fourteen appearances of *be'akherit hayyamim* (בְּאַחֲרִית הַיָּמִים), nine are apparently eschatological, based on reference in the immediate context to final victory, eschatological repentance, final restoration, final conflict, or an eschatological kingdom (Num 24:14; Deut 4:30; Jer 48:47; 49:39; Ezek 38:16; Dan 2:28, Is 2:2; Mic 4:1; Hos 3:5). If a consistent use of the phrase is granted in the Pentateuch, Jeremiah, and Daniel, as would likely be the case if each is the composition of a single author, then the remaining five instances are also accounted for (Gen 49:1; Deut 31:29; Jer 23:20; 30:24; Dan 10:14). In fact, on closer investigation, the respective contexts of Genesis 49:1 and Deuteronomy 31:29 also deal with much eschatological content (Gen 49:8–12; Deut 32–33). Thus, the usage of the phrase itself in these various contexts supports a meaning of "in the last/latter/end of days" as referring to the eschatological era, rather than "in the days to come" or any other phrase indicating merely the future generally. This result is supported by English translations and the Septuagint, which always uses a form of ἔσχατος, meaning "last," to translate this phrase.

Further confirmation arises from analysis of the word *'acherit* (אַחֲרִית). When this word is used temporally, as it is in *be'akherit hayyamim*, standard lexicons BDB and HALOT gloss it as "latter part," "close," or "end."[8] In

---

[8] The theological debate surrounding *be'akherit hayyamim* (בְּאַחֲרִית הַיָּמִים) can be seen even in the entries of *'acherit* (אַחֲרִית) in these two lexicons. Whereas BDB, the older of the two lexicons, explains that the phrase *be'akherit hayyamim* is "a prophetic phrase denoting the final period of the history so far as the speaker's perspective reaches; the sense thus varies with the context, but it often = the ideal or Messianic future," the more recent HALOT, without much explanation, also references the phrase along with the following bibliographic references, "Bentzen on Da 228 [Dan 2:28]; Vriezen VT Supp. 1:202f: non-eschatological Buchanan JNES 20:188ff; Akk. [transliterated Akkadian] in future days." What each of the scholars mentioned here believed is left as an exercise for the user of the lexicon but suffice it to say that "non-eschatological" and "in future days" show what the authors of this lexicon believe the phrase to mean. The core lexical data (i.e., from the Hebrew Bible) had not changed during the time between the publication of these two lexicons, but the controversy concerning the phrase had certainly continued. For more on this discussion, see T. Vriezen, "Prophecy and Eschatology," in *Congress Volume: Copenhagen, 1953*, Supplements to Vetus Testamentum, ed. G. W. Anderson (Leiden: Brill, 1953), 202, who asserts, "this expression has both a more general and a more restricted meaning: it

some contexts, *'akherit* appears together with its antonym, *re'shit* (רֵאשִׁית), meaning "beginning." For example, Deuteronomy 11:12 says that the eyes of the Lord are on the land "from the beginning [רֵאשִׁית] of the year, and even until the end [אַחֲרִית] of the year." Likewise, the Lord declares "the end [אַחֲרִית] from the beginning [רֵאשִׁית]" in Isaiah 46:10.[9] The juxtaposition of *re'shit* and *'akherit* clarifies the meaning of *'akherit* as "end," the proper antonym of "beginning," rather than "future," which is the antonym of "past."[10] The antonymous relationship between *re'shit* and *'akherit* even factors into the overall compositional strategy of the Pentateuch. It is probably no accident that the three major poetic sections appearing in conjunction with *be'akherit hayyamim* also contain the word *re'shit* and use it with the meaning of "beginning" or "first" (Gen 49:3; Num 24:20; Deut 33:21). Furthermore, Sailhamer notes that the *be'akherit*, meaning "in the last/latter/end" in *be'akherit hayyamim*, contrasts with *bere'shit* (בְּרֵאשִׁית), meaning "in the beginning," in Genesis 1:1.[11] Thus the temporal scope of the Pentateuch is not merely from the "beginning" (Gen 1:1) to Moses' death (Deut 34), even though this is the temporal scope of the historical events described in the Pentateuch, but it is from "beginning" to "end" by way of its prophetic, eschatological, Messianic vision.

Genesis 49:8-12, the Messiah, and the "Blessing of Abraham"

If *be'akherit hayyamim* (בְּאַחֲרִית הַיָּמִים) means "in the last days" (Gen 49:1), this phrase is one piece of evidence for the king described in Gen 49:8-12

---

may denote the future in general as well as the last days [e.g., Is 2:2; Mic 4:1; Jer 23:20; 30:24; 48:47; 49:39]." George Buchanan, "Eschatology and the 'End of Days,'" *JNES* 20 (1963): 188-93, argues that the phrase in the OT and its equivalents in the NT never require an eschatological meaning, which must be derived from additional context.

[9]The other verses that contain both words agree with this (Num 24:20; Job 8:7; 42:12; Eccles 7:8).

[10]Even though BDB also secondarily suggests "future" as a gloss, it explains it as meaning "a happy close of life." HALOT also secondarily suggests "future" as a gloss, but the passages cited in support (Is 46:10; Jer 29:11; Prov 23:18; 24:14) also involve an "end." Is 46:10 has already been discussed, and the other three passages involve a final state of blessing in which "hope" has become reality. One of the problems with the argument of Buchanan, "Eschatology and the 'End of Days,'" 188, is that he asserts without linguistic evidence that the antonym of *'akherit* is *lefanim* (לְפָנִים, "previously") via his analysis of the cognate *'akhar* (אַחַר, "after"). But such an approach to the meaning of *'akherit* through antonymity is not as direct and reliable as the one we have used.

[11]Sailhamer, *Pentateuch as Narrative*, 83 (including n. 6). The four instances of *be'akherit* (בְּאַחֲרִית) in Jeremiah are likewise paralleled by four instances of *bere'shit* (בְּרֵאשִׁית) in Jer 26:1; 27:1; 28:1; 49:34.

being the Messiah. Neither David nor Solomon reigned during "the last days" (see Acts 2:17; 2 Tim 3:1; Heb 1:2; Jas 5:3; 2 Pet 3:3-4). Relatedly, even though both David and Solomon ruled their Israelite "brethren" and enjoyed some power over neighboring nations (2 Sam 8; 1 Kings 10), the biblical record also points out major disruptions to their rule, such as Absalom's rebellion and Solomon's adversaries (2 Sam 12:10–19:43; 1 Kings 11:11-40), that seem to conflict with the ideal rule described in Genesis 49:8-12. Intertextual connections between this passage and other Messianic prophecies in Genesis provide further evidence that the Messiah is exclusively in view. The phrases "let your brothers praise you" and "let the sons of your father bow down to you" (Gen 49:8) closely parallel Genesis 27:29, "May the peoples serve you, and may the nations bow down to you; be lord over your brothers, and let the sons of your mother bow down to you," which was already argued in the previous chapter to be a Messianic prophecy. Moreover, just as the acts of "serving" and "bowing down" in Genesis 27:29 are used together throughout the Old Testament to express worship, so the acts of "praising" (Hiph. יָדָה) and "bowing down" (הִשְׁתַּחֲוָה) in Genesis 49:8 are directed toward God in the other two Old Testament passages in which they appear together (2 Chron 7:3; Ps 138:1-2).[12] The original naming of "Judah" (יְהוּדָה), a play on the verb *praise*, commemorated praising the Lord (Gen 29:35), which would be at odds with praising a mere human "in the last days" in Genesis 49:8. Therefore, the king in Genesis 49:8-12 can be reasonably understood as the same divine Messiah of Genesis 27:27-29. Both passages also are poetry and use jussive verbs (Gen 27:29, "may peoples serve you, and may nations bow down to you," "may the sons of your mother bow down to you"; Gen 49:8, "may your brothers praise you," "may the sons of your father bow down to you").

At the same time, the use of jussive verbs in the context of "enemies" (אֹיֵב) in Genesis 49:8 also connects to Genesis 22:17b ("may your seed possess [jussive] the gate of his enemies [אֹיֵב]"), Genesis 24:60 ("may your seed possess [jussive] the gate of his haters [שֹׂנֵא]"), and secondarily to

---

[12] E. W. Hengstenberg, *Christology of the Old Testament* (McLean, VA: MacDonald, 1972), 1:37, saw in Gen 49:8 "the slight allusion to a superhuman dignity of the tribe of Judah" in these two acts, through which "something divine is ascribed to Judah" and "he is raised above the merely human standing."

Melchizedek's blessing in Genesis 14:19-20 ("Blessed [בָּרוּךְ] be Abram ... and blessed [בָּרוּךְ] be God Most High, who has delivered your enemies [צָר] into your hand"). The conflict in all of these passages is in turn rooted in the "enmity" (אֵיבָה) of Genesis 3:15. Genesis 49:8-12 is thus closely intertwined with the network of Messianic prophecies in the preceding context (e.g., Gen 3:15; 22:17b; 24:60; 27:27-29) as well as with other passages that secondarily relate to the Messiah (e.g., Gen 14:18-20).

Just as the royal, and specifically the Messianic, aspects of the covenant promises to Abraham were passed down to Jacob in Genesis 27:27-29, so they are passed down to Judah in Genesis 49:8-12. The corporate aspects of these promises were also passed down to Jacob earlier (Gen 28:3-4, 13-14), but these aspects are now passed down to all twelve sons, not just Judah alone. As Genesis 49:28 summarizes, "This is what their father said to them, and he blessed [בֵּרַךְ] them, each man according to his own blessing [בִּרְכָה] he blessed [בֵּרַךְ] them."[13] Thus, whereas all of the Abrahamic promises were passed from Abraham to Isaac and then from Isaac to Jacob, the Messianic aspects of those promises were passed to Judah only and the corporate aspects to all twelve sons.

At the same time, although each son's reception of a "blessing" (Gen 49:28) suggests that the "blessing of Abraham" (Gen 28:4; see Gen 12:2) had been given to them, closer investigation of each blessing reveals that some do not sound like blessings at all. Whereas Joseph is "blessed" with many "blessings" (Gen 49:22-26), Reuben's "blessing" (Gen 49:3-4) recalls his sleeping with Bilhah, his father's concubine (Gen 35:22). The "blessing" of Simeon and Levi even includes the line, "Cursed [אָרוּר] be their anger" (Gen 49:7), which references their slaughter of the Shechemites following the rape of Dinah (Gen 34). Jacob evidently had not forgotten about any of these past misdeeds (see Gen 37:11). The mixed nature of the blessings in Genesis 49:3-27 suggests that the corporate aspects of the "blessing of Abraham" would not be fully enjoyed by the twelve sons/tribes in the near future. The comparison of Dan to a biting "serpent" (Gen 49:17) and the subsequent, "I wait for your salvation, LORD" (Gen 49:18) confirm this.

---

[13] The language and syntax here have some similarities to Gen 1:27-28.

On the surface level, to speak of the near future in Genesis 49:1-27 appears to contradict interpreting *be'akherit hayyamim* in Genesis 49:1 as "in the last days." Indeed, some have used this as an argument in favor of interpreting the phrase as meaning "in the future." After all, the "scattering" of Simeon and Levi within Israel (Gen 49:7) predicts that their portions of land will be absorbed within the boundaries of the other tribes.[14] This obviously did not take place "in the last days" but before the exile. In response to this apparent contradiction, the broader usage of *be'akherit hayyamim*, as surveyed above, still strongly supports a meaning of "in the last days." As a general rule, it is more reliable linguistically not to derive a new or modified meaning of a word or phrase based on its usage in one context. If this rule is upheld, then one solution is that "in the last days" in Genesis 49:1 does not necessarily mean that everything in Genesis 49:3-27 is eschatological. It only means at least some portion of it is. On the level of the composition of the Pentateuch as a whole, it has already been shown above that the use of this phrase in conjunction with a major poetic section is part of the top-level macrostructure of the Pentateuch. Furthermore, the compositional strategy at play here can be expressed quasi-mathematically as "major poetic section + 'in the last days' = Messianic prophecy."[15] This formula even holds for Exodus 15:1-18 (a major poetic section without "in the last days") and Deuteronomy 4:30 (which uses "in the last days" but not in conjunction with a major poetic section), neither of which have a Messianic prophecy in the immediate context. Note that this formula does not mean that Messianic prophecy in the Pentateuch must always be related to a major poetic section and "in the last days" (e.g., Gen 3:15; 27:29; Deut 18:15, 18), or likewise that eschatological content must always be linked to these two elements (e.g., Ex 15:1-18; Deut 4:30; 30:6). The formula specifically concerns major poetic sections and whether or not they directly predict the coming of the Messiah.

---

[14]Victor Hamilton, *The Book of Genesis: Chapters 18–50*, New International Commentary on the Old Testament (Grand Rapids: Eerdmans, 1995), 652, "Eventually Simeon is integrated into the tribe of Judah.... Levi is dispersed in the sense that the Levites are never given a territory of their own, but are divided among the remaining tribes."

[15]Kevin Chen, *Eschatological Sanctuary in Exodus 15:17 and Related Texts* (New York: Peter Lang, 2013), 70.

Genesis 49:8-12 and Joseph in the Narrative Context

By themselves, the phrase "in the last days" in Genesis 49:1, the seemingly perfect rule over brothers and nations, and the extensive intertextual connections to Genesis 27:27-29 and other Messianic prophecies already form a strong argument that the "lion of Judah" in Genesis 49:8-12 directly predicts the coming of the Messiah, who will rule the world and defeat his enemies. But what else does this passage say about the Messiah? How does it distinctly contribute to the Messianic vision of the Pentateuch? The readers of the Pentateuch would expect that this longest Messianic prophecy would say still more. In order to get at this "more" properly, Genesis 49:8-12 should be interpreted in light of the preceding narrative. This is exactly what is required for a proper understanding of the "blessings" of Reuben, Simeon, and Levi in Genesis 49:3-7, as explained above.

The same applies to the blessing of Judah in Genesis 49:8-12. However, whereas the blessings in Genesis 49:3-7 recall the sins of those three brothers, the blessing of Judah does not recall the sins of Judah, such as his initiation of the sale of Joseph as a slave (Gen 37:26-28) or the fiasco surrounding Tamar (Gen 38). This is surprising given Jacob's remembrance of his older brothers' sins. Moreover, while Genesis 49:8-12 does reference the preceding narrative concerning Judah (e.g., Gen 29:35), it primarily picks up on words and themes concerning another brother, Joseph, who receives his own blessing that also refers to parts of the narrative that concern himself (Gen 49:22-26). Although some commentators do not interpret Genesis 49:8-12 in light of the narrative context, the Pentateuch as a composition practically requires it, especially in view of the figurative speech and rare words in Genesis 49:8-12.[16] The exegesis of Genesis 49:8-12 is thus complex and easily confused because it requires properly relating it in different ways to both Judah and Joseph as they are each depicted in the narrative context.[17] We begin with the relation to Joseph, which is primary and more extensive.

---

[16] Victor Hamilton, *The Book of Genesis: Chapters 18–50*, 657, interacts with such an approach but basically rejects it. While he is right that sometimes this approach has gone too far, his commentary on Gen 49:8-12 does not make use of it enough, and only passingly acknowledges it regarding Gen 49:11 (662).

[17] For an example of such confusion, see, e.g., Edwin Good, "The 'Blessing' of Judah, Gen 49:8-12," *JBL* 82 (1963): 427-32. While "abandoning the tried but still unsuccessful messianic (or royal)

The starting point and basis for relating the blessing of Judah in Genesis 49:8-12 to Joseph in the preceding narrative is the similarity between "may the sons of your father bow down [הִשְׁתַּחֲוָה] to you" in Genesis 49:8 and Joseph's dreams about his brothers "bowing down" (הִשְׁתַּחֲוָה) to him in Genesis 37:5-11. Dreams are a major theme in the Joseph narrative (see the dreams of the cupbearer, baker, and Pharaoh in Gen 40–41), and Joseph's dreams are of particular, unifying importance. When Joseph has them, the narrator does not tell the reader whether these dreams about his brothers paying homage to him are from God. Given their existing hatred of him (Gen 37:2-4), his brothers' skepticism is not surprising, and even his father's rebuke is understandable. Ultimately, however, Jacob "kept the matter in mind" (Gen 37:11). Time would tell whether Joseph's dreams were from God, and Jacob would wait it out. Years ago, God had also given Jacob a dream, and Jacob himself had received a blessing that included rule over his brothers (Gen 27:29; 28:12). His dream and blessing, however, had included rule over the nations and a promise of land. In any case, it is as though the reader is also to keep in mind Joseph's dreams, which center on rule over his brothers. Are these dreams from God or not? As the story unfolds, it becomes clear (first to the reader and to Joseph, then to his brothers, and lastly to Jacob) that Joseph's dreams are from God. Despite the seeming reversal of his dreams through being sold into slavery and eventually imprisoned on false charges (Gen 37:28, 36; 39:20), Joseph

---

interpretation" (429), he does attempt to make connections to Gen 37:18-35 and Gen 38, in which Judah is at fault for selling Joseph into slavery and for his dealings with Tamar. While rightly recognizing the repetition of "prey" (טרף, Gen 49:9; 37:33) and the thematic repetition of the "dipping of a coat in blood" (Gen 49:11; 37:31) among some other connections that seem to be a stretch, Good interprets both of these as referring to Judah's "deception" of Jacob concerning Joseph's apparent death (429, 431). Following Good's approach though differing in interpretation especially of Gen 49:10-12, Calum Carmichael, "Some Sayings in Genesis 49," *JBL* 88 (1969): 439, remarks, "Judah is regarded by Jacob as the wild beast who tore Joseph." Good concludes that Gen 49:8-12 is "an ironic reflection on Judah's misdeeds in two earlier incidents [the other being Gen 38 for which he also believes there to be parallels]." Where Good errs is in his attempt to relate Gen 49:8-12 to Judah only, sometimes in questionable ways, when the passage relates primarily to Joseph. This is clear from Gen 49:8 (see below), but Good does not deal with this verse much, suggesting that it is a "late insertion" (428). Carmichael makes essentially the same mistake, only passingly noting the relationship between Joseph's dreams and Gen 49:8 (435). Our approach seems to answer Gordon Wenham, *Genesis 16–50*, Word Biblical Commentary (Dallas: Word, 1994), 475, whose objection to Good and Carmichael is that "the symbolic equations are far from obvious, and it demands Jacob's remarks being understood as criticisms of Judah rather than as praise. This is difficult in light of the explicitly positive v 8."

became Pharaoh's second-in-command and was put in charge of the storage of food during the years of plenty and the distribution of food during the famine (Gen 41:33-57). Since the famine reached the land of Canaan, Joseph's family was affected, and his brothers came to Egypt to buy food (Gen 42:1-5). In the process, his brothers came before Joseph and "bowed down" (הִשְׁתַּחֲוָה) to him (Gen 42:6). The reader now knows that Joseph's dreams have come true in the most improbable way.[18] Though his brothers did not realize what was happening, Joseph knew that they were his brothers (Gen 42:7-8) and that his dreams had come true (Gen 42:9). His brothers even unwittingly "bow down" (הִשְׁתַּחֲוָה) to Joseph several more times in the narrative (Gen 43:26, 28; cf. Gen 44:14; 50:18).

With so much emphasis on Joseph's dreams and their fulfillment in Genesis 37–50, it is all the more surprising that Jacob's blessing in Genesis 49:8-12 concern brothers "bowing down" (הִשְׁתַּחֲוָה) instead to Judah.[19] The important consequence, according to Sailhamer, is "that which was to happen to Joseph, and did happen in the course of the narrative (e.g., Gen 42:6), has been picked up by way of this image and transferred to the future of the house of Judah. That which happened to Joseph is portrayed as a picture of that which would happen to Judah 'in the last days.'"[20] In particular, the blessing of Judah in Genesis 49:8 intentionally refers to the Joseph narrative in Genesis 37–50 such that Joseph's brothers "bowing down" to him is re-presented and projected as a part of the Messianic vision of the Pentateuch. Just as Joseph's brothers bowed down to him, so the Messiah's brothers will also bow down to him "in the last days" (Hos 3:5). As a Messianic prophecy, Genesis 49:8-12 thus both directly predicts in itself the coming of the Messiah and at the same time uses intentional foreshadowing by selectively drawing on Joseph in the preceding narrative. In this respect, Genesis 49:8-12 is similar to Genesis 3:15, which also in itself directly predicts the coming of the Messiah and at the same

---

[18]Granted, the narrative does not explicitly deal with his parents bowing down to him (Gen 37:9-10). In an apparent reversal of Joseph's second dream, Joseph "bowed down with his face to the earth" before his father in Gen 48:12 (cf. Gen 27:29; 32:3).

[19]Jürgen Ebach, *Genesis 37–50*, Herders Theologischer Kommentar zum Alten Testament (Freiburg: Herder, 2007), 572, "thus it appears plainly unsettling, that such homage, which is correct just for Joseph in the story, now is rightly placed referred to Judah."

[20]Sailhamer, *Pentateuch as Narrative*, 235.

time uses intentional foreshadowing by alluding to Adam as king and priest in the preceding context. As was the case for the seed of the woman, one would expect that, with these same textual dynamics at play and its greater length, Genesis 49:8-12 will be a gold mine for the Messianic vision of the Pentateuch. The following will demonstrate that this is indeed the case.

Given the direct reference to Joseph's brothers bowing down to him in the blessing of Judah (Gen 49:8), the next question is to what extent does Genesis 49:8-12 re-present Joseph as intentionally foreshadowing the Messiah. The unifying function of Joseph's dreams in Genesis 37–50, along with Sailhamer's comments above,[21] suggests that there may be even more to the re-presentation of Joseph in Genesis 49:8-12. This begins to emerge further on closer investigation of the statement, "your hand will be on the neck of your enemies [אֹיְבֶ֫יךָ]" (Gen 49:8). While on the one hand the mention of "enemies" is compositionally related to the Messianic prophecies of Genesis 3:15 ("enmity"), Genesis 22:17b ("enemies"), and Genesis 24:60 ("haters"), it is also related to the Joseph story in Genesis 37–50. Joseph encountered quite a few enemies, including Potiphar's wife who falsely accused him (Gen 39:13-18) and the cupbearer who forgot him (Gen 40:23), but Joseph's primary enemies were his own brothers. This is clear at the outset of the story. When they saw that he was their father's favorite, "they hated [וַיִּשְׂנְא֫וּ] him and could not speak to him peaceably [לְשָׁלֹֽם]" (Gen 37:4). Then, when Joseph shared his first dream with them, "they hated [שְׂנֹא] him even more" (Gen 37:5, 8). Indeed, Joseph's brothers "were jealous [וַיְקַנְאוּ] of him" (Gen 37:11). The same verbs *hate* and *be jealous* also appear together in the context of conflict between Isaac and Abimelech/the Philistines (Gen 26:14, 27) and between Leah and Rachel (Gen 29:31, 33; 30:1). The conflict that Joseph experienced with his brothers especially parallels that of Cain and Abel and of Jacob and Esau, the latter of which takes on the added dimension of being recast as part of the Messianic vision of the Pentateuch (Gen 27:29). In Genesis 49:8, this recasting takes place through the underlying assumption in Genesis 49:3-27 that each

---

[21]Sailhamer, *Pentateuch as Narrative*, 235, though he does not trace this out further in his remarks on Gen 49:8-12 either in this work or in his *Genesis*, Expositor's Bible Commentary, rev. ed. (Grand Rapids: Zondervan, 2008), 324-25.

brother will become a forefather of a tribe of Israel (see Gen 49:28), which was not true for Cain or Esau/Edom. Thus, Joseph's conflict with his brothers, as part of his larger conflict with enemies in general that is represented in Genesis 49:8, is a picture of the conflict between eschatological "Judah" and his brethren, the nation of Israel. This agrees with the references to "your brothers" and "the sons of your father" immediately before and after "enemies" in Genesis 49:8 and with the delayed mention of "peoples" in Genesis 49:10.

In this way, the compositional relationship between "your hand will be on the neck of your enemies" in Genesis 49:8 and the Joseph narrative extends and clarifies the reader's understanding of the Messiah's enemies already mentioned in Genesis 3:15; 22:17b; 24:60. The opponents in these earlier passages are rightly equated with the serpent and his seed, including anyone who might fight against the Messiah (see Gen 14:20). But Genesis 49:8 is the first indication in the Pentateuch that the Messiah will be rejected specifically by Israel. Like Joseph, the Messiah would seek their "peace" (שָׁלוֹם, Gen 37:14; Mt 23:37), but on the whole they would reject him (Is 53:1). However, the beauty of the Joseph narrative is that these enemies from his own family are not destroyed by Joseph but are ultimately reconciled to him (see also Gen 33:1-11). His brothers had been his enemies and had done him immeasurable harm, but Joseph provided for them, revealed himself to them, forgave them, and brought them to live with him (see Ex 23:4-5). This informs our understanding of the Messiah's relationship to his "enemies" (Gen 49:8). In view of the Joseph story, there seem to be two kinds of enemies: those who are ultimately crushed (Gen 3:15; 14:20; Num 24:17) and those who are reconciled.[22] The former group opposes the Messiah to the bitter end, whereas the latter comes to a true knowledge of him and ceases to be among his enemies (Rom 5:8, 10; Col 1:21). In view of the hope expressed similarly in Amos 9:12 ("in order that they may possess [יָרַשׁ] the remnant of Edom [i.e., a longtime enemy] and all the nations upon whom my name is called [i.e., objects of salvation]"), it is possible that the Messiah's "possession" of the gates of enemies/haters in

---

[22]This distinction also resolves the tensions in biblical portrayals of Edom raised in Bradford Anderson, "Edom in the Book of Numbers: Some Literary Reflections," *ZAW* 124 (2012): 38-51. See also discussion of the serpent's seed and Jacob as a paradigm of the righteous in chap. 1.

Genesis 22:17b and Genesis 24:60 likewise concerns not only judgment of Edom/humanity and the nations but their salvation as well (see Gen 22:18; Acts 15:16-17).

This is even suggested, albeit not definitively, by the statement "your hand will be on the neck [עֹרֶף] of your enemies" itself. The placing of a hand on the neck of one's enemies is unparalleled in Scripture.[23] The closest possible parallels may be the placing of victors' feet on the necks of their enemies in Joshua 10:24 (see 2 Sam 22:41), the "seizing" of the neck of an enemy (Job 16:12), or the construction "hand on/against" (יָד followed by בְּ) as sometimes expressing conflict (Gen 16:12; Ex 7:4). In contrast, though using a different word for neck, Joseph's tearful reunion with his brother Benjamin and his father Jacob involved falling and weeping on the "neck" (צַוָּאר, Gen 45:14; 46:29; see Gen 33:4). His reconciliation with his other brothers involved kissing them and weeping on them, though no word for "neck" is used (Gen 45:15). The Joseph story may faintly hint at the reconciliation of some of the Messiah's enemies through this statement as well. Perhaps the use of a different word for "neck" (עֹרֶף) in Genesis 49:8 relates to its frequent use in conjunction with Israel having a "stiff neck" (קְשֵׁה־עֹרֶף, Ex 32:8; 33:3; Deut 9:6, 13; see Jer 7:26).

Be that as it may, the portrait of the Messiah's "enemies" is still enriched by the relationship between Genesis 49:8 and the Joseph narrative in Genesis 37–50. The relationship between the blessing of Judah and this narrative will reach a stunning climax in Genesis 49:9. In the first part of the verse, Judah is called a "lion's whelp" (גּוּר אַרְיֵה).[24] Other Scriptures associate a lion with power and authority (Prov 30:30), even with reference to the Lord Himself (Hos 11:10; Amos 3:8). The comparison of Judah to a powerful lion also fits with the comparison of Issachar (Gen 49:14), Dan

---

[23]This conclusion is based on our search for *hand* (יָד) in combination with the two words for "neck" mentioned in this paragraph. Substitution of the words *palm* (כַּף) and *right hand* (יָמִין) did not yield any results either.

[24]In a "dirge" for "the princes of Israel," Ezek 19:1-5 likewise refers to the "whelps" of a "lioness." But one of them who had become a ruler was caught (Ezek 19:3-4), and so was the next one (Ezek 19:5-9). The princes are then compared to branches of a vine that are strong enough to be "scepters" (שֵׁבֶט) of rulers (Ezek 19:10-11), but the vine is plucked up and its branches withered (Ezek 19:12). The intertextual relationship to Gen 49:9-10 is unmistakable, and along with it the implied need for the eschatological "lion's whelp" from Judah who will wield a "scepter" over the nations.

(Gen 49:17), Naphtali (Gen 49:21), and Benjamin (Gen 49:27) to various animals. The Messiah will rule his brothers like a mighty lion ruling other animals. Continuing with the next phrase, "from the prey, my son, you ascend," there are more links to Joseph in the Joseph story. The noun *prey* (טֶרֶף) is a cognate of the verb *tear (to pieces)*. On seeing Joseph's bloodied robe (Gen 37:32), Jacob was convinced that Joseph ("my son") had been devoured by a wild animal and said, "Joseph has surely been torn to pieces [טָרֹף טֹרַף]" (Gen 37:33). This statement is later recalled by Judah in Genesis 44:28. As was the case with "enemies" above, relating "prey" to the Joseph story reveals an additional shade of meaning. Whereas a lion certainly can be characterized as tearing prey (Num 23:24; Ezek 19:3,6), Joseph, on whom Genesis 49:8-12 is largely patterned, does not tear prey but instead is believed to have *been* torn to pieces by a wild animal *as* prey ("a harmful animal has eaten him," Gen 37:33). Likewise, while a mighty lion might "go up" after eating prey (Is 35:9; Jer 4:7; 49:19; 50:44; Joel 1:6; see Num 23:24),[25] from Jacob's perspective, Joseph had been torn to pieces and yet had lived again.[26] Jacob had thought he would "go down" to his son when it was his time to die (Gen 37:35), but instead Joseph ("my son") had first "gone up" from having been torn to pieces as prey (Gen 49:9).[27] Concerning this theme of resurrection, Jon Levenson remarks, "The story of Joseph in Genesis 37–50 is not only the longest and most intricate Israelite exemplar of the narrative of the death and resurrection of the beloved son, but also the most explicit."[28]

Jacob had been certain that Joseph was dead (using the infinitive absolute verbal form in standard fashion, "surely torn"). But apparent

---

[25] In fact, the first five passages involve a lion "going up" in order to wreak havoc. The "going up" is first and precedes the destruction. The order in Gen 49:9 is reversed. The lion "goes up" afterward. In keeping with the rule, Num 23:24 describes a lion that arises first and eats prey before lying down.

[26] This is not to say that Jacob's words in Gen 45:28 and Gen 46:30 should be translated "live again." In Gen 43:7, 27-28 and Gen 45:3, a similar construction means "still living." It is nevertheless suggestive. See also Gen 45:26-27; Ps 49:10.

[27] Contra Good, Carmichael, and Midrash *Bereishit Rabbah* 98. See also Rashi.

[28] Jon Levenson, *The Death and Resurrection of the Beloved Son* (New Haven, CT: Yale University Press, 1993), 143. He rightly notes that the theme of fratricide can be traced back to Cain and Abel. This theme is also found in relation to Jacob and Esau (Gen 27:41), the former having experienced a "symbolic death" through being "threatened with fratricide and condemned to exile and harsh servitude" but ultimately "returns a better man" (68).

certainties get overturned in the Joseph narrative. Likewise employing the typical use of the infinitive absolute verbal form, his brothers had expressed through rhetorical questions their own certainty that Joseph would never rule over them (Gen 37:8, "Will you surely be king [הֲמָלֹךְ תִּמְלֹךְ] over us, or will you surely rule [מָשׁוֹל תִּמְשֹׁל] over us?"), which was followed by another rhetorical question by their father to similar affect (Gen 37:10, "Will I and your mother and your brothers surely come [הֲבוֹא נָבוֹא] to bow down to you to the ground?"). As it turns out, contrary to the expectation of these three rhetorical questions, Joseph's brothers would "bow down" to him. Including Genesis 37:33, all four expressions of certainty in Genesis 37 at the outset of the Joseph narrative are overturned.[29] Moreover, from Jacob's perspective, the overturning of these certainties through the fulfillment of Joseph's dreams took place in spite of and even through death. In one sense, Joseph had to be hated by his brothers and experience much suffering in order for his dreams of rule to be fulfilled.

The verb *go up* is paralleled by the verb *arise* in the question, "Who will raise him?" (Gen 49:9), which will provide further support for the theme of resurrection suggested above. The key issue concerns what the question really means. Most modern translations render the question, "Who will a/rouse him?" Such a translation seems to be based on the idea that a powerful lion has lain down and should not be disturbed. The problem with this translation, however, is that the meaning of "rouse" or "arouse" is not well attested for the form of Hebrew verb used (Hiph. קוּם, *qum*). In fact, standard lexicons BDB and HALOT list only Genesis 49:9 and the nearly identical parallel in Numbers 24:9 as passages in which this form of the verb has such a meaning. In other words, these lexicons do not provide independent attestation for the meaning "a/rouse" in Genesis 49:9 and Numbers 24:9. For readers of English translations of the Bible, the problem of the meaning of Hiphil *qum* here is compounded by the similar spelling of the English words "arise/raise" and "a/rouse," which must also be recognized as distinct in meaning.

---

[29]This is not to say all such statements involving an infinitive absolute are overturned in the Joseph story. The ones Joseph speaks in Gen 40:15 and Gen 50:24-25, as well as the other two attributed to him in Gen 43:3, 7 hold true. The one his brothers speak in Gen 43:20 is likewise true, whereas the frightened one in Gen 50:15 is unfounded. The one the Lord uses to assure Jacob in Gen 46:4 naturally holds true. For discussion of Joseph's claim to "surely practice divination" in Gen 44:5, 15, see chap. 6 below.

Given this state of affairs, we are left to analyze *qum* and especially its Hiphil (often causative) form ourselves. This common verb means to "arise" in its basic form (Qal) and in its Hiphil form it means to "raise" or "raise up." This is well attested and has the support of standard lexicons. For example, Joshua "raised up" (or "set up") twelve stones in the middle of the Jordan river (Josh 4:9). Moses likewise "set up" the tabernacle (Ex 26:30; 40:2, 18). Hiphil *qum* can also mean to "establish," as in, "And I will *establish* my covenant with you [i.e., Noah]" (Gen 6:18). Oaths, vows, and words can also be "established" (Gen 26:3; Num 30:14-15; Deut 9:5; 1 Sam 1:23).

The most relevant subcategory of linguistic data is that which involves a living thing (or things) as a direct object, since Genesis 49:9 concerns a lion that has lain down. Frequently, Hiphil *qum* is used of "raising up" a person or a group of people for a specific purpose or task. In Judges 2:16, "the LORD *raised up* judges" for the purpose of delivering Israel. Later, he "raised up" prophets for the exiles in Babylon (Jer 29:15). Related to this, the Lord declares, "I am raising up the Chaldeans" (Hab 1:6) for judgment. In contrast, to "rouse" a living thing (or things) has more to do with awakening it from a resting state, which is expressed by a different verb, *'ur* (עוּר, Ps 44:23; 73:20; 108:2; Song 5:2). With reference to the mighty Leviathan (Job 41:1), the Lord says, "No one is so fierce that he *arouse* [עוּר] him" (Job 41:10; see Job 3:8; Deut 32:11). In the six verses in which both verbs appear in any form (e.g., including Qal *qum*), most of the time the context of the verse accordingly suggests arousal first, followed by arising.[30] This is especially clear in Ezra 1:5, where the Israelites whose spirits were "aroused" then "arose" to return to Judah. Likewise, the dead "will not be aroused from his sleep" and hence will not "arise" but will "lie down" in perpetuity (Job 14:12). This suggests that there is a subtle but important difference between the Hebrew verbs translated "raise" and "a/rouse" and that the question in Genesis 49:9 is more precisely translated, "Who will raise him?"[31]

---

[30]Besides Ezra 1:5 and Job 14:12 discussed below, the others are Judg 5:12; Ps 7:7; Is 14:9; 51:17. Of these four passages, only Ps 7:7 does not at least suggest this distinction, but it does not contradict it either. The fact that a person or group can be "aroused" to action (Jer 6:22; Zech 9:13), though partially overlapping with being "raised up" for a purpose or task, does not erase the distinction between the two words, as the usage surveyed in standard lexicons attests.

[31]Sailhamer, *The Meaning of the Pentateuch: Revelation, Composition, and Interpretation* (Downers Grove, IL: InterVarsity Press, 2009), 36, 222, 331, 335, 469, 475, 520, sometimes translates the question in this way but other times according to standard English translations.

There is still one more even narrower subcategory concerning Hiphil *qum* that further supports this result. In some cases, a weak person who has fallen is the object of the "raising." David fasted and laid down on the ground all night in grief, and the elders tried in vain to "raise him up" (2 Sam 12:16-17). Ecclesiastes 4:10, in discussing the benefits of companionship, says if one falls, his friend will "raise him up" (see Job 4:4; Ps 113:7). Similarly, Zion had fallen, and "there is no one to raise her up" (Amos 5:2). In an even closer parallel to Genesis 49:9, Deuteronomy 22:4 mentions an animal which has fallen on the road and needs to be "raised up." The meaning "a/rouse," which concerns only an initial stimulus after which the recipient actively responds, clearly does not fit any of these passages. What each party needs is not to be aroused but rather to be raised up, an effectual and more forceful act. This suggests the same for the lion which has stooped and lain down in Genesis 49:9.[32]

What appears to have happened in many interpretations of Genesis 49:9 is that the usual association of the lion with power and authority has dictated the interpretation of "from the prey, my son, you go up" and "who will raise him?" as reinforcing the ferocity of the lion. While understandable, consideration of the Hebrew word for "prey" in relation to Genesis 37:33; 44:28 suggests another meaning or a double meaning, and closer investigation of the precise meaning of Hiphil *qum* ("raise") suggests a different meaning from "a/rouse." Riffaterre's characterization of poetry agrees with this, "poetry expresses concepts and things by indirection."[33] Moreover, in regard to "raise" versus "a/rouse," the force of the question changes. Whereas the natural answer to "Who will arouse him?" is "No one would dare rouse a fearsome lion," the answer to "Who will raise him?" is not as clear.

To begin to answer this question, another connection to the Joseph story comes into play. In Joseph's first dream, his sheaf "arose" (*qum*, Gen 37:7). Now, near the end of the narrative, his father, who had kept

---

[32]In our comprehensive study of *qum* (Hiph.) and *'ur*, we did not find any passage that contradicted this result.

[33]Michael Riffaterre, *Semiotics of Poetry* (Bloomington, IN: Indiana University Press, 1978), 1, adds, "To put it simply: a poem says one thing and means another." Although we would not put it so starkly, for fear of implying agreement with reader-response hermeneutics, his basic observation about the frequent use of indirection in poetry is still valid.

these dreams in mind (Gen 37:11), asks, "Who will raise [Hiph. *qum*] him?" From the perspective of Jacob who spoke these words, Joseph's dream of "arising" over his brothers had been shattered by his death, but it ultimately came true through his resurrection from the dead. Jacob had been convinced that Joseph was in "Sheol" and could only be joined by "going down" there (Gen 37:35). Joseph's actual suffering also involved him twice being thrown into a "pit" (Gen 37:22, 24; 40:15), a word often used in close connection with Sheol and death (Gen 37:20; Ps 28:1; 30:4; 40:3; 88:4-7; Prov 1:12). Levenson relatedly refers to Joseph's "symbolic death" through "a threefold downward movement": into the pit where his brothers threw him (Gen 37:18-24), down to Egypt where he was sold as a slave (Gen 39:1), and into prison after being falsely accused by Potiphar's wife (Gen 39:20).[34] If Joseph's brothers ultimately became honest men, as Joseph's testing of their words suggests (Gen 42:11, 19, 31, 33-34), then even they thought he had died (Gen 44:20). This further explains both their dismay when Joseph revealed his identity to them (Gen 45:3) and Jacob's later declaration that this entire turn of events was the work of God, "I never expected to see your face, but now *God* has shown me even your offspring" (Gen 48:11). Joseph likewise interprets these amazing events specifically and emphatically as the work of God, as he declares, "God sent me before you. . . . God sent me before you. . . . You did not send me here but God, and he made me father to Pharaoh, lord to all his house, and ruler in all the land of Egypt" (Gen 45:5-8; see also Gen 50:20). Levenson also points out the Lord's presence with Joseph as the reason for his success while a slave in Potiphar's house and while in prison (Gen 39:2-6, 20-23) and that both successes are part of a series of "ascents" that answer Joseph's aforementioned threefold descent and "symbolic death."[35] Thus the answer to "Who will raise him [from the dead]?" so that his sheaf will arise over his brothers is "God will." By asking this rhetorical question, the same Jacob to whom the Lord had given a dream at Bethel long ago and who had seen his favorite son's related dream shattered by certain death but ultimately fulfilled by God through a sort of resurrection, now implies that "Judah" will be resurrected "in the last days" by God himself. Thus the climax of the

---

[34]Levenson, *Death and Resurrection*, 150-52.
[35]Levenson, *Death and Resurrection*, 152-53.

"descent"/"ascent" theme in Genesis 37–50 is not Joseph's becoming Pharaoh's second-in-command but its eschatological projection: the resurrection of the Messiah. He will "go up from the prey" because God will "raise him" from death. Jacob himself had tasted both the shock and life-giving power of these truths (Gen 45:26-27).

In further support of this answer to the question in Genesis 49:9, the Pentateuch and other Old Testament passages repeatedly affirm that the Lord will "raise up" (Hiph. *qum*) the Messiah. For instance, the Lord will "raise up" a prophet like Moses (Deut 18:15, 18; see chap. 7 below); David's seed to sit on his throne forever (2 Sam 7:12-13; 1 Chron 17:11); a Righteous Branch to rule Israel (Jer 23:5; see Jer 30:9); "one shepherd . . . my servant David" (Ezek 34:23); and the "fallen booth of David" (Amos 9:11). Who will raise up the Messiah? God will.

The fact that Jacob probably said these things with Joseph's "death" in mind suggests that he believed that God would not only "raise up" the Messiah for the task and purpose of ruling Israel and the nations (Gen 49:8, 10) but that he would raise him specifically *from the dead* to this end. Deuteronomy 18:15, 18 can be linked to Genesis 49:9 in the compositional strategy of the Pentateuch and the other passages correspondingly rooted in both Genesis 49:9 and Deuteronomy 18:15, 18 such that both the Pentateuch and the OT as a whole bear direct witness to the resurrection of the Messiah. Jacob's question is similarly posed in Genesis 49:9 LXX, "Who will raise him?" (τίς ἐγερεῖ αὐτόν) and in Numbers 24:9 LXX (τίς ἀναστήσει αὐτόν), and correspondingly answered both in the Septuagint in the aforementioned passages (using ἀνίστημι) and in many New Testament texts as well.[36]

---

[36] As representative examples, see ἀνίστημι in Acts 2:24, 32; 13:34; 17:31; and ἐγείρω in Acts 3:15; 4:10; 26:8; Rom 4:24; 8:11; 1 Cor 6:14; 15:15; 2 Cor 4:14; Gal 1:1; Eph 1:20. The NT also uses ἀνάγω in Rom 10:7 and Heb 13:20 of the resurrection. With reference to ἀνίστημι in 2 Sam 7:12 LXX, see Otto Betz, "Die Frage nach dem messianischen Bewusstein Jesu," *NovT* 6 (1963): 32-33. For more discussion of ancient interpretation of Gen 49:9, see Emmanouela Grypeou and Helen Spurling, *The Book of Genesis in Late Antiquity: Encounters Between Jewish and Christian Exegesis* (Leiden: Brill, 2013), 395-98. John William Wevers, *Notes on the Greek Text of Genesis* (Atlanta: Scholars, 1993), 825, assumes that Gen 49:9 MT means "who would rouse him" and that the LXX provides a literal translation. His comment on Num 24:9 LXX is consistent with this in his *Notes on the Greek Text of Numbers* (Atlanta: Scholars, 1998), 407. Also assuming this meaning of the MT is Martin Rösel, "Die Interpretation von Genesis 49 in der Septuaginta," *BN* 79 (1995): 62. Without providing as lengthy an argument as we have here, Hippolytus, cited in Mark Sheridan,

Still, the above interpretation can only hold if the lion stooping (כָּרַע) and lying down (רָבַץ) indicates that the mighty lion has died. Both acts are certainly things that lions and other animals can do as part of their normal course of life ("stoop," כָּרַע, Job 39:3; "lie down," רָבַץ, Gen 29:22; 49:14; Num 22:27; Ps 104:22; Ezek 19:2). Although these actions can be the result of weakness (Ex 23:5; Job 39:3), the individual verbs by themselves do not require this. The parallel passage in Numbers 24:9 substitutes *shakab* (שָׁכַב, which also means "to lie down") for *rabats* (רָבַץ), and by itself does not provide further insight. However, the pair of verbs in Numbers 24:9 has a close intertextual parallel in Judges 5:27, the only one of its kind in the Old Testament. With only a slight variation in word choice, Numbers 24:9 says, "he stooped [כָּרַע], he has lain down [שָׁכַב] like a lion, and like a lioness who will raise him?" Judges 5:27 poetically describes Sisera's death at the hands of Jael in this way, "between her feet he stooped [כָּרַע], he fell, he has lain down [שָׁכַב]; between her feet, he stooped [כָּרַע], he fell; in which place he stooped [כָּרַע], there he fell, destroyed." The pairing of these two verbs (even using the same verbal forms, i.e., Qal perfect, third masculine sg.) is found nowhere else in the Old Testament and suggests an intertextual relationship between Judges 5:27 and Genesis 49:9/Numbers 24:9. This is reinforced by the phrase "between her feet" (בֵּין רַגְלֶיהָ) that parallels "from between his feet" (מִבֵּין רַגְלָיו) in Genesis 49:10. Moreover, the crushing of an enemy's head by a woman (Jael) provides an arresting reminder and foretaste of the fulfillment of Genesis 3:15, as discussed in chapter one above. The manifold lexical, syntactical, thematic, and intertextual evidence, along with those that concern Genesis 49:8-12 in relation to Genesis 37–50, provide good evidence that the mighty lion that has "stooped" and "lain down" in Genesis 49:9 has also died. If this is still not enough to demonstrate his death, Genesis 49:11 will be the clincher, as will be shown in due course.

---

ed., *Genesis 12-50*, Ancient Christian Commentary on Scripture (Downers Grove, IL: InterVarsity Press, 2002), 329, similarly remarks, "He says the words 'After stooping down, you slept like a lion and a whelp' in order to show Christ sleeping during the three days of his burial. . . . Jacob also said, 'Who will wake him?' He did not say 'Nobody will wake him' but 'Who?' in order that we may understand that the Father woke the Son from the dead, as the apostle confirms [cites Gal 1:1]." Ambrose, also cited in Sheridan's volume, likewise sees Gen 49:9 as concerning Christ's "passion" and burial, followed by his "rous[ing] himself by his own power and the power of the Father" (330).

Another consideration in Genesis 49:9 is the phrase "my son." As pointed out above, this was how Jacob referred to Joseph, his favorite son (Gen 37:33, 35; cf. "your son," Gen 37:32). After becoming convinced of Joseph's death, Jacob called his new favorite, Benjamin, "my son" (Gen 42:38). On learning that Joseph is alive, he goes back to calling him "my son" (Gen 45:28; 48:19; cf. "your son," Gen 45:9; 48:2). Thus, when Jacob says "my son" in the narrative, he is always referring to his favorite son, usually Joseph. He only uses it to refer to Benjamin when he thinks that Joseph has died. This provides another link between the blessing of Judah in Genesis 49:8-12 and Joseph in the Joseph story. Just as Joseph's rule over his brothers and being raised from the dead to this end has been projected onto Judah, so has Joseph's status as his father's favorite, "my son." In fact, no other son in Genesis 49:3-27 is called "my son," not even Joseph. In the fatherly blessing concerning "the last days" (Gen 49:1), Judah overshadows Joseph in this respect as well. Joseph and his other brothers certainly are "the sons of Jacob" (Gen 49:2), but in the context of Genesis 49:3-27, none of them are the favorite son among other sons, the son *par excellence*. This ties into the use of the same title, "my son," as a Messianic title in Genesis 27:27, which was discussed in chapter two above. Because Genesis 49:8-12 would not be fulfilled by Judah himself, the title "my son" is fittingly applicable primarily to the Messiah (Ps 2:7).

At long last, we can move to Genesis 49:10-12. The theme of rule develops and becomes clearer in Genesis 49:10. In Genesis 49:8-9, Judah's brothers "bow down" whereas he "goes up" and is "raised" after himself humbly "stooping" and "lying down."[37] In Genesis 49:10, the "peoples" are also explicitly subject to Judah, to whom belongs their "obedience."[38] The rule of eschatological Judah over his brothers and the nations in Genesis 49:8, 10 matches the Messianic rule described in Genesis 27:29. Joseph's dreams of rule had only involved his family. Still, when the famine came "upon all the lands" (Gen 41:54), "all the land/earth" came to Joseph to buy food (Gen 41:57) because he was Pharaoh's second-in-command and had been put in charge of the food distribution (Gen 41:39-44). The

---

[37]See figure 2.2 in chap. 2 and the surrounding discussion concerning motion on a vertical axis.
[38]The Hebrew word יְקָהַה translated "obedience" here appears only once elsewhere in Prov 30:17, where it refers to obedience to one's mother.

"scepter" (שֵׁבֶט) and "ruler's staff" (מְחֹקֵק, Gen 49:10), as instruments of rule (Num 21:18; Judg 5:14; Ps 60:9), represent the kingship of the Messiah from the lineage of "Judah" that will be established "in the last days." In another Messianic prophecy, Number 24:17 says relatedly, "a scepter [שֵׁבֶט] will arise [קוּם] in Israel." Even the verb *qum*, discussed at length above in relation to the lion that has lain down (Gen 49:9) and to Joseph's sheaf (Gen 37:7), is repeated. The "star" in Numbers 24:17 that comes out from Jacob also recalls Joseph's second dream involving his brothers, as represented by eleven stars, bowing down to him (Gen 37:9), which further indirectly suggests that Joseph is a twelfth star. The difficult phrase, "until Shiloh [or "to whom it belongs"] comes" (עַד כִּי־יָבֹא שִׁילֹה, Gen 49:10), if connected to the following phrase, "and the obedience of the nations is his," appears to be clarified by Ezekiel 21:27, "until he comes, to whom the judgment belongs [עַד־בֹּא אֲשֶׁר־לוֹ הַמִּשְׁפָּט], and I will give it to him." The context here concerns a certain wicked "prince of Israel," whose day of judgment has come (Ezek 21:25). He will be dethroned and his kingdom ruined "until he comes, to whom the judgment belongs" (Ezek 21:27). If this phrase is an interpretation of "until Shiloh comes" by a later prophetic author, then both phrases seem to be best taken as referring to the coming of the Messianic king (see Deut 33:7; Mic 1:15). Similarly, Habakkuk 2:3 predicts, "For he/it will surely come [כִּי־בֹא יָבֹא] and will not delay."[39]

The last two verses in the blessing of Judah are the most difficult but will be shown below to relate to the Joseph story again in such a way that reinforces the important theme of the Messiah's death in Genesis 49:9. Interpreters have observed that Genesis 49:11-12 is held together by agrarian themes and words, such as *vine, donkey, choice vine, female donkey, wine, grapes,* and *milk*. In view of this, commentaries have often treated these verses as describing the enjoyment of an abundantly fruitful land.[40] While there is no question that such themes are at play in Genesis 49:11-12 and that they relate to Edenic and land themes that are an important part of Messianic prophecy (see Gen 27:27-28), comparison to Joseph in the Joseph narrative will at points reveal additional layers of intended meaning.

---

[39] Opting to read בא as a participle instead of an infinitive absolute, the LXX translates this, "For a coming one will come and will not delay."
[40] Wenham, *Genesis 16–50*, 478-79; Ebach, *Genesis 37–50*, 605.

At the same time, there will be points at which later Old Testament passages will appear to interpret and clarify the meaning of Genesis 49:11-12.

This is the case with the references in Genesis 49:11 to "his colt" (עִירֹה) and a "foal of his female donkey" (בְּנִי אֲתֹנוֹ). Although these two designators do not clearly refer to any passage in the Joseph story (the closest being Gen 32:16),[41] they appear in nearly identical fashion in the description of the Messiah in Zechariah 9:9 as "riding on a donkey [חֲמוֹר], on a colt [עַיִר], the foal of female donkeys [בֶּן־אֲתֹנוֹת]." Thus the author of Zechariah 9:9 appears to have read and interpreted these same two designators in Genesis 49:11 and clarified that their close association with the Messiah, whether through being ridden or tied, helps identify him. Moreover, Zechariah 9:10 contrasts the donkey, which is associated with "peace," with the "horse," which is often used for war (see Ex 14:9, 23; 15:1).[42] The tying of the donkey to a "vine"/"choice vine" has long puzzled commentators, who have wondered how something as flimsy as a vine could possibly serve as a hitching post for a donkey, who might even eat it. Some commentators have suggested that even if the donkey did eat the vine, there would be such abundance at that time that it would not matter. Another possibility is that the Messianic kingdom will bring rule over the animals as was originally intended in Genesis 1:26-28, and in such a restored world order it will be much easier to have an animal stay in one place than is commonly experienced (Num 22:22-30; Ps 32:9). Relatedly, although employing figurative language, the "vine" in Ezekiel 19:10-11 produces branches that are strong enough to be "rods of strength" and "scepters [שֵׁבֶט] of rulers." Yet another possibility is that the tying of "*his* colt," "the foal of *his* female donkey" is directly fulfilled by the implicit tying and explicit loosing of the donkey that Jesus used for the triumphal entry. Jesus apparently saw it as his own (Mt 21:2; Mk 11:2; Lk 19:30).

---

[41] A more common word for donkey appears repeatedly in the Joseph story (Gen 42:26-27; 43:18, 24; 44:3, 13; 45:23; 47:17; 49:14), but without clear connection to Gen 49:11.

[42] Despite having received much from the Egyptians (Gen 12:16; 13:2), Abraham did not take any horses (the earliest mention of horses in connection with Egypt is Gen 47:17), only donkeys, other animals, and servants (Gen 12:16; 13:2; 24:35). Neither did the wealth of Isaac or Jacob include horses (Gen 26:12-14; 30:43; 32:5; see 43:18). Accordingly, Moses returned to Egypt on a donkey (Ex 4:20).

In line with the theme of an abundant land, commentators have taken "he washes his garment [לְבֻשׁוֹ] in wine" as another indication of great bounty. They suggest that there are so many grapes and so much wine that people can even wash their clothes in it. The basic problem with this interpretation, however, is that it doesn't seem to make sense. Washing clothes in wine would not be effective, and as Good points out, "there is nowhere any indication that in the eschaton . . . that wine will be the ordinary medium of laundry."[43] This is where the Joseph narrative provides the necessary context for proper understanding. In this narrative, which has already been referenced several times in Genesis 49:8-10, there is a close parallel to Joseph's special "robe" (כְּתֹנֶת) being dipped in goat's blood (Gen 37:31). This arresting compositional connection suggests that "Judah," that is, the Messiah, will die a violent death, just as Jacob believed Joseph to have suffered (Gen 37:33).[44] The reference to the "blood [דַּם] of grapes" parallel to "wine" in Genesis 49:11 further strengthens the intended parallel. These connections had already been hinted at in Genesis 49:9 with the word *prey* but are now expressed in startling fashion here.

In view of Genesis 3:15, the first and foundational passage in the unfolding of the Messianic vision of the Pentateuch, the Messiah's violent death in Genesis 49:9, 11 should not be a complete surprise. In fact, it would be quite strange if the suffering and death of the seed of the woman were not picked up by other Messianic prophecies in the Pentateuch. To be sure, his suffering and death were alluded to in Genesis 22:1-19 concerning the sacrifice of Isaac, but they are again brought into the limelight in Genesis 49:8-12, which fittingly employs the Joseph story to this greater end. But not only does the blessing of Judah remind the reader that the Messiah will suffer a violent death, it also explains that he will "go up" and be "raised" from the dead (Gen 49:9), just as Joseph was from Jacob's perspective. Genesis 3:15 had not included this triumphal element of

---

[43]Good, "'Blessing' of Judah," 427.
[44]Good, "'Blessing' of Judah," 431, notices the same parallel but wrongly interprets it as an ironic reminder of Judah's deception in this matter. Though in a different way, Carmichael, "Some Sayings," 442-43, also misinterprets this parallel by relating it to Judah instead of Joseph, "The washing of Judah's own clothes in wine and in the imaginary blood of grapes, on the other hand, signifies the real death of Er and Onan. Jacob is speaking of the terrible justice meted out to Judah for his attempt to eliminate his favorite son, Joseph."

resurrection, and neither had any other instance of Messianic prophecy or intentional foreshadowing up to this point. Only Genesis 22:1-19 moves in this direction, but not with the clarity and force of Genesis 49:9. The Messianic vision of the Pentateuch thus includes both the Messiah's death and resurrection unto his fully realized rule over the world "in the last days."

There is much more to say about the washing of clothes in wine/the blood of grapes in relation to the dipping of Joseph's special robe in goat's blood (Gen 37:31; 49:11). To begin, what do we make of the different verbs, "wash" (כָּבַס) and "dip" (טָבַל)? They are certainly not synonyms, though they do have some overlap in meaning. This can be seen indirectly in 2 Kings 5:10-14. Though using a different word for "wash" (רָחַץ), the prophet Elisha commanded Naaman the Syrian to "wash" in the Jordan to be healed of his leprosy (2 Kings 5:10). Naaman initially objected, thinking that it would be better to "wash" in the rivers of Damascus (2 Kings 5:12). However, his servants insisted that he "wash" in the Jordan in obedience to the prophet (2 Kings 5:13), and so Naaman finally "dipped" (טָבַל) himself in it (2 Kings 5:14). In this case, Naaman "washed" by "dipping" himself in the water. This suggests that the word used for "wash" in Genesis 49:11 (see Is 7:3; 36:2) and the same word for "dip" are also similarly related, though not identical, in meaning.

Still more questions can be raised. What do we make of the dipping of Joseph's robe in blood as a deceptive act by others in Genesis 37:31-32 compared to Judah's own washing of his garment in wine/blood in Genesis 49:11? In view of the overwhelmingly positive tone of Genesis 49:8-12, it would be unnatural to take Judah's washing of his garment in wine/blood as a deceptive act. This further supports the idea that the Messiah will actually die, as Genesis 49:9 already suggests. On another occasion Joseph's clothes were also used by another person, Potiphar's wife, in order to deceive. One time he resisted her sexual advances to the point of fleeing the house (Gen 39:7-12). She had taken hold of his "garment" (בֶּגֶד), which he left behind in his haste to flee the scene. Recognizing that she could turn this "garment" (בֶּגֶד) into evidence against Joseph (Gen 39:13), she did exactly that (Gen 39:15-18). Both deceptive uses of Joseph's clothing by others were successful. A related pattern that arises here is that Joseph's clothes represent him and sometimes also his status. This is especially evident in the case of his "robe of many colors" (Gen 37:3), which signified that he was Jacob's favorite son. The stripping of that robe by his brothers was not a mere removal of his clothing but an attempt to strip him of his favored status and to shame him (Gen 37:23). Likewise, when Joseph came out of prison to hear and interpret Pharaoh's dreams, "he changed his clothes" (וַיְחַלֵּף שִׂמְלֹתָיו, Gen 41:14), presumably changing out of his prison clothes into something more suitable to wear in Pharaoh's presence. Shortly afterward, when he correctly interpreted the ruler's dreams and as part of the honor bestowed on him by Pharaoh, Joseph was clothed with "garments of fine linen" (בִּגְדֵי־שֵׁשׁ, Gen 41:42). Joseph's different appearance, which included his clothes, was undoubtedly a key reason why his brothers did not recognize him (Gen 42:7) and simply refer to their brother as "the man" (הָאִישׁ, Gen 42:30, 33; 43:3, 5, 7; likewise Jacob in Gen 43:6, 13-14). Though sometimes Joseph's clothes can be misleading—such as when his special robe was dipped in blood, when his garment was used against him by Potiphar's wife, or when his Egyptian clothes probably contributed to his brothers' inability to recognize him— they still represent him and often indicate his status. In relation to this thematic connection to the Joseph story, Judah's clothes in Genesis 49:11 accordingly represent him and his violent death. One who dies peacefully at a good old age does not end up in clothes that appear to have been washed in wine or the blood of grapes. This result fits perfectly with Isaac's enjoyment of the aroma of Jacob and "his clothes" (בְּגָדָיו) in Genesis 27:27. As was shown in chapter two above, Jacob and his clothes relate compositionally to the pleasing aroma of Noah's burnt offerings in Genesis 8:20-21. It is as though the Messiah's violent death will identify him on the one hand (Jn 12:32; Rev 5:6) and be a pleasing sacrifice and aroma to his father on the other (Rom 3:25; 1 Jn 2:2).

Sailhamer insightfully points out that Isaiah 63:1-3 draws on both Genesis 3:15 and Genesis 49:11 simultaneously.[45] The one who treads the winepress in Isaiah 63:1-3 such that his clothes are stained with the blood of his enemies bears a marked similarity to the one in Genesis 49:11 who washes his clothes in wine/blood. There is no denying the intertextual

---

[45] Sailhamer, *Meaning of the Pentateuch*, 239.

relationship between these texts. But does not relating the blood-stained clothes in Genesis 49:11 to the blood of *enemies* contradict the interpretation given above? Not necessarily, if polysemy is at work.[46] In the blessing of Judah in Genesis 49:8-12, we have already seen multiple levels of intended meaning at work with reference to "enemies" (Gen 49:8), "prey" (Gen 49:9), and the agrarian themes in Genesis 49:11-12. The "vine" and animals in Genesis 49:11 relate to a fruitful, peaceful land, whereas, in view of the Joseph story, the washing of his clothes in wine/blood relates to violent death. Thus it is possible for the blood on Judah's clothes in Genesis 49:11 to come from both the Messiah and his enemies. In fact, the shedding of the Messiah's blood and enemies' blood seems to be implied in Genesis 3:15, "He will crush your head, and you will crush his heel." Also, if Isaiah 63:1-3 is indeed alluding to Genesis 3:15, then the trampling of enemies in Isaiah 63:1-3 may implicitly recall the victor also being struck on the heel. Suggestively, the difficult Hebrew word *sutoh* (סוּתוֹ/סוּתֹה, "vesture") in the last line of Genesis 49:11, which appears only here in the Old Testament, appears to be derived from *sut* (סוּת), which means "incite." There may be at least a wordplay such that the Messiah not only washes his own clothes in blood but also bathes "his inciter" (סוּתוֹ/סוּתֹה) or enemy (see Job 2:3) in it as well.

It seems that agrarian themes continue to play in these different ways in Genesis 49:12, the finale of Judah's blessing. The Messiah's teeth being "white from milk [חָלָב]" does indeed suggest a time of abundance. After all, the Promised Land is often characterized as "flowing with milk [חָלָב] and honey" (Ex 3:8, 17; 13:5). Nevertheless, even an abundance of milk is no guarantee that the Messianic kingdom has arrived in its fullness, since it can relate to a diet of "curds and honey" eaten during a time of being dominated by foreigners (Is 7:22). To have eyes that are "dark from wine" also suggests abundance (Amos 9:13), while also seeming somewhat unbecoming of the Messiah (Prov 23:29-30). But since the Messiah's washing his clothes in wine/blood seems to focus on his death while not excluding victory over enemies, then perhaps the primary meaning is that he has drunk to the bottom the cup of the Lord's wrath (Is 51:17, 20-23;

---

[46]See discussion of polysemy in chap. 1 above.

Mt 26:39), again while not excluding his victory over his enemies (see discussion of Num 23:24; 24:8 in chap. 6 below). Along these lines, darkened eyes are associated with death in Psalm 13:3 (see also Ps 88:9-10).

Thus the meaning of Judah's blessing in Genesis 49:8-12 is significantly enriched by careful comparison to Joseph in the Joseph narrative. Such an analysis reveals first and foremost that the fulfillment of Joseph's dreams of his brothers bowing down to him will be overshadowed "in the last days" by the Messiah who will rule both his Israelite brethren as well as the nations (Gen 49:8, 10; 27:29). He will reconcile some of his enemies to himself, while defeating those who resist him to the end (Gen 49:8, 11). Moreover, just as Joseph's dreams were fulfilled despite and through death, so the Messiah will die a violent death but be raised to life by God (Gen 49:9, 11). Then his reign will be fully realized, and it will be characterized by peace and prosperity reminiscent of Eden (Gen 49:11-12).

GENESIS 49:8-12 AND JUDAH IN THE NARRATIVE CONTEXT

Although the blessing of Judah in Genesis 49:8-12 primarily relates to Joseph in Genesis 37–50, it also secondarily relates to Judah in the preceding narrative.[47] This is clear from the opening line, "You are Judah [יְהוּדָה], let your brothers praise [יוֹדוּךָ] you" (Gen 49:8), which closely parallels the naming of Judah in Genesis 29:35 by his mother Leah, "'This time I will praise [אוֹדֶה] the LORD.' Therefore, she called his name Judah [יְהוּדָה]." In contrast, the naming of her first three sons (Reuben, Simeon, and Levi) had been expressions of her attempt to gain her husband Jacob's love (Gen 29:32-34). Through his greater love for Rachel (Gen 29:30), Leah was effectively "hated" (שְׂנוּאָה, Gen 29:31, 33), and she relatedly experienced "affliction" (עֳנִי, Gen 29:32). In addition to the linking of Genesis 49:8 back to the naming of Judah in Genesis 29:35 through the words *Judah* and *praise*, the context of Judah's birth in Genesis 29:30-35 contains several words and themes that connect forward to the Joseph story in Genesis 37–50 (e.g., the twelve sons of Israel; favoritism/"love," Gen 37:3-4; "hate," Gen 37:4-5, 8; "affliction," Gen 41:52; see also "envy," Gen 30:1/Gen 37:11). Incidentally, the "praise" promised to Judah in Genesis 49:8 contrasts with

---

[47] For a treatment that overlaps with ours at points, see Bryan Smith, "The Central Role of Judah in Genesis 37–50," *BSac* 162 (2005): 158-74.

the inability of Joseph's brothers to speak "peaceably" to Joseph in Genesis 37:4.

Whereas some scholars mistakenly relate Genesis 49:8-12 primarily to Judah's past shameful misdeeds (i.e., his role in selling Joseph into slavery in Gen 37:26-28 and the Tamar incident in Gen 38),[48] Jacob's words in Genesis 49:8 clearly focus on Judah as a praiseworthy person (and not just in the eyes of his mother but of his brothers) and direct the reader to look for his positive qualities. Unlike what he said about Reuben, Simeon, and Levi in Genesis 49:3-7, Jacob did not bring up Judah's sins, even though he could have. In the process of inquiring after Judah's positive qualities in the narrative, we will see that these qualities include confession and repentance from sin. Along the way, additional reasons to link the portrayal of Judah in the narrative as intentionally foreshadowing the Messiah will be revealed. Due to the scarcity of lexical parallels (most of those relate to Joseph), the below analysis is mainly thematic, though still compositional.

It is clear from the narrative that Judah is consistently a leader of his brothers, for better or for worse. For example, Joseph's brothers, on seeing him coming, wanted to kill him (Gen 37:18-20). The firstborn, Reuben, objected and convinced them to throw Joseph in a pit (Gen 37:21-24). Although Reuben's plan was to ultimately rescue Joseph and return him to Jacob (Gen 37:22), Judah's idea to sell him into slavery won out (Gen 37:26-28), and Reuben was thwarted (Gen 37:29-30). Even though Judah's leadership was not exercised for a positive purpose here, later on in the narrative it would be. After the brothers had returned home from Egypt the first time, the food that they had brought back with them eventually ran out (Gen 43:2). Once again, the outcome, this time wholly positive, is secured by Judah instead of Reuben. Jacob firmly resisted the requirement that Benjamin accompany his brothers down to Egypt, and Judah, not Reuben, was the one who ultimately convinced Jacob to allow it (Gen 42:37–43:15). Thus, Judah was not only treated as a leader by his brothers but was also especially respected by his father (see Gen 46:28). Thus, although the words spoken to Judah "let the sons of your father bow

---

[48]See Good, "'Blessing' of Judah," 427-32; Carmichael, "Some Sayings," 435-44.

down to you" (Gen 49:8) primarily project Joseph's dreams and their fulfillment onto something even greater for Judah/Messiah, the theme of Judah's leadership in the preceding narrative also accords broadly with this statement.

Closer investigation of Judah's leadership in Genesis 43–44 yields still more insight. Whereas Reuben, who had already fallen from favor (Gen 35:22), tried to convince Jacob to allow Benjamin to go with them by letting his father kill his two sons if Benjamin did not return (Gen 42:37), Judah successfully offered himself as a "pledge" for Benjamin (Gen 43:9; 44:32). In contrast with Reuben's unappealing offer that could have involved even more loss of life, Judah's pledge involved taking personal responsibility for Benjamin's safety. According to other passages that describe this act, it was a serious, binding commitment that was not to be taken on lightly (Prov 6:1-5; 17:18). Due to the risk, such responsibility was not to be taken up for the sake of a stranger (Prov 11:15; 20:16). Aware of this responsibility ("my sin will be before you forever," Gen 43:9), Judah still did it for his brother.

The use of the verb *'arab* (עָרַב, "be a pledge or surety") in Genesis 43:9 and Genesis 44:32 provides a striking contrast with the cognate noun *'erabon* (עֵרָבוֹן, "pledge") in Genesis 38:17-18, 20.[49] There Judah had given his seal, cord, and staff as a "pledge" to Tamar (Gen 37:18), whom he had mistaken for a prostitute. This "pledge" served as a down-payment or guarantee that he would later send the promised full payment of a young goat (Gen 37:17). Although Judah did in fact send this full payment, it was never received (Gen 37:20-23) because it was not what Tamar was really after (Gen 37:11-14). In any case, when Judah called for her death because of her pregnancy, it was Judah's original pledge ("the seal and the cord and the staff") that revealed his responsibility and humiliated him (Gen 37:24-25). Compositionally, these two passages involving a "pledge" show the transformation of Judah. Whereas earlier he had pledged some of his belongings to an apparent prostitute as a guarantee of full payment later (see

---

[49]Of the modern commentaries surveyed, only Ebach, *Genesis 37–50*, 321-22, observes this connection. He thinks that, "Judah has learned something. He has learned that he himself is responsible, that he himself stands under obligation for the entire family." He also points out that the "pledge" in Gen 38 represents Judah himself and concerns his identity. This in turn relates to the above discussion of Joseph's clothes as it relates to his identity.

Prov 27:13), in Genesis 43:9 Judah pledges himself to his father for the noble purpose of preserving the lives of the whole family, which was in danger of starvation. Even in Genesis 38, after the truth came out, Judah humbly confessed, "She [Tamar] is more righteous than I [צָֽדְקָ֣ה מִמֶּ֔נִּי], because I did not give her my son Shelah" (Gen 38:26). He had broken his promise, which was insincere to begin with (Gen 38:11, 14). His repentance from his sexual sin is implied by the line, "and he did not know her again" (Gen 38:26). Furthermore, not only do Judah and his pledges undergo a transformation between Genesis 38 and Genesis 43–44, but so does his secret (and later public) shame in Genesis 38 compared to his being praised by his brothers and his exaltation over the whole earth in Genesis 49:8, 10.

The themes of Judah's leadership, confession, and repentance come to a head in his speech before Joseph in Genesis 44:14-34. By this time, Benjamin had gone down to Egypt with his brothers, who attempted to repay the money that was returned to them from their previous purchase of food (Gen 43:15-23). In the process, Joseph also saw Benjamin for the first time in years, which at the same time partially verified his brothers' earlier statements about Benjamin (Gen 42:13, 20). But Joseph wanted to know how they would treat this favored brother when under duress, so he had his silver cup placed in Benjamin's sack, which was later discovered (Gen 44:1-12). On his brothers' return (Gen 44:13), it is again Judah who takes the lead and serves as spokesman (Gen 44:14, 16). Judah's words and actions concerning Benjamin, Jacob's current favorite son, show a complete transformation compared to Judah's previous dealings with Joseph, the previous favorite son (Gen 37:26-28).

Reminiscent of his confession in Genesis 38:26, Judah humbly confesses, "What will we say to my lord, what will we speak? And how will we justify ourselves [וּמַה־נִּצְטַדָּ֑ק]? God has found out the guilt [עֲוֺ֣ן] of your servants" (Gen 44:16). Of course, neither Judah, Benjamin, nor any of their other brothers had done anything wrong in this instance, but they had lately been acutely aware of their sins committed against Joseph from long ago (Gen 42:21-22, 28, 35; 43:18, 33). Judah was thus leading his brothers in taking responsibility for their sins against Joseph, while at the same time taking responsibility presently for guilt that was not actually theirs. By refusing Judah's offer that all the brothers become his slaves (Gen 44:16-17), Joseph held firm to the original punishment that had been decreed (Gen 44:10), which allowed him to continue applying pressure to Judah and his other brothers. As Judah continued to intercede, he explained that Benjamin was his father's favorite son and must return home, lest great sorrow and even death come upon Jacob (Gen 44:18-31). Joseph would probably not have been surprised that Benjamin was Jacob's favorite, but this high-pressure situation revealed Judah's acceptance of this reality along with his concern for his father's well-being in relation to it. This is a marked contrast to Judah's callousness in Genesis 37:26-35. Furthermore, Judah revealed to Joseph that he had even put himself up as pledge for Benjamin (Gen 44:32) and accordingly offered himself as a substitute for Benjamin to be Joseph's slave for the rest of his life (Gen 44:33-34).

This moving turn of events demonstrates the complete transformation of Judah's attitude toward a brother favored over him. Earlier, rather than endure Jacob's favoritism of Joseph, Judah had Joseph sold as a slave. But now, rather than endure the harm caused to Benjamin and the sorrow inflicted on his father, Judah gives himself up as a slave to Joseph, the one he had sold as a slave years before. He offers himself as a substitute "in place of the youth" (תַּחַת הַנַּעַר, Gen 44:33). Hamilton notes the unusual way of referring to Benjamin as a "youth" (נַעַר), which appears for the first time in Genesis 43:8.[50] He is repeatedly referred to this way in Genesis 44:30-33 (see Gen 44:22), culminating with the phrase just cited from Genesis 44:33. The theme of substitution along with the words for "in place of" and "youth" parallel the substitution of the ram for Isaac in Genesis 22:12-13. The ram was offered "in place of [תַּחַת] his son [Isaac]" (Gen 22:13; see Gen 42:38), who is referred to as "the youth" (הַנַּעַר) in the previous verse (Gen 22:12). Just as the substitutionary sacrifice of the ram spared Isaac from death, so the substitutionary work of Judah would spare Benjamin from slavery.

The likelihood that Genesis 22:12-13 and Genesis 44:33 are compositionally related along the lines of a substitutionary sacrifice by the Messiah for a youth/son (see Ex 4:22-23; Hos 11:1) is further supported by the

---

[50] Hamilton, *Book of Genesis 18–50*, 541-42. Joseph is also called a "youth" in Gen 37:2; 41:12.

independent relationships of each of these two passages to Messianic prophecies in the Pentateuch (Gen 3:15; 22:17b-18; 49:8-12).[51] Suggestively, the same preposition meaning "in the place of" (תַּחַת, whose more common meaning is "under") in Genesis 22:13 and Genesis 44:33 is also used in the context of substitution on the lips of Jacob and of Joseph (Gen 30:2; 50:19), who on separate occasions ask in nearly identical fashion, "Am I in the place [תַּחַת] of God?" Neither of them were, of course. Jacob did not have the power to give Rachel children, and Joseph knew that he was not worthy of the servitude his brothers were offering (Gen 50:18). Neither Jacob nor Joseph could take God's place, but the Messiah both stands in God's place and will take our place as a sacrifice, for which he is worthy of worship (Rev 5:12).[52]

Thus, though largely thematic by necessity, the analysis of the blessing of Judah in Genesis 49:8-12 in relation to Judah in the preceding narrative also yields significant fruit. His praiseworthiness and leadership in Genesis 49:8 suggest the lines along which such an analysis should proceed. Even with this positive emphasis, the analysis still ends up being a holistic accounting of Judah that includes the reality of his past sins. More important than these sins, however, are Judah's confession and repentance from them. By properly responding to his sins, his leadership was sanctified and he became willing to pledge his own wellbeing and offer himself as a substitute on behalf of Benjamin, his favored brother. Rather than being driven by hatred, jealousy, callousness, lust, and shame, Judah became a positive example characterized by love, responsibility, humility, intercession, and self-sacrifice—qualities certainly worthy of praise. Judah's transformation justifies the glorious blessing given to him in Genesis 49:8-12 and the absence of any mention of his past sins, unlike his three older brothers (Gen 49:3-7). Fittingly, the last reference to Judah in the narrative is as a guide sent by his father to "show" (יָרָה, meaning "teach" in Ex 35:34) the way for his family to travel to Goshen in Egypt (Gen 46:28), which further supports his casting as an ultimately positive example who leads others to salvation and a savior (see Gen 18:19). Though used in other

---

[51] Both passages involve the Lord's love for Israel, like the special love that Isaac and Benjamin received from their fathers. See also Joseph in Gen 37:2-3.
[52] Suggestively, Moses will be "God to Pharaoh" (Ex 7:1). See chap. 4 below.

ways, the same verb is often used of the teaching ministry of priests (e.g., Lev 10:11; 14:57; Deut 17:10-11; 24:8). When considered alongside Judah's representation of his brothers and intercession in Genesis 44, there is a hint of his priestlike role. Judah's descendant, the Messiah of Genesis 49:8-12, though he would know no sin, will perfectly embody the same positive qualities and be praised and honored by his brothers. Like Leah, many more will say, "I will praise the LORD" (Gen 29:35).

CONCLUSION

The blessing of Judah in Genesis 49:8-12 is a goldmine of Messianic prophecy in the Pentateuch. Considered in relation to its immediate literary context alone (Gen 49:1-27), it is already recognizable as a prophecy of a powerful king to come from the line of Judah "in the last days" (Gen 49:1). This "lion" will reign over Israel and the nations as well as bring a return of Edenic abundance, in line with other Messianic prophecies such as Genesis 3:15 and Genesis 27:27-29. The compositional relationship of Genesis 49:8-12 to depictions of Joseph and Judah in the preceding narrative enrich its meaning even further. In regard to Joseph, it re-presents the fulfillment of his dreams of rule over his brothers as something that will happen again on a grander scale to the Messiah. Significantly, it also implies that the Messiah's kingdom will be realized through his violent death and his resurrection by God, just as it was for Joseph's rule from Jacob's perspective. In regard to Judah, Genesis 49:8 focuses on Judah as a leader who is worthy of praise and honor. Although he certainly was not so at first, he became a servant-leader marked by love, responsibility, humility, intercession, and self-sacrifice. In the last days, the Messiah will likewise lay down his life for others and be praised and honored by his brothers as the perfect embodiment of these same traits of his forefather.

4

PASSOVER AND THE SONG OF THE SEA

As the previous chapters have shown, the Messianic vision of the Pentateuch is firmly established in Genesis. The Messiah will be an individual male "seed" of a woman (i.e., "my son") who will defeat the serpent at the cost of his own life. Nevertheless, his father, God, will raise him from the dead to rule gloriously over Israel and the nations, who will worship him. The Messiah will also defeat his enemies once and for all, though some of them will repent and be reconciled to him before it is too late. Edenic peace and abundance will be restored as the Lord's blessing reaches all creation. The covenant promises made to Abraham will be fulfilled in this "lion of Judah" who will be both king and priest, like Adam was supposed to be and like Melchizedek was. These core elements have been established by a variety of Messianic prophecies ("lenses") and passages with intentional Messianic foreshadowing ("mirrors") that together form what is already an extensive, intricate network of texts within the Pentateuch.

Nevertheless, the Messianic vision of the Pentateuch is not yet complete. Although the next Messianic prophecy is not until Numbers 24:7-9, this vision will be extended in the intervening portion of the Pentateuch through several important instances of intentional foreshadowing of the Messiah. To mitigate the risk of overextending our argument, we limit ourselves to examples that are directly cited in the New Testament and those that can be readily supported by an exegesis of the Pentateuch (and Old Testament) itself. The first such instance that will be considered is the Passover (Ex 12). In 1 Corinthians 5:7, Paul calls Christ, "our Passover lamb." John the Baptist called Jesus, "the Lamb of God who takes away the sin of the world" (Jn 1:29; see also Jn 1:36). The four Gospels also link Jesus' death to the Passover (Mt 26:2; Mk 14:1; Lk 22:1-2, 15-16; Jn 18:39; 19:14).

Another text that will be discussed in this chapter is the Song of the Sea (Ex 15:1-18), which, although not intentionally foreshadowing the Messiah, relatedly concerns the Lord's everlasting kingdom (Ex 15:18). The reader should almost expect that there would be intentional foreshadowing of the Messiah in relation to the exodus because it is the most important and most extensive example of salvation in the Old Testament.

Slavery, Passover, and the Exodus

In order to properly understand the institution of the Passover in Exodus 12, it must be seen in the context of Israel's enslavement in Egypt and the exodus (Ex 1–15). The reader should also remember that this section and the entire book of Exodus are not independent literary works but part of the Pentateuch and its overarching compositional strategy. This means that Genesis 1–50, including the emerging Messianic vision of the Pentateuch that it casts, is part of the literary and compositional context of Exodus 1–15 and should be part of readers' preunderstanding as they read about Israel's slavery and liberation from Egypt. This vision has already presented Israel's final salvation as coming through the Messiah "in the last days" (Gen 3:15, 22:17b-18; 27:27-29; 49:1, 8-12). Therefore, Israel's exodus from Egypt, as essential as it is to the overall divine plan, was never intended to be their ultimate salvation. Moses was not from the line of Judah (Gen 49:8), but a future prophet like Moses would be (Deut 18:15, 18; see chap. 8 below). As will be seen, the biblical narrative in the opening chapters of Exodus repeatedly references Genesis, even as it provides necessary background for our analysis of the Passover and the Song of the Sea.

As the reader of the Pentateuch knows, the Israelites had been in Egypt since the time Jacob moved his whole family there because of a famine. Joseph was in Egypt already and arranged for them to live in Goshen (Gen 45:1–47:6). Like his father Jacob (Gen 47:29-31; 49:29–50:13), he gave orders that his body not have its final resting place in Egypt (Gen 50:24-25). Both Jacob and Joseph did this in faith, believing that the Lord would bring them out of Egypt to the Promised Land (Gen 48:21) in keeping with his covenant with Abraham. In the process of instituting this covenant, the Lord had predicted that prior to Israel's possession of the land they would be enslaved in a foreign country for four hundred years (Gen 15:13-16).

Exodus 1–15 fits directly into this framework. After Joseph's death (Ex 1:6), the "sons of Israel" were "fruitful," "multiplied," and "became extremely powerful" (Ex 1:7), thus carrying forward the blessing of Adam in Genesis 1:28, Noah in Genesis 9:1, and Abram in Genesis 12:2. In accordance with what the Lord had said to Abram long ago (Gen 15:13), a king of Egypt, feeling threatened by the Israelites, enslaved them (Ex 1:8-14). In contrast, Joseph had previously refused to enslave his brothers (Gen 50:18-21; see Ex 21:2-11). The Israelites' work of "building" (בָּנָה, Ex 1:11) with "mortar" (חֹמֶר) and "brick" (לְבֵנָה, Ex 1:14) recalls the Tower of Babel in Genesis 11:3-4 and suggests that they were being forced to build a human kingdom in competition with the Lord's. Nevertheless, Pharaoh's enslavement of the Israelites was futile, for his maltreatment of them only resulted in their greater increase (Ex 1:12). Pharaoh's oppression even extended to the murder of newborn Israelite boys, but this too was thwarted by Hebrew midwives and the survival of Moses (Ex 1:15–2:10), the future deliverer. The Lord not only had compassion on the Israelites in their bitter affliction but did so in faithfulness to his covenant with Abraham, Isaac, and Jacob (Ex 2:23-25). This covenant, as pointed out in previous chapters, has both individual, Messianic aspects and corporate aspects that concern Israel. While the latter is the focus of Exodus 2:23-25, the former should never be forgotten. In any case, the Lord's deliverance of the Israelites from Egyptian bondage in Exodus 3–15 should be understood as motivated by both compassion for the oppressed and faithfulness to the Abrahamic covenant.

These same two elements reappear when the Lord calls Moses to bring the Israelites out of Egypt (Ex 3:6-10, 15-17). At that time, the Lord also explained that Moses would be stubbornly resisted by Pharaoh (Ex 3:19). Nevertheless, Pharaoh's stubbornness would provide an occasion for the Lord to stretch out his hand and strike Egypt with all his wonders (Ex 3:20). When Pharaoh finally allows the Israelites to go, they will even leave with many possessions acquired from the Egyptians (Ex 3:21-22). Genesis 15:14 had predicted this same divine judgment and plundering of the Egyptians. The miracles that Moses would perform before Pharaoh (see Ex 4:21) included turning his rod into a snake (Ex 7:9-13) and the ten plagues (Ex 7–12), culminating in the plague of the firstborn and the Passover (Ex 12). But even before Moses had set out to return to Egypt (Ex 4:20), and before the nature of each plague is revealed to the reader, the death of Pharaoh's firstborn is already threatened (Ex 4:22-23). There is thus an indication that the Passover is on the horizon.

Significantly, the Lord calls Israel "my son, my firstborn" (בְּנִי בְכֹרִי, Ex 4:22). This sets up his message to Pharaoh, "Let my son go so that he may serve me. You were unwilling to send him. Behold, I am killing your son, your firstborn [בִּנְךָ בְּכֹרֶךָ]" (Ex 4:23). Pharaoh's mistreatment of Israel, the Lord's "son" and "firstborn," receives its just recompense in the Lord's killing of Pharaoh's firstborn son. Although sometimes overlooked, the title "my son" has already been strategically used of the Messiah in Genesis 27:27 and Genesis 49:9 (see chaps. 2-3 above). If this is not merely an expected way for Isaac to refer to Jacob (Gen 27:27) and Jacob to refer to Judah (Gen 49:9), then these two passages indicate that the Lord refers to the Messiah as "my son," as he does directly in Psalm 2:7.

This suggests that the references to Israel as the Lord's "son" in Exodus 4:22-23 are related to but overshadowed by the already established references to the Messiah as his "son" in Genesis 27:27 and Genesis 49:9.[1] Both Israel and their Messiah have the status of being the Lord's "son," but "in the last days," "my son" Israel will worship and praise "my son" the Messiah, who saves them (see Is 49:5). Accordingly, the Lord's purpose of delivering Israel ("my son") in Exodus 4:23 is that "he may serve [עָבַד] me." This is a very different picture from the one called "my son" in Genesis 27:27 and Genesis 49:9 who is *being* served by his Israelite brethren and the nations (Gen 27:29; 49:8, 10). In this respect, the strategic, varied use of "my son" in these passages parallels the use of "seed" in the patriarchal narratives and "servant" in the book of Isaiah (see also "firstborn" in Ps 89:27). Sometimes each term refers to Israel, but other times to the Messiah only. In each case, Israel is a compositional foil for the Messiah.

The next passage (Ex 4:24-26), though infamously difficult, also deals with themes related to the Passover. Despite the challenge of determining precisely whom the Lord was going to put to death (Ex 4:24, does "him" refer to Moses' son?) and why, Stephen Dempster points out that this passage is a "proleptic Passover" involving a son, the threat of death, the

---

[1] See the discussion of the related relationships between Isaac ("my son") and the seed of the woman in Gen 22:1-19 as well as between the Tower of Babel and Jacob's "ladder" in chap. 2 above.

shedding and likely application of blood ("she touched it [i.e., the foreskin] to his feet"), and circumcision, which was a requirement to celebrate the Passover (Ex 12:48).[2] Nahum Sarna's thorough analysis is worth citing:

> The featuring of the circumcision episode [Ex 4:24-26] following the reference to the first-born [vv. 22-23] provides an artfully wrought literary framework for the entire narrative, one that encompasses the struggle for liberation from Pharaoh's oppression. That struggle begins with Moses' setting out to return to Egypt (v. 20), and its successful conclusion is signaled by the death of the Egyptian first-born (12:29-36). This latter [passage] is followed immediately by the law requiring circumcision as the precondition for participation in the paschal sacrifice (12:43-49), which in turn is followed by the law of the first-born (13:1, 11-15).... In addition to the literary structure, there is also a functional correspondence between the blood of circumcision and the visible sign of the blood on the paschal sacrifice. In both instances, evil is averted on account of it (4:26; 12:7, 13, 22-23).[3]

Thus themes and language of firstborn, son, circumcision, blood, death, and salvation, culminating in the Passover, frame Israel's deliverance from Egypt (Ex 4:20-26; 11-13).

In view of this, Pharaoh's refusal to release the Israelites until the Passover is not entirely surprising. The careful crafting of the narrative leads the reader to expect that his firstborn son will eventually be put to death (Ex 4:23). The other plagues, despite their severity, would thus not secure Israel's deliverance. Whereas earlier the Lord had only mentioned the death of Pharaoh's firstborn, the plague of the firstborn would strike every Egyptian household, and even their animals (Ex 11:5). Indeed, this last plague would be brought "on Pharaoh and on Egypt" (Ex 11:1) and would be one for the ages (Ex 11:6). While there would be a "great cry in all the land of Egypt" (Ex 11:6), there would be peace and quiet among the Israelites (Ex 11:7). Hence, the deliverance of Israel, the Lord's firstborn son, contrasts not only with the death of Pharaoh's firstborn son but also with the Lord's punishment of Egypt a whole. The Egyptians themselves

---

[2]Stephen Dempster, *Dominion and Dynasty* (Downers Grove, IL: InterVarsity Press, 2003), 98. There is no need, however, to equate "feet" with genitals as Dempster does.
[3]Nahum Sarna, *Exodus*, JPS Torah Commentary (Philadelphia: Jewish Publication Society, 1991), 24-25.

acknowledged this when they urged the Israelites to leave quickly "because they said, 'All of us will be dead.'" (Ex 12:33). Their firstborns represented the whole nation, just as Pharaoh's and Israel's firstborns did.

Pharaoh's refusal to release the Israelites related not only to his desire to maintain control over his enslaved workforce (Ex 5:4) but also to their request to leave Egypt to "sacrifice," "celebrate a festival," and "serve" the Lord (Ex 3:18; 5:1-3, 8, 17; 8:25-29; 10:7-11, 24-27).[4] In other words, the issue was also worship, and the different kind of "service" that they would render to the Lord (see Ex 12:26). The contest for worship is also evident in the Lord's performance of superior signs (Ex 7:9-12; 8:19) and his judgment "upon all the gods of Egypt" (Ex 12:12). After the Passover, all Pharaoh's "servants" would "bow down" to the Lord as they urged the Israelites to leave (Ex 11:8).[5] Accordingly, when Pharaoh finally let the Israelites go, he said, "Go, serve [עָבַד] the Lord" (Ex 12:31). This is exactly what the Lord desired for Israel from the beginning (Ex 3:12; see Ex 20:2-6).

With this context in place, we may more closely consider the institution and observance of the Passover in Exodus 12. Its importance is immediately reinforced in Exodus 12:2 through the reorientation of time based on it, "This month is for you the head [רֹאשׁ; see Is 2:2] of months; it is for you first in the months of the year." The subsequent instructions focus on the "lamb" (שֶׂה) that each man is to select for his house on the tenth day of the month and slaughter at twilight on the fourteenth day (Ex 12:3-6). The spreading of the lamb's blood on the doorposts and lintel will be a "sign" so that the Lord will pass over the houses of the Israelites when he strikes down all the firstborn in Egypt that night (Ex 12:7, 12, 13).

As it relates to the Messianic vision of the Pentateuch, the starting point for exploring the Passover as intentionally foreshadowing the Messiah is the Passover lamb itself (Ex 12:3-5). The preceding discussion of the sacrifice of Isaac as a "burnt offering" in Genesis 22:1-19 (see chap. 2 above) likewise

---

[4]For a helpful analysis of the "three-day journey" requested in connection with this (Ex 3:18; 5:3; 8:27), see R. Alan Cole, *Exodus: An Introduction and Commentary*, Tyndale Old Testament Commentaries (Downers Grove, IL: InterVarsity Press, 1973), 71-72.

[5]Ex 12:31-32 suggests that the speaker has changed from the Lord to Moses. See Umberto Cassuto, *A Commentary on the Book of Exodus*, trans. Israel Abrahams (Jerusalem: Magnes, 1983), 133. William Propp, *Exodus 1–18*, Anchor Bible (New York: Doubleday, 1999), 345, notes the parallel to Ex 7:17, "where the personae of Deity and prophet merge. The prediction of 7:1, that Moses would become 'as a deity to Pharaoh,' thus is literally fulfilled."

centered on the lamb (שֶׂה) that will die as a substitute for a son (Gen 22:7-8, 13). In relation to the death of the (male) seed of the woman in Genesis 3:15, it was also argued that both Isaac and the lamb in Genesis 22:1-19 intentionally foreshadow the Messiah in their respective ways. The narrative patterning at work between Genesis 3:15 and Genesis 22:1-19 appears to extend to Exodus 12 as well. This time, the "son" that is spared is not Isaac but his progeny Israel (Ex 4:22-23), as represented by their firstborn sons (Ex 12:12-13) and even their firstborn animals (Ex 13:2, 12-15). At the same time, the Passover lamb that dies in place of a "son" corresponds to the Messianic "son" and his clothes in Genesis 27:27, which substitute Jacob for Esau, parallel the pleasing aroma of Noah's "burnt offerings" (Gen 8:20-21; see discussion of Ex 12:8-10 below), and are compositionally related to the Messiah's bloodstained clothes in Genesis 49:8-12, where the violent death of "my son" even relates to the salvation of Israel and the nations. Relatedly, the Messiah's forefather Judah offered to give himself up to slavery in place of his brother Benjamin (Gen 44:33), his father's beloved "son" (Gen 42:38), for the sake of the whole family.

A closer look at the description of the Passover lamb will confirm its relationship to the Messiah and his death. Its explicit identification as "male" (זָכָר, Ex 12:5) fits with the seed of the woman being a "he" and with Isaac and the "ram" being male (Gen 22:13). This is important because a "lamb" (שֶׂה) evidently can be female (see Lev 5:6-7).[6] Its young age ("the son of a year") corresponds to the term *youth* that is applied to both Isaac and Benjamin (Gen 22:12; 44:30-33; see chap. 3 above). Its being "without blemish" (תָּמִים), although a common requirement for sacrificial animals (e.g., Ex 29:1; Lev 1:3, 10), also describes the character of the godly (Gen 6:9; 17:1; Deut 18:13) and the work of the Lord himself (Deut 32:4).

Practically all these characteristics are found in the prediction of the Messiah's coming in Isaiah 52:13–53:12. He is "like a lamb led to the slaughter" (כַּשֶּׂה לַטֶּבַח יוּבָל, Is 53:7), whose death secures a "second exodus" (Is 52:11-12) from depraved "Babylon" (Is 48:20-21).[7] The substitutionary nature of his

---

[6]The person who cannot afford a "lamb" (שֶׂה) in Ex 12:7 can offer pigeons instead of a "female from the flock" (Ex 12:6).

[7]J. Alec Motyer, *The Prophecy of Isaiah* (Downers Grove, IL: InterVarsity Press, 1993), 420-22, recognizes the second exodus and Passover themes in Is 52:11-12 but denies that the Suffering Servant is being cast as a Passover lamb in Is 53:7 because he is also likened to a "ewe" (רָחֵל)

death is repeatedly emphasized, such as in Isaiah 53:5 ("pierced for our transgressions," "crushed for our iniquities," "the punishment that brought us peace," "by his wounds we are healed"), Isaiah 53:10 ("when you make his soul a guilt offering [אָשָׁם]"; see Lev 5:6-7, 15-19; 14:12-17, 21-28), Isaiah 53:11 ("he will bear their iniquities"), and Isaiah 53:12 ("he bore the sin of many and interceded for transgressors"). His youth is suggested through his comparison to "a young plant" (יוֹנֵק, Is 53:2; see Is 11:8; Num 11:12; Deut 32:25) and being "cut off" without a "generation" (Is 53:8), probably referring to posterity (see Gen 17:12; Ex 12:14; Job 42:16). His blamelessness is explicit in Isaiah 53:9 ("no violence has he done and there was no deceit in his mouth"). Moreover, the repetition of the word *lamb* (שֶׂה) five times in Exodus 12:3-5 is paralleled by five references to the Messiah using the word *he* (הוּא, Is 53:4, 5, 7, 11, 12), both of which answer the repetition of "the serpent" (הַנָּחָשׁ) five times in Genesis 3 (Gen 3:1, 2, 4, 13, 14). As pointed out in chapter one above, the pronoun *he* (הוּא) also relates to Messianic prophecies in Genesis 3:15; 15:3-4; 2 Samuel 7:12-14; 1 Chronicles 17:11-13; and Zechariah 6:13. Even the "dipping" (טָבַל) of hyssop into the lamb's blood (Ex 12:22) parallels the "dipping" of Joseph's special robe into goat's blood (Gen 37:31), which was already shown to be compositionally related to the Messiah's bloodstained garment in Genesis 49:11. No wonder Paul says, "*Our* Passover lamb, Christ, has been sacrificed" (1 Cor 5:7). He is "*the* lamb" that the sacrifice of Isaac and the Passover look forward to (Gen 22:7-8, 14). In a compositional sense, the reader of the Pentateuch can also look back on his saving death already revealed in Genesis 3:15.

The Passover lamb was to be both a sacrifice and a meal (Ex 12:8-10). The former is already obvious through the slaughter of the lamb and the use of its blood, but the roasting of its flesh over fire, including its head, legs, and inner parts, and the burning of anything left over associates it with "burnt offerings" that are a "pleasing aroma to the LORD" (Ex 29:17-18; Lev 1:8-9, 12-13; 8:20-21).[8] This provides yet another link to the sacrifice of

---

which "has no cultic use" (433). While granting Motyer's observation, the parallel use of "lamb" and "ewe" may correspond to the parallel use of "lion" and "lioness" in Gen 49:9/Num 24:9, perhaps suggesting the Messiah's identification with humanity created as male and female (Gen 1:27).

[8] A sin offering for the "anointed priest" (Lev 4:3-12) or for the whole congregation of Israel (Lev 4:13-21) seems to have been handled similarly (see Lev 4:8-12, 20-21). Since the blood of these

Isaac, who was supposed to be a "burnt offering" (Gen 22:2-3, 6-8, 13), and to the correspondence between the aroma of Jacob's clothes and Noah's burnt offerings (Gen 8:20-21; 27:27). The roasted Passover lamb was also to be eaten with "unleavened bread" (מַצָּה) and "bitter herbs" (מְרֹרִים, Ex 12:9; Num 9:11). The latter term is associated with suffering in Lamentations 3:15 as its cognates often are also (see Ex 1:14; 15:23; Job 13:26).[9] Exodus 12:33-34, 39 explains that one reason for unleavened bread was because the Israelites ate in haste and did not have time to wait for yeast to take effect (see Deut 16:3).

The Passover meal is thus linked to the Feast of Unleavened Bread (Ex 12:15-20), which suggests additional significance to yeast. The Israelites were commanded to "put an end to" (Hiph. שָׁבַת) yeast (שְׂאֹר) from their houses because anyone who ate anything "leavened" (חָמֵץ) would "be cut off" (Niph. כָּרַת) from Israel (Ex 12:15). Propp suggests that the verb *shabat* (שָׁבַת, "to cease") here and in Exodus 5:5 "may resonate with ... 'Sabbath,' ostensibly derived from the same root. ... The first and last days of [the Feast of] Unleavened Bread are days of rest (12:16)."[10] The effect is to relate the "cessation" of yeast from Israelite households to the Sabbath rest, both of which are results of the exodus. Their enslavement in Egypt presumably lacked such rest (Ex 5:5; Deut 5:15). Furthermore, the themes of bread, Sabbath, and divine commandments reappear concerning manna in Exodus 16:3-5, 14-30. Also in common with Passover are the gathering of sufficient food for the family (Ex 16:16-17; 12:3-4), the command to leave no food until the morning (Ex 16:19; 12:10), and language concerning food preparation (Ex 16:23; 12:9). The importance of observing the Sabbath in relation to gathering manna (not necessarily unleavened) in Exodus 16 strengthens the connection between yeast/unleavened bread and Sabbath in Exodus 12:15-20. But why were the

---

sin offerings was brought into the tabernacle (Lev 4:5-7, 16-18), none of their flesh could be eaten (Lev 6:25-30). See Jacob Milgrom, *Leviticus 1–16*, Anchor Bible (New York: Doubleday, 1991), 407, who notes that the other such offering that could not be eaten was "the bull of the high priest and he-goat of the community on Yom Kippur (16:27)." For parallels between the Passover meal and the consecration of Aaronic priests in Ex 29 and Lev 8 that suggest the Israelites' consecration through the Passover meal, see T. Desmond Alexander, *From Paradise to the Promised Land*, 3rd ed. (Grand Rapids: Baker, 2012), 205-6.

[9]In Deut 32:32 and Job 20:14, the cognate מְרֹרָה relates to poison or venom.
[10]Propp, *Exodus 1–18*, 402.

154

Israelites supposed to "cease" specifically from yeast? The reason seems to be that, during the Feast of Unleavened Bread, yeast temporarily represents something unclean. The idea of "temporary uncleanness" can also be found in Leviticus 19:23 regarding fruit borne by trees in the Promised Land that was to be regarded as "uncircumcised" (עָרֵל) for three years and could not be eaten during that time. The close connection between the Passover and the Feast of Unleavened Bread (Ex 12:6-8, 17-18) then suggests that one of the intended results of the Passover was the removal of yeast, that is, uncleanness.

The serious consequences of being "cut off" for those who eat anything leavened support the suggestion that yeast represents uncleanness during the Feast of Unleavened Bread. By extension, the same would apply to prohibitions against yeast in connection with several other sacrifices (e.g., Ex 23:18; Lev 2:11; 6:17 [MT v. 10]), though the exceptions in Leviticus 7:13 and Leviticus 23:17 suggest that this symbolism is not absolute. Nevertheless, Martin Noth points out that the intervening days between the Sabbaths at the start and end of the feast "are singled out only by an extremely emphatic demand for the eating of unleavened bread (vv. 15b, 19)."[11] Prohibitions against eating in the Pentateuch are commonly related to uncleanness (see "unclean for you," Lev 11:4-8, 26-28),[12] as well as defiling sacred things which likewise results in being "cut off" (Lev 7:18, 20-21, 25, 27; 17:10, 14; 19:7-8).[13] As is well known, yeast spreads through dough (Lk 13:21; 1 Cor 5:6; Gal 5:9), just like uncleanness is contagious and is easily spread (Lev 5:2-3; Hag 2:13-14). These considerations increase the likelihood that yeast represents uncleanness in Exodus 12:15-20. This in turn suggests a symbolic cleansing effect of the death of the Passover lamb, which accords with the death of the seed of

---

[11]Martin Noth, *Exodus*, Old Testament Library (Philadelphia: Westminster, 1962), 97.

[12]Seth Postell, *Adam as Israel: Genesis 1-3 as the Introduction to the Torah and Tanakh* (Eugene, OR: Wipf and Stock, 2011), 117-18, also points out the connection between dietary restrictions Lev 11 and the tree of the knowledge of good and evil in Gen 2:17; 3:3.

[13]See Milgrom, *Leviticus 1-16*, 457-58; Propp, *Exodus 1-18*, 403. Their discussion of what it means to be "cut off" is applicable to the Messiah's being "cut off" in Dan 9:26 (see Is 53:8), even though neither scholar makes this application. When Paul implies that incest with one's father's wife is a kind of "yeast" in 1 Cor 5:1, 6, this fits with an apparent compositional strategy in the Pentateuch concerning various crimes resulting in being "cut off" (Lev 18:8, 27). In the case of incest in 1 Cor 5, this means being "handed over to Satan" (1 Cor 5:5), but there is still the possibility of ultimate salvation, presumably if the offender repents (2 Cor 2:6-8).

the woman and his cleansing work as foretold in Genesis 3:15 (see also Is 52:15; Ps 110:4).

The spreading of the Passover lamb's blood on the "doorposts" (מְזוּזֹת, Ex 12:7, 22-23) also appears to be strategically related to writing the Shema on the "doorposts of your house" (Deut 6:9). Although "doorposts" also appear in Exodus 21:6, only in Deuteronomy 6:9 and similarly in Deuteronomy 11:20 does this word appear in connection with fathers teaching their children to love the Lord with all their heart, soul, and strength (Deut 6:5,7; 11:13, 18-19). Likewise, the meaning of the Passover "sacrifice" was to be taught to children by their parents (Ex 12:26-27). The importance of parental instruction is repeated twice more in connection with the Feast of Unleavened Bread (Ex 13:8-9, 14-16). The phrase "sign on your hand and frontlets between your eyes" in Exodus 13:16 (cf. Ex 13:9), Deuteronomy 6:8, and Deuteronomy 11:18 solidifies the compositional relationship between the Passover and the Shema. The parent-to-child instruction concerning the Passover is even called "the law of the Lord in your mouth [בְּפִיךָ]" in Exodus 13:9 (cf. Ex 12:49), which parallels the "words" which were to be "on your heart" (עַל־לְבָבְכֶם/עַל־לְבָבֶךָ) in Deuteronomy 6:6; 11:18. Although not explicitly stated, it seems that all of these passages involve divine instruction "on the heart" (see "remembrance" in Ex 13:9) and "in the mouth" (as implied by parental instruction). Significantly, to have a certain "commandment" and "word" "in your mouth and in your heart" (בְּפִיךָ וּבִלְבָבְךָ) is how Deuteronomy 30:14 characterizes the new covenant (see Josh 1:8; Is 59:21; Jer 31:33-34; Rom 10:8-10). These compositional relationships demonstrate that there are new covenant themes and dynamics at play in the application of the Passover lamb's blood to "doorposts" and the parent-to-child (hence person-to-person; cf. "disciple all the nations" in Mt 28:19) instruction concerning its meaning, the latter of which contrasts with its mere inscription on stone tablets (Ex 24:12; 31:18; Jer 31:32-33). The centrality of the Passover is also upheld in Deuteronomy 6:12, 20-24; 11:3-4, even though the Lord had done many other things for Israel since then (see Deut 1–5; 8:2; 11:5-6). Such new covenant themes and dynamics accord with the intentional foreshadowing of the Messiah through the institution of the Passover and Feast of Unleavened Bread in Exodus 12–13.

The Song of the Sea

Israel's departure on the night of the Passover (Ex 12:30-33) would not be the last time that they saw the Egyptians, who quickly regretted letting them go and pursued them (Ex 14:2-10). Nevertheless, this last obstacle provided another dramatic opportunity to manifest "the salvation of the LORD" (Ex 14:13) and allow the Lord to "be glorified" (Niph. כָּבֵד, Ex 14:4, 17-18). He accomplished this by parting the Red Sea (or "Reed" Sea) for the Israelites to pass through safely and returning it to its normal state to drown the Egyptians (Ex 14:21-29). Indeed, the Lord had "saved" (יָשַׁע) Israel, and they saw his power, feared him, and believed in him and in Moses (Ex 14:30-31; contra Num 14:9-11).

In response, Moses and the Israelites sang the salvation song of Exodus 15:1-18, known as the Song of the Sea. Although one of the four major poetic sections in the Pentateuch, it is unique in that it does not appear in conjunction with the phrase "in the last days" (Gen 49:1; Num 24:14; Deut 31:29) and as such does not directly predict the coming of the Messiah (cf. Gen 49:8-12; Num 24:7-9, 17-19; Deut 33:7; see chap. 3 above). It does not even intentionally foreshadow the Messiah like the other aforementioned passages do. Why even discuss it then in relation to the Messianic vision of the Pentateuch? The answer is that not only is the Song of the Sea compositionally related to the other major poetic sections as part of the overall structure of the Pentateuch, but it is also related to them lexically, thematically, and intertextually. Furthermore, the exodus, especially as depicted in the Song of the Sea, serves as a pattern for the eschatological "second exodus" that centers on the Messiah.[14] This patterning can even be detected in Exodus 15:1-18, as the analysis below will demonstrate.

Clear evidence of the influence of the Song of the Sea on descriptions of the second exodus can be found in other Old Testament passages, such

---

[14]For prophetic allusions to the exodus in general (not necessarily as represented in Ex 15:1-18), see John Day, "Prophecy," in *It Is Written: Scripture Citing Scripture: Essays in Honour of Barnabas Lindars, SSF*, ed. D. A. Carson and H. G. M. Williamson (New York: Cambridge University Press, 1998), 45-46; Samuel E. Loewenstamm, *The Evolution of the Exodus Tradition*, trans. Baruch J. Schwartz (Jerusalem: Magnes, 1992); Michael Fishbane, *Biblical Text and Texture: A Literary Reading of Selected Texts* (Oxford: Oneworld, 1998), 121-40; R. Michael Fox, ed., *Reverberations of the Exodus in Scripture* (Eugene, OR: Wipf and Stock, 2014).

as Isaiah 12. This chapter concludes Isaiah 1–12 and immediately follows a prediction of an eschatological exodus in Isaiah 11:10-16 that will be like the exodus from Egypt. On that day the Lord's anger will have turned away, and he will "comfort" his people (Is 12:1; see Is 40:1), as they sing "Yah, the LORD, is my strength and song; he has become my salvation" (Is 12:2) as they had long ago in Exodus 15:2. Psalm 118:14 also cites this line from Exodus 15:2 in the context of the saving power of the Lord's right hand (Ps 118:15; see Num 24:18; Ps 60:12; 108:13) and of "a stone that the builders rejected" (Ps 118:22; 1 Pet 2:7; see Is 1:11, 10). DiFransico points out the extensive allusions to the Song of the Sea as a whole in Micah 7:7-20 and concludes that these allusions are "intentional."[15] Although she believes that the defeat of a human enemy in Exodus 15:1-18 is "reinterpreted" in Micah 7:7-20 such that sin is personified as a "military enemy" (Mic 7:18-20),[16] the analysis below will show that within the Pentateuch itself the Song of the Sea has a far grander scope than the defeat of Pharaoh and his army, a scope that encompasses even Micah 7:7-20 and the defeat of sin.

The conflict between Israel and Pharaoh not only concerns the fulfillment of the Abrahamic covenant (see Ex 2:23-25; 3:6-10, 15-17) but also the conflict between the seed of the woman and the seed of the serpent in Genesis 3:15. Although (collective) Israel is not the (individual) seed of the woman (see chap. 1 above), the Israelites are still an essential part of the plan of salvation since the individual seed will be descended from them (Num 24:17) and will rule them and the nations (Gen 27:29; 49:8-10). This suggests that Pharaoh and the Egyptians are part of the seed of the serpent. After all, Pharaoh viciously opposed the multiplication of the Israelites, which advanced the Lord's plan of blessing at creation (Gen 1:28) that culminates in the Messiah (Gen 22:17b-18). Furthermore, Pharaoh relied on "sorcerers" and "magicians" who used "enchantments" (Ex 7:11, 22; 8:7) in an attempt to compete with the signs that the Lord performed through Moses (Ex 8:18-19; 9:11). Pharaoh's allegiance with the demonic realm firmly places him among the seed of the serpent. The casting of Pharaoh and Egypt as part of the seed of the serpent is generalized in other Old

---

[15]Lesley DiFransico, "'He Will Cast Their Sins into the Depths of the Sea . . .': Exodus Allusions and the Personification of Sin in Micah 7:7-20," *VT* 67 (2017): 191-95.
[16]DiFransico, "'He Will Cast Their Sins," 188, see also 197-203.

Testament passages. Ezekiel 32:2, though referring to another Pharaoh, compares him to "a sea monster [תַּנִּים] in the seas," a designation that associates him with the evil snake in the Garden of Eden (Is 27:1). Likewise, Psalm 74:13 poetically describes the Lord parting the Red Sea and breaking "the heads of [רָאשֵׁי] sea monsters in the waters." Thus the defeat of Pharaoh is linked to the defeat of the serpent's seed and the eschatological defeat of the serpent himself by the seed of the woman (Gen 3:15; Num 24:17).[17]

In contrast with the narrative account in Exodus 14, scholars have noted that Exodus 15:1-18 generalizes the Lord's victory over the Egyptians at the Red Sea.[18] Egypt and Israel are not directly mentioned. Instead the focus is on an "enemy" (אֹיֵב, Ex 15:6, 9), "those who rise up against you" (קָמֶיךָ, Ex 15:7), and the "people" he has "redeemed" (גָּאַל, Ex 15:13). Accordingly, Samuel Loewenstamm notes further that "a considerable number of biblical texts refer to the parting of the sea without any mention of the Egyptians."[19] Even the mention of Pharaoh once in Exodus 15:4 does not overthrow this generalizing tendency, since Pharaoh represents the serpent's seed, as argued above. Moreover, there is a wordplay on "Pharaoh" (פַּרְעֹה) with the word translated "locks" or "leaders" (פְּרָעוֹת) in connection with an "enemy" (אֹיֵב) in Deuteronomy 32:42. This verse is also part of a major poetic section (Deut 32–33) and describes the Lord's arrows and sword having their fill "from the head [רֹאשׁ] of the locks/leaders [Pharaohs?] of the enemy." This suggests an intertextual relationship between these two passages, and the additional reference to "head" provides a direct link back to Genesis 3:15. This link and inclusio is even more explicit in Deuteronomy 32:42 LXX through its translation "from [the] head of [the]

---

[17]The salvation of Egypt in Is 19:19-25 shows that these negative associations with Pharaoh (and Egypt) are not absolute, as is the case for "enemies" and "Edom" (see discussion in chap. 3 above).

[18]See my *Eschatological Sanctuary in Exodus 15:17 and Related Texts* (New York: Lang, 2013), 48, for a summary of the following scholars on this issue: Sarna, *Exodus*, 75; Terence E. Fretheim, *Exodus*, Interpretation (Louisville: John Knox, 1991), 165-66; Brian Russell, *The Song of the Sea: The Date of Composition and Influence of Exodus 15:1-21* (New York: Lang, 2007), 28.

[19]Loewenstamm, *Evolution of the Exodus Tradition*, 236. He cites Josh 4:22-24; Ps 66:5-6, 114:1-3; Is 11:15-16, all of which also mention the crossing of the Jordan (236-38). He also cites the following passages that only mention the crossing of the Red Sea: Josh 2:9-11; 5:1; Is 51:9-10; 63:12-14; Ps 77:14-20 (238-41). He concludes, "Common to all these texts, we may now assert, is the idea that the parting of the sea alone was sufficient to achieve eternal renown for Israel's God, and to demonstrate, both to Israel's satisfaction and that of the entire world, that He alone is God in the heavens above and on earth below" (241-42). Relatedly "the LORD vanquished not only the Egyptians but the sea itself as well" (251). He cites Ps 106:9-12 and 136:13-16 in support of this synthesis.

rulers of [the] enemies" (ἀπὸ κεφαλῆς ἀρχόντων ἐχθρῶν). Similar dynamics are also likely at play in Judges 5:2 ("when the leaders led [בִּפְרֹעַ פְּרָעוֹת] in Israel"), which is part of a long poem whose climactic conclusion (Judg 5:26-27) is intentionally patterned on Genesis 3:15 and Genesis 49:8-12. Judges 5 accordingly closes with the generalizing prayer, "So may all your enemies perish [יֹאבְדוּ כָל־אוֹיְבֶיךָ], LORD" (Judg 5:31).

The generalized presentation in Exodus 15:1-18 is also evident through the exclusive emphasis on the Lord as the sole agent of judgment and salvation. Unlike Exodus 14, there is no mention of Moses or his role in lifting up his staff or "stretching out" his "hand" (יָד) prior to the Red Sea parting and after the Israelites had crossed over (Ex 14:16, 21, 26-27). Instead, it is the Lord's "right hand" (יָמִין) that "shatters the enemy" (תִּרְעַץ אוֹיֵב, Ex 15:6) and thwarts the enemy's desire to "possess" (יָרַשׁ) with his "hand" (Ex 15:9; see Gen 15:3-4; 22:17b; 24:60). It is the Lord, not Moses, who "stretched out" (נָטָה) his right hand so that the enemy was swallowed up (Ex 15:12). It was this "mighty hand" (הַיָּד הַגְּדֹלָה) that the Israelites recognized in Exodus 14:31 and celebrated in song. The display of the Lord's "strong hand" (יָד חֲזָקָה) had indeed been foretold (Ex 3:19; 6:1) and would be remembered for generations (Ex 13:9; 32:11; Deut 4:34; Ps 136:12; Dan 9:15). Likewise, his "great arm" brings terror on the onlooking peoples (Ex 15:14, 16). Whereas the Lord's "right hand" is used to defeat the enemy (Ex 15:6, 12), his "hands" are used to establish a sanctuary (Ex 15:17). The majority of the Song of the Sea casts the Lord as a "man of war" (Ex 15:3) whose "right hand" triumphs over his enemies so that his glory is manifested beyond all other gods (Ex 15:12) and his kingdom triumphs forever (Ex 15:18). Brevard Childs characterizes the song as,

> directed completely to the praise of God and thus subordinates all the historical details of Israel's active involvement.... Often this description in praise of Yahweh is not directly related to the sea event, but ... celebrates Yahweh's glory as 'fierce in action,' 'doer of wonders' (v. 12).... the action is not confined to the Reed Sea event, but flows into a broader description of Yahweh's attributes.... The victory at the sea simply illustrates those same attributes which are continually celebrated throughout the Psalter.[20]

---

[20]Brevard Childs, *The Book of Exodus*, Old Testament Library (Philadelphia: Westminster, 1974), 250-51.

This strong emphasis on the Lord's distinctive work of judgment and salvation is also found in the other major poetic sections (Gen 49:18; Num 23:23; 24:23; Deut 32:4, 26-27, 36-41). But these same poetic sections also at points attribute a similarly distinctive work of judgment and salvation to the Messiah. This compositional relationship suggests that the generalization of the victory at the Red Sea is especially directed toward the Messiah's eschatological victory, not equally to all the Lord's saving acts in general. This is especially true for Exodus 15:14-17 (see discussion below). The Messiah is also cast as a warrior who defeats his enemies and saves the Lord's people (Gen 49:8; Num 24:8, 17-19; Deut 33:7). As a king who rules over the world "in the last days" and brings a return to Edenic abundance (Gen 49:1, 10-12; Num 24:5-7, 14), the Messiah is naturally understood to rule forever (see Is 9:7) just like the Lord in Exodus 15:18. Even the relative deemphasis of the Lord in Genesis 49 (only Gen 49:18, 24-25) in conjunction with a greater emphasis on the Messiah (Gen 49:8-12) is balanced by Exodus 15:1-18 and its resounding emphasis on the Lord as warrior and king. This balancing is particularly apt because of the relative proximity of Genesis 49 and Exodus 15, compared to the other major poetic sections. Numbers 23–24 emphasizes both the Lord and the Messiah (see chap. 6 below), and Deuteronomy 32–33 primarily emphasizes the Lord and the Messiah secondarily (see chap. 8 below). This compositional relationship between the Song of the Sea and the other major poetic sections thus suggests a connection between the Lord in Exodus 15:1-18 and the Messiah in Genesis 49:8-12, Numbers 24:7-9, 17-19, and Deuteronomy 33:7. From a compositional perspective, which detects an authorial strategy rather than a contradiction, the implication is that the Lord's distinctive work of judgment and salvation, including military victory over his enemies, salvation of his people, and his eschatological reign, are in complete harmony with the Messiah's. The suggestion that the Messiah is divine accords with this as well (see discussions of Gen 27:29; 49:8 in chaps. 2–3 above).

This is not to say, however, that the Song of the Sea is a direct Messianic prophecy or even that it intentionally foreshadows his coming like other passages, such as Jacob's ladder, the sacrifice of Isaac, or the Passover. Those narrative passages are closely intertwined with particular Messianic prophecies in the Pentateuch. Exodus 15:1-18 is different. Its focus is on the Lord and his distinctive work of judgment and salvation as exemplified at the Red Sea. Since the Song of the Sea already concerns the Lord himself (and potentially a divine Messiah by extension), the category of "intentional foreshadowing," which is used to describe the authorially intended proleptic casting of Jacob's ladder (and the memorial stone pillar), Isaac and the ram in Genesis 22:1-19, and the Passover lamb, does not seem to apply. Nevertheless, the casting of the Lord as warrior and king in the Song of the Sea and the similar casting of the Messiah in the other major poetic sections strongly suggests a compositional strategy linking the Lord and the Messiah. If the latter is indeed divine, then it becomes difficult at times to draw a sharp distinction between the two. While this certainly does not mean that the Messiah should be read into every mention of the Lord in the Pentateuch or Old Testament (e.g., Ps 2:2; 110:1), the compositional relationship of the Song of the Sea to the other major poetic sections, as well as the likelihood of the Messiah's divinity, at least suggests that the Lord's work of judgment and salvation and the Messiah's work are closely related and even identical at many key points. Indeed, the generalized nature of the Song of the Sea allows it to celebrate a victory over Pharaoh/Egypt while at the same time encompassing a future work of salvation, the second exodus. This is exactly what the aforementioned uses of Exodus 15:1-18 in Isaiah 12, Psalm 118, and Micah 7 strongly suggest.

The patterning of an eschatological second exodus after the one from Egypt is even discernible in the Pentateuch itself. Numbers 24:8 predicts that the Lord will bring the Messiah out of Egypt "in the last days" (Num 24:14) just as he had brought Israel out of Egypt (Num 23:22; see chap. 6 below). Likewise, the coming of a "prophet like Moses" (Deut 18:15, 18) suggests another prophet who will perform great signs to bring about a future exodus (Deut 34:8-10; see chap. 7 below). A second exodus may even be predicted by the Song of the Sea itself, which not only looks back to the victory over the Egyptians (Ex 15:1-12) but also looks forward to the Lord bringing Israel into the Promised Land (Ex 15:13-18). Norbert Lohfink has pointed out the parallel imagery between Exodus 15:8-10 and Exodus 15:14-17 concerning "passage through dangers threatening."[21] In

---

[21]Norbert Lohfink, *The Christian Meaning of the Old Testament*, trans. R. A. Wilson (Milwaukee: Bruce, 1968), 82.

both the retrospective and prospective parts of the song, there is a "narrow passage," a "danger zone" which people attempt to pass through. The attempt of Pharaoh/"the enemy" (Ex 15:4, 9) to pass through the waters ends in disaster (Ex 15:10). The Israelites' safe passage through waters, though implicit (Ex 15:13), is not strongly emphasized in the Song of the Sea as it is in Exodus 14:29. Rather, it is their safe passage through "the peoples" (Ex 15:14-15) that the song describes in greater detail (Ex 15:16, "until your people pass over [עָבַר], Lord, until this people you acquired pass over [עָבַר]"). The verb *pass over* can be used of traversing a body of water (Gen 32:11; Deut 2:14; Josh 4:1), including the Red Sea (Ps 78:13; 136:14). Lohfink remarks, "The threatening masses of nations correspond here to the masses of water on each side of the passage of the Egyptians. Just as Yahweh congeals the masses of water, so he now turns the nations to stone, so that Israel can pass between them, and they do not flow back together upon Israel."[22] Indeed, just as the peoples "heard" (שָׁמַע), "tremble" (רָגַז), and are seized by "writhing" (חִיל) in Exodus 15:14, so in the similar context of Psalm 77, God is "doing a wonder" (עֹשֵׂה פֶלֶא) among the "peoples" and redeeming his people with his "arm" (Ps 77:14-15; Ex 15:11, 13, 16), so that the waters "saw" (רָאָה), "writhe" (חוּל), and "tremble" (רָגַז, Ps 77:16). The waters and the peoples are thus parallel again. Deliverance from "many waters" and from enemies are also closely linked in Psalm 18:16-17 and Psalm 144:7.

Lohfink, however, interprets the song as "open-ended," whose purpose is to "provide a context of imagery in which differences in time are suppressed, and into which every act of God on behalf of his chosen people can be fitted."[23] He cites as examples the Lord's bringing Israel into Canaan, the crossing of the Jordan River in Joshua, and the casting of the return from exile as another exodus.[24] While his observations concerning the "pattern of imagery" in Exodus 15:8-10, 14-17 are very insightful, there is good reason for taking Exodus 15:14-17 as referring to only one future, climactic exodus, rather than to many saving acts that will fit this general pattern. Namely, other passages in the Pentateuch directly foretell a

---

[22]Lohfink, *Christian Meaning*, 83.
[23]Lohfink, *Christian Meaning*, 81-82.
[24]Lohfink, *Christian Meaning*, 84.

singular "second exodus" to be led by a Judahite king who will also be a prophet like Moses (Num 24:8; Deut 18:15-19; 34:10-12). Taken together, these passages are not left open to all future saving acts of the Lord, as Lohfink believes, but look forward to a specific, climactic one.[25] Nevertheless, if Lohfink's basic observation regarding the parallel "pattern of imagery" in Exodus 15:8-10, 14-17 is valid, along with our argument regarding the specificity of Exodus 15:14-17 (see below), then the Song of the Sea treats not only the exodus in general terms (Ex 15:1-12) but also specifically the second exodus.

That being said, many commentators do not mention any future "exodus(es)" in Exodus 15:13-18 and simply take this section as predicting Israel's crossing of the Red Sea and entrance into the Promised Land under Joshua. However, there are reasons to interpret it otherwise in addition to Lohfink's argument. Perhaps the easiest way to see this is to start at the end of the Song of the Sea, especially the last line, "The LORD will reign forever and ever" (יְהוָה יִמְלֹךְ לְעֹלָם וָעֶד, Ex 15:18). Although this can be taken as a universal statement that is always true (Judg 8:23; 1 Sam 8:7),[26] similar statements often relate to the realized reign of the Lord that finds fulfillment eschatologically. Psalm 146:10 resembles Exodus 15:18 more closely than any other passage in the Old Testament, but its syntax expresses a prayer and a hope, "May the LORD reign forever" (יִמְלֹךְ יְהוָה לְעוֹלָם). Exodus 15:18 can then be interpreted as a prediction. Michael Snearly observes that Psalms 146–150 serve as a conclusion to the Psalter and have many parallels to Psalms 1–2.[27] In particular, both Psalm 2:6 and Psalm 146:10 concern a king and Zion. The eschatological king on Zion in Psalm 2:6 is the Messiah, and the eschatological king in Psalm 146:10 is the Lord (see Ps 93:1; 95:3; 96:10; 97:1; 99:1).[28] The implied close relationship between the Messiah and the Lord is parallel to what has been observed above already in the major poetic sections in the Pentateuch.

---

[25] Dempster, *Dominion and Dynasty*, 32, 100, agrees with Lohfink's conclusion.

[26] Neither of these passages mention "forever," unlike Ex 15:18 and Ps 146:10.

[27] Michael Snearly, *The Return of the King: Messianic Expectation in Book V of the Psalter* (New York: T&T Clark, 2016), 178-81.

[28] Relatedly, Ps 66:7 ("He rules by his strength forever") follows a direct reference to the Song of the Sea in Ps 66:6 ("there, let us rejoice in him!") and appears in the context of "all the earth" worshiping him (Ps 66:1-5, 8; see Ps 67).

In further support of an eschatological interpretation of Exodus 15:18, Nebuchadnezzar's dream in Daniel 2 concerns "the last days" (Dan 2:28) and the Lord setting up a kingdom on earth that will last "forever," as represented by the "stone" that crushes all human kingdoms and then becomes a mountain that fills the earth (Dan 2:44-45). Furthermore, the reference to the stone suggests that the Messianic kingdom is specifically in view (Ps 118:22). What is hinted at in Daniel 2 is clarified in Daniel 7, a parallel passage within the book that also concerns four human kingdoms. Using the same language that is used of the Lord's kingdom as in Daniel 2:44 ("it will not be destroyed," "forever"), Daniel 7:13-14, 18 equates this with the Messianic kingdom. As perhaps might be expected, the same things are repeatedly said of the Lord's kingdom elsewhere in the book (Dan 4:3, 34; 6:26). Likewise, Chronicles describes David's "seed" as sitting on his own throne in his own kingdom (1 Chron 17:11-12, 14; 22:10) while at other times saying that he rules over the Lord's kingdom on the Lord's throne (1 Chron 17:14; 28:5; 29:23).[29] The Lord's eschatological kingdom and the Messiah's eschatological kingdom thus seem to be one and the same.

Although the crossing of the Jordan in Joshua 3:1-17 (and to a lesser extent the parting of the Jordan by Elijah/Elisha in 2 Kings 2:8, 14) bears much resemblance to the crossing of the Red Sea, it should not be too quickly equated with the crossing described in Exodus 15:14-16. The Canaanites did indeed "melt" (מוג) before Israel (Ex 15:15; Josh 2:9, 24; see מָסַס in Josh 2:11; 5:1), but the subsequent narrative reveals that some Canaanites remained in the land (Josh 13:13; 15:63; 16:10; 17:12-13; Judg 1:19-36) such that at the end of Joshua's life there still remained "very much land to possess" (Josh 13:1). A closer look at the enemies listed in Exodus 15:14-15 will clarify this. In Exodus 15:14 "writhing seizes the inhabitants of Philistia." However, when the Israelites departed from Egypt, the Lord intentionally led them away from the Philistines lest the *Israelites* retreat (Ex 13:17). Although the Israelites were supposed to possess Philistia (Ex 23:31; Josh 13:2-3), the Philistines not only remained in the land but caused trouble for Israel for many years (Judg 3:31; 10:6-11; 13-16). Dempster

---

[29]For a survey of others who have interpreted Ex 15:18 eschatologically, see my *Eschatological Sanctuary*, 52-53.

notes Philistia's domination of Israel at the end of the book of Judges, a situation that carries over into 1–2 Samuel.[30] This does not match the glorious entrance into the land described in Exodus 15:13-17. Likewise, Exodus 15:15 characterizes "the chiefs of Edom" as being "terrified," but their armed resistance to Israel passing through their land (Num 20:18-21) does not resemble the stunned silence of those watching the Lord's people pass by in Exodus 15:16. Similarly, although Moab did indeed dread the Israelites greatly as they passed through (Num 22:3), their king's plan to curse them (Num 22:4-6) also does not match the stunned silence of Exodus 15:16. These incongruities exist because the final defeat of Edom and Moab awaits the coming of the Messiah (Num 24:17-18).[31] The same is true of the Canaanites (Obad 20; Zech 14:21) and the Philistines (Is 14:29-32; Obad 19; Zech 9:6).[32] Even the "trembling" (רָגַז) foretold for the "peoples" in Exodus 15:14, though referenced again in Deuteronomy 2:25, instead perennially afflicted Israel who would "tremble" because of enemy nations (Deut 28:64-65; 2 Sam 7:10; 1 Chron 17:9; Is 14:2-3). But when the Lord's reign is realized in Zion, then "the peoples will tremble" (Ps 99:1-2; see Ex 15:14, 17-18; Joel 2:1).

Furthermore, a number of passages describe an eschatological "passing over/through" of the Lord's people. Isaiah 35:8 says that the unclean will not "pass through" the "way of holiness." Similarly, Isaiah 43:2 seems to imply that the redeemed will "pass through" waters and rivers, just as they had before (Is 51:10). In Isaiah 62:10, they are commanded to "pass through" gates onto a "way" and "highway." They likewise pass through a "gate" in Micah 2:13 (see Gen 28:17), preceded by "their king," a possible reference to the Messiah (Hos 3:5; see Mic 7:18; Zech 10:11). In Exodus 15:13, 16, this blessed people is "guided" (נָחָה), "redeemed" (גָּאַל), "led" (נָהַל), and "purchased" (קָנָה) by the Lord himself. The last verb recalls Melchizedek's proclamation of God Most High as "Possessor [קֹנֵה] of heaven and earth" (Gen 14:19; see Gen 14:22), while contrasting with the last covenant curse

---

[30]Dempster, *Dominion and Dynasty*, 131.
[31]The "Kenites" in Num 24:21 are a subgroup of the Canaanites (Gen 15:18-21), who are the focus of Num 21:1-3. The only nation in Ex 15:14-15 that goes unmentioned in these passages from Numbers is Philistia, which like Canaan, Babylon, and Assyria, is descended from Ham (see Gen 10:6-14).
[32]For more discussion, see my *Eschatological Sanctuary*, 49–52.

listed in Deuteronomy 28 of Israel wanting to sell themselves as slaves but having "no purchaser" (אֵין קֹנֶה, Deut 28:68).

The Lord's people in Exodus 15:17 will also be "brought" and "planted [like trees?] on the mountain" of his inheritance. Although it is tempting to equate this "mountain" with "the established place for your dwelling" and "the sanctuary your hands establish" as a reference to Solomon's temple, the absence of the preposition "on/in" (בְּ) prior to the latter two phrases leaves open the possibility that this sanctuary is the Lord's people themselves ("you will plant them on the mountain of your inheritance, the established place for your dwelling . . . the sanctuary, Lord, your hands established"; with "place"/"sanctuary" in apposition to "them").[33] In fact, a sanctuary that the Lord's own hands establish is better understood as something that he himself distinctively builds (Zech 6:12-13; Mt 16:18), rather than as referring to Solomon's temple or any other "humanmade" structure. Such a sanctuary established by divine hands would then be an eschatological sanctuary intertwined with the eschatological Zion described in passages such as Isaiah 2:2, Micah 4:1, and Psalm 146:10. An eschatological sanctuary in Exodus 15:17 agrees with the exclusive emphasis on the Lord's work in the Song of the Sea and with other passages that contrast what he does with his "hands" compared to what humans do with theirs (Is 66:1-2; Dan 2:34, 45; Mk 14:58; Acts 7:48; 2 Cor 5:1; Eph 2:11; Col 2:11; Heb 9:11, 24).[34]

Returning to DiFransico's recognition that Micah 7:7-20 repeatedly and intentionally alludes to the Song of the Sea, we can now see how even forgiveness of sin can ultimately be related to the Song of the Sea. As shown above, Pharaoh is part of the seed of the serpent, and the Lord's defeat of him is intentionally generalized and compositionally related to

---

[33] Childs, *Book of Exodus*, 250, though not arguing for this particular point, comments, "Above all, the display of divine power is to create for himself a people." If his people are the sanctuary, then they are the direct object of *all* the 2nd masculine sg. verbs with the Lord as subject in Ex 15:13-18.
[34] For extended treatment of Ex 15:17, see my *Eschatological Sanctuary*. Related to the NT passages cited, the LXX uses χειροποίητα consistently of idols (e.g., Lev 26:1, 30; Is 2:18; 10:11; Dan 5:4, 23). Contra John Sailhamer, *The Meaning of the Pentateuch: Revelation, Composition, and Interpretation* (Downers Grove, IL: InterVarsity Press, 2009), 572-73, 577, who believes that the "sanctuary" in Ex 15:17 is the Garden of Eden in Gen 2 and the kingdom in Ex 15:18 is "eternal" (past, present, and future), rather than eschatological. We recognize the Edenic imagery but still see good reason for taking the sanctuary and divine reign in Ex 15:17-18 as eschatological.

the other major poetic sections in the Pentateuch such that it also relates to the Messiah's eschatological defeat of the serpent and all his enemies. As shown in chapter one, to defeat the serpent and his seed is also to defeat sin, which he uses with great effectiveness, and death, which ensues after successful temptation. Contrary to DiFransico, sin has already been personified in Genesis 4:7 as an enemy ("sin is lying at the door . . . but you must rule over it"; see Rom 7:8-11).[35] When Genesis 3:15, Genesis 4:7, and Exodus 15:1-18 are properly interpreted in relation to one another, the Lord's salvation of his people and defeat of their enemies in Micah 7:19—culminating in "subduing" (יִכְבֹּשׁ, see Gen 1:28) their iniquities and casting "all their sins into the depths of the sea" (בִּמְצֻלוֹת יָם כָּל־חַטֹּאותָם, see Ex 15:4-5)—is not a "reinterpretation" of the Song of the Sea. Rather, if sin is one of the enemies that the Lord will triumph over so that he reigns forever and ever (Ex 15:18), then the Song of the Sea, though immediately directed toward the victory over Pharaoh, also applies to the eschatological victory over sin as part of the second exodus predicted in Exodus 15:14-16.

Conclusion

Although the reader must wait until Numbers 24 for the next Messianic prophecy, the exodus narrative provides an opportunity for the Messianic vision of the Pentateuch to unfold through the Passover and the Song of the Sea. The Passover lamb is intertextually related to the sacrifice of Isaac, the seed of the woman, and Judah's willingness to be a substitute for his brother Benjamin. While advancing the storyline, the institution of the Passover simultaneously depicts the Messiah (called "my son," in Gen 27:27; 49:9) as a blameless lamb whose death will substitute for Israel's firstborn and even Israel itself (called "my son" in Ex 4:22-23). Since the Passover is inextricably linked to the Feast of Unleavened Bread, the lamb's death is also linked to the "cessation" of yeast, which is likely a symbol of uncleanness. The Song of the Sea, as one of the four major poetic sections in the Pentateuch, also relates to the Messianic vision of the Pentateuch. It is not a Messianic prophecy, nor does it intentionally foreshadow the Messiah,

---

[35]DiFransico, "'He Will Cast Their Sins," 188, refers to "an unusual metaphor for sin" in Mic 7:7-20. While granting this, the more important point is that this metaphor is found already in Gen 4:7.

but the description of the Lord as a warrior-king who reigns forever strongly resembles the descriptions of the Messiah in the other major poetic sections (Gen 49; Num 24). Also, although directed immediately to the defeat of Pharaoh, the Song of the Sea generalizes realities about the Lord's salvation and judgment with a focus on the second exodus in Exodus 15:14-16. This eschatological exodus will center on the Messiah (Num 24:8; Deut 18:15, 18) and will result in the establishment of an eschatological sanctuary and an eschatological kingdom.

5

SHADOWS AT SINAI

The previous chapter has shown that the long stretch without Messianic prophecy between Genesis 49 and Numbers 24 does not mean that the Messianic vision of the Pentateuch has been temporarily set aside. On the contrary, the central example of past salvation in the Old Testament, the exodus, provides a vehicle for additional instances of intentional foreshadowing of the Messiah. This should not be surprising since the second exodus, which focuses on him, is patterned after the exodus from Egypt. Although the Song of the Sea (Ex 15:1-18) marks the completion of the exodus proper, the Lord's plan was never simply to bring Israel out of bondage but to bring them into the Promised Land in fulfillment of the Abrahamic covenant (Gen 15:13-21; Ex 15:13-18). In this sense, Israel's salvation was still incomplete because they were not yet settled in their own land. There was still a journey through the wilderness to be taken, including a planned stop at Mount Sinai (Ex 3:12).

The New Testament famously refers to several passages from Israel's time in the wilderness and at Mount Sinai as foreshadowing Christ in some sense. In John 6:32-35, Jesus references manna from heaven and calls himself "the true bread from heaven," "the bread of God," and "the bread of life."[1] Subsequently, he commands his hearers to eat this bread so that

---

[1] D. A. Carson, *The Gospel According to John*, Pillar New Testament Commentary (Grand Rapids: Eerdmans, 1991), 286-88, notes that based on Prov 9:5, "some Jewish authorities figuratively referred to the law of Moses, Torah, as 'bread,'" and that similar symbolism may be at work in John 6. He adds that one of manna's "chief functions was to serve as a type of the *true* bread from heaven." He also observes that "bread of God" sometimes refers to the "showbread" in the tabernacle (Lev 21:6, 8, 17) and "establish[es] a typological reading of the Old Testament." Carson interacts with Peder Borgen, *Bread from Heaven: An Exegetical Study of the Concept of Manna in the Gospel of John and the Writings of Philo* (Leiden: Brill, 1965), as does C. K. Barrett, *The Gospel According to St. John*, 2nd ed. (Philadelphia: Westminster, 1978), 289. While granting

they may live and even goes so far as to say that they should eat his flesh and drink his blood (Jn 6:50-56). In another famous passage, Paul recounts the experiences of the Israelites in the wilderness, whom he calls "examples" or "types" (τύποι; 1 Cor 10:1-6).[2] In the process, he makes the startling claim that "all ate the same spiritual food and all drank the same spiritual drink, for they drank from the spiritual rock that followed them; and the rock was Christ" (1 Cor 10:3-4). Likewise, the book of Hebrews takes the sacrificial system (Heb 7:27; 10:4-11) and especially its pinnacle, the Day of Atonement (Heb 9:7, 25; 10:1-3), as in some sense foreshadowing Christ and the new covenant.[3] Although unmentioned in the New Testament, Bezalel, the Spirit-filled man from the tribe of Judah who led the construction of the tabernacle (Ex 31:1-5; 35:30-33), is also highly suggestive in this regard. As was the case previously, the goal of the analysis below is not simply to point out parallels between these passages and the Messiah but to investigate the extent to which each intentionally foreshadows the Messiah in the compositional strategy of the Pentateuch.

We have deliberately limited ourselves to these passages because of their importance in the New Testament and their promise when analyzed compositionally, rather than attempting to delve, say, into the details of the various sacrifices, tabernacle articles, and other laws. We make this decision for practical reasons and not to dismiss possible fruitful discoveries. The preceding chapters have already pointed out what are probably intentional parallels between the Garden of Eden and the tabernacle, and more

---

the importance of parallel biblical passages, our discussion below argues instead for intentional foreshadowing.

[2]Joseph Fitzmyer, *First Corinthians*, Anchor Bible (New Haven, CT: Yale University Press, 2008), 380, is aware that this wording "encourages some commentators to indulge in typological interpretation" but characterizes this "mode of interpretation" as "born of later conceptions" and "sometimes strange to what Paul is saying in this passage." Gordon Fee, *The First Epistle to the Corinthians*, New International Commentary on the New Testament, rev. ed. (Grand Rapids: Eerdmans, 2014), 489, characterizes Paul's use of the OT here as "a mixture of type and analogy." Without necessarily disputing Fee's point regarding the various elements of Israel's experience cited in 1 Cor 10:1-5, our focus is on Paul's emphatic statement, "the rock was Christ," and the extent to which intentional foreshadowing may be at work.

[3]E.g., William Lane, *Hebrews 1–8*, Word Biblical Commentary (Dallas: Word, 1991), cxxiii, "The central section of Hebrews, extending from 8:1 to 10:18, provides abundant illustration of the manner in which the writer employs typology." Though just one of nine principles that he discusses concerning the use of the OT in Hebrews, he believes that "typological interpretation plays a key role in the developing argument in Hebrews."

importantly, the textual casting of the Messiah as a priest (Gen 3:15; 14:18-20) and a sacrifice (Gen 3:15; 22:1-14; 27:27; 49:8-12; Ex 12). Thus the tabernacle, the Aaronic priesthood, and the Levitical sacrifices indeed "have a shadow of the good things to come" (Heb 10:1; see Heb 8:5), not merely in the sense of being surpassed by something greater in the future, but also within the Pentateuch itself as a compositional "shadow" of the Pentateuch's central Messianic vision. For the present purposes, authorially intended "shadows" of the Messiah can even be discovered on the journey to and from Mount Sinai.

Manna from Heaven and Water from the Rock

Israel's exodus from Egypt led immediately to major challenges to their survival. They had nothing to drink (Ex 15:22-26), nothing to eat (Ex 16), and then nothing to drink again (Ex 17:1-7). Although this part of the narrative also includes their battle with Amalek (Ex 17:8-16) and the interaction between Moses and his father-in-law concerning how best to settle disputes for the Israelites (Ex 18), Israel's need for food and drink is a major theme of their journey from the Red Sea (Ex 15:22) to Mount Sinai (Ex 19:1-2) and of their time in the wilderness as a whole (Deut 8:3; Josh 5:12). This theme even frames both Israel's stay at Mount Sinai (note its conclusion in Numbers 10:11-13, followed by Numbers 11:4-35 concerning manna and quail) and their journey away from Sinai in Numbers 11–20 (see water from the rock in Num 20:1-13).[4]

Although Exodus 16 considered in isolation does not show that manna intentionally foreshadows the Messiah, it is compositionally related to other Messianic passages in the Pentateuch and the Old Testament. The analysis below will first link the *provision* of manna to the provision of salvation through the Messiah and then will secondarily link manna itself to the Messiah himself. In Exodus 16:4, the Lord says, "Behold, I am raining [Hiph. participle מַמְטִיר] bread from heaven [לֶחֶם מִן־הַשָּׁמָיִם] for you."

---

[4]Frank Polak, "Water, Rock, and Wood: Structure and Thought Pattern in the Exodus Narrative," *JANES* 25 (1997): 19, relatedly argues that the triad of water, rock, and wood dominates Ex 15:22–17:16 and unites the entire book of Exodus. William Propp, *Exodus 1–18*, Anchor Bible (New York: Doubleday, 1999), 606, counts "five spring narratives" in the Pentateuch, including also Ex 15:27 and Num 21:16-18. The latter passage does not significantly affect the literary framing argued for here.

Similarly, Psalm 78:24 says, "He rained [Hiph. מָטַר] manna upon them to eat; and the grain of heaven [וּדְגַן־שָׁמַיִם] he gave to them." Manna, which was so named because it was previously unknown to the Israelites (Ex 16:15; Deut 8:3, 16; see Is 53:1-3), is thus called both "bread from heaven" (Ex 16:4) and "grain of heaven" (Ps 78:24). Though in a different configuration, "grain" (דָּגָן) and "heaven" (שָׁמַיִם) also appear together in Isaac's blessing of Jacob in Genesis 27:28 ("may God give to you from the dew of heaven . . . and an abundance of grain"). Significantly, the heavenly provision of food here is directly tied to the coming of the Messiah, who brings pleasure to his father and rules the world (Gen 27:27, 29). It is as though the provision of manna ("bread from heaven") is a picture of the Messianic blessing as described in Genesis 27:28.

Furthermore, manna even seemed to arrive first in the form of "dew" (טַל, Ex 16:13-14; Num 11:9). Israel's enjoyment of "grain" and heavenly "dew" in Deuteronomy 33:28 is part of their eschatological salvation and the final defeat of their enemies (Deut 33:27, 29), which is accomplished by the Messiah (Num 24:17-19). Within the Pentateuch, "dew" (טַל) only appears in the Messianic blessing of Genesis 27:28 and the contrasting statement in Genesis 27:39 ("dew of heaven"), the manna passages of Exodus 16 and Numbers 11, and the often eschatological, final poetic section of Deuteronomy 32–33 (see Deut 32:2; 33:13). The intentional mention of "dew" as a type of precipitation is also suggested by the verb *rain* in Exodus 16:4 and Psalm 78:24, which also links to the Messianic prophecy of 2 Samuel 23:4.[5] The provision of manna, via its close association with dew, heaven, and grain, thus serves in the composition of the Pentateuch to intentionally foreshadow the provision of eschatological salvation through the Messiah.

Again configured differently but still strongly tied to the provision of food and precipitation from heaven, Isaiah 55:10 says that the Lord's saving "word" (Is 55:11-13; cf. Jn 1:1) is effective just like "the rain [הַגֶּשֶׁם] and the snow [that] come down from heaven [שָׁמַיִם] and do not return there but water the earth . . . and give seed to the sower and bread [לֶחֶם] to the eater." Reminiscent of Gen 27:27-28, the preceding context in Isaiah 55:1-3 has already established food and drink ("waters," "wine," "milk," "bread," "fatness")

---

[5] Polak, "Water, Rock, and Wood," 26, notes the water theme in the manna passage (the verb *rain* in Ex 16:4 and the noun *dew* in Ex 16:13-14).

as a metaphor for salvation through the Messiah. The "coming" and "eating" (Is 55:1) are intermingled with "listening" and "inclining the ear" to the speaker (Is 55:2-3). That spiritual food provided by God is in view here is implied by its being bought "without silver" (בְּלוֹא־כֶסֶף, Is 55:1; cf. Jn 6:5-7), which can only be exchanged for "what is not bread" (בְּלוֹא־לֶחֶם) and "what does not satisfy" (Is 55:2).

This is the same point Jesus is making in John 6:27, "Do not work for the food which perishes but the food which endures to eternal life, which the Son of Man will give to you" (cf. Jn 6:49). Note that in the narrative sequence of John 6 the nature of the "food" that the Messiah "gives" in John 6:27 is not yet clear. But when Jesus calls himself "the true bread from heaven" and "bread of God" (Jn 6:32-33), the implication is that he both *gives* the food (Jn 6:27) and *is* the food (Jn 6:32-33). There is a broad parallel to the Messiah being both priest and sacrifice, as mentioned previously (e.g., Gen 3:15). Jesus' invitation in John 6:35 to come and believe, and implicitly to eat and drink, unto eternal life (Jn 6:33, 40, 47) matches the invitation in Isaiah 55:1-3 and the promised blessing, "so that your soul will live." Participation in an "eternal covenant, the steadfast mercies of David" (Is 55:3) centers on the "eternal life" that Jesus, the Son of David, gives to all who believe in him (Jn 17:2). Psalm 89 also links the steadfast love and covenant faithfulness of the Lord to David (Ps 89:1-2, 24, 28, 33, 49) to the problem of death for "all the sons of Adam" (Ps 89:47-48).[6] In the Messianic son of David, all the nations will be blessed (Ps 72:17), even with "the blessing" of eternal life, which is like "dew" (Ps 133:3). But the way that he gives this eternal life to others is by laying down his own, as he makes clear in John 6:51, "the bread which I will give for the life of the world is my flesh" (see Jn 10:11, 15, 17, 18). The centrality of his death to the giving of life to others is likely the purpose of Jesus' instructions to eat his flesh and drink his blood in John 6:51-58 (cf. Jn 12:24).[7] The point is to partake by faith in the saving benefits of his death. If this was offensive

---

[6]Like Is 55:3, Ps 89:1-2, 24, 28, 33, 49 all use the word חֶסֶד ("steadfast love") and a word derived from the root אמן (usually denoting faithfulness). This collocation also appears in Deut 7:9; Ps 36:5; 40:10; 88:11; 92:2; 98:3; 100:5. In relation to Ps 89, the latter three are highly suggestive for Ps 93–100, which also emphasize the Lord as king.

[7]Andreas Köstenberger, *John*, Baker Exegetical Commentary on the New Testament (Grand Rapids: Baker, 2004), 215-16.

to his hearers, so would his resurrection be (Jn 6:60-62). As has already been shown, the Messiah's death and resurrection are at the core of the Messianic vision of the Pentateuch (Gen 49:9). If this vision is coherent, then the heavenly provision of food in the Messianic age (Gen 27:28), which is a picture of eschatological salvation, is accomplished through his death (Gen 3:15; 49:8-12) and partaken of by faith (Gen 15:6), just as John 6 says.

If Melchizedek does indeed intentionally foreshadow the Messiah (see chap. 2 above), then his bringing of food and drink in Genesis 14:18 (לֶחֶם וָיָיִן, "bread and wine") should also be related to the "raining" of manna, Israel's ongoing need for food and drink in the wilderness, and the offer of similar provisions in Isaiah 55:1-3. Moreover, Genesis 14:18 would also be compositionally related to the "grain and new wine" (דָּגָן וְתִירֹשׁ) promised to Jacob (Gen 27:28) as part of the Messianic prophecy in Genesis 27:27-29. Also suggestive is the personification of wisdom and her invitation, "Partake of my bread [לֶחֶם] and drink the wine [יַיִן] I have mixed" (Prov 9:5). Whereas she provides the food in this passage, her identification with a "tree of life" in Proverbs 3:18 comes closer to suggesting that she both provides the food and is herself (i.e., her fruit) the food. The preceding considerations thus suggest that the provision of manna intentionally foreshadows the eschatological salvation and heaven-sent blessings that the Messiah, "the wisdom of God" (1 Cor 1:24), brings and is in himself, especially in death.

The interrelationship of food and drink/water in several of these passages (see also Deut 8:15-16) bears on possible intentional foreshadowing concerning water from the rock (Ex 17:1-7; Num 20:2-13). Isaiah 55:1 had also invited "all who thirst" to come to the "waters." In comparison to the preceding investigation of manna, the analysis below will reveal an even stronger likelihood that the rock itself indeed intentionally foreshadows the Messiah, especially his suffering. Even though Moses was wrong to do it on the second occasion (Num 20:11-12; 27:14), the "striking" (נָכָה) of the rock is itself suggestive (Ex 17:6).[8] Moreover, the instrument used was

---

[8] That "Moses lifted up his hand" (וַיָּרֶם מֹשֶׁה אֶת־יָדוֹ) in Num 20:11-12 may also suggest his self-reliance (Deut 32:27; see the idiom "with a high hand [i.e., boldly]" in Ex 14:8; Num 15:30; 33:3). See also the exaltation of the Lord's hand in Ps 89:13 and Is 26:11 (also Mic 5:9?).

Moses' rod, which he used to strike the Nile (Ex 17:5; 7:20) and bring many other judgments on Egypt (Ex 8:5, 16; 9:23; 10:13; 14:16). The act of judgment cited in Exodus 17:5, however, was the first plague and involved a "striking" that resulted in "blood" (see Ex 12:12-13). This time, however, the role of water is reversed: it flows from a rock instead of being turned into blood.[9] Depicting a sort of salvation through judgment, striking the rock thus brings life, whereas striking the Nile brought death (Ex 7:21). The Messiah would also be "struck" (Zech 13:7; Mt 26:31) both by humans (Is 50:6) and by God (Is 53:4), and both blood and water would flow (Jn 19:34; 1 Jn 5:6, 8), the latter in more than one sense (Jn 4:10, 14; 7:37). As Isaiah 53:5 says, his "punishment" brings us "peace," and "by his stripes, we are healed." In Exodus 17:4-6, striking the rock even resolves the threat of Moses being "stoned" (סָקַל) by the people. Instead of Moses being struck to death by stones, he strikes a rock. Thus the striking of the rock not only preserves the lives of the thirsty Israelites (Ex 17:1) but also saves Moses' life, in a substitutionary manner no less. Though using a different word, the striking of the rock accords with the serpent striking (שׁוּף) the heel of the seed of the woman (Gen 3:15). This prophecy, as has already been shown, is compositionally related to several others in the Pentateuch concerning the Messiah's suffering and death (e.g, Gen 49:8-12; Ex 12:1-13).

Other significant intertextual relationships arise from the fact that the Lord was "standing" (עֹמֵד) "on *the* rock" (עַל־הַצּוּר) that Moses was to strike (Ex 17:6). In other words, Moses was not simply to strike any rock but only the one identified by the Lord by standing on it.[10] The specification of "the rock" (הַסֶּלַע) is maintained in Numbers 20:8-11. The themes of a specific rock (or stone) and the Lord "standing" on something are also found in Genesis 28:10-22 concerning Jacob's "ladder." As explained in chapter two above, Jacob took one of the stones at Bethel, used it as a pillow (Gen 28:11), and eventually set up this ordinary stone as memorial of the ladder in his dream (Gen 28:12, 18, 22). The description of this ladder is followed with the statement, "And behold, the LORD was standing [נִצָּב] on it" (Gen 28:13).

---

[9] Terence Fretheim, *Exodus*, Interpretation (Louisville: Knox, 1991), 190, "Just as Moses' striking the Nile led to water being unfit to drink, so here his striking the rock leads to water fit to drink."

[10] E.g., John Durham, *Exodus*, Word Biblical Commentary (Waco, TX: Word, 1987), 231, Moses is "to go along until he sees a rock Yahweh will designate by 'standing' upon it.... A specific rock is clearly intended."

Both Genesis 28:10-22 and Exodus 17:1-7 even involve dramatic proof of the Lord's presence for those who were unaware of it or doubted it. After waking up, Jacob exclaimed, "Surely the Lord is in this place, and I did not know" (Gen 28:16). The site where Moses struck the rock was named Massah and Meribah because the Israelites tested the Lord, saying "Is the Lord in our midst or not?" (Ex 17:7). What these parallels suggest is that "the stone" (הָאֶבֶן, Gen 28:18, 22) that represents the ladder that "the Lord was standing upon" (יְהוָה נִצָּב עָלָיו, Gen 28:13) corresponds compositionally to the "the rock" (הַצּוּר) that he "stands" (עֹמֵד) on in Exodus 17:6. Even the syntax of these verses is similar:

וְהִנֵּה יְהוָה נִצָּב עָלָיו	And behold, the Lord was standing upon it. (Gen 28:13)
הִנְנִי עֹמֵד לְפָנֶיךָ שָּׁם עַל־הַצּוּר	Behold, I am standing before you there on the rock. (Ex 17:6)

If this relationship is intentional, it implies that the rock that Moses struck intentionally foreshadows the Messiah, just as the ladder and the stone do in Genesis 28:10-22.[11] As demonstrated in chapter two above, the ladder that reaches the heavens contrasts with the Tower of Babel and is linked to the exalted Messiah in Genesis 49:8 via Joseph's dreams in Genesis 37:5-10. The stone represents this ladder, and the anointing of its "head" (Gen 28:18) carries kingly and priestly overtones. The rock in Exodus 17:6, however, is neither exalted nor anointed, but struck. In this way, the stone in Genesis 28:18, 22 and the rock in Exodus 17:6 balance one another with their respective emphases on glory and suffering. Genesis 3:15 has already prepared the reader for this paradox. The priestly seed of the woman will cleanse creation of uncleanness but will be bitten on the heel in the process. He will mediate between heaven and earth (Gen 28:12) but will also be struck (Ex 17:6). Likewise, the compositional relationship of Genesis 49:8-12 to the Joseph story shows that the kingly rule of the Messiah will be realized through death.

---

[11] The combination of "behold" and the Lord "standing [נצב/עמד] upon" something only appears elsewhere in the OT in Amos 7:7 and perhaps Gen 18:2 (since the arrival of the three men involve an appearance of the Lord; see vv. 1, 13-14). Ezek 3:23, which lacks the same use of the preposition עַל ("upon"), comes close.

The different words for "stone" (אֶבֶן, Gen 28:18, 22) and "rock" (צוּר, Ex 17:6) are even strategically reused as titles for the Lord in major poetic sections (Gen 49:24; Deut 32:4). In other words, whereas the Lord identified "the rock" in Exodus 17:6, in other Pentateuchal passages he is identified *with* the rock/stone itself. In Genesis 49:24, the same Jacob who set up a "stone" as a memorial at Bethel and returned to it years later (Gen 31:13; 35:1-15) referred to God at the end of his life as "the shepherd, the stone of Israel," who had guided him this whole time (Gen 48:15; see Is 30:29).[12] In other words, the stone pillar itself had not moved, but "the stone of Israel" which it represented had been with him all the time. If this "stone" is compositionally related to the "rock" in Exodus 17:6, then it provides one reason why Paul might have described the "rock" as having followed the Israelites in the wilderness (1 Cor 10:4).[13] The word translated "rock" (צוּר) in Exodus 17:6 is correspondingly used as a title for the Lord in Deuteronomy 32:4, "The Rock [הַצּוּר], his work is blameless." This context also says that he guided Israel through the wilderness (Deut 32:10-12).[14]

The repetition of "rock" in Deuteronomy 32 will further increase the likelihood that the rock that Moses struck intentionally foreshadows the Messiah. After Deuteronomy 32:4, the next time this word appears is in the context of the Lord's provision for Israel in the wilderness, "he suckled him with honey from the rock [סֶלַע], and oil from the flint [חַלְמִישׁ] of the rock [צוּר]" (Deut 32:13). The use of two different words for "rock" matches

---

[12]See Jürgen Ebach, *Genesis 37–50*, Herders Theologischer Kommentar zum Alten Testament (Freiburg: Herder, 2007), 627-28, who also traces additional connections to Shechem through the parallel title, "God, the God of Israel," that Jacob used there (Gen 33:18-20; see Gen 37:12-14; 48:22; "mountain slope" is a wordplay on "Shechem"). This line of poetry ("from there is a shepherd, the stone of Israel") is nevertheless difficult. See S. R. Driver, *The Book of Genesis* (London: Methuen and Co., 1948), 392, "The line undoubtedly expressed some thought parallel to that of clause *c* ["from the hands of the Mighty One of Jacob"]; but what exactly that thought was, it seems impossible now to discover." For more discussion, see Raymond de Hoop, *Genesis 49 in Its Literary and Historical Context* (Leiden: Brill, 1999), 198-205.
[13]John Sailhamer, *The Pentateuch as Narrative: A Biblical-Theological Commentary* (Grand Rapids: Zondervan, 1992), 277, also observes in this connection that God provides water from the rock at the beginning and end of Israel's time in the wilderness (Ex 17:1-7; Num 20:1-13).
[14]For a view similar to ours, see Peter Leithart, *Deep Exegesis: The Mystery of Reading Scripture* (Waco, TX: Baylor University Press, 2009), 37. See the remark on Ps 78:15-20, 35 by James Hamilton, *God's Glory in Salvation Through Judgment* (Wheaton, IL: Crossway, 2010), 97, "It would seem that Yahweh is being struck so that the people might drink." Cf. Abner Chou, *The Hermeneutics of the Biblical Writers: Learning to Interpret Scripture from the Prophets and Apostles* (Grand Rapids: Kregel, 2018), 110-13, 136.

the two different words used in Exodus 17:6 and Numbers 20:8-11. Though some scholars argue that Deuteronomy 32:13-14 concern a fruitful land instead of the wilderness (see Deut 8:7-8), the allusion to both episodes concerning water from the rock still stands.[15] The uncommon word for "flint" is accordingly related to the same provision as recounted in Deuteronomy 8:15. This word appears nowhere else in the Pentateuch, and aside from Number 20:8-11, the first word for "rock" in Deuteronomy 32:13 (סֶלַע) only appears once elsewhere in the Pentateuch in Numbers 24:21. Outside of Exodus 17:6, Deuteronomy 8:15, and Deuteronomy 32, the last word for "rock" in Deuteronomy 32:13 (צוּר) is not common in the Pentateuch either, appearing only in Exodus 33:21-22 and Numbers 23:9. Thus these three terms (צוּר, חַלָּמִישׁ, סֶלַע) strongly suggest an intertextual relationship between Deuteronomy 32:13 and these Pentateuchal passages concerning water from the rock, as well as the major poetic section in Numbers 23–24.

Significantly, the meaning of the Lord's provision of water from the rock in these passages is recast in Deuteronomy 32:13. It is not water that flows from the rock but instead "honey" and "oil." Eckhart Otto notes that the motif here, that is, that "Yahweh lets honey to be sucked from rock and oil from flint, links Deut 8:15, [where] Yahweh lets water gush from flint in the wilderness, which alludes to the water miracles in Ex 17:1-7 and Num 20:8-11 . . . with the motif of the abundance of the Promised Land. No longer water, but honey and oil flow from the rock."[16] The context of

---

[15] J. Gordon McConville, *Deuteronomy*, Apollos Old Testament Commentary (Downers Grove, IL: InterVarsity Press, 2002), 455, who thinks that whereas Deut 32:10-12 concern the wilderness, Deut 32:13-14 concern a fruitful land. Similarly, Jack Lundbom, *Deuteronomy: A Commentary* (Grand Rapids: Eerdmans, 2013), 879-83; Jeffrey Tigay, *Deuteronomy*, JPS Torah Commentary (Philadelphia: Jewish Publication Society, 1996), 303-4. The exhortation to remember the Lord while enjoying his provision in Deut 8:7-20 contrasts with the failure to do so in Deut 32:9-20. Deut 8 moves back and forth between the Lord's provision in the wilderness and in the land. Deut 32:10-14 certainly begins with the wilderness (Deut 32:10-12), and the abundance in Deut 32:13-14 arguably befits the Promised Land, although there is no clear transition between these two sections (with being borne on eagle's wings in Deut 32:11 even seemingly parallel to riding on the heights of the land in Deut 32:13; though see Ex 19:4) and the mention of "Bashan" (Deut 32:14) perhaps suggesting the east side of the Jordan (Num 21:33). It is possible that the ambiguity of Deut 32:13-14 allows it to relate to both the water from the rock episodes and Israel's later complacency in the land (Deut 31:20). The emphasis in Deut 32:10-14 is on the Lord's provision generally.

[16] Eckhart Otto, *Deuteronomium 23,16–34,12*, Herders Theologischer Kommentar zum Alten Testament (Freiburg: Herder, 2017), 2179.

Deuteronomy 32:13 emphasizes abundant provision through additional references to produce of the field, curds, milk, fat, the finest of wheat, the blood of the grape, and wine (Deut 32:13-14), much like Gen 27:27-28 and Isaiah 55. Deuteronomy 32:12-14 thus recasts the water from the rock in Exodus 17:6 and Numbers 20:8-11 into a picture of the Lord's abundant provision for the Israelites. Likewise, Psalm 78 characterizes this water supply as being "like the great depths" (כִּתְהֹמוֹת רַבָּה, Ps 78:15), which "flowed" (זוּב) and was "overflowing" (Ps 78:20; cf. Ps 105:41). The verb *flow* is more commonly used to describe the Promised Land as "flowing with milk and honey" (Ex 3:8).

Lest the reader think that "rock" as a title for the Lord in Deuteronomy 32:4 has been left behind in the description of his abundant provision (Deut 32:12-14), Deuteronomy 32:15 immediately refers to the Lord as "the rock of their salvation." Although he alone had provided for them, the Israelites grew complacent, "forsook God who made them," and "considered the rock of their salvation [צוּר יְשֻׁעָתוֹ] to be a fool." The strategic use of *rock* (צוּר) in Deuteronomy 32:4, 13, 15 demonstrates not only that the Lord is "the rock" in a general sense but also hints that "the rock," which abundantly provided for the Israelites but was rejected, was the Lord himself. The same "rock" even "gave birth" to the Israelites (Deut 32:18; note the marked use of *wayyiqtol* verb form as in Deut 32:13, 15) and handed them over to their enemies (Deut 32:30). The word *rock* is used two more times in Deuteronomy 32:31, 37 to express the Lord's incomparability compared to idols, which are an inferior kind of "rock" (see Num 24:21). Though the Lord as "rock" is not explicitly "struck" in Deuteronomy 32, he is relatedly forsaken, insulted, made jealous, provoked, and forgotten despite enduring labor pains (Deut 32:15-21; Prov 10:1). Deuteronomy 32 thus seems to interpret "the rock" in Exodus 17:6/Numbers 20:8-11 as representing the Lord himself, especially as one who abundantly provided for Israel. The intertextual relationship of Exodus 17:6 to Jacob's ladder/stone pillar suggests Messianic overtones in Deuteronomy 32. Furthermore, the theme of suffering is common to Exodus 17:6 and Deuteronomy 32, which fits the Messianic vision of the Pentateuch as expressed in Genesis 3:15 and Genesis 49:8-12.

There is one other Pentateuchal passage involving "standing" on a "rock." However, unlike Exodus 17:6, it involves *Moses* standing on a rock

(Ex 33:21). It uses the word for "stand" (נָצַב) found in Genesis 28:13 and the word for "rock" (צוּר) that is used in Exodus 17:6. The context is Israel's "great sin" (Ex 32:20) of the golden calf (Ex 32:1-6), which resulted in the Lord threatening to wipe them out completely (Ex 32:7-10). Through a combination of Moses' intercession (Ex 32:11-13, 30-32), his retributive actions (Ex 32:19-29), and divine judgment (Ex 32:35), the Lord's wrath subsided somewhat (Ex 32:14, 33-34). But the Lord's initial solution that his angel lead Moses and Israel henceforth into the Promised Land (Ex 32:34; 33:2) signaled a continuing problematic relationship between the Lord and Israel (Ex 33:4-5), which sharply contrasts with Moses' intimate "face to face" (פָּנִים אֶל־פָּנִים) relationship with the Lord (Ex 33:7-11). In the subsequent passage, Moses successfully appealed to the Lord that his "presence" or "face" (פָּנֶיךָ/פָּנַי) go with Israel (Ex 33:14-15), which is equivalent to "your going with us" (Ex 33:16; 34:9). Relatedly, Moses requested to know the Lord's "ways" (Ex 33:13) and "glory" (Ex 33:18), which the Lord granted and related to his goodness, name, mercy, grace, sovereignty, and justice (Ex 33:19; 34:1-7). But Moses was not allowed to see his "face" (פָּנַי) (Ex 33:20, 23) and had to "stand on the rock" (וְנִצַּבְתָּ עַל־הַצּוּר), be put "in the cleft of the rock" (בְּנִקְרַת הַצּוּר), and be protected by the Lord's "palm" (Ex 33:21-22).

In addition to the language and themes surrounding "standing on the rock," there are additional reasons to link Moses' experience as described in Exodus 33:21-22 to Exodus 17:6 and Genesis 28:13. As shown above, those two passages also emphasize the theme of the Lord's presence (Gen 28:16-17; Ex 17:7). The form "in our midst" (בְּקִרְבֵּנוּ) is common to Exodus 17:7 and Exodus 34:9. Furthermore, the specification of a "place with me" (מָקוֹם אִתִּי) for Moses' to stand in Exodus 33:21 is paralleled by the Jacob's recognition of the importance of the "place" (מָקוֹם) where he had spent the night (Gen 28:11, 16-17, 19). Both "places" were sites of divine revelation (Gen 28:12-15; Ex 34:5-7). Even the particle *behold* (הִנֵּה) recurs in Exodus 33:21 in connection with Moses' "standing" ("Behold, there is a place with me"; cf. Gen 28:13; Ex 17:6). The specificity of the "place" in Genesis 28 and Exodus 33:21 dovetails with the specificity of "the rock" and "the cleft of the rock" where Moses was to be protected, which in turn parallels the specification of "the rock" in Exodus 17:6 as pointed out above.

What appears to be happening compositionally is that Exodus 33:21-22 is being deliberately linked to the intentional foreshadowing of the Messiah in Genesis 28:10-22 and Exodus 17:6 while at the same time adding its own contribution to the Messianic vision of the Pentateuch by taking "the rock" in another direction. While it is still something to be stood on, the emphasis in Exodus 33:21-22 is on the rock as the divine means of protection for Moses. Contrary to what his "face-to-face" relationship with the Lord might imply if taken in isolation (Ex 33:7-11), even Moses cannot endure the presence/face of God without standing on this rock and being put by the Lord in "the cleft of the rock." These references to "the rock" are framed by the phrases "a place with me" and "my hand will cover you," which relate the protection provided by the rock to protection personally and directly provided by the Lord himself. This accords with the Lord as "the rock" in Deuteronomy 32:4 and explicit statements of the Lord as a protective "rock" (צוּר) frequently found in the Psalter (e.g., Ps 18:2, also סֶלַע; Ps 27:5; 31:2-3, also סֶלַע; Ps 62:2; 71:3, also סֶלַע). If Exodus 17:6 and Exodus 33:21-22 are intended to be understood in light of one another, then the rock that Moses struck, which had in a sense substituted for Moses (Ex 17:4-6), has even more clearly become his protection (Ex 33:20-23). Once again, "the rock" has saved Moses' life.

The cognate verb (נָקַר) of the noun *cleft* (נְקָרָה) appears in Isaiah 51:1 in connection with the righteous who are exhorted to "look to the rock from which you were hewn [הַבִּיטוּ אֶל־צוּר חֻצַּבְתֶּם] and to the quarry from which you were *dug out* [מַקֶּבֶת בּוֹר נֻקַּרְתֶּם]." The repeated language of "rock" and "cleft"/"dig out" in Exodus 33:21-22 and Isaiah 51:1 also parallels the striking of the rock in Exodus 17:6. The verb *hew* (חָצַב) in Isaiah 51:1 is used of hewing stone (2 Kings 12:13; 1 Chron 22:2; Job 19:24; Is 22:16), which involves an action closely related to striking.[17] The Septuagint reads the (unpointed) verbs חצבתם and נקרתם as active ("look to the strong rock *you hewed* and to the hole of the pit of *you dug out*"), further strengthening the intertextual connection to water from the rock in Exodus 17:6 and Numbers 20:8-11. Isaiah 51:2 continues with a related exhortation to "look to Abraham your father and to Sarah who travailed [in birth] for you

---

[17]See also the mountain quarries in Deut 8:9; 1 Kings 5:29; 2 Chron 2:2, 18. Similar to Is 51:1, pits and cisterns can also be "hewn" (Deut 6:11; Neh 9:25; Is 5:2; Jer 2:13).

[תְּחוֹלְלְכֶם]." The collocation of "rock" and "travail" recalls Deuteronomy 32:18 in which God, "the rock," similarly "travailed for you" (מְחֹלְלֶךָ). The Septuagint reading of Isaiah 51:1 can even be taken as especially distinguishing between the "rock you hewed" (Is 51:1) and Abraham/Sarah (Is 51:2). The noun *cleft* (נִקְרָה) in Exodus 33:22 suggestively appears in the plural in Isaiah 2:21 (the only other appearance in the Old Testament), where it concerns idolaters who are hiding in caves from the Lord (Is 2:19-21). They enter caves and clefts of "rocks" (צֻרִים, Is 2:19, 21; 57:5), whereas they had been instructed to enter "the rock" in Isaiah 2:10. As in Deuteronomy 32, this is a frequent title for the Lord in the book of Isaiah (see Is 8:14, also אֶבֶן; Is 17:10; 26:4; 30:29; 44:8), which overlaps with references to water from the rock (Is 48:21; 51:1) and to the Messiah (Is 28:16, אֶבֶן; Is 32:2, סֶלַע). In Isaiah 50:7, the Messiah sets his face "like flint" (כַּחַלָּמִישׁ) as he braves "those who strike" (Hiph. participle נָכָה) him and insult him (Is 50:6).[18] These manifold considerations suggest that Moses' striking of the rock with his staff in Exodus 17:6 intentionally foreshadows the fatal striking of the divine Messiah for the salvation of the world.

Bezalel, the Tabernacle Builder

Although unmentioned in the New Testament, there are good reasons to consider Bezalel, the leader of the tabernacle construction project, as intentionally foreshadowing the Messiah. Like Melchizedek king of Salem, Bezalel appears suddenly on the narrative scene. Unlike Melchizedek, he does have a genealogy. He is the son of Uri, the son of Hur, from the tribe of Judah (Ex 31:2), and his name means "in the shadow of God" (בְּצַלְאֵל). The importance of his name is suggested by the first thing that the Lord says about him to Moses, "See, I have called by *name* [רְאֵה קָרָאתִי בְשֵׁם] Bezalel" (Ex 31:2). Similarly, the first thing Moses says to Israel about him is, "See, the Lord has called by name [רְאוּ קָרָא יְהוָה בְּשֵׁם] Bezalel" (Ex 35:30). In the intervening context (Ex 33), one of the ways Moses' intimate relationship with the Lord is described is "you have found favor in my eyes and I know you by name [וָאֵדָעֲךָ בְּשֵׁם]" (Ex 33:17). In granting Moses' request to see his glory (Ex 33:18), the Lord says, "I will call on the name of

---

[18]Besides the three passages cited (Deut 8:15; 32:13; Is 50:7), the only other two appearances of "flint" in the OT are in Job 28:9 and Ps 114:8.

the Lord before you" (וְקָרָאתִי בְשֵׁם יְהוָה לְפָנֶיךָ, Ex 33:19). In fact, the Lord's calling on Bezalel's name (Ex 31:2; 35:30) frames his calling on his own name (Ex 33:19; 34:5). Not only does this suggest a sharing of the divine glory associated with the name of the Lord (Ex 33:18; 34:5-7), it even more strongly suggests the importance of Bezalel's name. If the latter is so, then it connotes his being especially under divine protection and blessing ("in the shadow [צֵל] of God"), as in Psalm 17:8; 36:8; 91:1 ("in the shadow of the Almighty"); Isaiah 25:4-5; 49:2; Ezekiel 17:23; and Hosea 14:8 (cf. Ps 23:4; Is 30:2-3; Ezek 31:17). There may even be an intentional wordplay and semantic overlap with the divine "image" (צֶלֶם; Gen 1:26-27) in which humanity was created ("in our/his image" [בְּצַלְמוֹ/בְּצַלְמֵנוּ], "in the image of God" [בְּצֶלֶם אֱלֹהִים]). Bezalel's ancestors' names, "Uri" (אוּרִי) and "Hur" (חוּר), are also plays on words for "light" (אוֹר) and "spirit" (רוּחַ), recalling Genesis 1:2-3.[19]

The tribe of Judah has already been singled out as the tribe from which the Messiah will come (Gen 49:8-12). But Bezalel certainly is not the Messiah. The era of the "last days" has not yet dawned, and he is not a king over Israel and the nations. Instead, he will lead the construction of the tabernacle. Moses directed the Israelites to Bezalel as the divinely appointed man who will lead them to its completion (Ex 35:30–36:1). And complete it he did, with no indication of Moses' involvement in making the components of the tabernacle even though Moses was the one who received the instructions (Ex 38:22). For this task, Bezalel was "filled" with "the Spirit of God" (Ex 31:3). The Spirit of God had also been in Joseph (Gen 41:38), the one on whom the Messianic prophecy in Genesis 49:8-12 was mostly patterned. In both cases, the result was that each person had wisdom—one to manage the storage and distribution of food (Gen 41:33, 39), the other to build the tabernacle (Ex 31:3). For both men, their wisdom involved the understanding of divine revelation, followed by its "translation" and application to creation. Joseph correctly interpreted Pharaoh's dreams, which were given by God (Gen 41:25, 28, 32), and then proposed appropriate measures to prepare for the upcoming famine. Bezalel's work

---

[19] Isaac Kalimi, *Metathesis in the Hebrew Bible: Wordplay as a Literary and Exegetical Device* (Peabody, MA: Hendrickson, 2018), 32, points out that "Hur" and "spirit" consist of the same three letters in reverse order.

on the tabernacle and all its furnishings (Ex 31:7-11) implicitly involved understanding the divine "pattern" revealed to Moses on the mountain (Ex 25:9, 40) and then making it an earthly reality. This pattern evidently still required the additional making of "plans" (מַחֲשָׁבֹת, Ex 31:4; 35:32-33, 35). Similarly, God himself, in concert with his own Spirit (Gen 1:2; Ps 33:6), created the heavens and the earth with wisdom (Gen 1:1; Prov 3:19; 8:22-31) according to his own "plans" (Ps 33:11; Is 55:8-9; Jer 29:11).

The only others in the Pentateuch described as having the Spirit in or on them were Moses, the seventy elders, and Balaam (Num 11:17-29; 24:2), and Joshua was the only one "filled" with a "spirit of wisdom" (Deut 34:9; cf. Num 27:18). Like the Messiah, Joshua was to lead the Israelites into the Promised Land to "possess" it (Deut 31:3) and be like a "shepherd" to them (Num 27:17).[20] Though he certainly was not the Messiah, since he was from the tribe of Ephraim (Num 13:8, 16) and did not bring permanent rest to Israel (Heb 4:8), there is a possibility that the Pentateuch at points intentionally foreshadows the Messiah through Joshua. In view of the different ways Joseph, Bezalel, Moses (see chap. 7 below), and perhaps Joshua each intentionally foreshadow the Messiah,[21] it is not surprising that later Old Testament passages predict that he will be filled with the Spirit (Is 11:2-3), even though the Pentateuch has no direct prophecy that says this. Accordingly, the same Spirit active at creation and in Joseph, Moses, Bezalel, and Joshua will also be at work in the new creation (Is 48:16; Ezek 36:26-27).

The work of the Spirit has been discussed by scholars as one of the many parallels between creation and the tabernacle. John Sailhamer also lists the repetition and structuring function of "And God said"/"And the LORD said," the parallels between the Garden of Eden and the tabernacle (see chap. 1 above), the Sabbath, and a "Fall" (see Ex 32).[22] In this scheme, the divine speech focusing on humankind on day six of creation (Gen 1:26-30) even parallels the sixth instance of divine speech concerning the tabernacle

---

[20]The description of him "going out" and "coming in" before the people (see also Num 27:21) is used of kings David and Solomon (1 Sam 18:16; 2 Chron 1:10).

[21]We have intentionally limited ourselves to a brief discussion of select Pentateuchal passages here. A full treatment of whether or not Joshua intentionally foreshadows the Messiah would require more discussion, especially concerning the book of Joshua.

[22]Sailhamer, *Pentateuch as Narrative*, 298-99.

(Ex 31:1) that focuses on Bezalel (Ex 31:2-11), who is a sort of "better Adam" and a partial picture of the seed of the woman. The completion of the "work" (מְלָאכָה) by this Spirit-filled man (Ex 31:3, 5; 39:43) fittingly led to the glory of the Lord "filling" the tabernacle (Ex 40:34-35). This "work" relates contextually to the Sabbath instructions in the same context (Ex 31:14-15; 35:2) and to the divine "work" and Sabbath at creation (Gen 2:1-3; Ex 20:9-10). Thus the "completion" (כָּלָה) of work (Gen 2:2; Ex 39:32; 40:33) and the purpose of the Sabbath relates to the glory of the Lord filling not only the tabernacle but all creation (Num 14:21; Ps 72:19; Is 6:3; Hab 2:14). It is as though Bezalel, functioning as Adam should have and whose work parallels the divine work at creation, provides a foretaste of the work of the seed of the woman in ushering in the glory of the Lord to all the earth in conjunction with eternal Sabbath rest (Gen 3:15; 49:8-12; Heb 4:9-11).

Further investigation reveals that the Messiah's rule as king and Bezalel's role in constructing the tabernacle are not two divergent tasks. In Exodus 15:17-18, the Lord's hands establish a sanctuary, and he reigns forever and ever. Furthermore, other Old Testament passages indicate that he will reign forever precisely from a sanctuary in Zion. In an eschatological context, Isaiah 24:23 predicts, "The LORD of Hosts reigns on Mount Zion." Similarly, the declaration that "the LORD reigns" in Psalm 99:1 is followed by the related "the LORD is great in Zion" (Ps 99:2) as well as a command to "worship at his holy mountain" (Ps 99:9; cf. Ps 146:10). Like the divine king who reigns there, Mount Zion itself "will not be moved; it remains forever" (Ps 125:1). As pointed out in chapter four above, the depiction of the Lord as a warrior-king in the Song of the Sea (Ex 15) resembles the depiction of the Messiah as a warrior-king in Genesis 49 and Numbers 24. Each depiction includes imagery related to a garden or sanctuary (Gen 49:11-12; Ex 15:17; Num 24:6). Like the Lord, the Messiah also reigns "on Zion, my holy mountain" (Ps 2:6), as both king and priest (Ps 110:1-4).

Accordingly, the two acts of building a "house" and reigning eternally are predicted of David's "seed" (2 Sam 7:12-13). Zechariah 6:12-13 also highlights these same acts and explicitly ties in his priestly status. In chapter one above, the use of the singular pronoun *he* in 2 Samuel 7:13 to refer to this seed was shown to indicate that David's "seed" refers to an individual, not his collective seed. Moreover, the intertextual relationship with Genesis 15:4 implies that this individual will be the fulfillment of both the Abrahamic and Davidic covenants. Hence, this individual is the Messiah, the son of David, and the son of Abraham (Mt 1:1). Unlike David, who was not allowed to build the temple because he had shed so much blood in various wars (1 Chron 22:8; 28:3), the Messiah will build a sanctuary and reign forever just like the Lord in Exodus 15:17-18. To be sure, the Messiah is also a mighty warrior, but he wins the decisive battle by laying down his own life (Gen 3:15). His eternal reign from a sanctuary leads back to Genesis 1–3 with the sanctuary-like Garden of Eden that the Lord God "planted" (Gen 2:8; Ex 15:17) for Adam both to rule (Gen 1:26) and to "serve" and "keep" like a priest (Gen 2:15).

The themes of priest/sanctuary, the Spirit, and the tribe of Judah in the Messianic vision of the Pentateuch converge in Bezalel and suggest the use of him to intentionally foreshadow the Messiah. Second Samuel 7 and the other Old Testament passages discussed above serve to further clarify this. When viewed together, Isaiah 11:2-3, Zech 4:6-7, and Zech 6:12-13 attribute the building of an eschatological temple to a Spirit-filled Messiah. Like a priest, Bezalel handles holy articles and has the ability "to teach" (לְהוֹרֹת, Ex 35:34; Lev 10:11; cf. Gen 46:28; Lev 14:57). Even though Solomon was also a temple-builder, he probably did not handle the holy articles. In particular, the ark was already made and was transported into the temple (1 Kings 8:1-4). It is even conceivable that Bezalel's descent from Judah, instead of Levi or Aaron, and his leadership of the apparently priestly task of constructing the tabernacle and its holy articles may serve as another link between Melchizedek, priest-king of Salem, and the Messiah, priest-king in Zion (Ps 110:1-4).[23] Furthermore, if it can be

---

[23]See Joshua G. Mathews, *Melchizedek's Alternative Priestly Order: A Compositional Analysis of Genesis 14:18-20 and Its Echoes Throughout the Tanak*, Bulletin for Biblical Research Supplements (Winona Lake, IN: Eisenbrauns, 2013), 97-112, which insightfully discusses Aaron, Jethro, and Melchizedek in the compositional strategy of the Pentateuch. See also the comment on 2 Sam 8:18 in John Sailhamer, *NIV Compact Bible Commentary* (Grand Rapids: Zondervan, 1994), 243, "The statement at the conclusion of the chapter that 'David's sons were priests' (NIV, 'royal advisers') is important in showing that David's kingship was envisioned by the author of Samuel as a form of priesthood. Certainly it was not of the Levitical priests since Zadok and Ahimelech were the Levitical priests. The kind of priests identified with the sons of David was

established that building the tabernacle is a priestly task, then so is building a house for the Lord's name (2 Sam 7:13). Bezalel's superiority to the Levitical priesthood could be suggested through his direct handling of these articles (including the ark) and the reality that without his prior ministry, the priests cannot even function as divinely commanded. Meanwhile, Aaron had fashioned the golden calf and led the Israelites to worship it (Ex 32:1-6). Although Moses was the one who set up the tabernacle (Ex 40:1-33), his role was as a facilitator, and the silence concerning his involvement otherwise suggests that he did not have the requisite "wisdom/skill." Instead, it was the "sons of Israel," led by Bezalel, who made the tent, curtains, poles, and furnishings (Ex 39:32-43). The honor of being its builder or project leader did not primarily belong to Moses (see Heb 3:2-6).

Bezalel's successful leadership of the Israelites to construct the tabernacle is a striking contrast to their catastrophic failures under Moses in the surrounding context (see chap. 9 below). While Moses should not therefore be blamed, the fact remains that the portrait of the Israelites in the narrative includes constant grumbling (Ex 15:24; 16:2, 7-8; 17:3), worship of the golden calf (Ex 32:1-6), worship of goat idols (Lev 17:7), and ultimately an unbelieving refusal to enter the Promised Land (Num 14:2-4, 11). While this contrast could lead to psychologizing about the reasons for Israel's different responses to each leader, a more productive line of inquiry, we believe, is to recognize the beauty of a people that was otherwise hopelessly unbelieving and rebellious willingly and sacrificially following the Spirit-filled leadership of Bezalel, who in the compositional strategy of the Pentateuch intentionally foreshadows the Messiah.

Not only is this supported through the above analysis, but additional new-covenant dynamics are at play in the narrative. One example is the aforementioned role of the Spirit (Ex 31:3). In fact, the only times the Spirit is mentioned in the entire literary account of Israel's stay at Mount Sinai (Ex 19–Num 10) is in connection with Bezalel (Ex 28:3; 31:3; 35:31).

---

apparently that which was already represented in Melchizedek, a priest-king (Ge 14:18-20). According to Ps 110, David himself recognized in the Davidic covenant of ch. 7 [2 Sam 7] a divine promise that his descendants were to be priests 'in the order of Melchizedek' (Ps 110:4). Also in the postexilic period, the hope of the restoration of the Davidic kingship centered on the expectation of a king who would also be a priest (cf. Zec 6:9-15)."

God's Spirit was at work in the crossing of the Red Sea (Ex 15:8, 10) and in the incident concerning Moses and the seventy elders (Num 11:17, 25-29) but not noted anywhere in between. Besides supporting Paul's sharp contrast between Sinai/Deuteronomic "law" and Spirit (e.g., Rom 7:6; Gal 5:18; 2 Cor 3:6), the activity of the Spirit explains Bezalel's success (Ex 35:21-29; 36:1-7), which is all the more surprising in view of Israel's catastrophic failures in the preceding, following, and present contexts (Ex 32:1-6). The sometimes-embarrassing tribe of Dan (Gen 49:17; Lev 24:11; Judg 1:34-35; 13:2-5; 18:1-31; Amos 8:14) even gets a starring role (Ex 31:6). Under the Spirit-filled leadership of the Judahite Bezalel, it is as though the reader gets a brief glimpse of what a new-covenant people looks like.

These new-covenant dynamics become even clearer through a closer look at the use of the word s/Spirit (רוּחַ) in this context. It was not only Bezalel who was "filled" with the "Spirit of God" and "with wisdom and understanding and knowledge and in all manner of work" (Ex 31:3; 35:31) but "all the wise of heart [כָּל־חַכְמֵי־לֵב] whom I have filled with the s/Spirit of wisdom" (Ex 28:3). In view of the "Spirit of wisdom" on Joshua as a reference to God's Spirit (Num 27:18; Deut 34:9), it is likely that those who were to make Aaron's garments in Exodus 28:3 were also, like Bezalel, filled with the Spirit. Cornelius Houtman refers to "the divine inspiration of the craftsmen, [which] guarantees that the clothing will satisfy YHWH's requirements."[24] Bezalel's assistant, Oholiab the Danite, was also "filled" with "wisdom of heart" (חָכְמַת־לֵב) for this work (Ex 35:34-35). Oholiab and "all the wise of heart" (כָּל־חֲכַם־לֵב) were to play a role in making "all that I have commanded you" (Ex 31:6). Not even Bezalel did the work of constructing the tabernacle alone (Ex 36:1-2). It is true that Bezalel did work directly on this project, including making the ark (Ex 37:1) and even "all that the LORD commanded him" (Ex 38:22), but the "wise" among the Israelites made the priestly garments (Ex 28:3; 39:1-31) so that "the sons of Israel did according to all that the LORD commanded them" (Ex 39:32). The alternation between singular and plural verbs concerning who was doing the work also supports the idea of a collaborative effort involving

---

[24]Cornelius Houtman, *Exodus*, Historical Commentary on the Old Testament, trans. Sierd Woudstra (Leuven: Peeters, 2000), 3:473.

Bezalel and the Israelites (Ex 36:8; 39:1-9).²⁵ When the Israelites brought all the components of the tabernacle to Moses, including the ark and the other furnishings (Ex 39:33-41), the narrative says that *they* completed "all the service" (כָּל־הָעֲבֹדָה) and "all the work" (כָּל־הַמְּלָאכָה, Ex 39:42-43). Bezalel had already been mentioned by name for the last time (Ex 38:22), and the progress of the narrative shifts more of the credit to the Israelites, as though they had accomplished "greater works" (Jn 14:12). Another effect of this shift is to avoid having Moses directly evaluate Bezalel (see Ex 39:43), which would imply Moses' superiority.

The phrase "wise of heart" is used several times in Proverbs of the godly who possess the more fully orbed wisdom that is rooted in the fear of the Lord (Prov 1:7). The "wise of heart receives commandments" (Prov 10:8), will have as his "servant" the "fool" (Prov 11:29), and will be called "discerning" (Prov 16:21). Several other passages speak of the "heart of the wise" or the like (Prov 16:23; 18:15; 23:15; Eccles 7:4; 8:5; 10:2). Such wisdom is tied to faith in the Lord (Prov 3:5-6) and to the "law" (תּוֹרָה) written "on the tablet of your heart" (עַל־לוּחַ לִבֶּךָ, Prov 3:1-3; see Prov 7:1-4), which are strong new covenant themes. This suggests that the tabernacle workers were not simply skilled but are cast in the narrative as acting like a new-covenant people.

The workers' inward motivation to participate supports this further. Not only had they been given the wisdom/skill to do the work by the Lord (Ex 31:6), but on hearing the call for "all the wise of heart among you" to help (Ex 35:10), "all whose hearts stirred them" (כֹּל אֲשֶׁר נְשָׂאוֹ לִבּוֹ) volunteered (Ex 36:2). This inward motivation was even shared by the people as a whole, who, on hearing the call to give raw materials (Ex 35:5-9), gave generously (Ex 35:21), both men and women (Ex 35:22). Without being threatened, their "hearts stirred them" (נְשָׂאוֹ לִבּוֹ) and their "spirits made them willing" (נָדְבָה רוּחוֹ אֹתוֹ, Ex 35:21). Their gifts included gold, yarn, linen, goat's hair, animal skins, and silver, bronze, acacia wood (Ex 35:22-24). Every woman who was "wise of heart" made fabric out of the raw materials (Ex 35:25-26), and the leaders donated precious stones, spices, and oil

---

²⁵Houtman, *Exodus* 3:420, 471. Houtman further distinguishes between the function of the singular verb in Ex 28:2 ("you will make") and "and you [sg.]" in Ex 28:1, which requires direct action by Moses (472).

(Ex 35:27-28). The offerings made every morning (Ex 36:3) ended up being so plentiful that "all the wise ones doing all the work of the sanctuary" (Ex 36:4) actually asked Moses to tell the people to stop (Ex 36:5-7). There was so much raw material that it had become "wise" to stop giving!

The picture of a Spirit-filled wise man of Judah leading a willing, wise people in the construction of the tabernacle closely corresponds to the Spirit-filled Messiah leading his multiethnic church (Rev 7:9). As was the case for Bezalel and the other workers, Jesus builds a "sanctuary" (i.e., the church; Mt 16:18), but the people of God also play an important role in "building" (Rom 15:2; 1 Cor 8:1; 14:3-5; Eph 4:29; 1 Thess 5:11). It is as though not only the tabernacle itself is a "copy and shadow" of heavenly things (Heb 8:5; cf. Heb 10:1), but so is Bezalel ("in the shadow of God") and the manner in which the tabernacle was successfully completed.

The Day of Atonement

The last example of intentional foreshadowing examined in this chapter is the Day of Atonement in Leviticus 16. It too is a "shadow at Sinai." Consistent with our treatments of other such passages, the goal of the analysis below is not simply to observe parallels between the Day of Atonement and the substitutionary death of Jesus (Heb 9:7, 25; 10:1-3) but how the Pentateuch itself casts the Day of Atonement as intentionally foreshadowing this final sacrifice in its own compositional strategy. In order to do this, Leviticus 16 must be investigated in its literary context.

The first thing that stands out from a simple reading of Leviticus 16 is its connection to the preceding context. Before giving any instructions about the Day of Atonement, Leviticus 16:1 sets the scene for the Lord's words to Moses as being "after the death of two of the sons of Aaron, when they approached the LORD and died." The reference here is to the death of Nadab and Abihu in Leviticus 10:1-3 following their offering of "strange fire." Subsequently, the Lord gave instructions directly to Aaron, which included a prohibition against alcohol (Lev 10:8-9). Whether or not Nadab and Abihu were intoxicated, the rationale seems to be the prevention of similar future offenses "when you enter the tent of meeting" so that "you will not die." Jacob Milgrom points out the similarly solemn priestly prohibitions in Exodus 28:43 (against improper dress),

Exodus 30:20 (against improper washing), Leviticus 21:23 (against physical blemish), and Ezekiel 44:21 (against drunkenness; parallel to Lev 10:9) and concludes that the larger issue is that "the disqualified may not enter the Tent under any circumstance" or approach the altar.[26] Although the prohibition against physical blemish in Leviticus 21:23 significantly does not include the death penalty, these instructions, including Leviticus 10:9, also served to protect the priests from holy divine anger. Explicit motives for the command in Leviticus 10:9 are given in Leviticus 10:10-11, "to distinguish between the holy and the profane [לְהַבְדִּיל בֵּין הַקֹּדֶשׁ וּבֵין הַחֹל], and between the unclean and the clean [וּבֵין הַטָּמֵא וּבֵין הַטָּהוֹר], and to teach the sons of Israel all the statutes which the LORD spoke to them by the hand of Moses."

This motive unifies the laws of cleanness and uncleanness in Leviticus 11-15, which as shown below will demonstrate the seamless connection between Leviticus 16 and all of Leviticus 10-15. For example, the conclusion to the dietary laws in Leviticus 11 explains that one motive for the preceding is "to distinguish between the unclean and the clean [לְהַבְדִּיל בֵּין הַטָּמֵא וּבֵין הַטָּהֹר], and between the animal that can be eaten and the animal which should not be eaten" (Lev 11:47). As before (Lev 10:3, 10), the core concern is still the holiness of the Lord and his people (Lev 11:44-45). Properly recognizing what is unclean and clean also underlies the laws concerning "leprosy" (צָרַעַת, Lev 13:59), including on a garment or a "plague of leprosy on a house" (Lev 14:34, 54-57). The conclusion of the regulations concerning bodily discharges similarly emphasizes the need for Israel to be "separate" (נָזַר) from "their uncleanness, lest they die in their uncleanness when they make my tabernacle [מִשְׁכָּנִי] unclean which is in their midst" (Lev 15:31). The verb *separate* and its cognate noun *separation* (נֵזֶר) are repeatedly used of the Nazirite in Numbers 6. Israel as a whole was similarly to be consecrated to the service of the Lord.

Thus Milgrom sees Leviticus 11-15 as "specifying the impurities that can pollute the sanctuary (15:31), for which the purgation rite of chap. 16 is mandated." This was the crime doubly committed in Leviticus 10 by Nadab

---

[26]Jacob Milgrom, *Leviticus 1-16*, Anchor Bible (New York: Doubleday, 1991), 613-14.

and Abihu "in life by their sin and in death by their corpses." Yet there has been no explanation of how the sanctuary itself will be purged. "This procedure," explains Milgrom, "is detailed in chap. 16."[27] Accordingly, atonement is made both for the priests and the people (Lev 16:6, 11, 17, 24, 30, 34) and also for the sanctuary itself (Lev 16:16, 18, 20, 33). Israel becomes "clean" from all their sins and "clean before the LORD" (Lev 16:30). The bronze altar is likewise "cleansed" (Lev 16:18-19).[28]

Not only is Leviticus 16 climactic in relation to Leviticus 10–15, it is also the climax of the entire sacrificial system, much of which is detailed in Leviticus 1–7. The gravity and elaborate ritual in Leviticus 16 far exceed any sacrifice described in Leviticus 1–7 or elsewhere. Moreover, John Hartley points out that this chapter also "prepares for the coming material on holy living [in Lev 17–26]. It may be said that the moral and spiritual energy for the people to fulfill the laws in chaps. 17–26 comes out of their finding complete expiation on the Day of Atonement. The ritual for the Day of Atonement thus appropriately stands before the laws on holy living."[29] Accordingly, R. K. Harrison calls Leviticus 16

> the ceremonial and theological pivot upon which the entire book of Leviticus turns. Previous legislation has dealt with the different kinds of sacrifices and the conditions under which they were to be offered, the emphasis being upon the provision for individual needs. Now the focus is upon the making of atonement for all the uncleannesses and sins of inadvertence of the entire Israelite congregation, beginning with the priesthood.[30]

While remembering that Leviticus is part of the Pentateuch and subsumed in its overall structure of a repeating sequence of narrative-poetry-epilogue,

---

[27] Milgrom, *Leviticus 1–16*, 1011. Similarly, Gordon Wenham, *The Book of Leviticus*, New International Commentary on the Old Testament (Grand Rapids: Eerdmans, 1979), 228, "The main purpose of the day of atonement ceremonies is to cleanse the sanctuary from the pollutions introduced into it by the unclean worshippers (cf. 16:16, 19). Without a purpose such as this there would have been little point in the high priest putting his life at risk by entering into the holy of holies. The aim of these rituals is to make possible God's continued presence among his people."

[28] See Wenham, *Book of Leviticus*, 232-33 (especially n. 11), for a discussion of which altar is referred to here. The "cleansing" of the rest of the tabernacle is not directly mentioned in Lev 16, though it is "atoned for" (Lev 16:16, 20, 33).

[29] John Hartley, *Leviticus*, Word Biblical Commentary (Dallas: Word, 1992), 217.

[30] R. K. Harrison, *Leviticus*, Tyndale Old Testament Commentaries (Downers Grove, IL: InterVarsity Press, 1980), 166-67.

these considerations demonstrate the importance of Leviticus 16 in its literary context and in the sacrificial system.³¹

The use of a "ram" (אַיִל) as a "burnt offering" (לְעֹלָה) for Aaron (Lev 16:3) and another for the people (Lev 16:5) in conjunction with an "appearance" (Niph. רָאָה) of the Lord (Lev 16:2) parallels the sacrifice of a "ram" as a "burnt offering" in place of Isaac and the naming of the site "the LORD will provide/see/appear [יראה]" in Genesis 22:13-14 (see LXX). Although this combination of terms is also used of the ordination of priests in Leviticus 9:2-4 (see chap. 2 above), especially the Lord's "appearing" (Lev 9:4, 6, 23), the "tragic aftermath" resulting from Nadab and Abihu's misdeed on the same day (see Lev 9:1, 8-21; 10:19),³² contrasts with the generally positive results of Genesis 22:1-18 and Leviticus 16. These two passages also clearly concern substitutionary sacrifice, unlike Leviticus 9:2-4. The ram in Genesis 22:13, as discussed in chapters two and four above, is further related to the lamb in Genesis 22:7-8 and the Passover lamb in Exodus 12:3-5. The narrative patterning that encompasses the death of the seed of the woman (Gen 3:15), the death of a ram/lamb in Isaac's place (and Judah's offer of himself as a slave in Benjamin's place),

---

³¹We have deliberately avoided attributing the level of importance to Lev 16 suggested in Hartley, *Leviticus*, 217, "It stands at the center of the Book of Leviticus, and, of course, the Book of Leviticus is the center of the Pentateuch." Going even further is L. Michael Morales, *Who Shall Ascend the Mountain of the Lord? A Biblical Theology of the Book of Leviticus* (Downers Grove, IL: InterVarsity Press, 2015), 28, who argues that Lev 16 is "the literary and thematic centre of the Pentateuch." His reasoning is based on the Pentateuch's traditional fivefold division and concentric structure, which centers on Sinai and Leviticus (23-27). Leviticus, in turn, centers on Lev 16 (27-28). In our view, one problem with this proposed structure of the Pentateuch is that it is based on the traditional division of the Pentateuch into five books, which does not necessarily correspond to the original, authorially intended structure of the Pentateuch. Sailhamer's proposal (narrative-poetry-epilogue) does not assume this fivefold division and better accounts for formal, literary indications of original, authorially intended structure. Morales' preference for the traditional fivefold division of the Pentateuch leads to his support of a book-level concentric structure in the Pentateuch that pairs Genesis with Deuteronomy, Exodus with Numbers, and holds up Leviticus as the center. Relatedly, the concentric (sometimes called chiastic) structure that Morales cites concerning Sinai (26) omits certain passages and as such is debatable. For example, the manna passages in Ex 16 and Num 11 are not accounted for, even though they frame Israel's stay at Mount Sinai. Although Num 11 is mentioned, it is only with respect to Moses needing help to lead Israel. For an alternate proposal based on "parallel structures," see John Sailhamer, *The Meaning of the Pentateuch: Revelation, Composition, and Interpretation* (Downers Grove, IL: InterVarsity Press, 2009), 366. As a general observation, it also seems that any concentric/chiastic proposal for the structure of the Pentateuch will automatically center on Sinai law and Leviticus.

³²Milgrom, *Leviticus 1-16*, 595-96.

and the death of the Passover lamb in place of Israel and their firstborn thus seems to extend to the complex sacrificial ritual in Leviticus 16.

This ritual centers on the "two male goats" (שְׁנֵי הַשְּׂעִירִם/שְׁנֵי־שְׂעִירֵי עִזִּים) offered as a "sin offering" (חַטָּאת) for Israel (Lev 16:5, 7-8), which reveals still more links to the Messianic vision of the Pentateuch. The goat that is "for the LORD" (Lev 16:8) is offered as a typical "sin offering" (Lev 16:9). The other goat, traditionally known as the "scapegoat" (עֲזָאזֵל), is sent away into the wilderness (Lev 16:10) after Aaron lays both hands on its head and confesses "all the iniquities [עָוֹן] of the sons of Israel, and all their transgressions [פֶּשַׁע] in all their sins [חַטָּאת]" (Lev 16:21; cf. Dan 9:24).[33] These are put on the goat's head, who "bears" (נָשָׂא) them to a "land which is cut off" (אֶרֶץ גְּזֵרָה, Lev 16:22). What these two goats depict is both a substitutionary death for sinners and the bearing of their sin to a faraway place. This of course is what the Messiah does. Whereas his "head" is anointed (Gen 28:18), that same innocent head must also bear the weight of the sins of the world (in relation to Gen 3:18, see the crown of "thorns" in Mt 27:29; Mk 15:17; Jn 19:2, 5). The high priest also had to "bear" (נָשָׂא) iniquity on his "forehead" (מֵצַח, Ex 28:38). In the Messiah's substitutionary death for the sake of "our transgressions" (פֶּשַׁע) and "our iniquities" (עָוֹן, Is 53:5), "he bore [נָשָׂא] the sin [חֵטְא] of many" (Is 53:12; cf. Is 53:11) so that our "sins" (חַטָּאת) have been cast into the depths of the sea (Mic 7:19) and our "transgressions" (פֶּשַׁע) are separated from us as far as the east is from the west (Ps 103:12). The different ways each of the two goats likely foreshadow the Messiah recall Isaac and the ram intentionally foreshadowing the Messiah in different ways in Genesis 22:1-18.

Mary Douglas notes the parallel between the two goats in Leviticus 16 and the two birds in Leviticus 14:4-7.[34] As part of cleansing a leper (Lev 14:2-4), one bird is sacrificed (Lev 14:5) and the live bird is released "into the open field" (עַל־פְּנֵי הַשָּׂדֶה) after being dipped in the blood of the bird that had been killed (Lev 14:6-7). She also observes that two birds are

---

[33] We take the obscure word *Azazel* in Lev 16:8, 10, 26 in the traditional sense of "scapegoat," in accordance with the LXX, Vulgate (*capro emissario*), and its etymology. The view that Azazel is a demon clashes with prohibitions against offerings to demons, including the "goat idols" in Lev 17:7. See Wenham, *Book of Leviticus*, 234.

[34] Mary Douglas, "The Go-Away Goat," in *The Book of Leviticus: Composition and Reception*, ed. Rolf Rendtorff and Robert Kugler (Leiden: Brill, 2003), 133.

similarly used for cleansing a house in Leviticus 14:49-53. However, whereas the bird and the goat that are killed in these two passages do seem to serve a similar purpose, the living bird is freed whereas the live goat bears sin to a desolate place.[35] The scapegoat is led at first by an appointed person before being released (Lev 16:21-22).

Nevertheless, there is another passage in the Pentateuch that mentions two goats. In Genesis 27:9, Rebekah instructs Jacob to retrieve "two good young goats" (שְׁנֵי גְּדָיֵי עִזִּים טֹבִים) for her to prepare to facilitate Jacob stealing his father Isaac's blessing. Although the immediate context does not explain why she needed *two* goats, the effect is to suggest an intertextual relationship to Leviticus 16. The two goats in Genesis 27 also have a dual purpose, though it is likely that both goats serve both purposes rather than each goat serving a different purpose as in Leviticus 16. The first and obvious purpose is to be food for Isaac (Gen 27:9-10, 14, 17, 19, 25). The second is the use of their "skins" to "clothe [Jacob's] hands and the smooth part of his neck" (Gen 27:16). The skins on his hands prove to be crucial when Isaac wants to feel Jacob and touches his "hairy" (שְׂעִרֹת) hands (Gen 27:21-23). The word *hairy* (שָׂעִר, Gen 27:11, 23) plays on both the proper noun "Seir" (שֵׂעִיר, Gen 32:4; i.e., the land of Edom) and one of the words for "goat" (שָׂעִיר) used in Leviticus 16. In effect, "the skins of the young goats" (Gen 27:16), which were killed in the process, resulted in Jacob being treated as though he were someone else. These goat skins covered and effectively substituted for Jacob's smooth skin (Gen 27:11, 16). A goat is also associated with substitution in Genesis 37:31, where Joseph's brothers slaughtered a "male goat" (שְׂעִיר עִזִּים) and dipped his "garment" (כֻּתֹּנֶת) in its blood. The goat's violent death and its blood represent Joseph's violent death and his blood. Though the animals are unspecified, Genesis 3:21 relatedly describes the Lord God making "garments of skin" (כָּתְנוֹת עוֹר) for Adam and Eve with which "he clothed them" (וַיַּלְבִּשֵׁם). Thus Genesis 3, Genesis 27, and Genesis 37 each involve both the substitutionary death of a goat/animal and a direct link to the Messianic vision of

---

[35]Contra Douglas, "Go-Away Goat," 134-36, who draws a parallel to pairs of brothers in Genesis, such as Isaac/Ishmael and Jacob/Esau. She asserts that "the text contrasts freedom [live animal, Ishmael, Esau] with the covenant [sacrificed animal, Isaac, Jacob]" and that the "wilderness" in Lev 16 indicates "a place outside the habitations of Israel" (136).

the Pentateuch (Gen 3:15; 27:27-29; 37:6-10). This suggests the same for Leviticus 16.

The scapegoat's journey to a "land which is cut off" (אֶרֶץ גְּזֵרָה, Lev 16:22) recalls the isolation of the unclean in Leviticus 11–15 (e.g., Lev 11:24-28, 31-32, 39-40, "unclean until evening"; Lev 12:4, "until the days of her cleansing are fulfilled"). Sin is the ultimate uncleanness, and its banishment via the scapegoat especially parallels the quarantining of the leper in Leviticus 13:4-5, 26, 31-33. A person whose leprosy was chronic had to cry out "Unclean, unclean" and live "alone," "outside the camp" (מִחוּץ לַמַּחֲנֶה, Lev 13:45-46; 14:3), where certain sin offerings are burned (Ex 29:14; Lev 4:12, 21; 8:17; 9:11; 16:27).[36] Thus, when the Suffering Servant is described as having been "cut off" (נִגְזַר) in Isaiah 53:8, it suggests not only his death but his isolation and loneliness (Ps 22:1; cf. Dan 9:26).[37]

The timing and annual observance of the Day of Atonement suggest additional ties to the Passover, which has already been argued to be an important part of the Messianic vision of the Pentateuch (see chap. 4 above). The Passover began on the tenth day of the first month (Ex 12:2-3), and the Day of Atonement was observed on the tenth day of the seventh month (Lev 16:29). Harrison remarks,

> Six months after the passover had been celebrated, the people were instructed to 'afflict themselves,' after which the high priest would make atonement for them. Like the passover, this ceremony had to be observed annually, and it marked the occasion when the entire religious community was mobilized before God in a joint act of confession and atonement. It was a time of great solemnity, unlike the annual feasts, and if fasting was involved in the preparatory self-discipline, as many interpreters think, it was the only ceremony that demanded such a communal exercise.[38]

Both passages (including the feast of Unleavened Bread) also involve an "everlasting statute," a Sabbath ("you shall not do any work"), and

---

[36]See discussion in chap 4 above. Still more passages associate being "outside the camp" with uncleanness or shame: Num 5:3-4; 12:14-15; Deut 23:10-14. This was also where the blasphemer and Sabbath-breaker were stoned (Lev 24:14, 23; Num 15:35-36).
[37]See the discussion of being "cut off" (כָּרַת) for eating anything leavened in chap. 4 above.
[38]Harrison, *Leviticus*, 167.

application to both "the native" and "the sojourner" (Ex 12:14, 16-17, 19, 48-49; Lev 16:29). In a related generalized instruction, Leviticus 16:17 forbids "any man" (כָּל־אָדָם) from being in the tent of meeting when the high priest makes atonement in the Holy Place (for other uses of "man," see Lev 1:2; 5:4; 6:3; 13:2, 9; 18:5). Insofar as yeast represents uncleanness in Exodus 12 (see chap. 4 above), this theme is also common to both the Passover and the Day of Atonement.

Much has happened since the first Passover and the exodus, especially in terms of Israel's failures (Ex 32; Lev 10:1-3; 17:7), and the Lord institutes a solemn ritual exactly halfway between annual celebrations of the Passover as a reminder of their need for cleansing. There is no feast or meal this time, not even of one including bitter herbs, only affliction of "their souls" (Lev 16:29, 31). Neither is there a reference to the deliverance from Egypt nor of passing down a redemption story from parents to children. What remains the same is the substitutionary death of a sheep/goat,[39] accompanied by a greater emphasis on Israel's uncleanness and the banishment of their sin through the scapegoat. These similarities and differences suggest that the Day of Atonement is compositionally related to the Passover.

But, as was the case for the Passover, there are good reasons to understand the Day of Atonement as falling short of the ideal. Eschatological victory and cleansing have already been tied to the coming of the Messiah in the last days (Gen 3:15; 49:1, 8-12). The cleansing and atonement accomplished on the Day of Atonement (Lev 16:30) thus implicitly will never measure up to what will be achieved by this eschatological priest-king (Is 52:15) and the Lord himself (Deut 32:43; Ezek 16:63; 36:25). Furthermore, the appearance of the Lord above the mercy seat in a cloud (Lev 16:2), which was produced by the smoke from Aaron's censer and obscured his view (Lev 16:13),[40] contrasts with Moses' "face-to-face" conversations with the Lord in Exodus 33:11. Although a "cloud" is also mentioned in this context (Ex 33:9-10; 34:5), Moses' encounter was still more direct and intimate than the high priest's in Leviticus 16. Indeed, the

---

[39]See BDB, HALOT. The "goat" (שָׂעִיר/שְׂעִירָה) is a subtype of a "lamb" (שֶׂה) in Lev 5:6-7 (cf. Num 15:11).
[40]Milgrom, *Leviticus 1–16*, 1014-15.

severely restricted access to the Holy Place (Lev 16:2) shows that the way back to the presence of the Lord and the original Edenic world is still largely closed.

Conclusion

This chapter has shown that the Messianic vision of the Pentateuch continues to advance even during Israel's time in the wilderness and at Sinai. Although there are no direct Messianic prophecies ("lenses") in this portion of the Pentateuch, there are several instances of intentional foreshadowing ("mirrors") that contribute important elements to its expanding Messianic vision. The intertextual relationship between the giving of manna in Exodus 16 ("I will rain bread from heaven" and its association with "dew") and the Messianic blessing in Genesis 27:28 ("dew of heaven," "grain") provides a significant link between manna and the Messiah within the Pentateuch itself. The striking of "the rock" in Exodus 17:6 recalls both the striking of the heel of the seed of the woman in Genesis 3:15 and Jacob's dream of a "ladder" and the stone pillar that represents it in Genesis 28:10-22, both of which we have already argued are part of the Messianic vision of the Pentateuch (see chaps. 1-2 above). In the compositional strategy of the Pentateuch, the Spirit-filled Judahite Bezalel (Ex 31:2-3), leader of the tabernacle project, is linked directly to the lion of Judah in Genesis 49:8-12, to the wise, Spirit-empowered Joseph (Gen 41:38-39) who himself intentionally foreshadows the Messiah, and even to the Lord himself who called him by name (Ex 31:2; 33:19; 34:5-6; 35:30). Lastly, the Day of Atonement in Leviticus 16, as a climactic passage in its literary context and in the entire sacrificial system, is part of the narrative patterning beginning with the sacrificial death of the seed of the woman (Gen 3:15) and encompassing the sacrifice of Isaac (Gen 22:1-18) and the Passover (Ex 12).

6

THE BRONZE SNAKE
AND BALAAM'S ORACLES

Although the Messianic vision of the Pentateuch continues to unfold through intentional foreshadowing related to the exodus and Israel's time in the wilderness, the recurrence of direct Messianic prophecy in Numbers 24 is important for several reasons. In addition to contributing new pieces to this vision, it shows that the eschatological plan of salvation laid out in Genesis remains unchanged. The Sinai law has indeed been given (and broken), but the Lord's salvation plan for Israel and the nations is the same as it has always been (Gen 3:15). If there were no Messianic prophecies after Genesis 49 and after the giving of the Sinai law, it would be easier to conclude that this law had perhaps replaced or merged with the Messiah in the divine plan of salvation (see chap. 9 below). While intentional foreshadowing of the Messiah related to the exodus and the stay at Mount Sinai suggests otherwise, such suggestions are largely contingent on an intertextual relationship to direct Messianic prophecy, which is primary in the Messianic vision of the Pentateuch. Though we believe these instances of intentional foreshadowing between Genesis 49 and Numbers 24 are indeed linked to Messianic prophecy in Genesis (see chaps. 4–5 above), direct Messianic prophecy post–Mount Sinai is still crucial for the Messianic vision of the Pentateuch, and Numbers 24, Deuteronomy 18, and Deuteronomy 33 serve as lynchpins of this vision, especially in relation to the giving of the Sinai/Deuteronomic law. In particular, the Messianic prophecy in Numbers 24:7-9, 17-19 has some of the most extensive description of the Messiah in the Pentateuch. Taking its two parts together, it is comparable in length to Genesis 49:8-12, the longest continuous Messianic prophecy in the Pentateuch.

One of the main purposes of this chapter is to argue for direct Messianic prophecy in Numbers 24 (a "lens") and to explain its contribution to the Messianic vision of the Pentateuch. Its context in the Balaam narrative (Num 22–24) necessitates an analysis of this literary context as well. Furthermore, these chapters are also related to Numbers 21 and the incident surrounding the bronze snake, cited by Jesus in John 3:14 as illustrative of his death on the cross. Although some scholars take this citation as simply an analogy or a type,[1] the discussion below will show that Numbers 21:4-9 probably involves intentional foreshadowing of the Messiah.

The Bronze Snake

In addition to the obvious fact that Numbers 21 precedes Numbers 22–24, there are more reasons to link this chapter to the Balaam narrative. First, Numbers 11–20 is framed by the provision of food (Num 11) and the provision of water (Num 20), a major theme during Israel's time in the wilderness (cf. Ex 15:22–17:7). Even the vocative used by Moses in Numbers 20:10, "O rebels" (הַמֹּרִים), plays on both the "bitter" (מָרִים) waters in Exodus 15:23 and the references to "Miriam" (מִרְיָם) in each context (Ex 15:20-21; Num 20:1). Second, Moses and Aaron's failure concerning water from the rock in Numbers 20 marks the complete failure of their generation of Israelites, except for Caleb and Joshua. The failure of the nation as a whole and their sentence to wander in the wilderness until death was already treated in Numbers 14, but Moses and Aaron's inclusion in the same fate awaited Numbers 20. They would not bring Israel into the Promised Land (Num 20:12), and Aaron died in Numbers 20:23-29 and was replaced as high priest by his son Eleazar. Moses' death outside the land also loomed (Num 27:12-14). The transitional nature of Numbers 20–21 is further shown through Israel's second approach to the land, which involved encounters with Edom (Num 20:14-21); Canaanites (Num 21:1-3); Sihon, king

---

[1] As analogy, see Abner Chou, *The Hermeneutics of the Biblical Writers: Learning to Interpret Scripture from the Prophets and Apostles* (Grand Rapids: Kregel, 2018), 34. Andreas Köstenberger, "John," in *Commentary on the New Testament Use of Old Testament*, ed. Gregory Beale and D. A. Carson (Grand Rapids: Baker, 2007), 435, also refers to "analogy" here and specifies that it is "part of a very broad exodus typology or Moses/exodus typology that pervades much of the Gospel" (437). Note John's use of "go down," "go up," and "heaven" in conjunction with Jacob's ladder (John 1:51), the bronze snake (John 3:13), and the bread of life (John 6:33, 38, 41-42, 50-51, 58, 62).

of the Amorites (Num 21:21-32); and Og, king of Bashan (Num 21:33-35; cf. Deut 2-3). In this regard, the repeated mention of Moab especially links Numbers 21 to Numbers 22-24 (Num 21:11, 13, 15, 20, 26, 28-29; 22:1, 3, etc.). The last time Moab had been mentioned in the Pentateuch was in the Song of the Sea (Ex 15:15).

While affirming the relation of Numbers 21 to its preceding context, these factors also give legitimacy to analyzing it in relation to the Balaam narrative in Numbers 22-24. For the present purposes, the most important connection that holds Numbers 21-24 together is the keyword *nakhash* (נחש), translated as "snake" (נָחָשׁ) or "omen" (נַחַשׁ). The two underlying Hebrew words share the same three consonants and differ only in their vowels. Israel is afflicted by "snakes" (נְחָשִׁים) in Numbers 21:6, and Moses mounts a "bronze snake" (נְחַשׁ נְחֹשֶׁת) for their healing in Numbers 21:9. Numbers 24:1 characterizes Balaam as someone who usually invokes "omens" (נְחָשִׁים). But the reality is that there is no "omen/snake" (נַחַשׁ) that can defeat Israel (Num 23:23). What is happening compositionally is that by the keyword *nakhash* (נחש), Numbers 21-24 is both being tied *together* in itself and tied *back* to the "enmity" between the seed of the woman (descended from Israel) and the seed of the serpent (נָחָשׁ) in Genesis 3:15, as well as to the Messiah's crushing the head of the serpent. Seth Postell has relatedly argued that the "snake" in the Garden of Eden is a prototypical Canaanite, which also links the battle with the Canaanites in Numbers 21:1-3 to Genesis 3.[2] The intentional relationship of Numbers 21-24 to Genesis 3 is further suggested by the removal of "*the* serpent" (הַנָּחָשׁ, Num 21:7; cf. Gen 3:1) via the bronze snake (Num 21:9) and sealed by the prophecy of the Messiah crushing the heads of his enemies, who are implicitly the serpent's seed (Num 24:17). Thus the defeat of the serpent as predicted in Genesis 3:15 frames Numbers 21-24 and is brought back to the forefront of the reader's attention. The phrase "he crushes the head" (מָחַץ רֹאשׁ) in Psalm 110:6 also draws Genesis 3:15 and Numbers 24:17 together by using the common terminology of "head" (רֹאשׁ, Gen 3:15) and "crush" (מָחַץ, Num 24:17) in a Messianic, eschatological context.

---

[2] Seth Postell, *Adam as Israel: Genesis 1-3 as the Introduction to the Torah and Tanakh* (Eugene, OR: Wipf and Stock, 2011), 121-24.

With the compositional relationship of Numbers 21 to Numbers 22–24 established, as well as that of Numbers 21–24 to Genesis 3, we may look more closely at the passage concerning the bronze snake in Numbers 21:4-9. Israel had just defeated the Canaanite king of Arad after making a vow to the Lord to "devote to destruction" (חָרַם) their cities if he helped them (Num 21:1-2; cf. Gen 28:20-22; Ps 132:1-2). Despite the Lord listening to their voice (Num 21:3; Deut 26:7; 33:7), the Israelites quickly became embittered while going around the territory of Edom (Num 21:4).[3] As was the case the first time they were near the "Red Sea," they complained about food and water (Num 21:5; Ex 15:26–17:7). The lone reference to the Red Sea since then was in connection with Israel's refusal to enter the Promised Land and the Lord's command that they "turn" to "the way of the Red Sea" (Num 14:25). Though just recently sentenced to die in the wilderness, the Israelites presumptuously tried to approach the land anyway and were soundly defeated by Amalekites and Canaanites (Num 14:40-44) who chased them all the way to "Hormah" (Num 14:45; 21:3; Deut 1:45). This time, however, they were unhappy with the manna that the Lord had already been providing (Num 21:5; cf. Num 11:6). While alleging that "there is no bread" (אֵין לֶחֶם), they contradicted themselves by saying "our soul loathes [קוּץ] this contemptible bread [לֶחֶם]."[4] The verb *loathe* is yet another link to Numbers 22–24 (see Num 22:3, "Moab felt loathing [קוּץ] because of the sons of Israel").

Israel's rejection of "bread from heaven" (Ex 16:4; see chap. 5 above) in Numbers 21:5 leads to another instance of intentional foreshadowing of the Messiah through the bronze snake. But the process involved the Lord's judgment on Israel's unbelief by sending "among the people the fiery snakes [הַנְּחָשִׁים הַשְּׂרָפִים], and they bit the people, and a great number of people from Israel died" (Num 21:6). In addition to its common usage for sacrifice or judgment, fire is associated with Babel/Babylon (Gen 11:3) and

---

[3] On the Lord listening, see Gen 16:11; 29:33; Deut 9:19; 10:10; for negative connotations, see Num 11:3; 12:2; Deut 1:45.
[4] Timothy Ashley, *The Book of Numbers*, New International Commentary on the Old Testament (Grand Rapids: Eerdmans, 1993), 404, notes that the rare word translated "contemptible" (קְלֹקֵל) may be a cognate of "curse" (קְלָלָה). Even if not, there is still the possibility of wordplay. If there is an intentional link, the suggestion that Israel has implied that the divinely provided "bread from heaven" is "cursed" is very serious. The theme of blessing and cursing (קָבַב/אָרַר) is an important one in the Balaam narrative (Num 22:6, 12; 23:7, 11, 20, 25; 24:1, 9-10).

with Egypt (Deut 4:20; 1 Kings 8:51; Jer 11:4), both of which have ties to the seed of the serpent (see chaps. 1 and 4 above). The Israelites then confessed to Moses their sin of speaking "against the LORD and against you" (contra Ex 14:31) and asked him to intercede for them before the Lord so that "he may remove the serpent from upon us" (Num 21:7). The Lord instructed Moses to make a snake that resembled those biting Israel (שָׂרָף, which can be used as a noun: Is 14:29; 30:6) and set it on a "pole" or "banner" (נֵס) (Num 21:8). Moses then made a "bronze snake" so that all who looked at it would live (Num 21:9).

The repetition of the word *snake* (נָחָשׁ) especially links Numbers 21:4-9 to Genesis 3. Remarkably, this word appears five times in each passage (Gen 3:1-2, 4, 13-14; Num 21:6-7, 9). There are no other passages in the Pentateuch or the Old Testament that have this characteristic. It has already been pointed out that the fivefold appearance of "snake" in Genesis 3 is matched by the fivefold appearance of "lamb" (שֶׂה) in Exodus 12:3-5 and "he" (הוּא, i.e., the Suffering Servant) in Isaiah 53 (Is 53:4-5, 7, 11-12). The effect is a very strong intertextual linkage between Genesis 3 and Numbers 21:4-9, along with their juxtaposition with Exodus 12:3-5 and Isaiah 53. Israel's failure concerning faith and food, along with their defeat and death by snakes (i.e., the seed of the serpent), casts Numbers 21:4-9 as a sort of "Fall" narrative. Their seemingly "ungrammatical" (see chap. 2 above) request that the Lord remove "*the* snake" (הַנָּחָשׁ, Num 21:7) makes perfect sense if Genesis 3 is also in view (Num 21:9; Deut 8:15).[5] Israel's problem here was not simply an isolated incident of being bitten by poisonous snakes. Rather, the same snake that tempted and defeated Adam

---

[5]Contra Baruch Levine, *Numbers 21–36*, Anchor Bible (New York: Doubleday, 2000), 88, who takes it "in the collective sense"; Ashley, *Book of Numbers*, 405. Likewise, Jacob Milgrom, *Numbers*, JPS Torah Commentary (Philadelphia: Jewish Publication Society, 1990) 174, who cites "the frog" in Ex 8:2 as a parallel. Milgrom's observation is valid, but Num 21:4-9 is still compositionally linked to Gen 3. Moreover, unclean spirits are compared to "frogs" in Rev 16:13, suggesting a broad parallel between "the frog" in Ex 8:2 and "the snake" in Gen 3/Num 21:7. Nobuyoshi Kiuchi, *Leviticus*, Apollos Old Testament Commentary (Downers Grove, IL: InterVarsity Press, 2007), 206, observes that some of the unclean animals in Lev 11:29-30 are amphibians. Egyptian magicians had power related to "snakes" (תַּנִּין, Ex 7:9-12, sometimes "sea monster," as in Gen 1:21; see נָחָשׁ in Ex 4:3; 7:15), "water" (מַיִם, Ex 7:22; see "river" in Ex 7:17-21), and frogs (which belong in the "river"; see Ex 8:7-11), but they confessed that they could not match the power of the Lord as demonstrated through the other plagues (Ex 8:18-19; cf. Ex 9:11). Apparently, their power was limited to water and the creatures in it. The Lord has power not only over the waters (Ex 15:1-18) but all things (Job 38–41).

and Eve was still defeating Israel. In both cases, the snake does not even have to "bear the sword" alone. Instead, Adam, Eve, and Israel bring themselves under divine judgment through their lack of faith. Even though the Sinai law had been given, Israel's failure in this case was not breaking one of its specific regulations per se (cf. Num 14:11; 2 Kings 17:14; Ps 78:22, 32). Obviously, the snake's head had not yet been crushed, and sin and death still reigned. Israel needed the seed of the woman to come and defeat these enemies.

The Messiah would not come at this moment (Num 24:17), but the Lord provided a picture of what it would be like when he comes "in the last days" (Num 24:14; see discussion of this phrase in chap. 3 above). Evidently, neither the Israelites' confession of sin ("we have sinned") nor Moses' intercession were enough (Num 21:7). The bronze snake still had to be made, set on a pole, and looked at in order for the Israelites to "live" instead of "die" (Num 21:8-9). Themes of life and death are of course a major part of Genesis 2–3 (Gen 2:7, 9, 17; 3:3-4, 22). The uncommon narrative syntax of Numbers 21:9 (three *weqatal* verb forms in "And it would be [וְהָיָה] if the snake bit a man, he would look [וְהִבִּיט] to the bronze snake and he would live [וָחָי]") suggests a generalized practice or principle, as it breaks the flow of the sequential storyline and often links the narrative world to the reader's world (e.g., Gen 2:24; 15:6; Ex 1:12; 33:7-11).[6]

John Sailhamer has pointed out a parallel between Exodus 17 and Numbers 20–21.[7] Both passages involve water from the rock (Ex 17:1-7; Num 20:1-13) followed by a miraculous victory over enemies (Ex 17:8-16; Num 21:1-3). Also referencing Numbers 14:43-45 and Numbers 24:20, he believes that this structure encourages an identification of the Amalekites in Exodus 17 with the Canaanites in Numbers 21:1-3. In our view, this structure also encompasses the bronze-snake passage immediately following. Similar to how Moses went up the mountain with "the staff of God"

---

[6]There are certainly passages that use the same kind of syntax but do not bear as much theological weight, such as Gen 32:33; 34:5. They do however still usually adhere to this same function in the text. As readers of biblical Hebrew are well aware, narrative syntax is dominated by the *wayyiqtol* verb form and complemented primarily by *qatal*. *Weqatal* and *yiqtol* are uncommon in narration, though common in direct speech.

[7]John Sailhamer, *The Pentateuch as Narrative: A Biblical-Theological Commentary* (Grand Rapids: Zondervan, 1992), 401-2.

in his hand (Ex 17:9) and "would lift [רוּם] his hand" (Ex 17:11; note the *weqatals* and *yiqtols* again), the bronze snake is "set" (שִׂים) on a "pole/banner" (נֵס, Num 21:8-9). Joseph likewise had been "set" (שִׂים) in a high place (Gen 45:8-9). Aaron and Hur similarly "set" (שִׂים) a stone for Moses to sit on (Ex 17:12), and the altar memorializing the subsequent military victory is called "The LORD is my banner" (נִסִּי, Ex 17:15). The word *banner* appears elsewhere only in Numbers 26:10 where it describes the death of Korah and his followers abstractly as a "sign" or "warning." Banners are frequently "lifted up" (רוּם/נָשָׂא) in the Old Testament (e.g., Is 5:26; 13:2; 18:3; 49:22; 62:10; Jer 4:6; 50:2; 51:12, 27), which suggests a parallel to Moses' lifting up his hands in Exodus 17:11 and his setting a snake on a "banner" in Numbers 21:8-9. Numbers 24:7 will also describe Israel's eschatological king as "exalted" (רוּם) and his kingdom as "lifted up" (נָשָׂא), which is the same combination of verbs used of the Suffering Servant in Isaiah 52:13 (cf. Is 6:1).

The implied "lifting up" of the bronze snake is important because of Jesus' words in John 3:14, "as Moses *lifted up* the snake in the wilderness, so must the Son of Man be lifted up." Accordingly, Isaiah 11:10 describes the Messiah ("the root of Jesse"; see Is 11:1; 53:2) as standing "as a banner of the peoples" (לְנֵס עַמִּים). Relatedly, the Lord "will lift up a banner for the nations" (וְנָשָׂא נֵס לַגּוֹיִם, Is 11:12). This highlights the fact that in Numbers 21:8-9 Moses not only had to make the bronze snake but lift it up by setting it on a banner/pole. The necessity of its being lifted up is further suggested by the "must" (δεῖ) in John 3:14 and the requirement that Moses' hands be upraised if Israel was to defeat the Amalekites (Ex 17:11-13). In Numbers 21:8-9, the lifting up of the bronze snake relates to fatally afflicted Israelites "seeing" (רָאָה) and "looking" (נָבַט) to it. Accordingly, Balaam in Numbers 24:17 testifies concerning the Messiah, "I see him" (אֶרְאֶנּוּ). In Numbers 21, Israel's deliverance from poisonous snakes thus depended not only on their confession and Moses' intercession but on the three additional actions of Moses making a bronze snake, Moses setting it on a pole/banner, and the Israelites seeing it. Reinforced by Isaiah 11:10-12, the compositional relationship of Numbers 21:4-9 to Numbers 20–24, Genesis 3, and Exodus 17, including the interrelated themes of manna and water from the rock, suggests that Moses' lifting of the bronze snake for the healing of the Israelites intentionally foreshadows the saving work of the Messiah. Just as the seed of the woman crushes the head of the snake (Gen 3:15), the lifting of the bronze snake is the answer to Israel's prayer that the Lord "remove the snake from upon us" (Num 21:7; cf. Ex 15:26).

What is the significance of the snake being made of "bronze"? It at least involves a wordplay because *nekhoshet* (נְחֹשֶׁת), the word for "bronze," is very similar to *nakhash* (נָחָשׁ), the word for "snake."[8] Its material (bronze; often associated with strength, e.g., 1 Sam 17:5-6) thus matches its form (a snake).[9] Obviously, the "bronze snake," though in a sense a "snaky snake" and in another a "strong snake," is only a representation of a snake, much less identical with "the snake" in Genesis 3. Within the Pentateuch, a parallel to this doubling of the root *nakhash* (נחשׁ) is Joseph's claim to "surely practice divination" (נַחֵשׁ יְנַחֵשׁ) with his silver cup (Gen 44:5, 15), which was part of his overall disguise as an Egyptian ruler (see Gen 41:42, 45; 42:23). Moses likewise was mistaken for an Egyptian by seven Midianite sisters (Ex 2:19).[10] The use of the infinitive absolute verbal form in Genesis 44:5, 15 ("surely practice divination") parallels others in the Joseph story, and the certainty expressed by those at the beginning of Genesis 37–50 is eventually overturned in the narrative (Gen 37:8, 10, 33; cf. Gen 44:28; see chap. 3 above). What this may faintly suggest, in addition to the primary purpose of removing "the snake" (Num 21:7), is that the lifting up of the "bronze snake" simultaneously relates to the reckoning of the innocent Messiah as a foreign, wicked man (see Is 50:7-9; 53:9). If the scapegoat intentionally foreshadows the Messiah (see chap. 5 above), then this coheres with the placement of all Israel's "iniquities," "transgressions," and "sins" on its head (Lev 16:20-21). Just as Joseph probably did not really practice divination, and neither he nor Moses were Egyptians (and thus part of the seed of the serpent; see chap. 4 above), the Messiah would not really be a snake, even though he was called Beelzebub, prince of demons (Mt 12:24-25, 27; Mk 3:22; Lk 11:15, 18-19). From Israel's perspective, their

---

[8] R. Dennis Cole, *Numbers*, New American Commentary (Nashville: Broadman and Holman, 2000), 347, observes the similarity of the words for snake, omen, and bronze but does not pursue it further.

[9] See Milgrom, *Numbers*, 174.

[10] Umberto Cassuto, *A Commentary on the Book of Exodus*, trans. Israel Abrahams (Jerusalem: Magnes, 1983), 25, "They thought him to be an Egyptian on account of his dress and speech."

eschatological salvation would come from what appears to be a foreign source (Jn 8:48; 9:29; Acts 6:14; 21:21; Rom 11:13-14) and a condemned man (Is 53:5; cf. Gen 39:20). The nations will also have a similar perception of the Messiah (see Acts 16:21; 17:18; 1 Cor 1:23), as hinted at through the reaction of the Midianite sisters to Moses. In support of the simultaneous significance of the bronze snake with respect to the Messiah and "the snake," John 12:31-32 links Jesus being "lifted up from the earth" to "the ruler of this world" being "cast out" (see Num 21:7). The subsequent question in John 12:34 about how Jesus can say that "the Son of Man *must* [δεῖ] be lifted up" provides yet another link to John 3:14-15. As in the Gospel of John, the "lifting up" of the Messiah in the Pentateuch thus relates to both his exaltation (Gen 28:12; 37:6-10; 49:8-10) and his suffering (Num 21:8-9).[11]

Sailhamer further notes the thematic parallel to Moses' "staff" (מַטֶּה) turning into a "snake" (נָחָשׁ) in Exodus 4:2-3 and the wordplay between "flee" (נוּס) and "banner" (נֵס).[12] In both passages, "the writer emphasizes the necessity of the people's faith in the sign" (Ex 4:30-31; Num 21:8). They must "see" it "before [their] eyes" and "believe." Although no human is able to perfectly keep the Lord's commandments so that he will "live" (חָיָה, Lev 18:5), sinners can still "live" if they look to the bronze snake (Num 21:8-9). Joseph, whose claim to practice divination may link him to the bronze snake, likewise "preserve[d] alive" (לְהַחֲיוֹת) a "remnant" for his family (Gen 45:7), was "set" (שִׂים) as a ruler (Gen 45:8-9), and saved the lives of "many people" (עַם־רָב, Gen 50:20; cf. Num 21:6). Whereas Moses fled from the real snake that his rod had become, sinners should turn toward the bronze snake on the banner. It is not to be feared (2 Kings 18:4) and it will certainly not bite. It is harmless and signifies the defeat of "the snake" (Gen 3:1; Num 21:7), which will ultimately succumb to the Messiah's "rod of iron" (שֵׁבֶט בַּרְזֶל, Ps 2:9). Though not identical, these two hard metals, bronze and iron, are frequently mentioned together (Deut 8:9; Jer 1:18; Ps 107:16). The snake had "deceived" (Hiph. נָשָׁא) Eve (Gen 3:13) but the bronze snake set on a "banner" (נֵס) intentionally foreshadows his

---

[11] Andreas Köstenberger, *John*, Baker Exegetical Commentary on the New Testament (Grand Rapids: Baker, 2004), 128, 384n38.
[12] Sailhamer, *Pentateuch as Narrative*, 402 (including n. 10).

defeat by the Messiah, himself a "banner" (Is 11:10; cf. Ex 17:15) who will be "lifted up" (רוּם/נָשָׂא, Is 11:12; 52:13) as a sin-bearer (נָשָׂא, Lev 16:22; Is 53:4, 12).

Before moving on to the Balaam narrative in Numbers 22–24, it is worth briefly noting that the context immediately following the bronze snake episode describes Israel's journey by stations through the wilderness and a certain suggestive "well" (בְּאֵר, Num 21:16-18). Although its preceding context is obscure (Num 21:14-15), the Lord's provision of water at this well not only recalls both passages about water from the rock (Ex 17:1-7; Num 20:1-13) but also uses terminology and themes in common with other passages related to the Messianic vision of the Pentateuch. The form "from there" (מִשָּׁם, Num 21:16; cf. Num 21:12-13, but note נָסְעוּ וַיַּחֲנוּ) also appeared in Genesis 49:24 concerning "the stone of Israel" (cf. Deut 4:29). The instruction to "gather [אָסַף] the people" (Num 21:16) and the word translated "lawgiver/ruler's staff" (מְחֹקֵק, Num 21:18) parallel Genesis 49:1, 10. This latter word also appears in Deuteronomy 33:21 along with "heads of the people" (רָאשֵׁי עָם), who in Deuteronomy 33:5 "gathered themselves, the tribes of Israel together" (בְּהִתְאַסֵּף רָאשֵׁי עָם יַחַד שִׁבְטֵי יִשְׂרָאֵל). Similarly, not only are "the people" mentioned (Num 21:16), but so are the "princes" (שָׂרִים) and "the nobles of the people" (נְדִיבֵי הָעָם, Num 21:18). Their digging in this verse (כָּרָה/חָפַר) parallels Isaiah 51:1 LXX (נָקַר/חָצַב), which via Exodus 17:6 and Exodus 33:21-22 associates both texts with Moses striking the rock (see chap. 4 above; Ps 21:17 LXX). Furthermore, the sentence, "Then Israel sang this song" (אָז יָשִׁיר יִשְׂרָאֵל אֶת־הַשִּׁירָה הַזֹּאת) in Numbers 21:17 parallels Exodus 15:1, "Then Moses and the sons of Israel sang this song" (אָז יָשִׁיר־מֹשֶׁה וּבְנֵי יִשְׂרָאֵל אֶת־הַשִּׁירָה הַזֹּאת). The parallel syntax and terminology in these two songs appears nowhere else in the Pentateuch and suggests a strategic relationship between the two songs. The Song of the Sea was sung to the Lord (Ex 15:1), but this latter song is sung to the well (Num 21:17). The focus on this well is emphasized through the repetition of the word *well* four times in Numbers 21:16-18. Israel did not need "water of a well" (מֵי בְאֵר) from Edom (Num 20:17) or Sihon (Num 21:22) because they had their own rock/well (see Deut 32:4, 13, 15; 1 Cor 10:4). The last phrase of Numbers 21:18 may even serve the dual purpose of not only referring to their next stop but also functioning as a conclusion to the song, "From the wilderness, a gift/Mattanah [מַתָּנָה]" (see NEB).[13]

Numbers 21:16-18, which is part of the interruption of the chronicle of Israel's wilderness travels in Numbers 21:10-13, 19-20, is thus intertextually linked to the water-from-the-rock episodes and to all four major poetic sections in the Pentateuch (Gen 49; Ex 15; Num 23–24; Deut 32–33). The compositional relationship of Numbers 21:16-18 to the Balaam oracles consists not only of being in the same immediate literary context but also of sharing several words and themes, such as "from there" (מִשָּׁם, Num 21:16; 22:41; 23:13, 27); a call to gather (Num 21:16; 24:14); "water" (מַיִם, Num 21:16; 24:6-7); a springing/going up (Num 21:17; 24:6, 9); "princes" (שָׂרֵי/שָׂרִים, Num 21:18; 22:8, 13-15, etc.); a staff, scepter, or rod (Num 21:18; 22:17; 24:17); and gift(s)/Mattanah (Num 21:18-19; 22:18; 24:13). There may also be a wordplay regarding the word for "well," *be'er* (בְּאֵר) and Balaam son of "Beor" (בְּעוֹר), which also appears four times in its own context (Num 22:5; 24:3, 15; 31:8).[14] The concentrated convergence of words and themes from all four major poetic sections in the Pentateuch and from the water-from-the-rock passages suggests that the "well" and the "song" in Numbers 21:16-18 are also compositionally linked to the Messianic vision of the Pentateuch. In particular, if the rock that was struck indeed intentionally foreshadows the Messiah (see chap. 5 above), then naturally so would the well to which the song in Numbers 21:17-18 is sung.

THE BALAAM NARRATIVE AND BALAAM'S ORACLES

In order to properly understand the Messianic prophecies in Balaam's third and fourth oracles (Num 24:3-9, 15-19), we must interpret them in light of

---

[13]See also Leningrad Codex and Philip Budd, *Numbers*, Word Biblical Commentary (Waco, TX: Word, 1984), 237.
[14]Deut 23:5 also refers to Balaam in this way. For yet another wordplay, see "make plain" (בָּאֵר) in Deut 1:5; 27:8; Hab 2:2. Seth Postell, Eitan Bar, and Erez Soref, *Reading Moses, Seeing Jesus: How the Torah Fulfills Its Goal in Yeshua*, 2nd ed. (Wooster, OH: Weaver, 2017), 76n1, further point out the wordplay between "Beor" and the adjective "foolish" (בָּעַר) in Prov 30:2 (more distantly, see "with craftiness," בְּעָרְמָה in Josh 9:4). Both are used in the context of "the oracle of the man" (נְאֻם הַגֶּבֶר, Prov 30:1; Num 24:3, 15; see 2 Sam 23:1). Another broader connection between these two texts is the sevenfold repetition that Balaam "took up his proverb," (וַיִּשָּׂא מְשָׁלוֹ) seven times (Num 23:7, 18; 24:3, 15, 20-21, 23). "Proverbs" are of course at the heart of the book of the same name (Prov 1:1; 10:1; 25:1), and the verb *take up* (נָשָׂא) is a cognate of the noun *burden* (מַשָּׂא) in Prov 30:1.

the Balaam narrative as a whole (Num 22–24).[15] As has already been pointed out, this section is closely tied to the preceding context and especially to Numbers 21:4-9 through the keyword *nakhash* (נָחָשׁ), meaning "snake" or "omen" (see Num 23:23; 24:1). The link between Numbers 22–24 and Genesis 3 is further strengthened through the common theme of a talking animal. Moreover, though used of the angel of the Lord's opposition to Balaam, the verb *satan* (שָׂטַן, "to oppose"), a cognate of which is "the adversary" (הַשָּׂטָן) in Job 1–2, appears in Numbers 22:22, 32, its only two occurrences in the Pentateuch. The solution to Israel and humanity's problem with their adversary, "the [talking] snake" is what it has always been—the seed of the woman who will crush its head (Gen 3:15) and the heads of its seed (Num 24:17), even as he is struck on the heel by it (Gen 3:15) and lifted up like a bronze snake on a pole (Num 21:8-9). This inclusio of intertextual allusions to Genesis 3:15 in Numbers 21–24 was also pointed out above.

Although Moab's opposition to Israel (Num 22:2-6) is broadly similar to the responses of Edom (Num 20:14), the Canaanite king of Arad (Num 21:1), Sihon (Num 21:21-31), and Og (Num 21:33-35), the extended attention given to Moab's opposition (Num 22–24), in conjunction with Balaam's oracles as one of the four major poetic sections of the Pentateuch, yields rich intertextual relationships to other key passages in the Pentateuch and its Messianic vision. As demonstrated above, Numbers 21–24 is compositionally related to Genesis 3. The discussion of Numbers 22–24 below will also show that the Balaam narrative is also deeply intertwined with Genesis 12:1-3 and the Abrahamic covenant, Pharaoh's oppression of the Israelites in Exodus 1, and the longest continuous Messianic prophecy in the Pentateuch in Genesis 49:8-12.

Sailhamer observes that "the Balaam story, which lies at the close of Israel's sojourn in the wilderness, parallels many of the events and ideas of the story of Pharaoh at the beginning of the book of Exodus. Both men, Pharaoh and Balak [king of Moab], were kings of large and powerful nations which represented a major obstacle to Israel's entering the Promised Land."[16] Both rulers were worried that the Israelites were too

---

[15]For an extended treatment of this passage, see Hedwige Rouillard, *Le Péricope de Balaam (Nombres 22–24): La Prose et les "Oracles"* (Paris: J. Gabalda et Cie., 1985).
[16]Sailhamer, *Pentateuch as Narrative*, 406.

"many" (רַב) and too "strong" (עָצוּם, Ex 1:7, 9; Num 22:3, 6) and took counsel against them (Ex 1:9-10; Num 22:4-6). Hedwige Rouillard relatedly points out the parallel between the phrase "covers the eye of the land" in Numbers 22:5, 11 and Exodus 10:5, 15, as well as the use of magic by Israel's enemies.[17] Sailhamer further notes that Exodus 1:10 connects Pharaoh's opposition to Israel's possession of the Promised Land and that Pharaoh's three attempts to suppress Israel (Ex 1:11-22) parallel Balak's three attempts to get Balaam to curse Israel (Num 24:10).[18] Pharaoh's first measure was enslavement (Ex 1:11-14), followed by a command to Hebrew midwives to kill newborn Hebrew boys (Ex 1:15-16), which when thwarted (Ex 1:17-21) was followed by a command "to all his people" to throw these newborn boys into the Nile (Ex 1:22). Although Balaam gave four oracles, only the first three were requested by Balak (Num 22:27–23:6, 13-17, 27-30), and the third and fourth are closely related (see Num 24:1-4, 15-16).[19] Sailhamer further points out that the parallel structure between Exodus 1–2 and Numbers 22–24 portrays "Moses [whose birth is narrated in Ex 2 after Pharaoh's three attempts] . . . as a prototype of the 'star of Jacob' [who is the focus of Balaam's fourth oracle]."[20] This patterning provides an important link between the Messiah, the prophet like Moses (Deut 18:15, 18), and the second exodus (see Num 24:8). Though not a true prophet (Num 24:1; 31:16), Balaam's superficial resemblance to one also ties into this theme (Num 22:35, 38; 23:5, 12, 16; 24:13). His hailing from "Pethor" (פְּתוֹר, Num 22:5), while certainly descriptive of his homeland (Deut 23:5),[21] plays on the root פתר ("interpret"/"interpretation") that is so frequently used in the Joseph narrative (Gen 40:5, 8, 12, 16, 18, 22; 41:8, 11-13, 15).

---

[17]Rouillard, *Le Péricope de Balaam*, 54-55.
[18]Sailhamer, *Pentateuch as Narrative*, 406.
[19]Likewise, Balaam struggles with his donkey on four instances (Num 22:22-30), with the last two closely related (Num 22:26-30).
[20]Sailhamer, *Pentateuch as Narrative*, 407. He also points out the thematic parallels between Pharaoh's three attempts and Balaam's first three oracles concerning oppression and numerical growth (Ex 1:12; Num 23:8, 10), the strength of Hebrew women and the theme of deception (Ex 1:19; Num 23:19, 24), and the command to throw Hebrew newborn boys into the Nile (Ex 1:22; Num 24:7). Also observing the repetition of the root כבד in both narratives (Ex 7:14; 8:15, 24, 32; 9:3, 7, etc.; Num 22:15, 17, 37; 24:11), Sailhamer concludes that they "are linked at the thematic, structural, and verbal levels" (408).
[21]For a detailed discussion of this, see Rouillard, *Le Péricope de Balaam*, 43-53.

The theme of "three times" also appears elsewhere in the Balaam narrative itself. The prophet struck his donkey "three times" (שָׁלֹשׁ רְגָלִים, Num 22:28), a phrase which itself is repeated three times in Numbers 22:28, 32-33. Although the idiom is different from the one used in Numbers 24:10 (שָׁלֹשׁ פְּעָמִים, "three times"), the likely intended parallel remains.[22] This is further supported by the similarity of "the LORD uncovered the eyes of Balaam" (וַיְגַל יְהוָה אֶת־עֵינֵי בִלְעָם, Num 22:31) and the Spirit of God causing Balaam to be as "one whose eyes are uncovered" (גְּלוּי עֵינָיִם, Num 24:4) in his third and fourth oracles (Num 24:4, 16). Whereas the parallel to Exodus 1-2 drew a connection between the Messiah and Moses, this parallel within Numbers 22-24 itself draws a connection between the Messiah and the angel of the Lord whom Balaam worships in Numbers 22:31 (cf. Num 22:23).[23] The angel's possession of a "drawn sword in his hand" (חַרְבּוֹ שְׁלוּפָה בְּיָדוֹ) resembles the description of the Messiah as a warrior in Numbers 24:17 as well as tying in with the portrayal of the Lord as divine warrior in the Song of the Sea (Ex 15:1-18). All these texts in turn relate to "the prince of the host of the LORD," who was described as a "man" with a "drawn sword in his hand," that Joshua encountered prior to marching against Jericho (Josh 5:13-15; cf. 1 Chron 21:16). The use of the verbs for "stand" (עָמַד/נָצַב, Num 22:23-24, 26, 31, 34) also recalls Jacob's ladder in Genesis 28:12-13 and the water-from-the-rock episode in Exodus 17:6 (see chap. 5 above). In chapter three above, the theme of "standing" in Genesis 28:12-13 was shown to relate to the exaltation of the Messiah in Genesis 49:9 via Genesis 37:5-10. The question from Genesis 49:9 in turn is repeated verbatim in Numbers 24:9: "Who will raise [Hiph. קוּם] him?" The verb *arise* (קוּם) is then picked up in Numbers 24:17, "A scepter will rise [קוּם] from Israel."

Balak's persistent desire to "curse" (אָרַר, Num 22:6) Israel put him in direct opposition to the Abrahamic covenant and the Lord's plan to bless all the families of the earth through the seed of Abraham (Gen 12:3). Moreover, his confidence in Balaam that "whoever you bless is blessed"

---

[22]Levine, *Numbers 21–36*, 157-58, observes that the phrase used in Num 22 appears elsewhere only in Ex 23:14, which is followed in Ex 23:17 by the more common phrase also used in Num 24:10. He sees a possible allusion to the "annual pilgrimage festivals," which is further supported by the word דֶּרֶךְ in Num 22:32.

[23]Postell, Bar, and Soref, *Reading Moses*, 77, 79.

(אֲשֶׁר תְּבָרֵךְ מְבֹרָךְ) "and whoever you curse is cursed" (וַאֲשֶׁר תָּאֹר יוּאָר) pits Balaam's evil spiritual power through "omens/snakes" (נחשׁ, Num 23:23; 24:1) against the Lord's omnipotence and the power of his Spirit. The Messiah through whom the Lord's blessing will be realized for Israel and the nations (Gen 27:29; Num 24:9) had not yet come, and Balak's attempt to get Balaam to curse Israel was hence an attack on both Israel and the Messiah, who would "rise" from them (Num 24:17). Balaam learned from the Lord himself that Balak's plan will not succeed (Num 22:12).

In Balaam's first oracle (or "proverb," מָשָׁל), Balak's worst fears were confirmed (Num 23:7-10). Balaam, who could only see the "outskirts [קְצֵה] of the people" (Num 22:41), proclaimed that not even one fourth of Israel's population could be numbered (Num 23:10).[24] The inability to "count" their "dust" directly links to the Abrahamic covenant (Gen 13:16). Relatedly, the Lord was not going to curse them (Num 23:8), and Balaam even wished that his "death" and "end" (אַחֲרִית) be like theirs (Num 23:10). Significantly, he also characterized Israel as holy ("dwells alone"; "does not consider itself among the nations," Num 23:9) and "upright" (Num 23:10). However, the generation of adult Israelites who had come out of Egypt was anything but holy and upright, and their "end" was death in the wilderness as those who persistently rebelled against the Lord (see Num 14:11, 32-33; 25:1; 26:64-65). The next generation also had the same heart problem (Deut 29:4). As T. Desmond Alexander observes, "The central chapters of Numbers provide a very negative portrait of the Israelites."[25] Nevertheless, the words *dwell* (שָׁכַן) and *alone* (בָּדָד) in Numbers 23:9 appear together elsewhere in the Pentateuch only in Deuteronomy 33:28, which describes Israel's secure dwelling as part of their eschatological salvation by the Lord.[26] Micah 7:14, which is part of an extensive allusion to the Song of the Sea (Ex 15:1-18; see chap. 4 above), likewise describes the Lord's people "dwelling alone" (שֹׁכְנִי לְבָדָד). Its additional mention of a "forest in the midst of a garden land/Carmel" (יַעַר בְּתוֹךְ כַּרְמֶל) links to the description of Israel's

---

[24]The Hebrew word translated "outskirts" is variously translated by English versions—e.g., "fraction" (ESV), "extent" (NKJV), "portion" (NASB). This general sense is supported by Num 23:13.
[25]T. Desmond Alexander, *From Paradise to the Promised Land*, 3rd ed. (Grand Rapids: Baker, 2012), 282.
[26]Budd, *Numbers*, 267, calls "this part of the poem . . . reminiscent of the blessing of Moses in Deut 33:28."

secure dwelling using garden imagery in Numbers 24:6. This implies that the Israel Balaam describes in this oracle is not simply the generation of Israelites that Balak felt threatened by, but at points the eschatological, ideal Israel that is holy and upright (Num 23:8, 10). Balaam's focus on this Israel will become increasingly evident in the subsequent oracles and will provide a natural connection to the Messiah in the third and fourth oracles.

Though frustrated on his first try to get Balaam to "curse" his "enemies" (לְקֹב אֹיְבָי, Num 23:11; cf. Num 24:10), Balak tried again. From "another place," Balaam again "from there" will only see the "outskirts" of the people (Num 23:13; cf. Num 22:41). He began his second oracle (Num 23:18-24) with a strong statement that God, unlike humans, will not lie or change his mind (Num 23:19), especially with regard to Israel and the Abrahamic covenant. He will not speak "and not establish it" (וְלֹא יְקִימֶנָּה). Hiphil *qum* (קוּם) reappears in the near context in Numbers 24:9, "Who will raise him?" This question, which is identical to the one in Genesis 49:9, has already been argued to be a rhetorical question concerning God raising the Messiah from the dead, rather than a rhetorical question warning against arousing a lion (see chap. 3 above). Since Hiphil *qum* in Numbers 23:19 has God as the subject, this provides additional support for taking God as the answer to the rhetorical question in Numbers 24:9. He will establish his word and he will raise up the Messiah. Indeed, he will establish his word to Israel and the nations *by* raising up the Messiah.

The Israel that Balaam saw in his second oracle matches the first oracle. While certainly not excluding the generation of Israelites who were in the wilderness, certain statements focus especially on eschatological, ideal Israel. There is no "wickedness" or "trouble" among them (Num 23:21). This pairing of words often concerns the act and consequences of sin (Job 4:8; 15:35; Ps 7:14; 10:7; Is 59:4). In Habakkuk 1:3, the pairing characterizes an evil society, and in Psalm 90:10 it even characterizes the whole of human existence under sin and death, apart from the salvation of the Lord. The Israel in Numbers 23:21 has escaped all these things, as a holy and upright people (Num 23:9-10). The Lord is with them, and the "shout of a king" is among them. The theme of a king will be developed in the next oracle (Num 24:7). God had brought Israel out of Egypt, and they were like a powerful ox (Num 23:22), as Moab had said (Num 22:4). The exodus, of course, did especially concern the generation of Israelites of Balaam's day, but it also rightly applied to Israel for all time, as though even future generations participated in it (e.g., Jer 2:6; Mic 6:4). In connection with this exodus (Num 23:22), there was indeed no "omen" (נַחַשׁ) that Balaam could pronounce against Israel (Num 23:23), and neither was there a "snake" (נָחָשׁ) that could finally defeat them (see Gen 3:15; Num 21:7-9). Rouillard also discusses the collocation of "omen/snake" with "divination" (קֶסֶם) and its parallel to Deuteronomy 18:10 (see 2 Kings 17:17; see chap. 7 below).[27] At the "appointed time" (עֵת) "what God has done" (מַה־פָּעַל אֵל) for Israel will be manifested (Num 23:23).[28] The verb pa'al (פָּעַל, "to do/make") used here is less common than 'asah (עָשָׂה, "to do/make") and provides a lexical link to its other four appearances in the Pentateuch, all in major poetic sections (Ex 15:17; Deut 32:4, 27; 33:11).

The collocation "Behold, a people" (הֶן־עָם) that begins Numbers 23:24 is parallel to Numbers 23:9b and perhaps also to Genesis 11:6, a fitting contrast with the builders of Babel/Babylon. Whereas eschatological Israel has already been described as a holy people (Num 23:9-10, 21), the reference in Number 23:24 is to a people that "will arise like a lioness, and like a lion will lift itself up" (כְּלָבִיא יָקוּם וְכַאֲרִי יִתְנַשָּׂא). The holy people is therefore also a powerful people that is like both an ox (Num 23:22) and a lion that does not "lie down [שָׁכַב] until it eats [אָכַל] prey [טֶרֶף] and drinks the blood [דָּם] of the slain" (Num 23:24). Many of these words and themes are shared with Genesis 49:8-12 and Numbers 24:7-9. This can easily lead to confusion between the Messiah and Israel if the differences go unnoticed. Significantly, the order of their arising and lying down is reversed. In Numbers 23:24 Israel as a lioness/lion arises first, eats, and then lies down. In Genesis 49:9 and Numbers 24:9, however, the Messiah as lion/lioness lies down first and then awaits someone to raise him. Both contexts involve the Messiah eating (Gen 49:9, 12; Num 24:8), but the relationship of his eating to his lying down and being raised is not clearly indicated. His going up from the prey in Genesis 49:9 also places his raising/going up as

---

[27]Rouillard, Le Péricope de Balaam, 304-5.
[28]On עֵת, see LXX, NASB. This form by itself can mean "now" (see BDB, HALOT; Judg 13:23; 21:22), but note the related constructions in Gen 18:10, 14; Ex 9:18; Josh 11:6.

his last action in contrast with it being Israel's first action in Numbers 23:24. The question, "Who will raise him?" is only asked about the Messiah, not Israel. The distinction and relationship between the Messiah and Israel is clarified in Numbers 24:17-18, which explains that the Messiah will come "from Israel" and gain a victory that Israel will share in.

Balak's frustration after Balaam's second oracle (Num 23:25) also proved to be temporary, as the king decided to try "another place" (Num 23:27). He stubbornly wished that "it will be right in the eyes of God" for Balaam to curse Israel "from there" (Num 23:27), but Balaam realized that "it was good in the eyes of the Lord to bless Israel" (Num 24:1). He even no longer invoked "omens/snakes" as he had previously. This time as he was beholding "Israel dwelling by their tribes" (cf. Num 22:41; 23:13), the "Spirit of God" came on the Gentile spiritist (Num 24:2; cf. Num 23:6 LXX). Fittingly, Balaam's third and fourth oracles involve an even more expansive vision that involves not only ideal, eschatological Israel and a passing reference to a "shout of a king" (Num 23:21) but an increased focus on this king and his relationship to Israel.

Balaam's heightened spiritual perception in the latter two oracles (Num 24:3-9, 15-19) is indicated emphatically through Numbers 24:3-4, 15-16, where he testifies of becoming a man whose "eye has been opened," who "hears the sayings of God," who "beholds a vision of the Almighty," who "falls down," and whose "eyes have been uncovered." The word "oracle" (נְאֻם), which is uncommon in the Pentateuch (Gen 22:16; Num 14:28) but very common in the Prophets, is used six times. The pagan prophet thus casts himself has having been blind previously but now able to see a prophetic vision (cf. Num 22:31-34). It is not that his first two oracles were any less reliable, but the Spirit of God in the last two oracles opened his eyes to "see" (רָאָה) the Messiah (Num 24:17; cf. Num 21:8; 22:31) who will come "in the last days" (Num 24:14).[29] Israel, however, is not in any way pushed aside. After describing his heightened spiritual state in the third oracle,

---

[29]In the Balaam narrative and in the Pentateuch, "setting [שִׂים] a word in the mouth" seems to be a relatively more mechanical way of communicating than the Spirit being on a person to speak (Ex 4:15; Num 22:38; 23:5, 12, 16; Deut 31:19; cf. 2 Sam 14:3, 19; Ezra 8:17). This distinction, however, may not be absolute in the OT (see Is 51:16; 59:21). Compare the "giving" (נָתַן) of words in the mouth (Deut 18:18; Jer 1:9; 5:14; Mic 3:5; similarly 1 Kings 22:23/2 Chron 18:22; Ps 40:3; Ezek 2:8; 3:3) and "saying what the Lord says" (Num 22:35; 23:16-17; 24:13).

Balaam again describes ideal, eschatological Israel (Num 24:5-6). Picking up on the theme of Israel's secure dwelling in the first oracle (Num 23:9), he praises "how good" (מַה־טֹּבוּ) their "tents" (אֹהֶל) and "dwelling places" (מִשְׁכָּן) are. The thought resembles Psalm 133:1, "How good [מַה־טּוֹב] and how pleasant it is when brothers dwell [יָשַׁב] together in unity." Similarly, Psalm 84:1 exclaims, "How lovely are your dwelling places [מַה־יְּדִידוֹת מִשְׁכְּנוֹתֶיךָ], Lord of Hosts!" Furthermore, Israel's holy and delightful home will resemble "gardens by a river," "aloes the Lord planted," and "cedars by the water" (Num 24:6). In other words, they will have effectively returned to the Garden of Eden.

Despite the difficulty of Numbers 24:7a (MT: "water will flow from his buckets, and his seed will be in many waters"; LXX: "a man will go out from his seed and he will be lord over many nations"),[30] this verse still recognizably shifts the focus from eschatological Israel to their eschatological "king" (מֶלֶךְ) and "his[/their?] kingdom" (מַלְכֻתוֹ, Num 24:7b).[31] Also, the verb *flow* (נָזַל, Num 24:7a) appears in the Pentateuch only in the other major poetic sections (Ex 15:8; Deut 32:2; cf. Judg 5:5). Related to Israel's return to paradise (Num 24:6) and their exaltation (Num 23:24), the Messiah also will be "exalted [רוּם] over Agag" and his kingdom "lifted up" (נָשָׂא). The theme of the Messiah's exaltation links back to the bronze snake, as mentioned above. Although the Hebrew text's reference to "Agag" seems to link Numbers 24:7 to 1 Samuel 15 and Esther 3, there is also significant ancient evidence for an alternate reading of "Gog," Israel's enemy "in the last days" who will "cover the land" (Ezek 38:16; see Num 24:7 LXX, Aquila, Symmachus, Theodotion, Samaritan Pentateuch). Along with the fact that the context of Numbers 24:7 does not quite fit Saul, David, Esther, or Mordecai, Ezekiel 38:17 claims that "Gog" was spoken of by prophets in "former days," which, if traced back to Numbers 24:7 LXX, would then be the more likely original reading.[32]

---

[30]For more discussion, Rouillard, *Le Péricope de Balaam*, 363-70.
[31]In view of passages such as 2 Sam 7:10-16, Is 9:7, and Jer 23:5-6 (see also 1 Sam 13:13; 1 Kings 9:5), it is difficult to draw a hard and fast distinction between the Messianic kingdom and Israel's eschatological kingdom.
[32]Sailhamer, *The Meaning of the Pentateuch: Revelation, Composition, and Interpretation* (Downers Grove, IL: InterVarsity Press, 2009), 244-45. For a discussion of Num 24:7 LXX, see John William Wevers, *Notes on the Greek Text of Numbers* (Atlanta: Scholars, 1998), 405-6.

In another intentional link to the second oracle, Numbers 24:8 declares that "God brings him out of Egypt; he has horns like a wild ox." Although some English translations instead read "God brings *them* out of Egypt" just as in Numbers 23:22, the pronominal suffix in that instance is plural ("them"), whereas the pronominal suffix in Numbers 24:8 is singular ("him"). Although singular pronouns and pronominal suffixes can refer to Israel, and as they do so elsewhere in Numbers 23:21-22 ("the LORD his God is with *him*, and a shout of a king is with *him* . . . like horns of a wild ox for *him*"), it is as though the use of the plural in Numbers 23:22 intentionally distinguishes Israel ("them") from their king ("him") in Numbers 24:8.[33] Numbers 24:7b has already begun to shift the focus to this king and this focus is maintained until the end of the third oracle (see Num 24:9).

The importance of recognizing Numbers 24:8 as Messianic prophecy is manifold. For starters, it shows that the Lord will bring the Messiah out of Egypt, as was fulfilled in Matthew 2:14-15. Furthermore, it casts the Messianic age as involving a second exodus. Just as the Lord had brought Israel out of Egypt the first time (Num 23:22), so he would bring the Messiah out from there a second time (Num 24:8). What he had done for his "son" Israel (Ex 4:22-23), he would also do for his "son," the Messiah (Gen 27:27; 49:9; Hos 11:1; see chaps. 2–3 above). The use of the exodus as a picture of eschatological salvation parallels and reinforces the same move in the Song of the Sea (see chap. 4 above), while at the same time indirectly linking this song to the coming of the Messiah. As argued in chapter three above, Genesis 49:8-12 also recasts much of the Joseph story in Genesis 37–50 as a picture of the Messiah.

By characterizing the Messiah as a powerful ox and devouring lion, Numbers 24:8 adds even more resemblances between eschatological Israel and their eschatological king (Num 23:22, 24). Once again, there should be no confusion of the two, since they are distinguished in the oracles themselves (e.g., Num 24:17). What will indeed take place is that

---

[33]Sailhamer, *The Meaning of the Pentateuch*, 519-20; Postell, Bar, and Soref, *Reading Moses*, 80-83; Seth Postell, "Numbers 24:5-9: The Distant Star," in *The Moody Handbook of Messianic Prophecy: Studies and Expositions of the Messiah in the Old Testament*, ed. Michael Rydelnik and Edwin Blum (Chicago: Moody Publishers, 2019), 293-96.

eschatological Israel will share many (but not all) characteristics with their Messianic king. Although the depiction of the Messiah in Numbers 24:7b-8 is primarily triumphant, it should also be noted that the statement, "God brings him out of Egypt," emphasizes the power of God rather than that of the Messiah, who is passive and presumably needs divine assistance. This could be taken as contradicting the immediate context, but the Messiah's great power in himself and his real experience of divine help coming from outside himself have already been set forth as part of the Messianic vision of the Pentateuch (Gen 49:8-12). Both aspects will also be set forth again in Messianic prophecies in Deuteronomy (see chaps. 7–8 below).

This paradox is clearest in the second half of Genesis 49:9, which is repeated nearly verbatim in Numbers 24:9 ("he stoops down, he lies down like a lion [רָבַץ כַּאֲרִי/שָׁכַב כַּאֲרִי], and like a lioness, who will raise him?").[34] In the context of Genesis 49:8-12 and against the backdrop of Jacob's experience of Joseph coming back from certain death, we argued at length in chapter three above that these lines predict the death and resurrection of the Messiah. He will rule the world in power but will also need God to "raise him" (Gen 49:8-10). If the purpose of the first part of Numbers 24:9 is to reaffirm this core piece of the Messianic vision of the Pentateuch, then the rhetorical question "Who will raise him?" serves as a reminder that the Messiah will be resurrected by God. Nevertheless, it is still true that Genesis 49:8-12 emphasizes the Messiah's suffering and violent death more than Numbers 24:7-9, which has a relatively greater emphasis on his triumphant defeat of his enemies. This difference is due to how each Messianic prophecy fits into its narrative context. Joseph's apparent violent death, longsuffering, and eventual reconciliation with his brothers provides direct support for the death and resurrection of the Messiah in Genesis 49:9, as well as a nuanced understanding of his "enemies" in Genesis 49:8. The Balaam narrative in Numbers 22–24 does not involve these themes, but in wanting to reaffirm the importance of his death and resurrection it simply picks up on Genesis 49:9 while emphasizing the Messiah's triumph over the wicked, in accordance with its own narrative

---

[34]Sailhamer's observation of the relationship of Num 24:9 to Gen 49:9 and Gen 27:29 (and Gen 12:3) is a major contribution to the Messianic vision of the Pentateuch. See Sailhamer, *Pentateuch as Narrative*, 408-9.

context concerning Moab's determined opposition. Thus, in Numbers 24:8, the Messiah "devours nations, his enemies, and crushes their bones, and crushes with his arrows" (cf. the similar description of Israel in Num 23:24), whereas in Genesis 49:11 the Messiah washing his garments in wine plays on both his violent death and his victory (cf. Is 63:1-3), just as his drinking wine and milk do in Genesis 49:12 (see chap. 3 above). The reality of the Messiah's death and resurrection remains the same in both Genesis 49:9 and Numbers 24:9, but they relate differently to their respective narrative contexts. The nations that remain "his enemies" (צָרָיו) to the end will indeed be devoured (Num 24:8; cf. Ps 2:1), but the Messiah's enemies who repent will become "his people" (עַמּוֹ, Deut 32:43; cf. Gen 49:8; Is 19:25).

By nearly repeating the final lines of Genesis 49:9, Numbers 24:9 not only reaffirms the centrality of the Messiah's death and resurrection but also does several other things. As the first Messianic prophecy since Genesis 49:8-12, Numbers 24:7-9 thus picks up Messianic prophecy where it left off in the Pentateuch. Intentional foreshadowing of the Messiah since that point has indeed advanced the Messianic vision, but the Messianic prophecy in Numbers 24:7-9 shows in its own way that the giving and breaking of the Sinai law has not changed the Lord's salvation plan for the world first set forth in Genesis 3:15. The Sinai/Deuteronomic law was never intended to be the means of salvation for Israel and the nations. Israel and the nations will still be saved by the "seed of the woman." He will come from the line of Judah to defeat the serpent and its offspring, and he will fulfill the Abrahamic covenant, especially through his death and resurrection (Gen 49:9; Num 24:9).

The conclusion of Balaam's third oracle in Numbers 24:9 provides yet another intertextual link to Messianic prophecy in Genesis, this time to Genesis 27:29.[35] There Jacob had stolen Isaac's blessing, which included abundance, rule, and the concluding statement, "Those who curse you are cursed, and those who bless you are blessed" (אֹרְרֶיךָ אָרוּר וּמְבָרְכֶיךָ בָּרוּךְ, Gen 27:29). In another nearly verbatim citation, Numbers 24:9 reads, "Those who bless you are blessed, and those who curse you are cursed" (מְבָרְכֶיךָ בָרוּךְ וְאֹרְרֶיךָ אָרוּר). Thus, with its two citations of Messianic prophecy

---

[35]Sailhamer, *Pentateuch as Narrative*, 408-9.

(Gen 27:29; 49:9), Numbers 24:9 strongly ties Balaam's third oracle to the Messianic vision of the Pentateuch and the fulfillment of the Abrahamic covenant (Gen 12:3).

After the third oracle, Balak became angry and "struck his palms together" (Num 24:10; cf. Num 22:23, 25, 27). He sent Balaam home (Num 24:11), but before leaving Balaam summoned Balak to hear "what this people will do to your people in the last days" (Num 24:14; Gen 49:1; Deut 31:28-29). Balaam's fourth and last oracle, with its greater focus on the Messiah, implies that what "this people [Israel] will do" to Moab will be led by their eschatological king who will defeat Moab and all their enemies. Though beginning in similar fashion to the third oracle (Num 24:3-4, 15-16), the fourth oracle is quickly directed to the Messiah (Num 24:17; cf. Num 24:5-6). To be sure, this last oracle still speaks of eschatological Israel (Num 24:18), but their victory, along with their holiness, security, greatness, power, and material wealth (Num 23:9-10, 21-24; 24:5-6), has been achieved by their eschatological king (cf. 1 Cor 1:30; Eph 1:3). Moreover, there is an overall trend in Balaam's four oracles of a gradual shift of emphasis from eschatological Israel to the eschatological Messiah (see Num 23:21; 24:7b-9, 17-19). Indeed, Balaam testified of Israel in his first oracle, "I see them . . . I behold them" (אֲשׁוּרֶנּוּ . . . אֶרְאֶנּוּ, Num 23:9), and of the Messiah in his last oracle, "I see him [אֶרְאֶנּוּ] but not now, I behold him [אֲשׁוּרֶנּוּ] but not near" (Num 24:17).

In the fourth oracle, the Messiah's coming "not now" and "not near" (Num 24:17) accords with his coming "in the last days" (Num 24:14; see chap. 3 above). As a "star" that comes forth "from Jacob" (Num 24:17), he is an Israelite, a "star" among many "stars" (cf. Gen 15:5), and distinguishable from Israel as a whole (cf. Is 49:5-6). As a "scepter" (שֵׁבֶט) who "will rise from Israel" (Num 24:17), he is the Judahite king who wields a "scepter" over the nations in Genesis 49:10. His "crushing" (מָחַץ) the heads of Moab and the "forehead [?] of all the sons of Seth" (Num 24:17; Jer 48:45) seems to apply the Messiah's crushing the serpent's head in Genesis 3:15 to the serpent's seed also. Edom, who like Moab had opposed Israel (Num 20:14-21), will ultimately become a "possession" (יְרֵשָׁה) of the Messiah and Israel (Num 24:18). The cognate verb of "possession" had been used in Genesis 22:17 and Genesis 24:60 of the Messiah "possessing" the gate of his enemies as heir to the covenant promises made to Abram (Gen 15:3-4; see chap. 2 above). As mentioned already (see chap. 1 above), the entire clause "And Seir, his enemies, will be a possession" (וְהָיָה יְרֵשָׁה שֵׂעִיר אֹיְבָיו) in Numbers 24:18 plays on the entire clause "may your seed possess the gate of his enemies" (וְיִרַשׁ זַרְעֲךָ אֵת שַׁעַר אֹיְבָיו) in Genesis 22:17b. This matches the depiction of the Lord's eschatological kingdom in Obadiah 17-21, in which Israel will "possess" (יָרַשׁ) their enemies, and Edom will have no "survivor" (שָׂרִיד, Num 24:18, 19). Like a fire, the house of Jacob will "devour" (אָכַל) Esau (Obad 1:18), just as they, like a lion, "devour" (אָכַל) their enemies in Numbers 23:24. The word *city* is also repeated in Numbers 24:19 and Obadiah 20. All this will come to pass because "one from Jacob" will "rule" (רָדָה, Num 24:19), as humanity should have from the beginning (Gen 1:26, 28).

Numbers 24 concludes with three brief oracles (or "proverbs," to make a total of seven sayings of prophetic wisdom) that concern the destruction of more enemy nations (Num 24:20-24), followed by Balaam and Balak going their separate ways (Num 24:25). Amalek (Num 24:20) was Israel's first enemy after leaving Egypt (Ex 17:8-13), and the Lord's pledge to "surely blot out the remembrance of Amalek" (Ex 17:14), is thus linked to the coming of the Messiah in Numbers 24. Whereas Israel's "end" is desirable (Num 23:10), Amalek's "end" will be destruction (Num 24:20). Assyria will take "Cain" captive (Num 24:22) but will itself be afflicted by the "ships from Kittim" (Num 24:24; Dan 11:30). The question, "Alas, who will live when God appoints this?" (Num 24:23; cf. Ps 89:48), suggests fearsome judgment (Mal 3:2), even the day of the Lord (Mal 4:5).

Conclusion

Insofar as Messianic prophecy, on which intentional foreshadowing of the Messiah largely depends, is the backbone of the Messianic vision of the Pentateuch, Numbers 21–24 refocuses this vision. Through the use of the keyword *nakhash* ("snake"/"omen") and the theme of the defeat of the serpent and its seed, these chapters are bound together and to Genesis 3 and its prophecy of the seed of the woman. While setting forth the bronze snake in Numbers 21 as intentionally foreshadowing both the serpent's defeat and the Messiah's exaltation, the narrative in Numbers 22–24 also brings together threads from the Abrahamic covenant and the exodus. These important themes in the Pentateuch converge and find their integration point in Balaam's oracles, which describe eschatological Israel and their eschatological king, the Messiah. He will be the focus of the second exodus (Num 24:8), and he will crush the heads of his enemies and give Israel final victory (Num 24:17-18). As was the case in the previous Messianic prophecy in Genesis 49:8-12, his work will center on his death and resurrection (Gen 49:9; Num 24:9). The revelation of this gospel depends on the Spirit of God (Num 24:2), who can enable even a Gentile sorcerer to see and proclaim the Messiah.

7

THE PROPHET LIKE MOSES

The Messianic prophecies in Numbers 24:7-9, 17-19 not only refocus the Messianic vision of the Pentateuch after Israel leaves Mount Sinai but also cast the Messiah's coming in terms of a second exodus (Num 23:22; 24:8). In so doing, Numbers 23–24, the third major poetic section of the Pentateuch, links up with the Song of the Sea (Ex 15:1-18), the second major poetic section of the Pentateuch. Exodus themes likewise play a major part in the next Messianic prophecy concerning the "prophet like Moses" in Deuteronomy 18:15-19. Unlike Messianic prophecies in Genesis which precede the Exodus narrative (Ex 1–15), the Messianic prophecies in Numbers and Deuteronomy follow it and draw deeply on themes related to the exodus and Moses in the preceding literary context. As such, these prophecies more directly link the Messiah to the second exodus as its central human figure, just as Moses was in the exodus from Egypt. But as Genesis 27:29 implies, the Messiah is also "served" and "bowed down" to as divine (see chap. 2 above). His relationship to the Lord thus surpasses even Moses' "face-to-face" one. The discussion below will show that Deuteronomy 18:15-19 is indeed a Messianic prophecy, explain its significance, and relate it to the Messianic vision of the Pentateuch. In order to do this, the context of this well-known passage must be investigated. Deuteronomy 34:10 will also play a key role.

Deuteronomy 18:15-19 in Context

The prediction of a "prophet like Moses" (Deut 18:15, 18) is nestled in a passage concerning prophets in Deuteronomy 18:9-22. Jack Lundbom observes that prophets are also the focus of Deuteronomy 13:1-5, which along with Deuteronomy 18:9-22 forms an inclusio around Deuteronomy 13–18.[1] The outermost part of this literary frame specifically concerns false prophets who might lead the people astray (Deut 13:1-3; 18:20-22). Lundbom observes that the test concerning whether a prophet's word comes true in Deuteronomy 18:22 "complements" the earlier test concerning the prophet's doctrine and worship in Deuteronomy 13:1-3.[2] Such an inclusio that warns against false prophecy and idolatry on the one hand, and on the other hand commands obedience to a future "prophet like Moses" is fitting for at least two reasons. First, Moses as a prophet was central to the exodus and the giving of the Sinai/Deuteronomic law, and hence also to the very existence and wellbeing of Israel as the Lord's people. Consequently, impostors must be exposed while at the same time maintaining expectation for a future prophet like Moses who will lead an eschatological exodus and instruct the nations (Is 11:10-16; 42:1-4; Hos 1:11; 12:13; Mic 7:14-15). Second, the implied emphasis of the inclusio is a fitting development of Deuteronomy 12, which focuses on proper worship at "the place [מָקוֹם] the LORD your God will choose" (Deut 12:5, 11, 14, 18, 21, 26). One of the defining characteristics of false prophets is their attempt to lead people after other gods (Deut 13:2, 5). Incidentally, the theme of a special "place" of worship is also found in relation to Bethel, "the gate of heaven" (Gen 28:16-19), and the Lord's self-revelation to Moses (Ex 33:21; 34:8), two passages which have been discussed previously (see chaps. 2 and 5 above). The emphasis of Deuteronomy 12 on eating and joy (Deut 12:7, 18) also generally parallels Melchizedek's bringing of "bread and wine" in Genesis 14:18.[3]

---

[1]Jack Lundbom, *Deuteronomy: A Commentary* (Grand Rapids: Eerdmans, 2013), 555.
[2]Lundbom, *Deuteronomy*, 555.
[3]See J. Gordon McConville, *Deuteronomy*, Apollos Old Testament Commentary (Downers Grove, IL: InterVarsity Press, 2002), 223, "The picture of worship as community feasting and rejoicing is one of the hallmarks of Deuteronomy's depiction of Israel before God.... The rejoicing of Israel is a response to the promised blessings.... The feasting is in itself a participating in the blessings given." Taking it a step further, "This rejoicing of the people of God is no accidental extra, but is essential to the picture, and even has an eschatological quality" (231). Accordingly, McConville does not simply equate the "place" in Deut 12 with Jerusalem but takes its anonymity as expressing "an irreducible openness. The recognition in the historical books that Jerusalem corresponds to the chosen place (1 Kgs. 8:29) should not be confused with an irreversible claim on Jerusalem's behalf by Deuteronomy. This idea, that history could end in a specific place with its institutional trappings, runs counter to the thrust of Deuteronomy itself, which is perfectly

Duane Christensen sees a relationship between the instructions in Deuteronomy 13:1-5 and the Balaam narrative. He argues, "Balaam was a diviner who performed signs and wonders, and who received from YHWH a word in the night, presumably by means of dreams (Num 22:7, 8, 13, 19, 20)."[4] Although there is no biblical record of him performing signs and wonders, Balaam was a diviner (Num 24:1) who would ultimately play a role in turning the Israelites after other gods (Num 31:16; cf. Num 25), just as Deuteronomy 13:1-5 warned. Relatedly, as noted in the previous chapter, the terms "omen/snake" (נָחַשׁ) and "divination" (קֶסֶם) in Deuteronomy 18:10 provide a direct link to Balaam's dark practices in Numbers 23:23.[5] Signs and wonders (Deut 13:1-2) are associated with the Lord's plagues against Egypt (Ex 7:3; Deut 4:34; 6:22; 7:19), which he performed through Moses and Aaron (Ex 4:8-9, 17, 21; 7:9-10). Hence, false prophets who performed such miracles were implicitly competing with the Lord's mighty works through his chosen prophet, just as the Egyptian magicians attempted to match the signs that Moses and Aaron performed. Such mighty works are directly linked to the "prophet like Moses" in Deuteronomy 34:10-11, which shows that Deuteronomy 13:1-5 is linked to both passages that concern this future prophet. As shown in the previous chapter, the Balaam narrative is itself intertextually linked to the exodus narrative through the narrative patterning of Balak after Pharaoh, the parallels between the birth of Moses and the prophecies of the Messiah in Balaam's third and fourth oracles, and the casting of the Messiah's coming as central to the second exodus in Balaam's third oracle (Num 24:8). Deuteronomy 13:1-5 is thus also linked to the exodus, the second exodus, the Messiah, and the prophet like Moses through these intertextual relationships.

Christensen also points out that the warning against false prophets in Deuteronomy 13:1-3, 5 surrounds a restatement of the "great commandment" (i.e., the *Shema*) in Deuteronomy 13:3-4 (see Deut 6:5). Whether or not

---

echoed in Jeremiah's critique, with its direct reference to our present chapter (Jer. 7:11-15; note v. 12)" (232).

[4] Duane Christensen, *Deuteronomy 1–21:9*, Word Biblical Commentary (Nashville: Nelson, 2001), 270. Relatedly, he asserts, "The law in 13:2-6 [English: vv. 1-5] was used to shape the story of Balaam in Num 22."

[5] In the only other OT passage using these two roots, the biblical author of Kings characterizes the northern kingdom of Israel as guilty of such sins (2 Kings 17:17) at the end of a long list of sins (vv. 7-17).

Israel "listens" (שְׁמַע) to the "words" (דָּבָר) of a false prophet "tests" (נָסָה) whether they truly "love the LORD" with all their heart and soul (Deut 13:3). Accordingly, the stern commands to "listen" (שְׁמַע) to the "words" (דָּבָר) of the prophet like Moses (Deut 18:15, 18-19) should be understood as a key part of obeying "in the fullness of time" (Gal 4:4) the same "great commandment," which also begins with "Listen" (שְׁמַע, Deut 6:4; cf. Deut 4:1; 5:1; 9:1). Obedience to this prophet is thus linked to Deuteronomy's broader emphasis on obedience to the Lord's commands generally. Thus "listening" concerns not only the static legal corpora that are recorded in the Deuteronomy (and the Pentateuch) but also the words of the prophet like Moses (Is 42:1-4). If this prophet is an eschatological prophet or even the Messiah (as will be argued below), then this listening and obedience further relates to faith in this Messianic prophet-king. After all, Israel was also supposed to believe and obey Moses (Ex 4:1, 5, 8-9, 31; 14:31; 19:9), even though they often did not (e.g., Ex 16:2-3; 17:2-4; 32:1; Num 12:1; 16:3).

In addition to being related to Deuteronomy 13:1-5, Deuteronomy 18:9-22 is also connected to its immediately preceding context that contains instructions concerning various leaders. Judges, priests, and kings are dealt with in Deuteronomy 16:18–18:8. There is likely a sense in which the "prophet like Moses" is the climax of this section of Deuteronomy.[6] The "judges and officials" (שֹׁפְטִים וְשֹׁטְרִים) in Deuteronomy 16:18-20 are charged to execute "justice" (מִשְׁפָּט) and "righteousness" (צֶדֶק), consistent with those Moses appointed earlier in Deuteronomy 1:15-17 (see Ex 18). The apparent disruption to the flow of thought in Deuteronomy 16:18-20 with instructions concerning idolatry (Deut 16:21-22) is linked back to the themes of judges and judgment through the description of the judicial process for alleged idolatry (Deut 17:2-7). Common themes and language further link this process to Deuteronomy 13, including the portion specifically concerning prophets (Deut 13:1-5). These commonalities include the specification of types of possible offenders (Deut 13:1, 6, 12-13; 17:2), idolatry (Deut 13:2, 6-7, 13; 17:3), thorough investigation (Deut 13:14; 17:4), punishment by stoning led by witnesses (Deut 13:6, 9-10; 17:5-7), and purging evil from their midst (Deut 13:5; 17:7). A "judge" explicitly

---

[6]McConville, *Deuteronomy*, 285, "The climactic final position of this section stresses the primacy of Israel's affairs of the divine word."

reappears in Deuteronomy 17:8-9 in conjunction with difficult cases (see Deut 17:12). Priests are also especially involved in such situations (Deut 17:9, 12). Instructions concerning the king are famously the subject of Deuteronomy 17:14-20, with "the priests, the Levites" making another appearance in Deuteronomy 17:18 (cf. Deut 17:9; 18:1; 27:9). The whole tribe of Levi has no portion of land but is to be provided for by portions of sacrificial offerings and by the offering of firstfruits (Deut 18:1-8; cf. Deut 10:9; 12:12, 19; 14:27-29; 16:11, 14).

The instructions in Deuteronomy 18:9-22 begin with a prohibition against "the abominations of those nations" that Israel will encounter in the land (Deut 18:9). These include child sacrifice and divination (Deut 18:10-14), which leads to the promise of a prophet like Moses (Deut 18:15). This figure contrasts with the various kinds of spiritists just listed and with Balaam (Num 24:1). Unlike such mediums who speak messages from the demonic realm, the prophet like Moses speaks directly on behalf of the Lord himself. The idea is that the Israelites do not need to seek spiritists or mediums because the Lord will put his own words into this prophet's mouth for them to hear (Deut 18:18-19). Whereas the instructions concerning the king included special mention of him remaining under the authority of Scripture and the priests (Deut 17:18-20; cf. Deut 20:2), the authority of this prophet is not qualified in this way. Rather than suggesting that the prophet like Moses was somehow above divine law (see Deut 13:1-5), it instead seems to assume his complete conformity to it along with his possession of divine authority. Of course, not all who claim to have such status should be automatically believed (Deut 18:20-22).

J. Gordon McConville observes that there is a difference between the Lord "raising up" the prophet like Moses (Deut 18:15, 18) compared to his "choosing" (בָּחַר) the priest and king (Deut 17:15; 18:5). Although McConville suggests that the underlying reason has to do with whether or not there is an official installation to the office,[7] what cannot be disputed is that the "raising up" in Deuteronomy 18:15, 18 "emphasizes the initiative of Yahweh (Amos 2:11; Jer 29:15)."[8] The Lord had indeed "chosen" the Levites (Deut 18:5; cf. Deut 10:8; Ex 32:26-29) and wanted the Israelites to set over

---

[7]McConville, *Deuteronomy*, 302.
[8]Richard Nelson, *Deuteronomy*, Old Testament Library (Louisville: Westminster, 2002), 235.

themselves the king that he had "chosen" (Deut 17:14), but only the prophet like Moses is specifically said to be "raised up" by the Lord.⁹ The "judges and officials" were accordingly appointed by the people (Deut 16:18).

On the level of the composition of the Pentateuch and its Messianic vision, the Lord's act of "raising up" (Hiph. קוּם) the prophet like Moses provides yet another link to the Balaam narrative, specifically its Messianic prophecies in the third and fourth oracles. Numbers 24:9 had asked, "Who will raise [Hiph. קוּם] him?" Relatedly, Numbers 24:17 predicted that "a scepter will rise [Qal קוּם] from Israel." These passages are at the heart of the Messianic vision of the Pentateuch and also relate to Genesis 49:9, which asks the same question as Numbers 24:9 (see chap. 3 and 6 above). Genesis 49 and Numbers 24, as has been pointed out already, contain the most extensive Messianic prophecy in the Pentateuch. As an important lexical link between Deuteronomy 18:15, 18 and these Messianic prophecies in the Pentateuch and others in the Old Testament (e.g., 2 Sam 7:12; Jer 23:5-6; 30:9; Ezek 34:23; Amos 9:11; 1 Chron 17:11), the word *raise up* suggests an identification of the prophet like Moses with the Messiah himself. The answer to "Who will raise him up?" (Gen 49:9; Num 24:9) is, "God will" (Num 23:19), and Deuteronomy 18:15, 18 further explains that he will be a prophet like Moses. Numbers 24:8 has already placed the Messiah at the center of the second exodus ("God brings him out of Egypt"), and the parallel between Pharaoh's three attempts to suppress the Israelites followed by the birth of Moses, and Balak's three attempts to get Balaam to curse Israel followed by the Messiah-saturated fourth oracle (Num 24:17-19) also suggests that the Messiah will be a Moses-like figure in the second exodus. As noted earlier, the characterization of the Messiah as a warrior in Numbers 24 also matches the depiction of the Lord in his victory over Pharaoh at the Red Sea in Exodus 15:1-18.

What else might it mean to be a prophet specifically "like Moses"? It certainly means that this prophet will have important resemblances to

---

⁹Eckhart Otto, *Deuteronomium 12,1–23,15*, Herders Theologischer Kommentar zum Alten Testament (Freiburg: Herder, 2016), 1497-98, "But in contrast to the king, which is chosen by the Lord, but should be appointed by the people, the 'prophet like Moses' is appointed only by the Lord." He continues, "But in contrast to the appointment of the king the addressees of Deuteronomy have no part in the appointment of the prophets. It is the work of the LORD alone. Not once is Moses involved in it."

Moses. At the same time, it does not mean that he will somehow be identical to Moses. In other words, although he will be "like Moses" in a meaningful sense, there will also be at least some areas in which he is different. Deuteronomy 18:15-18 explains that he will be an Israelite ("from your midst, from your brothers") and that he will bear unique responsibility as a mediatorial spokesperson who will deliver the Lord's words to his people (Deut 18:16-18).[10]

The incident recalled in Deuteronomy 18:16-17 is Israel's request for Moses to become their mediator at Mount Sinai after hearing the Ten Commandments directly from the Lord (Deut 18:16; 5:5, 24-27; Ex 20:18-21).[11] The Lord's granting of their request (Deut 5:28; 18:17) is not necessarily a wholehearted endorsement because the phrase that may be translated "[all] that they have spoken they have spoken *well*" can instead mean "[all] that they have spoken they have spoken *thoroughly*" (see Hiph. יָטַב, Deut 9:21; 13:15; 17:4; 19:18; 27:8; Hos 10:1; Mic 7:3). Perhaps the ambiguity of the Hebrew verb corresponding to the English adverbs *well* or *thoroughly* (הֵיטִיבוּ) allows for a negative spin in Deuteronomy 5:29, where the Lord wishes that Israel had a heart to fear and obey him for their own good (Qal יָטַב), but a positive spin in Deuteronomy 18:17-18, where the Lord promises a prophet like Moses.[12] Another difference between the two recountings in Deuteronomy 5 and Deuteronomy 18 is that in Deuteronomy 5:27 Israel specifically requests Moses as their permanent mediator, and his mediation is the answer to this request (Deut 5:28-31). In contrast, although Israel still requested not to hear the voice of the Lord anymore in Deuteronomy 18:16, the request for Moses to be their

---

[10]Rashi reduced the meaning of a prophet being "like Moses" to his being an Israelite and interpreted this verse as a reference to a prophetic succession: "As I am from your midst, from your brothers, he will raise up for you in my place, and so from prophet to prophet." Although possible grammatically ("a prophet from your midst, from your brothers, like me," Deut 18:15; "from the midst of their brothers, like you," Deut 18:18), there are significant problems with this interpretation (see below).

[11]Ex 20:18-21 in the Samaritan Pentateuch includes related portions from Deut 5 and Deut 18. See Yoon-Hee Kim, "'The Prophet Like Moses': Deut 18:5-22 Reexamined Within the Context of the Pentateuch and in Light of the Final Shape of the TaNAK" (Ph.D. diss., Trinity Evangelical Divinity School, 1995), 60-63.

[12]Deut 29:4 implies that Israel did not have such a heart (also Jer 32:39). Moreover, Israel's desire to remove themselves from the immediate presence of the Lord (Ex 20:18-21; Deut 5:24-27) contrasts with the importance of the Lord's presence emphasized elsewhere (Ex 3:14; 33:14-16).

mediator is absent. Accordingly, their concern here is answered in Deuteronomy 18:17-18, not through Moses but through the promise of a "prophet like Moses."[13] Whereas Moses' mediation was ultimately a failure on multiple fronts (e.g., Ex 32:1-6; Num 11:11-15; 20:12), the future prophet's perfect mediation will achieve eschatological salvation.

To speak of Moses' "mediation" suggests that Moses not only acted as a prophet but also as a priest. Indeed, his frequent intercession on behalf of Israel reinforces this aspect of his ministry (e.g., Ex 15:25; 32:11-13; Num 14:13-19; 27:15-17). But Moses acted not only as prophet and priest, but also as a ruler. While granting the Lord's supremacy over Moses and Israel, Moses was clearly the nation's human leader. For example, Exodus 18:13-27 describes Moses "judging" (שָׁפַט) the disputes of the people (Ex 18:13, 16). Even after he accepted the wise advice of his father-in-law Jethro to appoint God-fearing "princes" (שַׂר) to help "judge" (שָׁפַט) these disputes, Moses was still the highest human authority who handled cases that were too difficult for the other leaders (Ex 18:21-22). While priestly themes can also be detected in Exodus 18:15 ("the people come to me to inquire of God"), Exodus 18 clearly sets forth Moses as the top-ranking human leader of Israel whose authority to "judge" encompasses all the affairs of the nation. It is probably no accident that Moses had been rejected earlier as "prince and judge" (שַׂר וְשֹׁפֵט, Ex 2:14). To act as a supreme judge of the nation is one of the key responsibilities of a king. Israel's later request for "a king to judge us" was repeatedly expressed in these same terms (1 Sam 8:5-6, 20). Accordingly, Solomon's prayer for wisdom was so that he could "judge your people" (לִשְׁפֹּט אֶת־עַמְּךָ) as the supreme human ruler of the land (1 Kings 3:9). The Lord as king also "judges" (Ps 96:10, 13; 97:1-2; 98:6, 9; 99:1, 4). Although the "judges" also "judged" (e.g., Judg 3:10; 10:2-3; Ruth 1:1), they were distinct from kings (Judg 17:6; 21:25), whose authority exceeded theirs. The closest that the Pentateuch may come to directly calling Moses a king is in Deuteronomy 33:5.[14] But even if the interpretation of this verse is disputed, it is still clear that Moses

---

[13] Mark O'Brien, "Deuteronomy 16.18–18.22: Meeting the Challenge of Towns and Nations," *JSOT* 33 (2008): 170, calls this "a clever move."

[14] See John Sailhamer, *The Pentateuch as Narrative: A Biblical-Theological Commentary* (Grand Rapids: Zondervan, 1992), 477.

operated as a quasi-king of Israel in the scope of his authority (see also the desire for a new "head" in Num 14:4). In other words, the Pentateuch presents Moses as a prophet and priest, and probably also as a kind of ruler or king.

Moses' ministry as prophet and priest is detectable in Deuteronomy 18:15-18, which suggests that the prophet like Moses will also bear priestly characteristics as a mediator between the Lord and his people. These priestly themes link to the Pentateuch's vision of the Messiah. As we have already seen, the first Messianic prophecy in the Pentateuch already includes a priestly aspect in his person and work. The seed of the woman in Genesis 3:15 removes uncleanness by crushing the head of the serpent and shedding his own blood (see chap. 1 above). Furthermore, insofar as Melchizedek, Jacob's ladder, and Bezalel intentionally foreshadow the Messiah and his priesthood (see chaps. 2 and 5 above), the corresponding passages also highlight the priestly side of the Messiah. Though Joseph's most obvious role was as a ruler, the narrative also presents him as a quasi-priest through his marriage to a priestess (Gen 41:45, 50; 46:20; see chap. 3 above). But in addition to having characteristics like a king and priest, Joseph also resembles a prophet through his experience of dreams (Gen 37:5-10) and his interpretation of dreams (Gen 40-41; cf. Num 12:6). Thus Joseph, like Moses, also has attributes of a prophet, priest, and king. The narrative presentations of these two men are compositionally related to one another and together intentionally foreshadow the Messiah as a prophet, priest, and king. They are even narratively linked in Exodus 13:19, where "Moses took the bones of Joseph with him" out of Egypt (cf. Gen 50:24-26; Ex 1:8). As already shown, Genesis 49:8-12 re-presents Joseph as a picture of the Messiah and his eschatological reign. Its emphasis on the Messiah as a king is balanced by the emphasis in Deuteronomy 18:15-18 on the Messiah as prophet and priest. Even in these respective emphases, the apparently missing elements are not totally lost. The Messiah's death in Genesis 49:9, 11-12 is a central part of his priestly ministry, as Genesis 3:15 has already established, and Joseph's prophetic characteristics loom in the preceding narrative just as Moses' kingly characteristics are evident in the literary context as well.

A Prophet Like Moses: An Individual or a Succession?

Some commentators, however, do not believe that Deuteronomy 18:15-19 concerns an individual prophet.[15] Obviously, if the prophet like Moses does not refer to an individual, then Deuteronomy 18:15-19 cannot be a direct prophecy of the Messiah. Since this is a crucial interpretative issue related to the Messianic vision of the Pentateuch, we deal with it at length here. Walter Brueggemann attempts to strike a balance, "The text seems to assume a single prophet in time to come, though it is possible in the perspective of Deuteronomy that the verse envisions a succession of prophets."[16] In view of the fact that all prophets mediate the Lord's word to the people as Moses did (Deut 18:16-17), McConville takes it a step further, "The 'raising up' of a prophet need not refer to a single act, or a single individual, therefore [i.e., because Deuteronomy is oriented toward life in the land]. It rather envisages a succession of prophets."[17] More forcefully, Nelson remarks, "In spite of the literal singularity of 'a prophet' . . . it seems obvious that a series of prophets is meant (cf. 17:14-15, where more than one king is undeniably in view)."[18] Jeffrey Tigay likewise confidently asserts, "The singular is clearly meant collectively, referring to a succession of prophets, just as the singular 'king' in 17:14-20 refers to any and all kings, and 'the Levite' here in 18:6 refers to many Levites."[19] His commentary on this verse explicitly references its polemical application to Christian and Muslim interpretations of the prophet as an individual and as predicting Jesus or Mohammed respectively. Indeed, Tigay's position is essentially the same as Rashi's from the Middle Ages. While diversity of opinion on the "prophet like Moses" is to be expected for a passage studied by so many throughout the ages, it even appears to be intertwined with the very foundation of three major world religions.

---

[15]For an extensive survey of the history of interpretation of this passage, see Kim, "Prophet Like Moses," 34-102.

[16]Walter Brueggemann, *Deuteronomy*, Abingdon Old Testament Commentaries (Nashville: Abingdon, 2001), 194.

[17]McConville, *Deuteronomy*, 303. Likewise, Otto, *Deuteronomium 12,1–23,15*, 1497, believes the verb "he will raise" has "an iterative connotation." Also J. A. Thompson, *Deuteronomy*, Tyndale Old Testament Commentaries (Downers Grove, IL: InterVarsity Press, 1974), 212.

[18]Nelson, *Deuteronomy*, 234-35.

[19]Jeffrey Tigay, *Deuteronomy*, JPS Torah Commentary (Philadelphia: Jewish Publication Society, 1996), 175.

The previous section of this chapter has already given several reasons for taking this prophet as an individual, such as his relation to the Messiah through the Balaam narrative, the verb *raise up*, and Moses/Joseph as prophet, priest, and king. Though some modern commentators have taken the "prophet like Moses" as an individual,[20] a more thorough argument for an individual interpretation of this prophet is necessary. In addition to the use of the singular in Deuteronomy 18:15, 18 and the intertextual connections to the Messianic passages mentioned above, a deciding factor is that the Pentateuch treats Moses as a unique prophet, a prophet *par excellence*. Accordingly, "prophet like Moses" cannot refer to a succession of prophets because to be "like Moses" by definition distinguishes Moses and the prophet like him from all other prophets. In this case, the apparent parallel between the singular "prophet" in Deuteronomy 18:15, 18 and the representative singular "king" in Deuteronomy 17:14-15 would not be a true parallel because the singular "prophet" is further specified as being uniquely "like Moses."

Clear support for Moses' uniqueness is found in Numbers 12:1-8. When Miriam and Aaron criticized their brother for marrying a Cushite woman (Num 12:1-2), the Lord called all three siblings together (Num 12:4-5) and explained Moses' unique status and calling to them directly (Num 12:6-8). Unlike the typical "prophet" that the Lord communicates with in a "vision" (מַרְאָה) or "dream" (חֲלוֹם) (Num 12:6; cf. Gen 15:1; 28:12; 31:10-11; 37:5-10; 46:2; Num 24:4, 16), Moses, "my servant," is special and "faithful in all my house" (Num 12:7), perhaps suggesting his greater authority and access (see Gen 39:4-9). The Lord speaks to him "mouth to mouth and plainly [מַרְאֶה], and not in riddles. He looks upon [נָבַט] the likeness of the LORD" (Num 12:8). In other words, the directness of communication between the Lord and Moses as part of their intimate relationship distinguishes Moses from other prophets. To be sure, Moses had seen a "great vision" before (Ex 3:3), which he shortly became afraid to "look upon" (נָבַט, Ex 3:6), but Moses later enjoyed such a close relationship with the Lord that the Lord spoke to him "face to face [פָּנִים אֶל־פָּנִים], as man speaks to his friend" (Ex 33:11).

---

[20]See Kim, "Prophet Like Moses," 87-89.

Thematically, this especially intimate relationship between Moses and the Lord parallels the Messiah's unique status and relationship to the Lord as "my son" (Gen 27:27; 49:9). The prophet *par excellence* parallels the son *par excellence* (see chap. 3 above). Both individuals are said to be outstanding among "your brothers" (אַחֶיךָ, Gen 49:8; Deut 18:15, 18). If these figures are two different people, their uniqueness would be diminished because there would be two individuals who share the honor of being exalted over their Israelite brethren (cf. Deut 17:15). From this perspective, it would be very strange for the Messianic "Lion of Judah" (Gen 49:9) to share such glory with another Israelite, the prophet like Moses who leads the second exodus, while the Messiah himself is merely brought out of Egypt (Num 24:8) as a more passive participant. However, if the prophet like Moses is the Messiah, then his uniqueness remains fully intact.

Although the king of Israel was also to be from "your brothers" (Deut 17:15), special attention was given to preventing "his heart from being lifted up over his brothers" (רוּם־לְבָבוֹ מֵאֶחָיו, Deut 17:20). As pointed out above, there is no corresponding concern to keep in check the exalted status of the prophet like Moses. Neither of course is the Messiah's authority reined in. On the contrary, he will be "lifted up [רוּם] over Agag/Gog and his kingdom will be exalted" (Num 24:7). Indeed, the kings of Israel needed such an exhortation to humility, but the prophet like Moses and the Messiah seem to have no need of the same.

As in Numbers 12:1-8, the intimate, "face-to-face" relationship between the Lord and Moses is reiterated in connection with a "prophet like Moses" in Deuteronomy 34:10. This makes plain that a special intimacy with the Lord is one of the defining characteristics of this prophet. Deuteronomy 34:11-12 further highlights Moses' role in performing miracles related to the exodus, which suggests that the prophet like Moses will also both perform miracles to bring about the second exodus and be the central figure in this eschatological deliverance. The centrality of the Messiah to the second exodus has already been established in Numbers 24:8. However, the Messiah is passively brought out of Egypt in Numbers 24:8 whereas the prophet like Moses presumably brings about the second exodus triumphantly through signs and wonders. Furthermore, insofar as the Passover lamb in Exodus 12 intentionally foreshadows the Messiah (see chap. 5

above), his death will be part of the climax of this eschatological deliverance. But such a paradox should not lead us to abandon the identification of this eschatological prophet with the Messiah. His death will lead to the miracle of his resurrection, and both Genesis 49 and Numbers 24 alternatively emphasize the Messiah's power in himself to defeat his enemies and his receiving divine help to "raise him" (Gen 49:9; Num 24:9). The very first Messianic prophecy in the Pentateuch (Gen 3:15) has already set forth the paradox of his victory and his death as a key integration point for its Messianic vision. Indeed, the emphasis on the Messiah's authority as the prophet like Moses in Deuteronomy 18 and Deuteronomy 34 is balanced accordingly by his need for divine help in the intervening Messianic prophecy in Deuteronomy 33:7 (see chap. 8 below).

Another possible objection to an individual referent for the prophet like Moses is the contrast with false prophets in Deuteronomy 18:20-22. A proper contrast with false prophets, it may be argued, would be true prophets generally, not just an individual prophet like Moses. But as Kim observes, the false prophet (Deut 18:20-22), like the prophet like Moses (Deut 18:19), claims to speak in the Lord's "name."[21] Next, she points out the difference between the anarthrous "prophet" (נָבִיא, Deut 18:15, 18) and "*the* prophet" (הַנָּבִיא, Deut 18:20, 22) as an intentional "distinction between the two terms" and concludes that what is being communicated is not "an antithetical relationship between true prophets versus false prophets. Rather it focuses on false prophets who would misuse either God's name or God's message."[22] Although perhaps counterintuitive on the surface, the anarthrous "prophet" (like Moses) in Deuteronomy 18:15, 18 thus refers to an individual, whereas "the prophet" in Deuteronomy 18:20, 22 refers to false prophets generally. Her basic argument seems to hold also for Deuteronomy 13:1-5, which, though beginning with an anarthrous "prophet" who ambiguously "arises" with miraculous power (Deut 13:1), focuses on "the prophet" who promotes idolatry (Deut 13:2-5). The anarthrous "prophet" in Deuteronomy 13:2 parallels the anarthrous "prophet like Moses" in Deuteronomy 18:15, 18. The former "arises in your midst" (יָקוּם בְּקִרְבְּךָ) from an unknown source, but the latter the Lord "from your

---
[21] Kim, "Prophet Like Moses," 246-47.
[22] Kim, "Prophet Like Moses," 248.

midst . . . will raise up" (יָקִים . . . מִקִּרְבְּךָ). Once it is clear in the context of Deuteronomy 13:1-5 that the former is an impostor (Deut 13:3), the false prophet is always referenced with an article: "that prophet" (הַנָּבִיא הַהוּא); "that dreamer of the dream" (חֹלֵם הַחֲלוֹם הַהוּא). In Deuteronomy 18:20, 22, "the prophet"/"that prophet" is directly described as an impostor and is always referenced with an article. Indeed, there is nothing inherently illogical about predicting the coming of an individual prophet like Moses while also warning against those false prophets who might claim the same authority.

A related objection is Nelson's view that Deuteronomy 18:15-22 is "an etiology for the institution of prophecy" whose scope encompasses all true prophets.[23] Indeed, as Lundbom observes, Deuteronomy 18:15-19 is "the only passage in any of the OT law codes to discuss the [genuine] prophet."[24] On this basis, it could be argued that an individual interpretation of the "prophet like Moses" leaves the prophetic succession without an adequate basis in the Pentateuch. Without disputing Lundbom's point about Pentateuchal legal codes, the Pentateuchal *narrative* does speak of prophets besides Moses and the prophet like him. Abraham was a "prophet" (Gen 20:7) and Miriam was a "prophetess" (Ex 15:20). Even more importantly, Moses wished that all the Lord's people were "prophets" (Num 11:29), as the seventy elders had been (Num 11:25-27). In view of these other passages in the Pentateuch that concern prophets, it is not necessary to require Deuteronomy 18:15-22 to the bear all the weight of explaining the origin of the institution of prophecy. Abraham, not Moses, was the first "prophet," and the prophet like Moses will bring about an outpouring of the Spirit on all flesh so that they "prophesy" (Joel 2:28-29) in fulfillment of Moses' wish in Numbers 11:29. Until that day, Abraham, Miriam, Moses, and many other genuine prophets and prophetesses provide a foretaste of what is to come.

Another key piece of evidence for an individual referent for the prophet like Moses in Deuteronomy 34:10 is the statement, "And a prophet never arose in Israel like Moses" (וְלֹא־קָם נָבִיא עוֹד בְּיִשְׂרָאֵל כְּמֹשֶׁה). Since the age of the prophets began with Samuel (see Acts 3:24; 13:20), this statement appears

---

[23]Nelson, *Deuteronomy*, 234-35.
[24]Lundbom, *Deuteronomy*, 556.

to be at least a retrospective evaluation of prophets who have come and gone but who do not measure up to the stature of Moses. Even granting Miriam and Deborah as prophetesses (Ex 15:20; Judg 4:4), the anonymous prophet in Judges 6:8, and the "man of God" in Judges 13:6, 8, the statement in Deuteronomy 34:10 still makes the best sense if many prophets from Samuel onward had already come and gone. Incidentally, this suggests that Deuteronomy 34:10, though still inspired (see Deut 34:10 LXX; cf. 2 Tim 3:16), was added to the original Mosaic Pentateuch by a later prophetic author.

Modern translations, however, do not always make clear this retrospective evaluation. For example, the NIV reads, "Since then, no prophet has risen in Israel like Moses." Most other English translations read similarly (cf. ESV, KJV, NASB, NKJV, RSV). If such translations accurately reflect the meaning of the Hebrew text of Deuteronomy 34:10, then it seems only to imply a passage of time since Moses' death, not necessarily the coming and going of many prophets. As such, it is conceivable that the origin of this statement could have been from Joshua's lifetime or the period of the judges. However, this is not what the Hebrew text expresses (וְלֹא־קָם נָבִיא עוֹד; "and a prophet never arose"). The key to proper interpretation of this statement is the word *'od* (עוֹד) and its relationship to the rest of the clause. Although this word by itself can mean a variety of different things ("still," "yet," "again"), its presence in this particular syntactical construction—that is, preceded by *lo'* (לֹא, "not") and a *qatal* verb—is well attested in the Old Testament.[25] As such, it does not simply mean that something has not happened or has not happened *yet* but expresses a sense of finality with respect to a defined set of past circumstances inferred from the literary context. In other words, with respect to a particular, complete situation viewed retrospectively, something never happened.

Blenkinsopp and Sailhamer both hold a similar view, and we attempt to thoroughly prove it with the examples below.[26] In some cases, לֹא ("not")

---

[25] The order is different in 2 Chron 20:33, with עוֹד first. As such, it means that, "the people still had not set their heart toward the God of their fathers" (וְעוֹד הָעָם לֹא־הֵכִינוּ לְבָבָם לֵאלֹהֵי אֲבֹתֵיהֶם).

[26] Joseph Blenkinsopp, *Prophecy and Canon: A Contribution to the Study of Jewish Origins* (Notre Dame, IN: University of Notre Dame Press, 1977), 86, says that this construction "never means 'not yet' with the implication 'it hasn't happened yet but it will later.' Following attested usage it must on the contrary be translated 'never again,' 'never since' or 'no longer' with no limitation of time unless expressly stated." Our view, as the subsequent discussion shows, allows for both a summative evaluation of the prophetic age and the coming of an eschatological prophet like

+ *qatal* verb + עוֹד expresses absolute finality (i.e., something never happened and never will again). For example, Joshua 5:12 says, "and there was no manna anymore for the sons of Israel" (וְלֹא־הָיָה עוֹד לִבְנֵי יִשְׂרָאֵל מָן) after they entered the land of Canaan. Likewise, in the exceptional incident of Saul summoning Samuel from the dead, Saul recognized that, "God departed from me, and he does not answer me anymore [וְלֹא־עָנָנִי עוֹד]" (1 Sam 28:15). Concerning the abundance of spices brought by the Queen of Sheba, 1 Kings 10:10 states, "Never again did so many spices come" (לֹא־בָא כַבֹּשֶׂם הַהוּא עוֹד לָרֹב). Other passages with לֹא ("not") + *qatal* verb + עוֹד that describe a situation in the past that continues permanently are Joshua 2:11; 2 Kings 2:12; 2 Chronicles 13:20; Psalm 88:5; and Ezekiel 33:22.[27]

But this construction can also simply express that something never happened (or didn't happen anymore) with respect to a defined set of past circumstances without implying that it never happened again in an absolute sense. For example, after Eli blessed Hannah as she prayed to have a son (1 Sam 1:17), "her face was not sad anymore" (וּפָנֶיהָ לֹא־הָיוּ־לָהּ עוֹד, 1 Sam 1:18). This probably does not mean that Hannah never felt sadness again, but rather that she did not feel sad anymore specifically about her barrenness. Likewise, when the Queen of Sheba saw Solomon's splendor and "there was no spirit in her anymore" (וְלֹא־הָיָה בָהּ עוֹד רוּחַ, 1 Kings 10:5; 2 Chron 9:4), this does not mean that she remained breathless for the rest of her life but that her visit to Solomon was characterized by breathless awe. Again, when Job's friends "did not answer him anymore" (לֹא־עָנוּ עוֹד, Job 32:15-16), this does not necessarily mean that they never again answered any of Job's questions for the rest of their lives but that they stopped trying to answer Job in this particular situation. Joshua 5:1 may also fall into this category (see Josh 9:1-2).

Moses. See also John Sailhamer, *Introduction to Old Testament Theology: A Canonical Approach* (Grand Rapids: Zondervan, 1995), 247-48.

[27] See also passages where the *qatal* verb is a helping verb used together with an infinitive construct. The usage is essentially the same as when the *qatal* is the only verb. It can describe something that never happened in a defined set of past circumstances and which may or may not have happened subsequently. In the following list, those passages that concern a "relative" finality are indicated. For יָסַף, see Gen 8:12; 38:26; Judg 13:21; 1 Sam 7:13 (relative); 1 Sam 27:4; 2 Sam 2:28; 2 Kings 6:23 (relative? see 2 Kings 6:24); 2 Kings 24:7. Num 32:14 also involves יָסַף in a different construction. For יָכֹל as helping verb, see Ex 2:3; Judg 2:14 (relative); 2 Sam 3:11. For אָבָה, see 1 Chron 19:19. For יָדַע, see Eccles 4:13.

Our comprehensive survey of these לֹא ("not") + *qatal* verb + עוֹד constructions shows that Deuteronomy 34:10 also expresses a sense of finality with respect to a defined set of past circumstances (i.e., the prophetic age), without necessarily implying absolute finality. It is indeed saying that a prophet like Moses "never came," not merely that he "has not come since" or "has not come yet," even though these are also true. Nevertheless, these latter translations fail to do justice to the inferred complete, past situation that such a לֹא ("not") + *qatal* verb + עוֹד construction implies.

As a syntactical point of comparison, the related construction of לֹא ("not") + *yiqtol* verb + עוֹד is well attested as commonly expressing that something will never happen again in the future. As representative examples, Jeremiah 3:16-17 says that Israel "will never again say [לֹא־יֹאמְרוּ עוֹד], 'the ark of the covenant of the LORD' ... and will never remember it [וְלֹא יִזְכְּרוּ־בוֹ] ... and it will not be made again [וְלֹא יֵעָשֶׂה עוֹד]." Likewise, at that time the Lord promises, "And I will remember their sins no more" (וּלְחַטָּאתָם לֹא אֶזְכָּר־עוֹד, Jer 31:34). The sense of finality with respect to the future expressed in these statements is confirmed by other passages (Gen 8:21-22; 9:11, 15; 17:5, etc.).[28] This is in keeping with the frequent use of the *yiqtol* in direct speech with reference to the future. Since the future is, by definition, open ended, לֹא ("not") + *yiqtol* verb + עוֹד expresses something that will never happen and is inherently absolute. On the other hand, *qatal* in narrative is frequently used with reference to the past, and the construction לֹא ("not") + *qatal* verb + עוֹד correspondingly expresses finality with respect to a defined set of past circumstances, with this "finality" being either relative to those circumstances or absolute by nature of those same circumstances.

This defined set of past circumstances, we believe, is not merely the coming and going of some Israelite prophets (which, if still ongoing, is open ended and neither complete nor clearly defined), but the entire succession of Israelite prophets including the exilic and postexilic prophets (Ezra 5:1; Ezek 1:1-3; Hag 1:1; Zech 1:1). Excluded in the retrospective

---

[28]It is possible that on rare occasions this construction indicates the foreseeable future (e.g., Ex 9:29; Deut 17:13; 19:20), which is not necessarily absolute. Sometimes the construction refers to a desired future (e.g., Lev 17:7; Num 18:5, 22; Deut 10:16; 13:17; 28:68), which may or may not have been realized. Compare the absolute prohibitions using אַל + *yiqtol* + עוֹד in Ex 36:6; Deut 3:26.

statement of Deuteronomy 34:10, of course, is John the Baptist, who is a special case (Mt 11:9-11) as "Elijah" who immediately precedes the Messiah as his forerunner (Mal 4:5; Mt 11:14) and is part of the Messianic age (Is 40:3; Mt 3:1-3; Mk 1:1-4). The view that Deuteronomy 34:10 refers to Moses' superiority to all Israelite prophets is well represented by scholars.[29] Although these same scholars come up with various ways of reconciling this interpretation of Deuteronomy 34:10 with the Lord's promise to raise up a prophet like Moses,[30] the simplest solution, in our view, is to interpret Deuteronomy 18:15, 18 and Deuteronomy 34:10 together as saying that all the prophets have come and gone (i.e., as the defined set of past circumstances and complete situation viewed retrospectively) but the promised prophet like Moses is yet to come. Psalm 74:9 even seems to adopt this same perspective with explicit reference to the cessation of prophecy, "There is no prophet anymore and there is not one with us who knows how long" (אֵין־עוֹד נָבִיא וְלֹא־אִתָּנוּ יֹדֵעַ עַד־מָה). This psalm also refers to the destruction of the sanctuary (Ps 74:3-7) as it recalls the Lord's past deliverance of Israel from Egypt (Ps 74:12-15) and prays for him to remember

---

[29]Tigay, *Deuteronomy*, 175, 339; McConville, *Deuteronomy*, 477-78; Nelson, *Deuteronomy*, 397; Thompson, *Deuteronomy*, 212, 320; Christensen, *Deuteronomy 21:10–34:12*, Word Biblical Commentary (Nashville: Nelson, 2002), 873. Contra Lundbom, *Deuteronomy*, 947-48, who thinks that the reference is to "8th-cent. prophets who had arisen recently" and notes that "Jeremiah appears to understand himself as this 'prophet like Moses.'" Brueggemann, *Deuteronomy*, 289, affirms Moses' incomparability while also noting a parallel to Josiah (2 Kings 23:25), "a Moses-like figure ... Josiah is Moses who reappears in royal garb."

[30]Most take "a prophet like Moses" in Deut 18 to refer to a prophetic succession which takes on the prophetic role "like" Moses, while Deut 34 refers to equality with Moses (which no one attained); e.g., Tigay, *Deuteronomy*, 175; Christensen, *Deuteronomy 1–21:9*, 409, "For Moses to say that the prophet to come will be 'like me' refers to the role Moses played as God's messenger, not to his person [in view of Deut 34:10]"; Nelson, *Deuteronomy*, 397, remarks, "Prophets like Moses would appear [i.e., Deut 18:15, 18 as a prophetic succession], but none would have his unmediated access to Yahweh's presence [as Moses is described in Deut 34:10]." Also seemingly in this category is McConville, *Deuteronomy*, 477, who takes Deut 34:10 as an "affirmation of Moses' incomparability as a prophet" but interprets Deut 18:15 as referring to a prophetic succession (303). The problem with taking the "prophet like Moses" in Deut 18:15, 18 as merely referring to Moses' *role* as prophet is that it largely removes the significance of the future prophet being "like Moses" because the designation "prophet like Moses" in the end is hardly distinguishable from simply being a "prophet." Differently, Thompson, *Deuteronomy*, 212-13, argues, "The sense of the passage [Deut 18:15-22] is that a succession of prophets would arise to continue the work of Moses who surpassed them all (34:10). In later times, particularly after the cessation of prophecy, an individual interpretation was given to this passage and 'the prophet who should come' became a figure associated with the Messianic age and sometimes identified with the Messiah Himself (cf. Jn. 1:21, 45; 6:14; 7:40; Acts 3:20-22; 7:37, *etc.*)."

"the covenant" (Ps 74:20). The coming of the Messiah is also related to the Lord's faithfulness to his covenant (Lk 1:72).

What About Joshua, Elijah, or Jeremiah as the Prophet Like Moses?

In arguing for an individual, Messianic interpretation of the prophet like Moses, we have not yet dealt with other individuals that have been set forth by commentators as this prophet, including Joshua, Elijah, and Jeremiah.[31] In order to do justice to this important aspect of the debate, we explain these views below along with additional reasons for excluding these candidates as fulfillments of Deuteronomy 18:15, 18. Obviously, the above arguments for a Messianic interpretation apply across the board to these three men and all other individual candidates. Nevertheless, it is still helpful to see additional specific reasons that apply to Joshua, Elijah, and Jeremiah.

There are several reasons why Joshua might be equated with the prophet like Moses.[32] He was Moses' successor (Num 27:15-23) and had the "spirit of wisdom" (Deut 34:9). As such, Moses' authority over the nation was transferred to Joshua (Num 27:20; Deut 34:9). Moreover, the crossing of the Jordan led by Joshua is an explicit parallel to the crossing of the Red Sea led by Moses (Josh 4:23). Joshua was relatedly "exalted" (גִּדַּל) by the Lord before all Israel so that they feared him just as they had feared Moses (Josh 4:14). The Lord had also promised to be with Joshua just as he had been with Moses (Josh 1:5; cf. Josh 1:17). There is no question that Joshua had many similarities to Moses, such as his leadership of the nation, his empowerment by the Spirit (Num 11:17, 25; 27:18), his leading the nation across a body of water miraculously, and the presence of the Lord with him.

Nevertheless, these similarities do not mean that Joshua was the prophet like Moses. Although he had the Spirit on him and so had characteristics of a prophet (Num 11:29; 27:18), the Pentateuch's last word on Joshua characterizes him more as a wise man (Deut 34:9), whose authority and power,

---

[31]There are even a few who mention Samuel in this connection. For further discussion, see Peter Miscall, *1 Samuel: A Literary Reading* (Bloomington, IN: Indiana University Press, 1986), 1-3, 44-46; Dale C. Allison, *The New Moses: A Matthean Typology* (Minneapolis: Fortress, 1993), 31-35.

[32]See Hans Barstad, "The Understanding of Prophets in Deuteronomy," *SJOT* 8 (1994): 236-51.

even if he is counted as a prophet, did not match Moses' (Deut 34:10-12). Joshua was not the prophet like Moses, since, as Kim points out, he "is eliminated by the larger context of the Pentateuch."[33] From "his youth" (Num 11:28), Joshua was Moses' "servant" (מְשָׁרֵת, Ex 24:13; 33:11). This title was even used after Moses' death (Josh 1:1). Moses' authority over Joshua is also implied through Moses changing Joshua's name from Hoshea (Num 13:16). Even when Joshua was publicly installed as Moses' successor, he only received "*some* of [Moses'] authority [מֵהוֹדְךָ]" (Num 27:20), presumably not all of it. Kim further cites Moses' initiation of the leadership transition (Num 27:15-17; contra Deuteronomy 18:15, 18); Joshua's need for priestly guidance involving the Urim, unlike Moses (Num 27:21); and the implied greater authority of Moses through the laying of hands on Joshua (Num 27:18; Deut 34:9).[34] Later, Joshua's success depended on his obedience to Moses' written instruction, the Pentateuch (Josh 1:7-8, 13; 4:10; 8:30-35). Joshua's obedience to Moses was commendable (Josh 11:15), but the picture of Joshua that emerges is not of one whose authority matches, much less exceeds, Moses', as it will for the prophet like Moses (Deut 18:15-19).

Another individual candidate for the prophet like Moses is Elijah.[35] He was a "prophet" (1 Kings 18:36) who "like Moses" worked signs and wonders on behalf of Israel (Deut 34:11-12; 1 Kings 17–18). He also parted a body of water (the Jordan River) with his cloak (2 Kings 2:7-8), just like Moses parted the Red Sea with his staff (Ex 14:16). Furthermore, Elijah's parting of the Jordan is connected with the transfer of his "spirit" to Elisha, his successor (2 Kings 2:9, 15; cf. 2 Kings 2:11,16). The impartation of the Spirit who was on Moses to Joshua was also a key part of that succession (Num 11:17, 25; 27:18). Elijah even experienced a special encounter with the Lord at "the mountain of God, Horeb" (1 Kings 19:8-18) just as Moses had (Ex 33:18–34:8). But it is here that an important difference between Elijah and Moses is revealed. Whereas the literary context of Moses' encounter emphasized his intimate, "face-to-face" relationship with the Lord

---

[33]Kim, "Prophet Like Moses," 207. Her helpful discussion of Joshua and the prophet like Moses (190-207) is the basis for much of the present paragraph.
[34]Kim, "Prophet Like Moses," 201-2, 205.
[35]See Havilah Dharamraj, *A Prophet Like Moses? A Narrative-Theological Reading of the Elijah Stories*, Paternoster Biblical Monographs (Milton Keynes, UK: Paternoster, 2011).

(Ex 33:7-11), Elijah, on the contrary, "wrapped his face with his cloak" (וַיָּלֶט פָּנָיו בְּאַדַּרְתּוֹ) (1 Kings 19:13). Although parallel to Moses hiding his face when called at the burning bush at Horeb earlier in his life (Ex 3:1-6), Elijah's action does not match the profile of Moses and the prophet like Moses as having a "face-to-face" relationship with the Lord (Deut 34:10). Indeed, the context of Moses' special encounter with the Lord in Exodus 33–34 also discusses his use of a "veil" (מַסְוֶה) when speaking to the Israelites because they were afraid of the glory shining from his face (Ex 34:29-35). As a shield for the Israelites, this veil would be removed when Moses went before the Lord (Ex 34:34). Elijah's use of his cloak as a shield places him and his encounter with the Lord in 1 Kings 19 on a lower level than Moses and his encounter(s) in Exodus 33–34. Thus, Elijah, though a "prophet" who was "like Moses" in several ways, was not the "prophet like Moses" as characterized in Deuteronomy 34:10 as having a "face-to-face" relationship with the Lord.

One more individual candidate for the prophet like Moses is Jeremiah. Moshe Weinfeld lays out parallels between Deuteronomy 18:18 ("and he will speak to them all which I command him . . . and I will put my words in his mouth") and the call of Jeremiah ("and all which I command you, you will speak. . . . Behold, I have put my words in your mouth," Jer 1:7, 9).[36] Lundbom also points out that both Moses and Jeremiah initially objected to their calling because they were not good speakers (Ex 4:10-17; Jer 1:6).[37] While there is no disputing the correspondence between these passages, among others, in Deuteronomy and Jeremiah (e.g., Deut 4:29; Jer 29:13), there are broader contextual reasons for rejecting Jeremiah as the "prophet like Moses." Jeremiah did not perform miraculous signs, as Deuteronomy 34:11-12 leads us to expect of the prophet like Moses. Also, although he did predict the second exodus (e.g., Jer 3:14-18; 23:1-8; 29:10-14), Jeremiah did not actually bring it pass. But the prophet like Moses will lead this eschatological deliverance and bring Israel permanently into the Promised Land (Num 24:8; Deut 34:10-12). Thus, although Jeremiah was

---

[36] Moshe Weinfeld, *Deuteronomy and the Deuteronomic School* (Oxford: Clarendon, 1972), 359.
[37] Jack Lundbom, *Jeremiah: Prophet Like Moses* (Eugene, OR: Wipf and Stock, 2015), 3, also draws a parallel between Jeremiah's vision of the almond tree (Jer 1:11-12) and Moses' encounter with the burning bush (Ex 3:2-6). See Lundbom, *Jeremiah 1–20*, Anchor Bible (New York: Doubleday, 1999), 232-35.

a prophet and resembled Moses and the prophet like Moses in some respects (Deut 18:18; Jer 1:7, 9), he is not the prophet like Moses either.

We are not denying that Joshua, Elijah, and Jeremiah were all "like Moses" in some ways. Elijah and Jeremiah were even "prophets," and Joshua at least resembled a prophet through the Spirit being on him. Nevertheless, none of them match the profile as defined by Deuteronomy 18:15-19, Deuteronomy 34:10-12, and relevant related passages. If the prophet like Moses refers to an individual, then the rejection of these other candidates also indirectly supports a Messianic interpretation by process of elimination. That being said, we must also bear in mind that such an interpretation does not imply that the Messiah is "like Moses" in every respect, as though he were somehow identical to him. He is indeed the "prophet like Moses" as defined by Deuteronomy 18:15-19, Deuteronomy 34:10-12, and relevant related passages, but he is also different from Moses in at least some ways.

Most importantly, the Messianic prophet *like* Moses is an eschatological prophet who is also *greater* than Moses. Moses, after all, did not lead Israel into the Promised Land, but the prophet like Moses will lead them there and give them permanent rest (Hos 1:11; Heb 4:8). Brueggemann pithily expresses the paradox of Moses as "banned but unequaled."[38] Moses delivered the Israelites out of Egypt with signs and wonders, but the prophet like Moses, with even greater signs and wonders (Jn 9:32; 15:24), will secure a final deliverance of his people from captivity "in the last days" (Gen 49:1; Num 24:14), in fulfillment of the original salvation promise of Genesis 3:15. Like Moses, he is worthy of being an object of faith (Ex 14:31; 19:9), but unlike Moses he will never lapse into sin (Num 20:12; 27:14). The great authority that Moses had will be overshadowed by the prophet like Moses' absolute authority (Deut 18:15, 18-19), and the burden that was too heavy for Moses at times (Num 11:11-14; cf. Ex 17:12; 18:14, 17-18) he will fully bear to the very end (Lev 16:21-22; Is 53:4, 12).

CONCLUSION

The Messianic vision of the Pentateuch takes another significant step forward in Deuteronomy 18:15-19. We learn through this passage that not

---

[38] Brueggemann, *Deuteronomy*, 287.

only will the Messiah's death as a Passover lamb secure the second exodus (Ex 12) and that he will be brought out of Egypt (Num 24:8), but he will also be a "prophet like Moses" who will perform miracles in leading people from all nations out of bondage and into the Promised Land (see Ps 107). Like Moses, he will have an especially intimate, "face-to-face" relationship with the Lord, which is elsewhere characterized as that of a favored son (Gen 27:27; 49:9). As a priestly mediator like Moses, he will have divine authority and speak the very words of God. In all these things, he is both like Moses and greater than Moses. The Lord's "raising up" of this prophet, his exaltation over his brothers, his centrality to the second exodus, and his coming during the eschatological era (Deut 18:15, 18; 34:10) show that the prophet like Moses is indeed the Messiah himself (Gen 49:1, 8-9; Num 24:8-9, 14). Deuteronomy 18:15-19 is both a "lens" of direct prophecy and a "mirror" that selectively draws on Moses as intentionally foreshadowing the Messiah.

8

THE BLESSING OF JUDAH

In the previous chapter, we argued that the promise of a "prophet like Moses" in Deuteronomy 18:15-19 is a Messianic prophecy that is thoroughly intertwined with the Messianic vision of the Pentateuch. Along the way, we discussed Deuteronomy 34:10-12, which, though a reminder and interpretation of the Messianic prophecy in Deuteronomy 18:15-19, is not itself a Messianic prophecy. As such, the last, though perhaps the most obscure and debatable, Messianic prophecy in the Pentateuch is the blessing of Judah in Deuteronomy 33:7. At first glance, this verse does not look like a Messianic prophecy at all, and indeed most commentators have interpreted it as referring to the tribe of Judah. Nevertheless, these challenges have not led us to abandon it in relation to the Messianic vision of the Pentateuch. After all, it is part of Deuteronomy 32–33, the last and by far the longest of the four major poetic sections in the Pentateuch (cf. Gen 49:1-27; Ex 15:1-18: Num 23:7-10, 18-24; 24:3-9, 15-19). These two chapters are also preceded by the phrase "in the last days" (Deut 31:29). The combination of this eschatological phrase with a major poetic section has already yielded key Messianic prophecies in Genesis 49 and Numbers 24. We believe that this same combination in Deuteronomy 32–33 yields another Messianic prophecy in Deuteronomy 33:7, which in its brevity and enigmatic nature resembles the first Messianic prophecy in Genesis 3:15. We will first set the eschatological stage through a selective treatment of Deuteronomy 32 before dealing directly with Deuteronomy 33.

THE CONCLUSION OF THE CANONICAL PENTATEUCH AND DEUTERONOMY 32

The canonical Pentateuch ends with a bang.[1] Blessings and curses for obedience and disobedience to the Lord's commands are pronounced in

---

[1] We use the word *canonical* here because we do not know exactly how the original Pentateuch ended. As argued previously, Deut 34, though also "inspired" (2 Tim 3:16), was probably added by a later prophetic author (cf. Deut 33:1).

Deuteronomy 27–28, followed by Moses' candid but discouraging remark in Deuteronomy 29:4, "And the Lord until this day has not given you a heart to know, or eyes to see, or ears to hear." In other words, this second generation of Israelites after the exodus was characterized by the same spiritual dullness that characterized the previous rebellious, unbelieving generation that was sentenced to die in the wilderness (Num 14:11, 21-23, 27-29). What this strongly suggests is that the curses for disobedience, rather than the blessings for obedience, will be the primary experience of the Israelites henceforth. But not all is gloom and doom in the final chapters of the Pentateuch. Though assuming the exile, in which the curses for disobedience have reached their climax with Israel banished from the Promised Land (Deut 28:63-68; 29:27-28), Deuteronomy 30:1-14 sets forth the hope of eschatological salvation, which includes national conviction over sin and wholehearted repentance (Deut 30:1-2, 8, 10), the Lord regathering Israel to the land and restoring them (Deut 30:3-5, 9), his circumcision of their hearts so that they keep the *Shema* (Deut 30:6; cf. Deut 30:11-14; Deut 6:5), and his defeat of their enemies (Deut 30:7). Evidently, the Sinai/Deuteronomic law itself would not actually bring "blessing," and the creational and Abrahamic blessing would come to Israel and the nations through the new covenant "in the last days."

The same themes of Israel's exile for their disobedience and the Lord's eschatological deliverance of them from "there" (Deut 30:1, 3-4) are found in Deuteronomy 31–32. Moses will not lead the Israelites into the Promised Land, but under Joshua they are to enter and destroy the nations who live there (Deut 31:2-8; cf. Deut 7:1-5). Nevertheless, Moses emphatically predicts that after his death the Israelites will still rebel against the Lord by turning to idols (Deut 31:16-22). As a result, the Lord's "anger will burn against them," and he will "forsake them" and "hide [his] face from them" so that "many disasters and distresses" come upon them (Deut 31:17). The Lord even has Moses write down a "song" and teach it to the Israelites as a "witness" against them in future generations when all these things come to pass (Deut 31:19-22, 30). This song is Deuteronomy 32:1-43. The "Book of the Law" would also be a "witness" against Israel (Deut 31:26). Joshua through Kings should thus be read with the expectation of Israel's eventual exile.

The Blessing of Judah

Tragically, Israel's rebellion and idolatry would take place even as they enjoyed blessings that the Lord himself had given them. After he brings them into a fruitful land, "they will eat and be satisfied and grow fat and turn to other gods and serve them" (Deut 31:20). This is exactly what Deuteronomy 8:10-20 had warned against (cf. Deut 4:25-27). Moses himself knew their "rebellion" and "stiff neck" and expected things to get worse after he died (Deut 31:27), as he also called "heaven and earth" as witnesses against Israel (Deut 31:28; 30:19; 32:1). Including the "song" and the "Book of the Law" (Deut 31:19, 22, 26), this amounts to at least the "two or three witnesses" required to establish every matter (Deut 19:15; cf. Deut 17:6).

Moses further explains that these disasters will come upon Israel "in the last days" (Deut 31:29). On the level of the structure and compositional strategy of the Pentateuch, this shows that Deuteronomy 32–33, like Genesis 49 and Numbers 23–24, is a major poetic section associated with this eschatological phrase in the immediate literary context. However, whereas the other two poetic sections more clearly involve Messianic prophecy, the coming of the Messiah is not so obvious here. In fact, the phrase "in the last days" in Deuteronomy 31:29 is directly tied to Israel's experience of the Lord's wrath because of their idolatry. This appears to be unrelated to the coming of the Messiah, while simultaneously reinforcing the nature of the song in Deuteronomy 32:1-43 as a "witness" regarding Israel's idolatry and experience of divine judgment. Thus, it seems to associate the phrase "in the last days" not so much with the Messianic age but with the Lord's punishment of Israel for their idolatry. Indeed, his hiding his face (Deut 32:20) and his burning "anger" (Deut 32:22) tie back to Deuteronomy 31:17-18, and his jealousy (Deut 32:21) in connection with "fire" (Deut 32:22) relates further back to his being a "consuming fire, a jealous God" (Deut 4:24; cf. Deut 5:9; 6:15; 9:3). Likewise, the "disasters" (רָעוֹת) of "famine," violent "beasts," and the "sword" (Deut 32:23-25) also recall the "disasters" in Deuteronomy 31:17, 21, while simultaneously drawing on the curses for disobedience (Deut 28:17-18, 22-26, 30-33, 38-42). At the same time, the "venom of things that crawl in the dust" (Deut 32:24) reaches all the way back to the antagonism of the serpent that started in the Garden of Eden (Gen 3:15; Num 21:6; Deut 8:15; Mic 7:17). In Deuteronomy 28, the fact that these "curses" (Deut 28:15) will "come upon you" (וּבָאוּ עָלֶיךָ), "overtake [נָשַׂג] you," and "pursue [רָדַף] you" (Deut 28:22, 45) further suggests their personification as "enemies" (Deut 28:25; cf. Ps 23:5), who are frequently characterized similarly (e.g., Gen 34:27; Ex 14:9; 15:9; 1 Sam 12:12; 2 Kings 25:5; Ps 7:5; Lam 1:3). This theme of enmity provides another compositional link back to the promise of the seed of the woman in Genesis 3:15, which further suggests the eschatological scope of Deuteronomy 32. As mentioned above (see chap. 4 above), the conclusion of the song also links back to Genesis 3:15 through the defeat of "the head of the locks/leaders of the enemy" (Deut 32:42), which leads to joy for the nations (Deut 32:43). This link is even stronger in the LXX through its rendering, "the head of the rulers of the enemies."

Even a surface reading of Deuteronomy 32:1-43 reveals that this song bears witness not only to Israel's future idolatry and judgment by the Lord but also his ultimate salvation of them. In Deuteronomy 32:26-27, the Lord is justly angry enough to wipe out "their memory" forever (cf. Ex 17:14), but he refrains because of the boast of the "enemy" (אוֹיֵב) and "their adversaries" (צָרֵימוֹ) that, "Our hand is lifted up, and the LORD has not done [פָּעַל] all this." As indicated by the three preceding uses of the verb *pa'al* (פָּעַל), all of which are in major poetic sections of the Pentateuch, eschatological Israel will be a testimony to "what God has done [פָּעַל]" (Num 23:23), in relation to "the established place" the Lord "made" (פָּעַל, Ex 15:17) and his perfect "work" (פֹּעַל, Deut 32:4; cf. Hab 1:5). Even more to the point, Deuteronomy 32:36-43 plainly declares that "the LORD will judge his people and have compassion on his servants" (Deut 32:36) and concludes with him "atoning" for his land, his people (Deut 32:43). The subjugation of enemies, first mentioned in the song in Deuteronomy 32:27, is also a major theme in Deuteronomy 32:30-35, 41-43, just as it is in the other major poetic sections (Gen 49:8; Ex 15:4-7, 9-10, 14-16; Num 23:24; 24:8, 17-24). In Deuteronomy 32:36-39, the Lord's victory shines brilliantly against the backdrop of his people's utter helplessness (Deut 32:36) and the demonstrable impotence of all other gods (Deut 32:37-38; cf. Ex 15:11; Mic 7:18). His "hand" (Deut 32:39-41) will again be manifested as it was in the Song of the Sea (Ex 15:6, 12, 16-17; note also "sword" in Ex 15:9; Deut 32:41). His taking of an oath in Deuteronomy 32:40 parallels his oath to Abraham in Genesis 22:16-18 to fulfill the Abrahamic covenant through a "seed"

(Gen 22:17; Deut 33:7), defeat his enemies (Gen 22:17; Deut 32:41), and bring blessing to all nations (Gen 22:18; Deut 32:43). His lifting of his hand for the oath in Deuteronomy 32:40 relates to both the certain fulfillment of the two oaths and his thwarting of the exaltation of the enemy's hand (Deut 32:27).

As it turns out, Israel's "enemies" (Deut 32:27, 31) are also the Lord's "adversaries" and "haters" (Deut 32:41). This parallels the Messiah's defeat of his and Israel's enemies in Numbers 24:8, 17-19, which roots both passages in the "enmity" between the seed of the woman and the serpent along with his seed in Genesis 3:15. Once again, the Pentateuch attributes the same action to both the Messiah and the Lord. The Lord's "repayment" (שָׁלֵם) of enemies in Deuteronomy 32:35, 41, along with the divine title "Most High" (עֶלְיוֹן, Deut 32:8; cf. Num 24:16), also recalls Melchizedek, king of "Salem" (שָׁלֵם), priest of God "Most High" (עֶלְיוֹן), who blessed the Lord for delivering Abram's "adversaries" (צָר) into his hand (Gen 14:18-20). The theme of a divine warrior in Deuteronomy 32:39-43 parallels that of the Song of the Sea, as well as matching the profile of the Messiah in Genesis 49 and Numbers 24. The verb *make atonement* (כִּפֶּר, Deut 32:43) further casts the Lord himself in the role of a priest (see Ezek 16:63; 36:25) and parallels passages that cast the Messiah in the same role (e.g., Gen 3:15; 14:18-20; 28:10-22; 49:8-12; Ex 31:2-5; Deut 18:15-19). The picture in Deuteronomy 32:43 of the "nations, his people" (גּוֹיִם עַמּוֹ) shouting for joy (cf. "nations, his adversaries" [גּוֹיִם צָרָיו] in Num 24:8), the Lord avenging the "blood of his servants," defeating his enemies, and cleansing his people is undoubtedly descriptive of eschatological salvation. The salvation of the nations is implicit in Genesis 3:15 (as a promise for the entire human race) and explicit in the covenant promises to Abraham (e.g., Gen 12:3; 17:4-5; 18:18; 22:18; 26:4), as well as in the prophets (e.g., Is 19:25; 42:6; 49:6). Moreover, as we have already seen, the use of the term *rock* of both water from the rock and the Lord who was scorned and forgotten when Israel became complacent (Deut 32:4, 13, 15, 18; cf. Deut 31:20) is linked to other water-from-the-rock passages in the Pentateuch and its overall Messianic vision (see chap. 5 above).

Thus even the phrase "in the last days" in Deuteronomy 31:29 can still be related to the Messianic age. Though it certainly is explicitly connected to the judgment of Israel's idolatry in Deuteronomy 31:29, this destruction and exile is directly linked to the coming of the Messiah because it is this situation of desperate need out of which he will deliver Israel. The timing of his arrival will not coincide with their enjoyment of the Lord's blessings in the Promised Land but rather with circumstances that provoke an acute awareness of their utter helplessness. Thus, Deuteronomy 32:1-43, though not containing what may be classified as Messianic prophecy, nevertheless is intertextually related to the Messianic vision of the Pentateuch (see Ex 15:1-18) and in its ultimate focus on eschatological salvation is inextricably linked to the deliverance the Messiah will bring.

The Blessing of Jacob

The Song of Moses concludes in Deuteronomy 32:43, but poetry continues in Moses' blessing of the twelve tribes in Deuteronomy 33. It is as though the Lord's eschatological victory has finally brought blessing to Israel and the nations. In its literary form and content, Deuteronomy 33 especially parallels Jacob's blessing of his twelve sons in Genesis 49:1-27.[2] Even in that literary context this fatherly blessing was already presented as not merely related to his sons as individuals but to the tribes that they would become (Gen 49:28). So much, of course, has happened since that time—the sojourn in Egypt, the exodus, the giving of the Sinai law, the failure of the first generation to enter the Promised Land, and the preparation for a transition of leadership from Moses to Joshua.

As a general rule, Jacob's blessings of his twelve sons in Genesis 49:1-27 focus on the tribes that will descend from each man. This is explicit for Simeon/Levi (Gen 49:5-7), Zebulun (Gen 49:13), Issachar (Gen 49:14-15), Dan (Gen 49:16-18; cf. Judg 13:1-5), and Asher (Gen 49:20). Even the blessing of Reuben (Gen 49:3-4) implicitly transfers the blessings of the firstborn to Judah and Joseph (Gen 49:8-12, 22-26) and thus dramatically affects the tribe that will come from Reuben's line. The blessing of Naphtali is obscure (Gen 49:21), though still often taken as referring to the tribe of

---

[2] For a helpful survey of the history of interpretation of both blessings, see Joel Heck, "A History of Interpretation of Genesis 49 and Deuteronomy 33," *BSac* 147 (1990): 16-31.

Naphtali,[3] and Gordon Wenham likewise comments regarding the blessing of Benjamin (Gen 49:27), "Clearly, the future military exploits of the tribe of Benjamin are in view [e.g., Judg 3:15-30; 5:14; 20:1-48; 1 Sam 10–14]."[4] This same basic pattern is confirmed in Deuteronomy 33, and the overall parallel between the two blessings in Genesis 49 and Deuteronomy 33 is well recognized by commentators.[5] In relation to the structure of the Pentateuch, we should also recall that both blessings involve the main human character calling an audience together to listen (Gen 49:1; Deut 31:28). Furthermore, both Jacob and Moses are about to die (Gen 49:29-33; Deut 31:14; 33:1; 34:5).

We will deal with the complex case of the blessing of Joseph momentarily, but this pattern shows that the focus on an individual Judahite instead of the tribe of Judah as a whole in Genesis 49:8-12 is exceptional among the blessings of Genesis 49:1-27. Furthermore, the parallel nature of Genesis 49 and Deuteronomy 33 (along with the connections to the Messianic vision of the Pentateuch discussed below) suggests that the blessing of Judah in Deuteronomy 33:7 also refers to an individual Judahite, the Messiah, just as Genesis 49:8-12 does. In this case, the brother who is praised by all his brothers (Gen 49:8) and the "lion" (Gen 49:9) who rules the other animals (Gen 49:14, 17, 21, 27; cf. Is 11:6-9) would be the same Judahite who needs to be brought to "his people" in Deuteronomy 33:7. If this is true, both Genesis 49 and Deuteronomy 33 not only deal with each tribe generally but also specifically highlight an individual king to come from the line of Judah "in the last days" (Gen 49:1, 8-12; Deut 31:29; 33:7). As in Genesis 49, most of the blessings in Deuteronomy 33 clearly concern

---

[3]For detailed discussion, see Gordon Wenham, *Genesis 16–50*, Word Biblical Commentary (Dallas: Word, 1994), 482-83; Stanley Gevirtz, "Naphtali in 'The Blessing of Jacob,'" *JBL* 103 (1984): 513-21. For our purposes, we observe that both commentators interpret this blessing in terms of the tribe of Naphtali. Though necessarily brief, Derek Kidner, *Genesis*, Tyndale Old Testament Commentaries (Downers Grove, IL: InterVarsity Press, 1967), 232, agrees.

[4]Wenham, *Genesis 16–50*, 487. Kidner, *Genesis*, 233, likewise refers to "the dash and spirit of the tribe" and adduces Judg 5:14 and Ps 68:27 as additional evidence.

[5]E.g., Wenham, *Genesis 16–50*, 469; Jürgen Ebach, *Genesis 37–50*, Herders Theologischer Kommentar zum Alten Testament (Freiburg: Herder, 2007), 573-74; J. Gordon McConville, *Deuteronomy*, Apollos Old Testament Commentary (Downers Grove, IL: InterVarsity Press, 2002), 467-68, who also notes the parallel to the aged Isaac's blessing in Gen 27:1-40; Eckhart Otto, *Deuteronomium 23,16–34,12*, Herders Theologischer Kommentar zum Alten Testament (Freiburg: Herder, 2017), 2235, believes that Deut 33:6-25 "presupposes" Gen 49:2-27 and "should be read as a corrective complement."

tribes rather than individuals. The blessing of Benjamin in Deuteronomy 33:12 is ambiguous, but the blessings of Reuben and Naphtali (Deut 33:6, 23), which were not as clear in Genesis 49, naturally relate to their tribes. Such would be expected of Moses' blessing of the Israelites by their "tribes" at this point in their history (Deut 33:1, 5; cf. Deut 31:28).

In order to further support the point about the blessing of Judah being focused on an individual in Deuteronomy 33:7 as in Genesis 49:8-12, we must account for the blessing of Joseph (Deut 33:13-17), which is also focused on an individual in Genesis 49:22-26. His blessing is comparable in length to Judah's and focuses on Joseph's fruitfulness (Gen 49:22),[6] the Lord's helping him against his enemies, and the outpouring of "blessings" on "the head of Joseph" (Gen 49:23-26). He is even singled out as "prince of his brothers" (נְזִיר אֶחָיו, Gen 49:26).[7] Abundant blessings and the singling out of Joseph is repeated in Deuteronomy 33:13-16. However, the last line of this latter blessing clarifies how such things will be fulfilled, "Such are the ten thousands of Ephraim, and such are the thousands of Manasseh" (Deut 33:17). In other words, the blessing of Joseph, for all its emphasis on Joseph as an individual, is ultimately related to the two tribes descended from him. This had already been hinted at in his earlier blessing through the wordplay between "fruitful bough" (פֹּרָת, Gen 49:22) and the naming and full inheritance of "Ephraim" (אֶפְרַיִם, Gen 41:52; 48:5, 20).

On the other hand, the extensive use of Judah as a picture of the Messiah in Genesis 49:8-12 should be kept in mind (see chap. 3 above). Accordingly, the portrayals of Joseph in the *poetic* blessings of Genesis 49:22-26 and Deuteronomy 33:13-17 also have several elements in common with Messianic prophecies in the Pentateuch. These include his enjoyment of divine "blessings" (Gen 49:25-26; Deut 33:13-16), his exaltation over his brothers (Gen 49:26; Deut 33:16), and his comparison to an ox with mighty horns who defeats the nations (Num 24:8; Deut 33:17; Ps 2:8; 18:42-43). Like Isaac's blessing of Jacob in Genesis 27:28 that includes the prayer that God give "from the dew of the heavens" (מִטַּל הַשָּׁמַיִם)

---

[6]Contra Wenham, *Genesis 16–50*, 484, who instead takes the difficult בֵּן פֹּרָת as "wild ass."
[7]Kristin Swenson, "Crowned with Blessings: The Riches of Double-Meaning in Gen 49,26b," *ZAW* 120 (2008): 424, argues, "It appears that those who are responsible for the final version of this poem sought to associate Joseph with the best traits of a king while deliberately avoiding such outright identity."

and "from fatness of the earth" (מִשְׁמַנֵּי הָאָרֶץ; see chap. 2 above), Joseph is blessed "from the excellence of heaven, from dew" (מִמֶּגֶד שָׁמַיִם מִטָּל, Deut 33:13) and "from the excellence of the earth and its fullness" (מִמֶּגֶד אֶרֶץ וּמְלֹאָהּ, Deut 33:16; cf. Gen 49:25). These parallels suggest that it is not only the narrative portrayal of Joseph that mostly precedes Genesis 49:8-12 but also the poetic portrayal of Joseph in these blessings that intentionally foreshadows the Messiah, even though the latter follow Genesis 49:8-12 in the literary context. Hence, the emphasis on Joseph as an individual in Genesis 49:22-26 and Deuteronomy 33:13-17 is ultimately directed to the tribes of Ephraim and Manasseh (Deut 33:17) on the one hand and to additional intentional foreshadowing of the Messiah on the other. The latter may help explain why Jesus being called a "Nazarene" (Ναζωραῖος) fulfilled "the prophets" (Mt 2:23), since the title may be a wordplay on "prince" (נְזִיר) in Genesis 49:26 and Deuteronomy 33:16 (cf. Judg 13:5, 7, נָזִיר, ναζιραῖος).

The individual focus of Genesis 49:8-12 is therefore truly exceptional and suggests a similar focus in Deuteronomy 33:7. However, many commentators interpret this blessing of Judah as referring to the tribe of Judah when in battle, such as when led by Davidic kings (see Rashi).[8] Another option is to take "bring him to his people" as relating to the separation of the tribe of Judah from the northern kingdom.[9] Nevertheless, the individual, Messianic focus of Genesis 49:8-12, along with the compositional relationship between Genesis 49 and Deuteronomy 33, still suggests an individual, Messianic interpretation of Deuteronomy 33:7.

The blessing of Judah in Deuteronomy 33:7 consists of a prayer on behalf of Judah. As shown by the petition, "Hear, O LORD, the voice of Judah," this verse is *Moses'* prayer (see Ps 90) that the Lord would hear *Judah's* prayer (see Ps 89 as a prayer for the coming of eschatological "Judah"). Although the words of Judah's prayer are not explicitly stated, the reference to the

---

[8]See Targum Onkelos; Jeffrey Tigay, *Deuteronomy*, JPS Torah Commentary (Philadelphia: Jewish Publication Society, 1996), 323; Duane Christensen, *Deuteronomy 21:10–34:12*, Word Biblical Commentary (Nashville: Nelson, 2002), 848-49.

[9]Richard Nelson, *Deuteronomy*, Old Testament Library (Louisville: Westminster, 2002), 389. For brief discussions of this view, see McConville, *Deuteronomy*, 470, who also remarks that this verse "has no messianic hint, unlike Gen. 49:8-12"; Jack Lundbom, *Deuteronomy* (Grand Rapids: Eerdmans, 2013), 925.

Lord being "help from his adversaries" (עֵזֶר מִצָּרָיו) suggests that deliverance in the midst of conflict is in view. More difficult are the precise meanings of "and you will bring him to his people" (וְאֶל־עַמּוֹ תְּבִיאֶנּוּ) and the obscure "[with] his hands he contends for himself" or "through his own hands strive for him" (יָדָיו רָב לוֹ).[10] To complicate the interpretation of "you will bring him" even more, John William Wevers, based on the division of εἰσέλθοισαν ("may they enter") into εἰσέλθοις ἄν ("may you enter"), believes that the Septuagint translator of Deuteronomy 33:7 "had no separation of the tribe from the rest of Israel in mind; it is the Lord who is implored to come (literally enter in) to his people."[11]

Rather than looking merely at the biblical history of the tribe of Judah in relation to Deuteronomy 33:7, we believe that the possibility of an individual referent suggests different intertextual relationships. Jeffrey Tigay, though taking this verse as referring to Judah in battle, notes the wordplay on "his hands" (יָדָיו) and "Judah" (יְהוּדָה), which is similar to Genesis 49:8 ("Judah," "praise [יָדְךָ]," "hand"). To this parallel may be added the similarity between "and you will bring him to his people" (וְאֶל־עַמּוֹ תְּבִיאֶנּוּ) and the last line of Genesis 49:10, "until he comes [יָבֹא] to whom it belongs and to him is the obedience of the peoples [עַמִּים]." Furthermore, the words *hand, contend, help,* and *adversary* draw on Joseph's conflict with his enemies and the Lord's helping him to overcome them in Genesis 49:23-25. The Messiah's defeat of his enemies, of course, is a major aspect of the Messianic vision of the Pentateuch (Gen 3:15; 22:17b; 24:60; 49:8; Num 24:8, 17-19). Deuteronomy 33:7 and Numbers 24:8 even have the phrase "his adversaries" in common (cf. Gen 14:20; Deut 32:41, 43), and this theme of enemies is reinforced both through other Messianic prophecies and through allusions to the blessing of Joseph in Genesis 49:23-25.

These intertextual relationships strengthen the likelihood that Deuteronomy 33:7 is indeed referring to an individual, the Messiah. As such, we believe that it is a prayer that the Lord bring the Messiah to his people in

---

[10]Tigay, *Deuteronomy*, 323. For more discussion, see Christensen, *Deuteronomy 21:10–34:12*, 848-49; Lundbom, *Deuteronomy*, 925.

[11]John William Wevers, *Notes on the Greek Text of Deuteronomy* (Atlanta: Scholars, 1995), 542, calls εἰσέλθοισαν "a reading based on a wrong division of words in old uncial texts in which words were written together. The plural is barely sensible, and is an obvious mistake." See also Frank Moore Cross and David Noel Freedman, "The Blessing of Moses," *JBL* 67 (1948): 193, 203.

fulfillment of Genesis 49:8-10 (cf. Num 24:8). The fact that the Messiah needs the Lord to answer his prayer for deliverance from his enemies accords with his need for divine help already established in Genesis 49:9 and Numbers 24:8-9. Relatedly, the Suffering Servant in Isaiah 50:7-9 remains confident that "the Sovereign LORD helps [יַעֲזָר־] me" and "the one who declares me righteous is near." Therefore he asks, "Who will contend [יָרִיב] with me?" and "Who will declare me guilty?" If we are correct about Deuteronomy 33:7, the Messiah's implied prayers for deliverance from his enemies also provide a foundation for a similar understanding of prayers such as "My God, my God, why have you forsaken me?" in Psalm 22:1 along with many others in the Psalter.

Though Deuteronomy 33:7 is indeed brief and obscure, we believe that the preceding considerations make a Messianic interpretation preferable to others. Other Davidic kings did also pray for help in battle (e.g., 1 Sam 30:8; 2 Kings 19:15-19; 2 Chron 13:14; 14:11; 20:5-12), but these kings are less frequently mentioned in the Pentateuch (Gen 17:6, 16; 35:11; Deut 17:14-20) and are not the focus of its central Messianic vision. None of them came "in the last days" (Gen 49:1; Deut 31:29) or are the subject of the parallel blessing of Judah in Genesis 49:8-12. The tribe of Judah was indeed separated from the northern tribes during and following the reign of Rehoboam, but it seems that the northern tribes are primarily responsible for rejoining the house of David since they are the ones who rebelled and left (1 Kings 12:16), not the other way around. Accordingly, Hezekiah sent to "all Israel" and "wrote letters to Ephraim and Manasseh" inviting them to the temple in Jerusalem to celebrate the Passover (2 Chron 30:1-9). Even if Deuteronomy 33:7 does allude to Judah's separation from his brothers in Genesis 38 or to Joseph being sold into slavery in Genesis 37, the primary considerations concerning the future fulfillment of Deuteronomy 33:7 remain the same, and the arguments for a Messianic interpretation are still intact.

THE ESCHATOLOGICAL SALVATION OF ISRAEL

With the appearance of "in the last days" in Deuteronomy 31:29 prior to Deuteronomy 32–33 and the eschatological scope of Deuteronomy 32 demonstrated above, readers might expect Deuteronomy 33 as a whole to have an eschatological outlook. This is indeed the case, and it is even more eschatologically focused then Deuteronomy 32, which also concerns Israel's idolatry and judgment. But Deuteronomy 33, in contrast, is thoroughly concerned with Israel's tribes enjoying the Lord's blessings in the land forever. Significantly, just as the "nations" share in the joy of the Lord's victory in Deuteronomy 32:43, so the "peoples" are also the objects of the Lord's love in Deuteronomy 33:3, as well as his worshipers alongside Israel in Deuteronomy 33:19. The Fall of Genesis 3 had affected all humanity, but in Deuteronomy 33 it is as though the creational "blessing" has been fully given to them (Gen 1:28; Deut 33:1) after an eschatological atonement (Deut 32:43).

Unlike Jacob's blessing in Genesis 49, Moses' blessing in Deuteronomy 33 "apportions no blame"[12] to any of the tribes but genuinely "blesses" each of them. Whereas Reuben's sin with Jacob's concubine was recalled in Genesis 49:3-4, Moses prays more positively (though admittedly reservedly) in Deuteronomy 33:6, "Let Reuben live and not die, and let his men be few." Likewise, Levi was included in the sin of killing the Shechemites and the punishment of being scattered in Israel in Genesis 49:5-7, but in Deuteronomy 33:8-11, the Levites are commended as faithful servants of the Lord and teachers of Israel. Moses' prayer that the Lord "strike [מָחַץ] the loins of those who rise up against him [Levi]" (Deut 33:11; cf. Ex 15:7) recalls the Lord's defeat of Israel's enemies in Deuteronomy 32:27, 39-43 (note מָחַץ, Deut 32:39) and the Messiah's defeat of his (מָחַץ, Num 24:8, 17). Benjamin is no longer a ravenous wolf (Gen 49:27) but instead "the beloved of the Lord," who "rests [שָׁכֵן] between his shoulders" (Deut 33:12). He "rests securely [יִשְׁכֹּן לָבֶטַח] on him [i.e., the Lord]," just as the whole nation "dwells securely [בֶּטַח . . . וַיִּשְׁכֹּן], alone" in the land (Deut 33:28). Eschatological Israel had been similarly described in Numbers 23:9 (Mic 7:14; Jer 23:6; see chap. 6 above). Issachar is no longer doing "forced labor" (Gen 49:15),[13] but rather he rejoices in his tents

---

[12]McConville, *Deuteronomy*, 468. He believes that Dan (v. 22) is the only tribe without "a clear comment on or wish for the tribes' blessing," but we argue below that even what is said to Dan can be interpreted positively.

[13]Contra Joel Heck, "Issachar: Slave or Freeman? (Gen 49:14-15)," *JETS* 29 (1986): 385-96, who believes that Gen 49:8-27 is entirely positive. We remain unconvinced based on the negative connotations associated with מַס־עֹבֵד ("forced labor"; cf. Josh 16:10; 1 Kings 9:21), the root of the

as he and Zebulun call "peoples" to a "mountain" and offer "sacrifices of righteousness" (Deut 33:18-19; cf. Ps 4:5; 51:19). The treasures of "seas" and "sand" (Deut 33:19) relate back to Zebulun's territory along the seashore (Gen 49:13), which had always been useful for trade but is now linked to the worship of the Lord.

J. Gordon McConville explains, "The Blessing of Moses fittingly forms part of the climax of the book of Deuteronomy.... It puts flesh on the theme of covenant blessing... a vivid picture of the possession and filling of the land."[14] Walter Brueggemann further observes that "the blessing functions in an anticipatory and efficacious willing of the future of Israel" and that, "the poem, in the context of a Deuteronomic expectation of exile, becomes an act of hope, asserting the conviction that YHWH's powerful blessing and providential resolve for goodwill finally overcome every historical circumstance of negation."[15] It is as though the conclusion of the Song of Moses with the Lord's defeat of his enemies and atonement for "his land, his people" (Deut 32:43) leads to a description of Israel living in the land peacefully forever in Deuteronomy 33.[16] Access to Eden has been reopened.

Before continuing our survey of the blessings of the tribes with Gad and Dan, we should point out that while many statements pertain only to the tribe addressed (e.g., Deut 33:8-10, 16), several seem to apply to that tribe as representative of the whole nation. The latter category includes not only the aforementioned defeat of Levi's enemies (Deut 33:11) and Benjamin's secure dwelling (Deut 33:12), but also Joseph's likeness to a bull (Deut 33:17; Num 23:22) and Zebulun/Issachar calling peoples to worship the Lord at a mountain (Deut 33:18-19; Is 55:5; 56:6-7; cf. Is 2:2-4; 60:3-14). Also included is the experience of abundant divine blessing by Joseph, Naphtali, and Asher (Deut 33:13-16, 23-24, 29).

---

verb *bear a load* (סָבַל, see Ex 1:11; 2:11 5:4-5; 6:6-7; Ps 81:6; Is 9:4), and the comparison of Dan to a serpent in Gen 49:17.

[14]McConville, *Deuteronomy*, 473.

[15]Walter Brueggemann, *Deuteronomy*, Abingdon Old Testament Commentaries (Nashville: Abingdon, 2001), 284.

[16]See Otto, *Deuteronomium 23,16–34,12*, 2238, "Through the connection to the Song of Moses in Deut 32, the blessing of Moses has a still greater timespan in view, insofar as it now as a promise is directed to the future of the addressees of Deuteronomy after the end-times, eschatological battle of peoples announced in Deut 32."

Whereas Zebulun and Issachar are directly linked in Deuteronomy 33:18, Gad and Dan are linked through the lion/lioness inclusio, "like a lioness he rests" (כְּלָבִיא שָׁכֵן, Deut 33:20) and "whelp of a lion" (גּוּר אַרְיֵה, Deut 33:22).[17] The latter phrase famously appears in Genesis 49:9, "Judah is the whelp of a lion." Since this phrase appears only once elsewhere in the Old Testament (Nahum 2:11), the interpretation of Genesis 49:9 and Deuteronomy 33:22 must be properly related to one another. Moreover, Genesis 49:9 also includes the phrase "like a lioness," after which it is asked, "Who will raise him?" The only other animal comparison in Deuteronomy 33, Joseph as an ox (Deut 33:17), was already seen above to likewise be related to the Messiah.[18] If Genesis 49:9 (and likewise Num 24:9) is a prophecy about the Messiah (an eschatological, individual "Judah"), then why are Gad and Dan associated with these same animals in Deuteronomy 33:20-22?

First, we should remember that Numbers 23:24 also compared Israel to a lion and a lioness, but in a way distinct from the comparison of the Messiah to the same animals in Numbers 24:9. In chapter six above, we showed that Israel as a lion/lioness "arises" first and then does not lie down until finished eating, whereas the Messiah lies down and awaits someone to "raise him." We also argued that Israel's triumph and power results from participation in the Messiah's victory in Numbers 24:17-19. This important result also applies to Deuteronomy 33:20-22. In both cases, eschatological Israel resembles the Messiah in some respects and shares in his triumph. At the same time, both contexts are careful to distinguish between the Messiah and eschatological Israel, including Gad and Dan. For example, the question "Who will raise him?" is not asked in connection with Gad or Dan, just as it was not asked with respect to Israel in the Balaam oracles.

But still more can be said. Unlike the other tribal blessings, Gad's blessing not only highlights the tribe of Gad but especially "the one who enlarges Gad" (Deut 33:20). Several commentators take this as the lone

---

[17] I would like to thank Tracy McKenzie for alerting me of the importance of this passage and discussing it with me. He in turn credited our colleague Seth Postell.

[18] Heck, "History of Interpretation," 23-25, rightly notes that all three animal comparisons in Deut 33 are positive and are fewer than the five or six (depending on how one reads Gen 49:22) animal comparisons in Gen 49.

instance of a blessing rendered to God for helping a tribe.[19] Tigay also points out the parallel to Genesis 9:26 where Shem's blessing actually blesses "the LORD, the God of Shem." What has not been explored by these commentators is the possibility that the subject of subsequent verbs in Deuteronomy 33:20-21a is also the Lord. After all, the subjects of these verbs are unstated and must be supplied by the context, "Blessed be the one who enlarges Gad, like a lioness he rests, and will tear off an arm, even a head. And he provided the firstfruits for himself" (Deut 33:20-21). The interpretive question is this: is it Gad who rests like a lioness, tears prey, and provides for himself, or is it "the one who enlarges Gad," even the Lord, who does these things? In our opinion, the latter interpretation is a better explanation of this difficult passage.

To put it plainly, we believe that the Messiah/the Lord is the one who not only "enlarges Gad" but also rests like a lioness, tears prey, and provides the "firstfruits" for himself. The reason why this interpretation can work is because the Messiah is himself divine (see discussion of Gen 27:29 in chap. 2 above). As the Lord himself, he can enlarge Gad (the Messiah himself will also take possession of land), but as the Messiah he can rest like a lioness and tear off an arm or even a head, as other Messianic prophecies would lead us to expect (Gen 49:9; Num 24:8-9, 17). Notably, the verb for "rest" (שָׁכַן), though similar in meaning, should be distinguished from the verbs translated "lie down" (שָׁכַב/רָבַץ) in Genesis 49:9 and Numbers 24:9. We argued in chapter three above that the latter verbs concern the death of the lion/lioness prior to the question, "Who will raise him?" In Deuteronomy 33:20, however, it may depict a lioness which has lain down and is devouring its prey. As observed above, the verb for "rest" (שָׁכַן) expresses Benjamin's/Israel's peaceful dwelling in the land in Deuteronomy 33:12, 28 (cf. Num 23:9; 24:2). In Deuteronomy 33:21, the subject briefly shifts (without fully changing) to the Lord, "And he provided the firstfruits for himself" (וַיַּרְא רֵאשִׁית לוֹ). This translation is supported by S. R. Driver and Duane Christensen, both of whom base it on the syntactical parallel to Genesis 22:8, "God will provide for himself the lamb for a burnt offering,

---

[19]Tigay, *Deuteronomy*, 331; Christensen, *Deuteronomy 21:10–34:12*, 853; Georg Braulik, *Deuteronomium II, 16,18–34,12*, Die Neue Echter Bibel (Würzburg: Echter, 1992), 242. Though not highlighting its uniqueness, see Lundbom, *Deuteronomy*, 934. Contra McConville, *Deuteronomy*, 472.

my son" (אֱלֹהִים יִרְאֶה־לּוֹ הַשֶּׂה לְעֹלָה בְּנִי).²⁰ Driver also adduces 1 Samuel 16:1 as syntactical parallel: "I have provided for myself a king among his sons (רָאִיתִי בְּבָנָיו לִי מֶלֶךְ). Christensen further cites the use of the word *firstfruits* (רֵאשִׁית) with reference to Reuben, Jacob's "firstborn" (בְּכוֹר) and "firstfruits/first" (רֵאשִׁית) in Genesis 49:3. The latter word is also famously translated "beginning" in Genesis 1:1 and Proverbs 1:7 (see the suggestive Prov 8:22). These same two nouns appear together with the same meanings in Deuteronomy 21:17; Ps 78:51; 105:36. Although Driver and Christensen see the syntactical parallel in Genesis 22:8 as merely illustrative of what they believe to be Gad's choice of the best part of the land for himself (Num 32), we believe that "he provided firstfruits for himself" in Deuteronomy 33:21 refers to the Lord providing for himself the Messiah, his "firstfruits" and "firstborn" (see Ps 89:26-27), as "the lamb," just as Genesis 22:8 declared he would. Abraham's naming of the site "The LORD will provide" because "on a mountain of the LORD it will be provided" (Gen 22:14; see "mountain" in Deut 33:19) suggests that a climactic divine provision was yet to come. In chapters two and four above, we discussed the relationship of the sacrifice of Isaac in Genesis 22:1-18 to the death of the male seed of the woman in Genesis 3:15, the sacrifice of the Passover lamb in Exodus 12, and the substitutionary death of the Suffering Servant in Isaiah 53. In other words, we believe that "he provided firstfruits for himself" in Deuteronomy 33:21 is not only syntactically parallel to Genesis 22:8 but intentionally alludes to it, and it does so in such a way that Genesis 22:8 also serves as a gateway to still more intertextually related passages.

This interpretation preserves the continuity of the grammatical subjects in Deuteronomy 33:20-21 and better accounts for the difficulty of applying Deuteronomy 33:21 to the tribe of Gad. Concerning the former, the Lord/Messiah enlarges Gad, the Messiah rests like a lioness and tears prey, and the Lord provides the firstfruits (the Messiah) for himself. In the latter two examples, the shift of emphasis to the Messiah and then briefly to the Lord is not a complete change of the subject of the verbs in these lines since they

---

[20] S. R. Driver, *A Critical and Exegetical Commentary on Deuteronomy*, International Critical Commentary (New York: Charles Scribner's Sons, 1909), 411 (see footnote), who is followed by Peter Craigie, *The Book of Deuteronomy*, New International Commentary on the Old Testament (Grand Rapids: Eerdmans, 1976), 400n36. See Christensen, *Deuteronomy 21:10-34:12*, 853.

still concern the triune Godhead. Taking Gad as the referent of the lioness and of the provider not only requires a major change of focus from "the one who enlarges Gad" to Gad itself but also results in major difficulties in understanding the content of Gad's blessing as a whole. Cross and Freedman see little hope for a synthesis that can account for the opening line of Deuteronomy 33:20 since "there is no connection between the first colon and those which follow, however the first words are interpreted."[21] Tigay sees similar problems with the last part of Deuteronomy 33:21 ("he performed the righteousness of the LORD and his judgments with Israel"): "It is not obvious how this statement relates to Gad."[22] David Noel Freedman even thinks that the whole of Deuteronomy 33:21 "has nothing to do"[23] with Gad. As a further indication of the difficulty of Deuteronomy 33:21, Freedman takes the "lawgiver's portion" (חֶלְקַת מְחֹקֵק) and the accomplishment of "the righteousness of the LORD" as descriptive of Moses, who is also associated with "the heads of the people" in Deuteronomy 33:4-5.[24]

But this and other complicated proposals are unnecessary once it is recognized that the word translated "lawgiver" is strategically used with reference to the Messiah in Genesis 49:10 ("the scepter will not depart from Judah, nor the lawgiver/ruler's staff [מְחֹקֵק] from between his feet"). Regardless of how the Hebrew word in question is best translated in each case, Genesis 49:10 links the "lawgiver/ruler's staff" to the tribe of Judah, not to Moses, his tribe (Levi), or Gad. In fact, the singular "lawgiver/ruler's staff" (מְחֹקֵק) is never used of Moses but only of Judah (Ps 60:7; 108:8) or the Lord (Is 33:22).[25] The only other appearance of this term in the Pentateuch is in Numbers 21:18 ("scepter/staff"), in connection with Moses "gathering" (אָסַף) the people (Num 21:16; Deut 33:5) to sing about the well dug by the

---

[21] Cross and Freedman, "Blessing of Moses," 208.
[22] Tigay, *Deuteronomy*, 332.
[23] David Noel Freedman, "The Poetic Structure of the Framework of Deuteronomy 33," in *The Bible World: Essays in Honor of Cyrus H. Gordon*, ed. Gary Rendsburg (New York: Ktav, 1980), 34.
[24] Freedman, "Poetic Structure," 34-35; Christensen, *Deuteronomy 21:10–34:12*, 854. Tigay, *Deuteronomy*, 331-32, rejects the equation of "lawgiver" with Moses, instead reading the Hebrew word translated "lawgiver" (מְחֹקֵק) as "digging tool." He nevertheless suggests a possible allusion of "when they [the heads of the people] gathered" in the LXX to Gad and Reuben presenting their request for land before Moses and the leaders (Num 32:2, 25) and the possible misplacement of the whole of Deut 33:21b in relation to Deut 33:5.
[25] The Qal plural is used in Judg 5:9 of the "lawgivers of Israel" and Polel plural in Judg 5:14 of those from "Machir," son of Manasseh, son of Joseph (Gen 50:23).

"princes" and "nobles" of Israel (Num 21:17-18). We have already discussed the connection of this passage to water-from-the-rock passages (Ex 17:5-6; Num 20:8-11) and to the Messianic vision of the Pentateuch (see chaps. 5 and 6 above). If the "lawgiver" in Deuteronomy 33:21 is the Messiah, then the "lawgiver's portion" (חֶלְקַת מְחֹקֵק) can be understood in accordance with Deuteronomy 32:9, "The LORD's portion is his people" (עַמּוֹ יְהֹוָה חֵלֶק). Then the Messiah's "portion" would also be his people, with the grammatical subject in Deuteronomy 33:21 shifting back to the Messiah who comes with "the heads of the people" (Deut 33:21). The uncommon verb translated "came" (אָתָה) is also used of the Lord in Deuteronomy 33:2 and reinforces this parallel between the Messiah and the Lord. The difficult term *safun* (סָפוּן) is often translated "reserved" in this verse, but the better-attested meaning of its root concerns "paneling" (1 Kings 7:3, 7; Jer 22:14; Hag 1:4) and may be a faint allusion to the temple (1 Kings 6:9, 15; cf. Ex 15:17).[26] The Messiah's "inheritance" includes the "nations" and "ends of the earth" as well (Ps 2:8). It is not hard to see how such a savior-king could perform "the righteousness of the LORD and his judgments with Israel" (Deut 33:21; cf. Ps 22:31).

If the blessing of Gad in Deuteronomy 33:20-21 is indeed thoroughly concerned with the Lord and his "firstfruits" Messiah, then perhaps the gathering of "the heads of the people, the tribes of Israel together" under a "king" in Deuteronomy 33:5 should be interpreted in light of it, instead of the other way around with reference to Moses (Deut 33:4). It would certainly fit the theme of "gathering" at the highest structural level of the Pentateuch (Gen 49:1; Num 24:14; Deut 31:28). It is "there" that the Messiah rules in the midst of his people (Deut 33:21; Gen 49:24), obedient "peoples" offer "sacrifices of righteousness" (Gen 49:10; Deut 33:19), and water flows unto eternal life (Num 21:16-18; Ps 133:1-3; Ezek 47:1-12; Jn 4:14). Godly leaders will gladly gather around him (Deut 33:5, 21), whereas enemy leaders will be put away (Deut 32:42; note ἄρχων in the LXX in these passages). Accordingly, Moses prays, "Bring him to his people"

---

[26]Contra LXX, which seems to combine the form סָפוּן with the following word, וַיֵּתֵא. See Freedman, "The Poetic Structure of the Framework of Deuteronomy 33," 33. The result is a divergent translation, "when the rulers were gathered together with the leaders of the peoples" (MT: "paneled, and he came with the heads of the people").

(Deut 33:7). Further supporting the interconnection of Deuteronomy 33:5, 7, 21 is that each verse contains a *wayyiqtol* verb form, which is uncommon in poetry.

In our interpretation of the blessing of Gad, it is apparent that the comparison to a "lioness" in Deuteronomy 33:20 does not necessarily describe Gad itself but could instead concern the "one who enlarges Gad," the Lord/Messiah. Dan, however, is certainly compared to the "whelp of a lion" in Deuteronomy 33:22, and although this should not lead to confusion with the "lion of Judah" any more than should the comparison of Israel to a lion/lioness in Numbers 23:24, we have yet to thoroughly explain why Dan is compared to this animal. One important reason is to show the resemblance of eschatological Israel/Dan to their Messianic king. They participate in his victory and power as a lion/lioness (Num 23:24; 24:8-9, 18; Mic 5:8-9). The perfect priest-king (Gen 3:15; 14:18) enables Israel to fulfill their intended role as a kingdom of priests (Ex 19:6; Is 61:6; Dan 7:18). Although the Messiah's people do not, for example, become divine like him, in many important ways his people resemble him (see Hos 4:9; 1 Jn 2:6; 3:3). In specifically likening eschatological Dan to the Messiah, Deuteronomy 33:22 especially highlights this tribe's transformation from the most infamous animal, a serpent (Gen 49:17), to the most glorious one. The contrast between these two associations could hardly be any stronger. Jacob's earlier comparison of Dan to a serpent associated this tribe with the evil serpent in the Garden of Eden and hinted at Dan's future failures (Lev 24:11; Judg 1:34-35; 13:2-5; 18:1-31; Amos 8:14), but Moses' blessing of Dan centers on his likeness to his Messiah and his sharing in Messianic glory. Through association with the eschatological king of Israel, this tribe's shame has been substituted for unspeakable honor. Similar dynamics were at play in Exodus 31:6 with the Danite Oholiab who was the top assistant to the Spirit-filled Judahite, Bezalel, in the construction of the tabernacle (see chap. 5 above).

The last two tribal blessings of Naphtali and Asher (Deut 33:23-24) emphasize favor ("full of favor," שְׂבַע רָצוֹן; "favored of his brothers," רְצוּי אֶחָיו). It is as though such favored status, which in the patriarchal period was only enjoyed by one brother (e.g., Esau or Jacob, Joseph or Benjamin), is now the experience of every "brother" and the tribes descended from them (see

Deut 33:16). Naphtali's eschatological "inheritance" (יְרָשָׁה, Deut 33:23) has been won by the Messiah (Num 24:17-19) in fulfillment of the Abrahamic covenant (Gen 15:3-4; 22:17b-17; 24:60) and is a window into all Israel's inheritance (Obad 17-21; cf. Ex 6:8; Deut 33:4). The meaning of Asher's name as "happy/blessed" (אָשֵׁר, Gen 30:13) paves the way for the concluding statement about all Israel: "Happy/blessed are you [אַשְׁרֶיךָ], Israel! Who is like you, a people saved by the LORD?" (Deut 33:29). Significantly, the question "Who is like you?" had been rhetorically asked of the Lord concerning his incomparable power in Exodus 15:11, and indeed "there is none like the God of Jeshurun [i.e., Israel]" (cf. Deut 33:5; Is 44:2), as Deuteronomy 33:26 declares.[27] But in Deuteronomy 33:29, the same question is now asked of Israel, who as the object of the Lord's incomparably glorious salvation, shares this overwhelming honor. Evidently, the Lord does not simply enjoy his glory in isolation or abstractly but magnifies it through those he saves, who also participate in it. He is also called "the shield of your help" (מָגֵן עֶזְרֶךָ, Deut 33:29). The word *help* links back to Deuteronomy 33:7, 26, and its use in conjunction with *shield* links to still more passages (Ps 28:7; 33:20; 115:9-11), some of which are related to the Messianic vision of the Pentateuch (Gen 14:20; 15:1-2, Eliezer means "my God is help"; Ps 89:18-19).

In fulfillment of Genesis 3:15 and parallel to Deuteronomy 32:42, the Lord will drive out the "enemy" (אוֹיֵב) and say, "Destroy!" (הַשְׁמֵד, Deut 33:27). Earlier, "he said" (וַיֹּאמֶר) to punish Israel for their foolishness and sin (Deut 32:20), and even "said" (אָמַרְתִּי) to destroy them completely (Deut 32:26), but never again. The prayer that Moses "said" (וַיֹּאמַר) for Judah in Deuteronomy 33:7 would be heard, and what the enemy might have said will be thwarted (Deut 32:27). The abundance of "speaking" for the purpose of blessing in Deuteronomy 33 parallels the divine speech in Genesis 1 (and relatedly the blessing of Abraham) and suggests a new creation in Deuteronomy 33 (see Deut 32:6).[28] An additional link to Genesis 1 is the use of light/sun imagery in Deuteronomy 33:2, "The LORD

---

[27] The Hebrew word יְשֻׁרוּן from which *Jeshurun* is transliterated appears to be a play on "upright" (יָשָׁר). Eschatological Israel is characterized as *yesharim* (יְשָׁרִים) in Num 23:10. The use of *Jeshurun* in Deut 32:15 would then be ironic.

[28] For lexical, syntactical, and thematic parallels to Gen 3, see Nachman Levine, "The Curse and the Blessing: Narrative Discourse Syntax and Literary Form," *JSOT* 27 (2002): 195-97.

comes from Sinai, and he dawns [זָרַח] upon them from Seir, he shines [יָפַע] from Mount Paran" (see Gen 1:3, 14-18; Ps 50:1-2; Hab 3:3). As pointed out in chapter one above, the "rule" of the sun is thematically parallel to the rule of humanity (Gen 1:26-28; 3:15), and several passages in the Prophets compare the Messiah's coming and his reign to the sunrise (2 Sam 23:3-4; Is 9:2 [MT v. 1]; Is 42:6, 49:6; 60:1-3; Mal 4:2 [MT 3:20]). Also suggestive for Genesis 1:3, 14-18 and Deuteronomy 33:2 in relation to the Messianic vision of the Pentateuch are Numbers 24:17 LXX, "A star will *dawn* [ἀνατελεῖ] from Jacob" and Is 63:1, "Who is this who comes from Edom [מֱאֱדוֹם]?" Edom and "Seir" (Deut 33:2) are closely related (e.g., Gen 32:3; 36:8; Ezek 35:15), and the bloodstained garments in Isaiah 63:1-3 have already been argued to be related to the Messiah's wine-soaked garments in Genesis 49:11 (see chap. 3 above). As in Deuteronomy 33:2, the Lord's coming likewise involves a divine display of power involving mountains in Judges 5:4-5; Psalm 18:7; 97:5; 144:5; and Isaiah 64:1-3.

The parallels between Genesis 1–3 and Deuteronomy 32–33 function as a sort of inclusio for the Pentateuch and a resolution of the central problems set forth in its first chapters. This resolution is prophetic in the sense that it had not yet been realized when the Pentateuch reached its "final form." Although only briefly described in Genesis 3:15, the prophetic picture of eschatological salvation through the Messiah has been filled out by the rest of the Pentateuch, especially Deuteronomy 33. Israel will peacefully enjoy "grain," "new wine," and "dew" in the land (Deut 33:28), a combination which is uniquely tied to the eschatological blessings brought by their Messiah in Genesis 27:28.[29] He will be the priest-king that Adam failed to be (Gen 3:15; see chap. 1 above), and Israel's "enemies" will "cringe" (כָּחַשׁ) before them (Deut 33:29), just as they will before the Lord and his king (2 Sam 22:45; Ps 18:44; 66:3; 81:15). Just like that, the eschatological salvation of Israel is directly tied to the coming of the Messiah once more at the end of the last and longest poetic section of the Pentateuch (see also discussion of Numbers 23–24 in chap. 6 above), and with one last reminder of the coming "prophet like Moses" in

---

[29] These three terms appear together in only these two passages.

Deuteronomy 34:10 (see chap. 7 above), the Pentateuch and its Messianic vision come to a close.

Conclusion

The Messianic vision of the Pentateuch comes to a climactic conclusion in Deuteronomy 32–33, the last and longest poetic section of the Pentateuch. Prefaced by the phrase "in the last days" (Deut 31:29), Deuteronomy 32:1-43 is not only a song that predicts the future failure, idolatry, and punishment of Israel, but also one that ultimately proclaims the Lord's eschatological salvation. As Genesis 49:1 and Numbers 24:14 have already implied, salvation "in the last days" will be accomplished by the Messiah (Gen 49:8-12; Num 24:7-9, 17-19). Many "disasters," culminating in exile, will indeed come upon Israel (Deut 31:17, 21; 32:23), but the Lord will relent for the sake of his own great name (Deut 32:26-27; cf. Ex 32:11-14; Num 14:13-23) and "have compassion on his servants" when they are at their weakest point (Deut 32:36). In one last battle, he will defeat his enemies (Deut 32:39-42), even as he brings shouts of joy to the "nations" and "makes atonement for his land, his people" (Deut 32:43). The themes of a divine warrior-priest are directly connected to the Messianic vision of the Pentateuch (Gen 3:15; 27:27-29; 49:8-12; Num 24:7-9, 17-19; see Ex 15:1-18), and the connection of Deuteronomy 32–33 to this vision becomes even clearer with the blessing of Moses in Deuteronomy 33.

In view of the strong structural and thematic parallels to Jacob's blessing of his sons in Genesis 49:1-27, the brief blessing of Judah in Deuteronomy 33:7 is properly interpreted as referring to an individual Judahite, in accordance with the corresponding blessing of Judah in Genesis 49:8-12. Though enigmatic when taken in isolation, the themes in Deuteronomy 33:7 of coming to his people, victory over enemies, and need for divine help are well established in the Messianic vision of the Pentateuch (e.g., Gen 49:8-10; Num 24:8-9, 17-19). The Messiah is not relegated to this single verse in Deuteronomy 33 either because it is he/the Lord "who enlarges Gad" (Deut 33:20-21) and "like a lioness rests." Relatedly, Dan will be transformed from the likeness of a serpent into "a whelp of a lion," resembling the Messiah himself in power and honor (Gen 49:17-18; Deut 33:22). In the end, Israel will live securely in the land, happily enjoying all the blessings that the Lord intended for them (Deut 33:28). The "peoples" will also share in the Messiah's eschatological salvation, as equal recipients of the Lord's love (Deut 33:3) and worshipers who have likewise been saved by grace (Deut 33:19; cf. Deut 32:36) and had their blood avenged (Deut 32:43). The covenant promises to Abraham concerning "all the families of the earth" will be fulfilled and access to the Garden of Eden restored but with one major difference: the serpent and his seed have been driven out, destroyed, and humiliated forever (Deut 33:27, 29; cf. Rom 16:20).

9

THE REPEATED BREAKING
OF THE SINAI/DEUTERONOMIC LAW

An argument for the centrality of a Messianic vision to the Pentateuch would not be complete without sufficiently accounting for the Sinai/Deuteronomic law. Although we have argued, based on Messianic prophecy after Israel's departure from Mount Sinai (i.e., Num 24; Deut 18; 33), that the giving of the Sinai law did not change the Pentateuch's own vision for eschatological salvation through the Messiah (see chap. 6 above), a more extensive argument for prioritizing the Messiah above the Sinai/Deuteronomic law in the theology of the Pentateuch may still be helpful. After all, many traditional interpretations of the Pentateuch have simply equated it with this law. Nevertheless, as we argued in this book's introduction, the term *Pentateuch* refers to the "book" that Moses wrote (Gen 1–Deut 34), whereas the "law," though sometimes also referring to this *book* (e.g., Mt 7:12), in other passages refers only to the *laws* that were given at Mount Sinai mostly from Exodus 20 onward (see Rom 3:21 for both uses of "law"). To avoid confusion, we have consistently used "Pentateuch" to refer to the former and "Sinai/Deuteronomic law" to refer to the latter. But even with such a distinction between the Pentateuch as a book and the laws that dominate the second half of Exodus, Leviticus, and Deuteronomy, many would still hold that the central message of the Pentateuch is the giving and keeping of the Sinai/Deuteronomic law. The purpose of this chapter is to further support our view that this central message is instead focused on the Messiah and the new covenant, with the Sinai/Deuteronomic law serving an important but supporting role as a contrastive backdrop for the Pentateuch's Messianic vision. Though perhaps counterintuitive, we believe that the Messiah is primary and the

Sinai/Deuteronomic law secondary in the compositional strategy of the Pentateuch.

The Narrative Context for the Giving of the Sinai Law

A fundamental interpretive step for understanding how the Messiah and not the Sinai/Deuteronomic law can be central to the authorially intended message of the Pentateuch is the recognition that the giving of the Sinai law takes place in a narrative context. Indeed, the Pentateuch as a whole is a narrative that begins with creation and ends with Moses and the Israelites on the brink of the Promised Land. As such, every passage in the Pentateuch has a broader narrative context that must be accounted for in order to fully understand its meaning in the overall compositional strategy. The narrative context for the giving of the Sinai law is Israel's exodus from Egypt (Ex 1:1–15:21), their journey from the Red Sea (Ex 15:22–18:27), their stay at Mount Sinai (Ex 19:1–Num 10:10), and their departure from this mountain (Num 10:11-12). Furthermore, this law was given through Moses (Jn 1:17; Acts 7:38) at precisely this point in the Pentateuch's storyline. It was not given, say, to Adam in the Garden of Eden or to the patriarchs. Galatians 3:17 deliberately contrasts the promises given to Abraham with the Sinai law, "which came 430 years later."

If the broader context of a passage is always essential to rightly understanding it, then the fact that the Sinai law began to be given in Exodus 20 and not somewhere else in the Pentateuch affects what the author intends for readers to understand about the giving of this law. Some of the laws, of course, concerned Israel as a nation and would have been nonsensical if given in an earlier period (e.g., Ex 21:2). But even a law that expresses an eternal truth or principle fits into its immediate context in a unique way. The particular law itself remains the same, but its proper understanding in relationship to the Pentateuch as a whole depends partially on its narrative context. For example, the seventh commandment is, "You shall not commit adultery" (Ex 20:14). Although the meaning of this particular law itself would not change no matter where it was found in the Pentateuch, a proper accounting for the meaning of the Ten Commandments in their fullness does not simply interpret this foundational legal code in isolation from its context. The meaning of each commandment does have a standalone component as expressing enduring divine truth or principle, but a more thorough reckoning of the literary context of the Ten Commandments might explore additional questions such as: Why did the Lord give the Ten Commandments at this point in Israel's history and not at some other time? Why were the Ten Commandments given first, and what relationship do they have to the many other laws that are given in the subsequent context? To what extent were the Ten Commandments new information for the Israelites? Didn't they already know, for example, about the Sabbath (Ex 16:23-30)? Relatedly, on what basis was Cain held accountable for murder (Gen 4:6-12), and how did Joseph know that sleeping with Potiphar's wife would have been to "sin against God" (Gen 39:9)? All these questions relate not only to the laws themselves but also to their relationship to the narrative context—that is, the Sinai law in relation to the compositional strategy of the Pentateuch.[1]

This leads to a second step for understanding how the Messiah and not the Sinai/Deuteronomic law occupies center stage in the theological message of the Pentateuch. As will be shown, the narrative context of the giving of the Sinai law intends to present this law not merely as foundational for the nation of Israel but also as a temporary, inherently limited system that is inferior to the Messiah's coming and the new covenant. While we affirm the historical significance of the Lord giving the Sinai law to Israel along with its great importance as an expression of the divine will, its narrative context raises additional important issues regarding the purpose of the Sinai/Deuteronomic law in the Pentateuch's compositional strategy. If, for example, the Ten Commandments were not entirely new information, then it seems that the giving of the Sinai law served as a formal codification of Israel's foundational law. Without disputing the importance of the Sinai/Deuteronomic law in the national history of Israel, its foundational role in this history does not necessarily mean that the

---

[1]The seminal work of John Sailhamer deals with this issue extensively and has provided a basis for much (but not all) of the subsequent discussion; see, e.g., his "The Mosaic Law and the Theology of the Pentateuch," *WTJ* 53 (1991): 241-61; *The Pentateuch as Narrative: A Biblical-Theological Commentary* (Grand Rapids: Zondervan, 1992), 46-59; *The Meaning of the Pentateuch: Revelation, Composition, and Interpretation* (Downers Grove, IL: InterVarsity Press, 2009), 374-98. For discussion of these laws in the life of the Christian, see James Todd III, *Sinai and the Saints: Reading Old Covenant Laws for the New Covenant Community* (Downers Grove, IL: InterVarsity Press, 2017), 31-44. He also deals with the Ten Commandments specifically on pp. 89-107.

Pentateuch's main purpose is to promote observance of this codified law as a means of salvation. Rashi's comment on Genesis 1:1 that the Pentateuch could have begun with the Passover law in Exodus 12:2 ends up only further highlighting the problem of equating the Pentateuch with Sinai/Deuteronomic law. There is no getting around the fact that the Pentateuch does not begin with legal material and instead is a narrative that describes, among other things, the giving of the Sinai/Deuteronomic law at length.

THE THEME OF ISRAEL'S REPEATED BREAKING OF THE SINAI/DEUTERONOMIC LAW

The Pentateuch does not simply describe the giving of the Sinai/Deuteronomic law and the importance of keeping it but also makes painfully clear that Israel did not keep this law. Thus, the Pentateuch is as much about the *breaking* of the Sinai/Deuteronomic law as it is about this law itself. An obvious example of this is the golden calf incident in Exodus 32. While Moses was on Mount Sinai receiving more laws, the Israelites, with the help of their future high priest Aaron, were at the foot of the mountain breaking the most fundamental law prohibiting idolatry (Ex 20:4). They could not plead ignorance because they had all heard the Ten Commandments directly from the Lord himself (Deut 5:4). Just a few months before (Ex 19:1), they had also experienced the Lord bringing them out of Egypt and across the Red Sea. Even Moses' temporary absence because of his mediation on their behalf was an arrangement that they requested (Ex 20:18-21). Before the giving of the Sinai law was even complete, its core tenet had already been broken. The picture of Moses as Israel's representative on Mount Sinai receiving more laws (about how the Lord would dwell among them in the tabernacle, Ex 25:8) while the people were at the foot of the mountain worshiping the golden calf could hardly be more tragic. The Sinai law was being given and broken at the same time.[2]

---

[2]Taking it a step further, Sailhamer held that the Sinai law was added because of Israel's transgressions, based on Gal 3:19. See *Pentateuch as Narrative*, 273, 387; *Introduction to Old Testament Theology: A Canonical Approach* (Grand Rapids: Zondervan, 1995), 272-89; *Meaning of the Pentateuch*, 40-42. Relatedly, see Nanette Stahl, *Law and Liminality in the Bible* (Sheffield: Sheffield Academic, 1995), 17, "The most common construction of the generic tension between law and narrative in the Bible is that the law is undermined by the narrative that enacts it."

Israel's breaking of the Sinai law in Exodus 32 was no isolated incident. Whereas the worship of the golden calf was initiated by the people with the cooperation of Aaron (Ex 32:1-2), the priests were fully responsible in Leviticus 10. The priests had just been consecrated in Leviticus 8–9 when two of Aaron's sons, Nadab and Abihu, offered "strange fire" before the Lord, "which he had not commanded them," and were put to death by the Lord as a result (Lev 10:1-2). Both people and priests were thus equally guilty as lawbreakers. In a passing comment explaining the reason for commanding the Israelites to bring their sacrifices to the Tent of Meeting (Lev 17:3-6), the Lord reveals that the Israelites, even after the exodus, had been sacrificing to "goat idols" and "prostituting themselves" (זנה) after them (Lev 17:7; cf. Amos 5:25-26 LXX; Acts 7:42-43). Israel's unfaithfulness and rebellion were thus a chronic problem. This core problem resurfaces periodically in the narrative, such as in the case of the blasphemer (Lev 24:10-23) and the ultimate failure of this entire generation of Israelites (Num 14:11). Lest the reader mistakenly come away with the impression that this problem was limited to one generation of Israelites, Moses describes the next generation of Israelites likewise as spiritually dull (Deut 29:4) and predicts that they and future generations will turn to idols (Deut 4:25; 31:16, 27-29). The same spiritual dullness persisted into the days of Isaiah (Is 6:9-10), Jesus (Mt 13:13-15), and Paul (Rom 11:7-10, 25). Even before the Israelites entered the Promised Land, their exile from it as punishment for idolatry was a foregone conclusion (Deut 4:26-28; 30:1). They would experience the curses of the covenant instead of its blessings (Deut 28).

Israel's constant failure to trust the Lord and listen to his instructions (Num 14:11) seem to be cast by the Pentateuch as representative of humanity generally. Before Israel existed as a nation, the same pattern of sin already had thoroughly infected the entire human race. Adam, the first and representative human (אדם), failed to keep the Lord's commands in the Garden of Eden. The narrative in Genesis 3 even implies that Eve's lack of confidence in the Lord and his word led to the breaking of the divine command (Gen 3:1-6). This rebellion not only intentionally foreshadows Israel's failure to keep the Sinai law, as Seth Postell has shown, but also characterizes the central problem of all human beings (Is 24:5; Hos 6:7).[3]

---

[3] Seth Postell, *Adam as Israel: Genesis 1–3 as the Introduction to the Torah and Tanakh* (Eugene, OR: Wipf and Stock, 2011).

This is borne out through the utter wickedness of "humankind" (אָדָם) before and after the flood (Gen 6:5; 8:21) and the rebellion of "the sons of Adam" (בְּנֵי הָאָדָם) at the Tower of Babel (Gen 11:5). Accordingly, Jeremiah characterizes both the nations and Israel as going after "the stubbornness of their [evil] heart" (Jer 3:17; 7:24; 9:14; 11:8, etc.). All of them (us) have been unfaithful to the Lord and are idolaters (Jer 2:11; Ps 96:5; Rom 1:18-23).

The Pentateuch itself thus implies that Israel did not and would never experience divine blessing through the Sinai/Deuteronomic law because they would never fulfill the condition of obedience to it (see Deut 27:26). The nations likewise were and are in rebellion against the Lord and justly subject to his wrath (see Gen 8:21; 9:25; 11:3-4). Therefore, if there is to be any salvation for Israel and the nations, it must come from the Lord himself, apart from Sinai/Deuteronomic law system (Rom 3:21). The Pentateuch itself reveals that this salvation comes through the Messianic seed of Abraham through whom all the families of the earth will be blessed (Gen 12:3), just as God intended at creation (Gen 1:28). Along with those from other nations (Gen 18:18; 22:18), Israel will one day bless their Messiah and be blessed themselves (Gen 27:29; Num 24:9). He will defeat the serpent (Gen 3:15) and decisively "atone" for "his people" and bring joy to the nations (Deut 32:43). Such considerations suggest that the Pentateuch has intentionally presented the Sinai/Deuteronomic law as an ultimately ineffective and hence temporary system for Israel. In contrast, eschatological salvation through the Messiah is the consistent teaching of the Pentateuch from beginning to end. Even the exodus intentionally foreshadows the eschatological second exodus that this "prophet like Moses" will lead (see chaps. 4, 6, 7 above), and the giving of the Sinai/Deuteronomic law and Israel's constant failure to keep it clarifies their need for salvation to come from outside themselves. They need the cleansing, forgiveness, grace, and transformation that come from the Lord alone.

Such blessings come through the new covenant. The Pentateuch itself even depicts both the Lord and Moses as longing for the new era it will bring. In Numbers 11:29, Moses' wish, "Would that [מִי יִתֵּן; lit. 'Who will give'] all the people of the LORD were prophets, that the LORD would put [יִתֵּן] his Spirit on them!" would begin to be fulfilled through the Messiah's coming and the new covenant when the Spirit is poured out "on all flesh"

(Joel 2:28-29; Acts 2:16-33). Likewise, the Lord's wish in Deuteronomy 5:29, "Would that [מִי יִתֵּן] they had such a heart in them to fear me and to keep all my commands all the days" will be fulfilled through the Lord's own work of circumcising Israel's hearts after the exile (Deut 30:6; cf. Jer 31:31-34; 32:39; Rom 2:29). He similarly wished that their spiritual dullness (Deut 29:4, "the LORD has not *given* you a heart to know . . . until this day"; cf. Is 1:3) would be replaced by understanding and wisdom (Deut 32:29; cf. Deut 4:6).

Thus the Pentateuch's themes of Messiah and Sinai/Deuteronomic law do not conflict in any way. Both relate to the message of salvation that this foundational book sets forth and are two sides of the same coin. On the one hand, the Pentateuch directly declares that this salvation comes "in the last days" through the Messiah who will defeat his enemies, cleanse creation, atone for his people, and rule the world. On the other hand, the Pentateuch also shows that Sinai/Deuteronomic law, despite its binding nature, revelation of the Lord's character, and value for governing Israel justly, was not given "in the last days" and would never be the means of eschatological salvation, as shown through Israel's chronic failure to keep it. Though the principles it expresses are eternal (e.g., truths about God, moral commands, concern for justice), the Sinai/Deuteronomic law as a system is temporary, inherently limited, and will be superseded when the Lord's *torah* is written on the hearts of his people (Jer 31:33). The Sinai/Deuteronomic law does not include the provision of the Spirit and as such is both inferior to the new covenant and ineffective as a means of blessing (Rom 8:3-4). The Pentateuch simultaneously emphasizes both the giving of the Sinai/Deuteronomic law to Israel and their breaking of it, and in so doing affirms both the importance of this law and its inability to save. When paired with the eschatological salvation through the Messiah set forth in the Pentateuch, its presentation of the Sinai/Deuteronomic law should not lead to myopic zeal for law keeping but to humble, patient hope in the Messiah's coming. Even the earliest readers of the Pentateuch, who lived under this law, could have discerned this focus.

Problems on the Journey to Mount Sinai and Their Continuance

Another important part of the narrative context of the giving of the Sinai law is the preceding narrative of Israel's journey to Mount Sinai from the

Red Sea, which in turn is linked to the exodus from Egypt. When the Lord called Moses at the burning bush at "the mountain of God, Horeb [i.e., Mount Sinai]" (Ex 3:1), he predicted Moses' success and his bringing Israel out of Egypt to serve God on this same mountain (Ex 3:12). This was to be a stop along the way to the Promised Land (Ex 3:8). A closer look at the section of narrative that concerns Israel's journey to Mount Sinai (Ex 15:22–17:7) reveals major problems with their relationship with the Lord. These problems worsen during these travels and worsen still more during their stay at Mount Sinai. As such, the worsening relational issues between Israel and the Lord are also a significant part of the narrative context of the giving of the Sinai law and shed light on the proper understanding of the Sinai/Deuteronomic law in the compositional strategy of the Pentateuch.

Israel's downward spiral began very quickly. When they had just crossed the Red Sea, they "feared the LORD and believed in the LORD and in his servant Moses" (Ex 14:31) and praised the Lord in the Song of the Sea (Ex 15:1-18). But this "spiritual high" was short-lived. After going three days in the wilderness without finding water and then finding only bitter water at Mara (Ex 15:22-23), Israel "grumbled against Moses, saying, 'What shall we drink?'" (Ex 15:24). Although their need for water was legitimate, the verb *grumble* (לוּן) is consistently used with a negative connotation related to Israel's lack of faith (e.g., Ps 59:15). In Numbers 17:10, the Lord took Israel's "grumblings" so seriously that they would die if these complaints continued. At Mara, Israel grumbled against Moses rather than praying to the Lord, as Moses did (Ex 15:25). The contrast with the Song of the Sea just three days ago is unmistakable. Whereas Israel had recently recognized the Lord's "mighty hand" (Ex 14:31) and given him glory in song, now Israel was fixated on Moses as the one presumably responsible for addressing their thirst. Moses of course was incapable of providing water for them, and his prayer to the Lord suggests a better way in which Israel could have responded. Moses' direct cry to the Lord resulted in the Lord "teaching" him (Hiph. יָרָה, cf. Ex 4:12, 15; Ps 32:8) concerning a "tree" (עֵץ, Ex 15:25).[4] Through this trial, the Lord "tested" Israel, and their actual

---

[4]The themes of wisdom and a life-giving tree recall both well-known trees in the Garden of Eden (Gen 2:9) and the personification of wisdom as a tree of life in Prov 3:13-18. See also Ps 1:2-3.

spiritual condition was revealed. Their walk with the Lord was not what it had appeared to be just a few days before.

The themes of grumbling, testing, and relational distance between Israel and the Lord continue in Exodus 16–17. Though again related to a legitimate need, this time for food, Israel "grumbled against Moses and Aaron" (Ex 16:2), going so far as to wish that they had died in Egypt along with many Egyptians (Ex 16:3). Such words totally undermined the Lord's compassion and faithfulness in bringing them out of Egypt (Ex 2:24-25), as well as disregarding his recent appeal that they "diligently listen" to his voice so that he would not afflict them as he had afflicted the Egyptians (Ex 15:26). The Israelites' glorification of life in Egypt through selective remembrance of the food they used to eat was a serious misrepresentation of their previous oppressed condition (Ex 16:3). Furthermore, their attribution of evil motives to Moses and Aaron ("you brought us out into this wilderness to kill this whole assembly with hunger") demonstrated not only a lack of faith in their leaders but also unbelief in the Lord himself (Ex 16:7-8), whom they seem to have forgotten. The Lord's provision of manna served not only to meet their genuine need but also to "test" Israel again to see if they would follow his instructions concerning its collection (Ex 16:4-5). They failed on both counts (Ex 16:19-20, 27), and the Lord voiced his frustration, "How long will you refuse to keep my commandments and my laws [מִצְוֹתַי וְתוֹרֹתָי]?" Things are getting worse. Israel seems to have forgotten the Lord, and the Lord himself was becoming frustrated with them. Israel was still not addressing the Lord directly as they had recently (Ex 15:1-18), and Moses was repeatedly mediating between them and the Lord (Ex 15:24-25; 16:2-6, 11-12).

When Israel needed water again (Ex 17:1), they "contended" with Moses, "grumbled" against him, and accused him again of wanting to kill them (Ex 17:2-3). As before, Moses "cried out to the Lord" (Ex 17:4; 15:25), who faithfully provided water again, this time from the rock (Ex 17:5-6). Israel's anger had reached the point that Moses feared that they were about to stone him (Ex 17:4), but the Lord's method of provision allowed for violence to be done only to "the rock" that Moses was to strike with his staff (Ex 17:5-6). The naming of this place "Massah and Meribah" would serve as a reminder of Israel's "contention" with Moses and their "testing" the Lord (Ex 17:7). The latter involved an unjustifiable questioning of the

Lord's presence in their midst and is directly forbidden in Deuteronomy 6:16 (cf. Mt 4:7; Lk 4:12; Acts 5:9). They had already been given ample evidence of this reality through the miracle at Mara and the provision of manna and quail in conjunction with a visible manifestation of the Lord's glory (Ex 16:10), to say nothing of the plagues against Egypt and the crossing of the Red Sea. At the same time, the strife and testiness between Israel and the Lord and Moses is intertwined with the provision of water from the rock, which we have argued intentionally foreshadows the Messiah (see chap. 5 above). The striking of the rock not only "saves" Israel from thirsting to death but also saves Moses from being stoned. The theme of divine provision in the midst of rising tensions between Israel and an individual Israelite who is the divinely appointed instrument of salvation parallel both the Joseph story (Gen 37) and the Suffering Servant in Isaiah.

The Israelites' arrival at Rephidim (Ex 17:1) was evidently not far from "Horeb," where the rock was struck (Ex 17:6). The meeting between Jethro and Moses in Exodus 18 likewise took place at "the mountain of God" (Ex 18:5). Israel's journey to Mount Sinai is also referenced in Exodus 19:1-2. The downward trend in their relationship with the Lord would continue here, with the exceptions of the construction of the tabernacle (see discussion of Bezalel in chap. 5 above) and the census and orderly arrangement of the camp (Num 1:19, 54; 2:34; 3:42, 51; 4:49; 5:4). Israel's worsening problems can be seen not only through their aforementioned sins during this period (Ex 32; Lev 10:1-3; 17:7; 24:10-12) but also through their other interactions with the Lord and Moses. Israel's arrival at Mount Sinai would not end their "drift away" from the Lord that began after the Song of the Sea (cf. Heb 2:1).

Israel's increasing relational distance from the Lord during their recent journey, as evidenced by faithless grumbling, prayerlessness, disobedience, and testing the Lord, is further manifested at Mount Sinai through their fear, physical distance from the Lord, and request for Moses to be their mediator. On the third day in which they were to meet with the Lord (Ex 19:10-15), they "trembled" (Ex 19:16) and instead "stood far away" (Ex 20:18, 21). The physical distance between Israel and the Lord reflects their increasingly distant relationship. They were indeed "far away" from God (Jer 2:5). Having heard the Ten Commandments directly from the Lord himself (Deut 5:4), their request, "may God not speak with us"

(אַל־יְדַבֵּר עִמָּנוּ אֱלֹהִים, Ex 20:19; cf. Deut 5:24-27), seems to contradict the Lord's repeated appeals to Israel to "diligently listen" to his voice (Ex 15:26; 19:5). Their petition for Moses to permanently serve as their mediator was driven by their own fear (Ex 20:20; Deut 5:5), which was so intense that they imagined that they would die if they heard the voice of the Lord again (Ex 20:19; Deut 5:24-26).[5] Even their promise to obey Moses seems to have been motivated by this fear (Ex 20:19; Deut 5:27). But being utterly terrified of the Lord is not the same thing as having genuine "fear of the LORD" that keeps a person from sinning, as Moses' exhortation implies, "Do not fear, for God has come to test you, in order that the fear of him [i.e., 'the fear of the LORD'] might be upon you, that you might not sin" (Ex 20:20). Proverbs 3:7 teaches, "Fear the LORD and turn away from evil" (cf. Job 1:1), but the Israelites' "fear" at Mount Sinai resulted in distancing themselves from the Lord (Ex 20:18, 21) rather than turning away from sin. Indeed, its effects would be short-lived, and they would soon be found committing the "great sin" of worshiping the golden calf in Exodus 32. In one sense, this is not surprising because it is impossible to avoid sin while at the same distancing oneself from the Lord (cf. Gen 17:1, "Walk before me and be blameless). The problems between the Lord and Israel reached a climax when he threatened to wipe them out completely and start over with Moses (Ex 32:10).

Even after Moses successfully interceded for Israel so that the Lord did not give full vent to his wrath (Ex 32:11-14), the underlying problems remained. Israel was still not walking with the Lord (cf. Gen 5:24; 6:9), and the relational distance between them and the Lord continued to grow. When Moses came down from Mount Sinai in Exodus 34:29, the skin of his face was shining. Because the Israelites "were afraid to draw near him" (Ex 34:30), Moses would put a veil over his face (Ex 34:33-35). The original reason for Moses' permanent mediation was Israel's fear of hearing the Lord's voice directly (Ex 20:18-19), but now they were also afraid of their mediator's shining face. As Nanette Stahl observes, "The mediator himself is mediated by the veil: even Moses' own face becomes unendurable to the people."[6] They had fallen a long way from praising the Lord in song in

---

[5]For more on the Lord's comment that they spoke "thoroughly" in asking for Moses' permanent mediation (Deut 5:28; 18:17), see the discussion in chap. 7 above.
[6]Stahl, *Law and Liminality*, 70.

Exodus 15:1-18 and hearing the Ten Commandments directly from him in Exodus 20:1-17. Moses' permanent mediation institutionalized an indirect relationship between the Lord and Israel, and the use of the veil in Exodus 34:33-35 indicates that this indirect relationship had become even more indirect. Likewise, Israel's faithlessness and grumbling continued after they left Mount Sinai (Num 11:1, 4-6; 14:2, 27; 16:11, 41), and they would again incite the Lord to wipe them out completely (Num 14:12; 25:11).

The giving of the Sinai law and the repeated solemn injunctions to keep it had no lasting effect on the hearts of Israel. To make matters worse, the consequences for Israel's rebellion became more severe, since "the law brings wrath" (Rom 4:15). Their grumblings on the way to Mount Sinai displeased the Lord but did not result in any punishment (Ex 15:22–17:7), whereas their later faithlessness was met with plague and death (Ex 32:35; Num 11:33; 14:37; 16:46-50). Israel's responsibility became greater, and their punishment also became greater. The Sinai law was given to a people that had already drifted away significantly from the Lord. Based on their recent track record, the reader of the narrative should have little hope that they will keep the Sinai law. Indeed, rather than halting their downward slide, this law even more clearly manifested it. The fact that Israel had just been explicitly prohibited from worshiping idols in Exodus 20:4-5 makes the sin of the golden calf all the more heinous in Exodus 32:1-6. As Paul says in Romans 7:13, "Through the commandment, sin might become exceedingly sinful." Thus the Sinai law did not solve the existing problem of Israel's increasingly distant relationship with the Lord that began shortly after crossing the Red Sea but instead magnified it. The narrative context of the giving of this law thus suggests that it was more of a stopgap than a solution (Gal 3:23-25). The real solution is the new covenant and its promise of "my law" being written on the hearts of Israel and Judah, who will all know the Lord (Jer 31:31-34). This covenant will not be broken and will include provision for the forgiveness of sins.

The Theme of the Lord's Salvation in Exodus

Another relevant consideration related to this same section of the Pentateuch is the theme of the Lord's salvation. This theme is unmistakable in the Exodus narrative (Ex 1–15), but it also carries over into Israel's journey to Mount Sinai, in such a way that it even informs our understanding of the Sinai law and its purpose. During the call of Moses, the Lord told him in advance that Pharaoh would not allow the Israelites to go "without a strong hand" (Ex 3:19) and that the Lord would stretch out his "hand" and "strike Egypt with all my wonders" (Ex 3:20). These included the plagues, which reached their climax in the Passover and plague of the firstborn (Ex 4:21-23). Prior to the plague of hail, the Lord even declared that he could have wiped out Egypt already, but he raised up Pharaoh for the very purpose of showing his power and displaying his glory in all the earth (Ex 9:15-16). In other words, the sovereign, almighty Lord deliberately chose to demonstrate his salvation in drawn-out fashion, and Pharaoh played merely a supporting role in this cosmic drama. After being finally delivered from the Egyptians at the Red Sea, the Israelites recognized the Lord's "mighty hand" (Ex 14:31) and glorified the Lord in song (Ex 15:1-18).

Though this "spiritual high" was short-lived, the praise expressed to the Lord is nonetheless significant. With respect to the glory due to the Lord for his salvation, Israel's singing of the Song of the Sea is one of the primary purposes of the exodus and one of the high points of the Pentateuch. It is also the Pentateuch's longest continuous expression of praise to the Lord. Eschatological salvation will likewise result in songs of praise that glorify the Lord (e.g., Is 12; Ps 96; 98; 149; Rev 5:9-14; 15:3-4). The exodus itself is still central to Exodus 1–15 as a display of the Lord's faithfulness, compassion, and power, but it was important for his people Israel to recognize these things and give him glory as their "strength and song" (Ex 15:2). The Lord's glory does not merely exist in an objective sense but also needs to be recognized and responded to by human beings, especially his people. Without this spontaneous song of praise, Israel would have experienced relief from their suffering in Egypt but not necessarily as something that the Lord did specifically for them (see Num 23:23). The song triumphantly declares the truth that the Lord alone delivered them from Pharaoh and Egypt (see chap. 4 above). He was their Savior (cf. Deut 32:12).

The strong emphasis in the Song of the Sea (Ex 15:1-18) on the Lord's salvation and the glory he deserves for it carries over into Israel's journey to Mount Sinai and beyond. Soon after leaving the Red Sea, the Israelites encountered difficulties that showed that they still needed the Lord just as much as they did when they were slaves in Egypt. Without water

(Ex 15:22-23), food (Ex 16:3), and water again (Ex 17:1), they would have died. The high drama of the plagues against stubborn Pharaoh were past, but the reality of their complete dependence on the Lord to sustain their lives remained the same. His "testing" of his people at Mara (Ex 15:25) even implies that the difficulties that Israel encountered in the wilderness were also orchestrated intentionally by the Lord to remind them of their constant need of him (cf. Ex 16:4; Deut 8:2-3). Egypt was in the rear-view mirror, but Israel was not to forget the diseases that the Lord afflicted the Egyptians with, since they were not exempt from the same fate (Ex 15:26). Nevertheless, he was not only the warrior who had delivered them from Pharaoh in the recent past (Ex 15:3) but was always, "the LORD your God, your healer" (Ex 15:26). Indeed, he miraculously and salvifically turned the bitter water into sweet water at Mara, provided manna daily for them to eat, and provided water from the rock. Furthermore, the victory over the Amalekites showed that "the LORD is my banner" (Ex 17:15), and the Lord summarized the whole journey to Mount Sinai as his having "carried" them "on eagles' wings" (Ex 19:4). Just as he could have destroyed Egypt instantly but chose instead to use a means that more fully manifested his power, so it would seem that the Lord could have given Israel an easier journey to Mount Sinai and the Promised Land (see Ex 13:17-18; 15:27) but chose instead to test them and show them that they would continue to need his salvation just as much as before.[7] He was more than capable to show himself to be the same savior, warrior, and healer that he had always been.

The glaring problem is that Israel was woefully unaware of this truth, as their troubles on the journey to Mount Sinai demonstrate. The faith that they briefly had in the Lord and Moses (Ex 14:31) quickly turned into grumbling and blaming Moses. Even the Lord's attempt to encourage faith in his chosen prophet (Ex 19:9) was ultimately unsuccessful (Ex 32:1). In such a spiritual condition, there was no way that Israel would keep the Lord's commands. Nevertheless, they promised four times that they would obey (Ex 19:8; 20:19; 24:3, 7). While fear likely played a factor in these

---

[7] See Frank Polak, "Water, Rock, and Wood: Structure and Thought Pattern in the Exodus Narrative," *JANES* 25 (1997): 30, "Divine guidance is not limited to the deliverance from Egypt, but pertains to all spheres of life."

promises, the idea that they would keep the Lord's commands also reflected an unwarranted self-confidence and a disconnect with reality.

Though well intentioned, these subtly self-reliant promises of obedience, as they are cast in the narrative, conflict with Israel's actual ongoing need for the Lord as savior and healer. Their complete dependence on the Lord to deliver them from Egypt and to provide food and water for the journey was not on their minds at Mount Sinai. Instead, Israel implicitly assumed that they could keep the Lord's commands, and this despite recent evidence to the contrary (Ex 16:20, 27-28). What Israel's recent difficulties and failures should have led them to deeply realize is that they always needed the Lord's salvation just as much as they did when they were in Egypt. The giving of the Sinai law, even with its serious charges to keep it and grave consequences for disobedience, did not change this. Their best efforts to keep it would not be the means to their salvation. Instead, this law was supposed to, among other things, more clearly show Israel's need for the Lord's salvation through their failure to keep it. They would need rescue from the curses, wrath, and exile that they would bring on themselves through their disobedience. This deliverance would need to include cleansing, forgiveness, restoration, transformation, and regathering from exile. As was the case in the exodus, this eschatological salvation will be accomplished by the Lord, to his own glory. The Messianic vision that permeates the entire Pentateuch positively paints a picture of this glorious divine work.

The misunderstanding of the Sinai law that the Israelites fell into is the same one that readers of the Pentateuch are also susceptible to. In essence it is the affirmation that the Lord has given the Sinai/Deuteronomic law and as such it must be kept, which is then equated with the meaning of the Pentateuch. Though the premise is true, such a treatment of the Sinai/Deuteronomic law actually fails to fully appreciate the purpose of this law in the narrative context of the Pentateuch as a whole. It is effectively an incomplete, reductionistic, and ultimately incorrect response to this law as it is presented in the compositional strategy of the Pentateuch and can quickly lead to a misconstrual of the Pentateuch's intended meaning. Mistakenly understood in this way, a common response to inevitable disobedience to divine law is to commit oneself to keep it in the future. But without the circumcision of the heart (Deut 30:6), the core issues of human sinfulness remain (Gen 8:21), and the pattern of disobedience continues. Even if the lawbreaker also asks for divine pardon, there is no definitive basis in the Sinai/Deuteronomic law itself for such mercy from a holy God. To make matters worse, without a fundamental change in a person's understanding of the Sinai/Deuteronomic law and its purpose, the cycle of disobedience and recommitment cannot be broken. People tragically accumulate more and more divine wrath to be poured out on them even as they affirm the importance of divine law and repeatedly commit themselves to keep it. Over time, this arrangement can become increasingly human-centered and legalistic, with the Lord on the periphery as the one who gives authority to his law and metes out consequences related to it. This is a far cry from walking with the Lord in close relationship (Gen 5:24; 6:9; Ex 33:11) without fear (1 Jn 4:18).

To be sure, the Sinai/Deuteronomic law was useful for the governance of Israel and must be kept on penalty of curse and death, but the Pentateuch also makes clear that the solution to humanity's inevitable failures to keep this law is not simply trying again but the unilateral salvation of the Lord and his Messiah, who will rule in "justice and righteousness" (Is 9:7 [MT v. 6]). He will die a sacrificial death for his people, bring blessing to all nations instead of curse, and bring his people back to the Promised Land. Rather than becoming trapped in a never-ending cycle of the importance of divine law, disobedience, and recommitment, the Pentateuch sets forth the way of salvation as beginning similarly with the importance of divine law but then uses our inevitable disobedience as a stepping stone to our need for forgiveness and transformation through the Messiah and the new covenant. Whereas the former approach to the Sinai/Deuteronomic law constantly turns back inwardly on this law and ourselves, the latter leads us away from this legal system and away from ourselves to the Messiah and to faith in him (Rom 3:21-22; Gal 3:24). The difference is one of life and death.

Conclusion

The Sinai/Deuteronomic law and the extended attention given to it does not in fact conflict with the Messianic vision of the Pentateuch. When interpreted in its narrative context and not only in terms of its specific commands and solemn charges to obedience, this law can be recognized for the contrastive element that it is. While certainly expressing the Lord's character and providing valuable insight into what a just society might look like, Israel's repeated failures to keep the Sinai/Deuteronomic law show that the Pentateuch is as much about these failures as it is about this law itself. It is difficult to imagine how a book that so clearly spells out Israel's past, present, and future failures to keep the Sinai/Deuteronomic law could have the keeping of this law for salvation as its central message. If the Pentateuch bears a coherent message, as we believe it does, then its central idea is actually that Israel, though under the Sinai/Deuteronomic law for a period of time and bound to keep it (Gal 3:23-25; 4:4-5), will not be saved through it but through the Messiah and the new covenant "in the last days." Israel's drifting away from the Lord while on the way to Mount Sinai further suggests the Sinai law's provisional nature and inherent limitations for a people whose relationship with the Lord was already far from ideal. Relatedly, the theme of the Lord's salvation that is so clear in Exodus 1–15 also subtly permeates the subsequent chapters that focus on the Sinai law. Although blessings were promised for obedience to the Sinai/Deuteronomic law (Deut 28:1-14; see Lev 26:3-13), in actuality curses would be the end result (Deut 30:1). But the Sinai/Deuteronomic law was never the Lord's plan of salvation in the first place. From the beginning, salvation for the human race would come through the seed of the woman (Gen 3:15) who would bring divine blessing to all the families and nations of the earth (Gen 12:3; 18:18; 22:18), including Israel (Deut 33). The giving of the Sinai/Deuteronomic law did not change this salvation plan in any way (Num 24:7-9, 17-19; Deut 18:15-18; 32–34) and even shines the spotlight on it all the more by ruling out this law and our works as a means of salvation, "for if righteousness is through the law, then Christ died for nothing!" (Gal 2:21).

CONCLUSION

"One does not fully appreciate a landscape in one day." Monet remarked that at first he merely cultivated his now famous water lilies in Giverny without any thought of painting them. Then suddenly, he testified, "I had a revelation of the magic of my pond. I took my palette. From this moment, I have had almost no other model."[1] The French impressionist's experience can undoubtedly be generalized for many other discoveries, including that of the Messianic "landscape" of the Pentateuch. Its rich and beautiful vision of the Messiah is not immediately apparent to the reader but emerges with greater clarity and splendor as one key passage after another is carefully studied and related to the others. As was the case for Monet and his water lilies, there may even be a period of time during which the Messianic glory that shines brilliantly through the Pentateuch and its compositional strategy goes largely unnoticed. The Bible itself suggests this possibility by its insistence that a full understanding of itself requires meditation on it (Josh 1:8; Ps 1:2) and the Lord's help (Ps 119:18; Lk 24:45).

As a work of genius, beauty, and glory, the Bible itself is a powerful testimony to the triune God and the gospel of Jesus the Messiah proclaimed on its pages. The goal of this book has been to lead the reader to recognize and be captivated by the intrinsic Messianic glory found in the Pentateuch, even as Paul was transformed by his own unique vision of the resurrected Jesus while on the Damascus Road (Acts 9:3-6; 22:6-10; 26:12-18; see Caravaggio's painting *The Conversion of Saint Paul*).

---

[1] Fondation Claude Monet, "Quotations," accessed December 2017, www.fondation-monet.com/en/claude-monet-2/quotations/. For a slightly different English translation of this quote, see Vivian Russell, *Monet's Water Lilies* (Boston: Bulfinch Press, 1998), front flap, 29.

Presumably having overhauled his previous Pharisaic understanding of the Old Testament, he subsequently devoted his life to preaching the gospel of Jesus the Messiah from its pages, including the Pentateuch (Acts 26:22-23; 28:23). We have attempted to show that direct Messianic prophecies ("lenses") and passages that intentionally foreshadow the Messiah ("mirrors") contribute to a sweeping Messianic vision that is the center of the Pentateuch's theological message. Each of these passages makes a unique contribution to the Messianic theology of the Pentateuch as a whole. The complex network of Messianic prophecies and instances of intentional foreshadowing is more than the mere sum of its parts. As a coherent web of texts, it is synergistic, and at times the Messianic import of one passage depends on or is clarified by an intertextual relationship to another Messianic passage (or passages). This is especially true for those passages that intentionally foreshadow the Messiah, which we have attempted to show are almost always intertextually related to direct Messianic prophecy. We leave as an open question for further research whether or not there are additional Messianic prophecies or examples of intentional foreshadowing of the Messiah that we have not discussed. The latter, we believe, is especially likely.

Thus Moses really did self-consciously write about the Messiah as the primary focus of the Pentateuch (Jn 5:46), even as he simultaneously told the story of creation, the patriarchs, and the birth of Israel. We recognize that much of the weight of our argument rests on our interpretation of Genesis 3:15, several passages that relate to "seed of Abraham" (e.g., Gen 15:3-4; 22:17b-18; 24:60), Genesis 27:27-29, and Genesis 49:8-12, which is why our analysis of those passages has been so detailed. These texts are themselves interrelated, with Genesis 3:15 as the foundation. But if we are correct about these passages being Messianic prophecies that together foretell the coming of an eschatological, divine-human, priest-king who will die sacrificially, rise again, defeat the serpent and his enemies, rule Israel and the nations, and bring divine blessing to all creation, then our basic understanding of the content of the Messianic vision of the Pentateuch holds. These Messianic prophecies in Genesis would then provide many connection points for intertextuality with the various examples of intentional foreshadowing of the Messiah found throughout the Pentateuch (e.g., Isaac/ram, Jacob's ladder, Passover lamb, "the rock"), not to mention the Messianic prophecies in Numbers 24, Deuteronomy 18, and Deuteronomy 33. Incidentally, the Pentateuch would also set forth a highly developed Christology, on par with that of the New Testament.

We also recognize that although the Pentateuch has been in its final form for well over two thousand years, readers have not often perceived the Messianic vision we hold that it sets forth. The primary reason for this, we believe, is the natural but misguided equation of the Pentateuch with the Sinai/Deuteronomic law, which is deeply entrenched in both Christian and Jewish interpretation. Insofar as readers mistakenly view the Pentateuch primarily as a legal code, its inherent Messianic glory will not shine through it. Nevertheless, when the Pentateuch's emphasis on the breaking of the Sinai/Deuteronomic law is recognized, this law can then be seen for the temporary and inherently limited system that it always was. As such, the Pentateuch itself presents a "theology of the Sinai/Deuteronomic law" that, while certainly affirming its divine origin and the consequent importance of keeping it, also demonstrates its inadequacy as a means of salvation and blessing, in contrast with the Messiah and the new covenant "in the last days." From beginning to end, salvation belongs to the Lord (Gen 3:15; Ex 14:13; Rev 7:10; 19:1). The Sinai/Deuteronomic law not only "looks forward" to the coming of the Messiah, as "having a shadow of the good things to come" (Heb 8:5), but from its inception was already overshadowed by the Messianic prophecies that both precede it in the Pentateuch (literarily and historically) and lay out the unchanging divine plan of eschatological salvation.

The Messianic vision of the Pentateuch provides a promising starting point for Old Testament theology and biblical theology, concerning which issues of unity, continuity, and discontinuity have long been debated. If the authorially intended meaning of the Pentateuch centers on the coming of the Messiah, and if the Pentateuch is the foundation of the entire Old Testament which is wholly consistent with it, then it suddenly becomes plausible that the Old Testament might likewise center on the Messiah and the new covenant much like the New Testament does. To prove this is of course beyond the scope of the present work, but we believe it can be done. Several other books in the Old Testament can also be characterized as having a "Messianic vision" (e.g., Isaiah, Psalms), and all the Old Testament books, related to one another compositionally and intertextually, together cast a coherent Messianic vision.[2]

In this way, the present book also serves to partially address some of the classic problems of Old Testament theology and biblical theology, especially as it relates to the problem of the Sinai/Deuteronomic law. Although we can affirm "progressive revelation" in the sense that the books of the Bible were written over the course of many centuries and that history culminates in Christ who reveals God in a climactic way, our view of the meaning of the Pentateuch does not require invoking "progressive revelation" as a unifying principle for biblical theology. This is because the meaning of the Pentateuch that Moses intended is the gospel of the Messiah. As such, its theology is in complete harmony with the New Testament, and there is no need to invoke "progressive revelation" to relate the message of the Pentateuch to the message of the New Testament through a scheme that emphasizes a chronological unfolding of divine truth. The messages are one and the same. As it relates more broadly to Old Testament theology and biblical theology, it remains to be shown that the message of the Old Testament is also this same gospel.

We close with one last quote from Monet that expresses what we hope is increasingly the experience of our readers as they study the Bible and behold its Messianic vision: "Each day I find something even more beautiful than the day before."[3]

---

[2] For one proposal, see John Sailhamer, "The Messiah and the Hebrew Bible," *JETS* 44 (2001): 5-23.
[3] Letter to his friend Frédéric Bazille, written from Honfleur, July 15, 1864, as cited and translated in Richard Kendall, ed., *Monet by Himself*, trans. Bridget Strevens Romer (Edison, NJ: Chartwell Books, 1989), 20.

BIBLIOGRAPHY

Alexander, T. Desmond. "Further Observations on the Term 'Seed' in Genesis." *TynBul* 48, no. 2 (1997): 364-68.

———. "Messianic Ideology in the Book of Genesis." In *The Lord's Anointed: Interpretation of Old Testament Messianic Texts*, edited by Philip Satterthwaite, Richard Hess, and Gordon Wenham, 19-39. Grand Rapids: Baker, 1995.

———. *From Paradise to the Promised Land*. 3rd ed. Grand Rapids: Baker, 2012.

Allison, Dale C., *The New Moses: A Matthean Typology*. Minneapolis: Fortress, 1993.

Anderson, Bradford. "Edom in the Book of Numbers: Some Literary Reflections." *ZAW* 124 (2012): 38-51.

Ashley, Timothy. *The Book of Numbers*. New International Commentary on the Old Testament. Grand Rapids: Eerdmans, 1993.

Auerbach, Erich. "Figura." In *Scenes from the Drama of European Literature*, 11-76. New York: Meridian, 1959.

———. *Mimesis*, translated by Willard Trask. Princeton, NJ: Princeton University Press, 1953.

August, Jared M. "The Messianic Hope of Genesis: The 'Protoevangelium' and Patriarchal Promises." *Themelios* 42, no. 1 (2017): 46-62.

Baker, David L. *Two Testaments, One Bible: The Theological Relationship Between the Old and New Testaments*. 3rd ed. Downers Grove, IL: InterVarsity Press, 2010.

Barrett, C. K. *The Gospel According to St. John*, 2nd ed. Philadelphia: Westminster, 1978.

Barstad, Hans. "The Understanding of Prophets in Deuteronomy." *SJOT* 8 (1994): 236-51.

Beale, Gregory. *The Temple and the Church's Mission*. New Studies in Biblical Theology. Downers Grove, IL: InterVarsity Press, 2004.

Betz, Otto. "Die Frage nach dem messianischen Bewusstein Jesu." *NovT* 6 (1963): 20-48.

Blenkinsopp, Joseph. *Prophecy and Canon*. Notre Dame, IN: University of Notre Dame Press, 1977.

Blomberg, Craig. *Matthew*. New American Commentary. Nashville: Broadman and Holman, 1992.

Bock, Darrell. *Acts*, Baker Exegetical Commentary on the New Testament. Grand Rapids: Baker Academic, 2007.

Borgen, Peder. *Bread from Heaven: An Exegetical Study of the Concept of Manna in the Gospel of John and the Writings of Philo*. Leiden: Brill, 1965.

Braulik, Georg, *Deuteronomium II, 16,18–34,12*. Die Neue Echter Bibel. Würzburg: Echter, 1992.

Brown, Raymond. "The History and Development of the Theory of a Sensus Plenior." *CBQ* 15 (1953): 141-62.

———. "The Problems of 'Sensus Plenior.'" *ETL* 43 (1967): 460-69.

———. "The 'Sensus Plenior' in the Last Ten Years." *CBQ* 25 (1963): 262-85.

———. *The 'Sensus Plenior' of Sacred Scripture*. Baltimore: St. Mary's, 1955.

Brueggemann, Walter. *Deuteronomy*. Abingdon Old Testament Commentaries. Nashville: Abingdon, 2001.

Buchanan, George. "Eschatology and the 'End of Days.'" *JNES* 20 (1963): 188-93.

Budd, Philip. *Numbers*. Word Biblical Commentary. Waco, TX: Word, 1984.

Calvin, John. *Commentaries on the First Book of Moses Called Genesis*. Calvin's Commentaries, translated by John King. Grand Rapids: Baker, 2003.

Carmichael, Calum. "Some Sayings in Genesis 49." *JBL* 88 (1969): 435-44.

Carson, D. A. *The Gospel According to John*. Pillar New Testament Commentary. Grand Rapids: Eerdmans, 1991.

Cassuto, Umberto. *A Commentary on the Book of Exodus*, translated by Israel Abrahams. Jerusalem: Magnes, 1983.

———. *A Commentary on the Book of Genesis, Part II: From Noah to Abraham: Genesis 6:9–11:32*, translated by Israel Abrahams. Jerusalem: Magnes, 1964.

Chan, Alan Kam-Yau. *Melchizedek Passages in the Bible: A Case Study for Inner-Biblical and Inter-Biblical Interpretation*. Berlin: De Gruyter, 2016.

Chen, Kevin. *Eschatological Sanctuary in Exodus 15:17 and Related Texts*. New York: Lang, 2013.

Childs, Brevard. *The Book of Exodus*. Old Testament Library. Philadelphia: Westminster, 1974.

Chou, Abner. *The Hermeneutics of the Biblical Writers: Learning to Interpret Scripture from the Prophets and Apostles*. Grand Rapids: Kregel, 2018.

Christensen, Duane. *Deuteronomy 1–21:9*. Word Biblical Commentary. Nashville: Nelson, 2001.

———. *Deuteronomy 21:10–34:12*, Word Biblical Commentary. Nashville: Nelson, 2002.

Cole, R. Alan. *Exodus: An Introduction and Commentary*. Tyndale Old Testament Commentaries. Downers Grove, IL: InterVarsity Press, 1973.

Cole, R. Dennis. *Numbers*. New American Commentary. Nashville: Broadman and Holman, 2000.

Collins, Anthony. *A Discourse of the Grounds and Reasons of the Christian Religion*. London, 1724. Repr., Eugene, OR: Wipf and Stock, 2005.

Collins, Jack. "A Syntactical Note (Genesis 3:15): Is the Woman's Seed Singular or Plural?" *TynBul* 48, no. 1 (1997): 139-48.

Craigie, Peter. *The Book of Deuteronomy*. New International Commentary on the Old Testament. Grand Rapids: Eerdmans, 1976.

Craigie, Peter, and Marvin E. Tate. *Psalms 1–50*. 2nd ed. Word Biblical Commentary. Nashville: Nelson, 2004.

Cross, Frank Moore and David Noel Freedman. "The Blessing of Moses." *JBL* 67 (1948): 191-210.

Danielou, Jean. *From Shadows to Reality: Studies in the Biblical Typology of the Fathers*. London: Burns and Oates, 1960.

Davidson, R. M. "Typological Structures in the Old and New Testaments." Th.D. diss., Andrews University, 1981.

Day, John. "Prophecy." In *It Is Written: Scripture Citing Scripture: Essays in Honour of Barnabas Lindars, SSF*, edited by D. A. Carson and H. G. M. Williamson, 39-55. New York: Cambridge University Press, 1998.

De Beaugrande, Robert and Wolfgang Dressler. *Introduction to Text Linguistics*. New York: Longman, 1981.

De Hoop, Raymond. *Genesis 49 in Its Literary and Historical Context*. Leiden: Brill, 1999.

De Lubac, Henri. *Medieval Exegesis: The Four Senses of Scripture*, translated by E. M. Macierowski. 3 vols. Grand Rapids: Eerdmans, 2000.

Delitzsch, Franz. *Messianic Prophecies in Historical Succession*, translated by Samuel I. Curtiss. Edinburgh: T&T Clark, 1891.

Dempster, Stephen. *Dominion and Dynasty: A Theology of the Hebrew Bible*. New Studies in Biblical Theology. Downers Grove, IL: InterVarsity Press, 2003.

Dharamraj, Havilah. *A Prophet Like Moses? A Narrative-Theological Reading of the Elijah Stories*. Paternoster Biblical Monographs. Milton Keynes, UK: Paternoster, 2011.

DiFransico, Lesley. "'He Will Cast Their Sins into the Depths of the Sea . . . ': Exodus Allusions and the Personification of Sin in Micah 7:7-20." *VT* 67 (2017): 187-203.

Douglas, Mary. "The Go-Away Goat." In *The Book of Leviticus: Composition and Reception*, edited by Rolf Rendtorff and Robert Kugler, 121-41. Leiden: Brill, 2003.

Drew, Elizabeth. *Poetry: A Modern Guide to Its Understanding and Enjoyment*. New York: Dell, 1959.

Driver, S. R. *The Book of Genesis*. London: Methuen and Co., 1948.

———. *A Critical and Exegetical Commentary on Deuteronomy*. International Critical Commentary. New York: Charles Scribner's Sons, 1909.

Duffy, Kevin. "The 'Sensus Plenior' of Scripture: A Debate and Its Aftermath." *LS* 38 (2014): 228-45.

Durham, John. *Exodus*. Word Biblical Commentary. Waco, TX: Word, 1987.

Ebach, Jürgen. *Genesis 37–50*. Herders Theologischer Kommentar zum Alten Testament. Freiburg: Herder, 2007.

Ede, Franziska. *Die Josefsgeschichte*. Berlin: De Gruyter, 2016.

Edenburg, Cynthia. "How (Not) to Murder a King: Variations on a Theme in 1 Sam 24; 26." *SJOT* 12 (1998): 64-85.

Elowsky, Joel C., ed. *John 1–10*. Ancient Christian Commentary on Scripture. Downers Grove, IL: InterVarsity Press, 2007.

Ernesti, Johann August. *Institutio interpretis Novi Testamenti*. 5th ed. Leipzig: Libraria Weidmannia, 1809.

Fairbairn, Patrick. *The Typology of Scripture*. Philadelphia: Daniels and Smith, 1852.

Fee, Gordon. *The First Epistle to the Corinthians*. New International Commentary on the New Testament. Rev. ed. Grand Rapids: Eerdmans, 2014.

Fishbane, Michael. *Biblical Text and Texture: A Literary Reading of Selected Texts*. Oxford: Oneworld, 1998.

Fitzmeyer, Joseph. *First Corinthians*. Anchor Bible. New Haven, CT: Yale University Press, 2008.

Fohrer, Georg. *Exegese des Alten Testaments*. Heidelberg: Quelle und Meyer, 1973.

Fox, R. Michael, ed. *Reverberations of the Exodus in Scripture*. Eugene, OR: Wipf and Stock, 2014.

France, R. T. *The Gospel of Matthew*. New International Commentary on the New Testament. Grand Rapids: Eerdmans, 2007.

Freedman, David Noel. "The Poetic Structure of the Framework of Deuteronomy 33." In *The Bible World: Essays in Honor of Cyrus H. Gordon*, edited by Gary Rendsburg, 25-46. New York: Ktav, 1980.

Frei, Hans. *The Eclipse of Biblical Narrative: A Study in Eighteenth and Nineteenth Century Hermeneutics*. New Haven, CT: Yale University Press, 1974.

Fretheim, Terence. *Exodus*. Interpretation. Louisville: Knox, 1991.

Gaffin, Richard B. "The Redemptive-Historical View." In *Biblical Hermeneutics: Five Views*, edited by Stanley Porter and Beth Stovell, 89-110. Downers Grove, IL: InterVarsity Press, 2012.

Gevirtz, Stanley. "Naphtali in 'The Blessing of Jacob.'" *JBL* 103 (1984): 513-21.

Glenny, W. Edward. "Typology: A Summary of the Present Evangelical Discussion." *JETS* 40 (1997): 627-38.

Goldsworthy, Graeme. *According to Plan: The Unfolding Revelation of God in the Bible*. Downers Grove, IL: InterVarsity Press, 2002.

———. *Gospel-Centered Hermeneutics: Foundations and Principles of Evangelical Biblical Interpretation*. Downers Grove, IL: InterVarsity Press, 2006.

Good, Edwin. "The 'Blessing' of Judah, Gen 49:8-12." *JBL* 82 (1963): 427-32.

Goppelt, Leonhard. *Typos: The Typological Interpretation of the Old Testament in the New*, translated by Donald Madvig. Grand Rapids: Eerdmans, 1982.

Grypeou, Emmanouela and Helen Spurling. *The Book of Genesis in Late Antiquity: Encounters Between Jewish and Christian Exegesis*. Leiden: Brill, 2013.

Gundry, Stanley. "Typology as Means of Interpretation: Past and Present." *JETS* 12 (1969): 233-40.

Gunkel, Hermann. *Genesis*, trans. Mark Biddle. Macon, GA: Mercer, 1997.

Hagner, Donald. *Matthew 1-13*. Word Biblical Commentary. Dallas: Word, 1993.

Hamilton, James. *God's Glory in Salvation Through Judgment*. Wheaton, IL: Crossway, 2010.

———. "The Seed of the Woman and the Blessing of Abraham." *TynBul* 58 (2007): 253-73.

———. "The Skull Crushing Seed of the Woman: Inner-Biblical Interpretation of Genesis 3:15." *SBJT* 10 (2006): 30-54.

Hamilton, Victor. *The Book of Genesis 1-17*. New International Commentary on the Old Testament. Grand Rapids: Eerdmans, 1990.

———. *The Book of Genesis 18-50*. New International Commentary on the Old Testament. Grand Rapids: Eerdmans, 1995.

Harrison, R. K. *Leviticus*. Tyndale Old Testament Commentaries. Downers Grove, IL: InterVarsity Press, 1980.

Hartley, John. *Leviticus*. Word Biblical Commentary. Dallas: Word, 1992.

Hays, Richard. *Echoes of Scripture in the Letters of Paul*. New Haven, CT: Yale University Press, 1989.

———. *Echoes of Scripture in the Gospels*. Waco, TX: Baylor University Press, 2016.

Heck, Joel. "A History of Interpretation of Genesis 49 and Deuteronomy 33." *BSac* 147 (1990): 16-31.

———. "Issachar: Slave or Freeman? (Gen 49:14-15)." *JETS* 29 (1986): 385-96.

Hengstenberg, E. W. *Christology of the Old Testament*, 2 vols. McLean, VA: MacDonald, 1972.

Hess, Richard. *Studies in the Personal Names of Genesis 1–11*. Winona Lake, IN: Eisenbrauns, 2009.

Hirsch, E. D. *Validity in Interpretation*. New Haven, CT: Yale University Press, 1967.

Houtman, Cornelius. *Exodus*. Historical Commentary on the Old Testament. 3 vols. Translated by Sierd Woudstra. Leuven: Peeters, 1993–2000.

———. "What Did Jacob See in His Dream at Bethel? Some Remarks on Genesis XXVIII 10–22." *VT* 27 (1977): 337-51.

Kaiser, Walter. "The Single Intent of Scripture." In *The Right Doctrine from the Wrong Texts?*, edited by Gregory Beale. Grand Rapids: Baker, 1994.

———. Review of *The Lord's Anointed: Interpretation of Old Testament Messianic Texts*, edited by Philip Satterthwaite, Richard Hess, and Gordon Wenham, in *JETS* 42 (1999): 99-102.

———. *The Uses of the Old Testament in the New*. Repr., Eugene, OR: Wipf and Stock, 1985.

Kalimi, Isaac. *Metathesis in the Hebrew Bible: Wordplay as a Literary and Exegetical Device*. Peabody, MA: Hendrickson, 2018.

Keener, Craig S. *Acts: An Exegetical Commentary (15:1–22:35)*. Grand Rapids: Baker, 2014.

Keil, C. F. and Franz Delitzsch. *Commentary on the Old Testament: The Pentateuch*. Peabody, MA: Hendrickson, 1996.

Kendall, Richard, ed. *Monet by Himself*, translations by Bridget Strevens Romer. Edison, NJ: Chartwell Books, 1989.

Kidner, Derek. *Genesis*. Tyndale Old Testament Commentaries. Downers Grove, IL: InterVarsity Press, 1967.

Kim, Yoon-Hee. "'The Prophet Like Moses': Deut 18:55-22 Reexamined within the Context of the Pentateuch and in Light of the Final Shape of the TaNAK." Ph.D. diss., Trinity Evangelical Divinity School, 1995.

Kiuchi, Nobuyoshi. *Leviticus*. Apollos Old Testament Commentary. Downers Grove, IL: InterVarsity Press, 2007.

Klappert, Bertold. "'Mose hat von mir geschrieben': Leitlinien einer Christologie im Kontext des Judentums Joh 5,39-47." In *Die Hebräische Bibel and ihre zweifache Nachgeschichte: Festschrift für Rolf Rendtorff zum 65. Geburstag*, edited by Erhard Blum et al., 619-40. Neukirchen-Vluyn: Neukirchener, 1990.

Köstenberger, Andreas. "John." In *Commentary on the New Testament Use of Old Testament*, edited by Gregory Beale and D. A. Carson, 415-512. Grand Rapids: Baker, 2007.

———. *John*. Baker Exegetical Commentary on the New Testament. Grand Rapids: Baker, 2004.

Kraus, H. J. *Psalms 1–59*, translated by Hilton C. Oswald. Minneapolis: Fortress, 1993.

Kugel, James. *The Ladder of Jacob*. Princeton, NJ: Princeton University Press, 2006.

Lai, Paul. "Jacob's Blessing on Judah (Genesis 49:8-12) within the Hebrew Old Testament: A Study of In-textual, Inner-textual, and Inter-textual Interpretation." Ph.D. diss., Trinity Evangelical Divinity School, 1993.

Lampe, G. W. H. "Typological Exegesis." *Theology* 56 (1953): 201-8.

Lane, William. *Hebrews 1–8*. Word Biblical Commentary. Dallas: Word, 1991.

Leithart, Peter. *Deep Exegesis: The Mystery of Reading Scripture*. Waco, TX: Baylor University Press, 2009.

Leonard, Jeffery M. "Identifying Inner-Biblical Allusions: Psalm 78 as a Test Case." *JBL* 127 (2008): 241-65.

Levenson, Jon. *The Death and Resurrection of the Beloved Son*. New Haven, CT: Yale University Press, 1993.

Levine, Baruch. *Numbers 21–36*. Anchor Bible. New York: Doubleday, 2000.

Levine, Nachman. "The Curse and the Blessing: Narrative Discourse Syntax and Literary Form." *JSOT* 27 (2002): 189-99.

Link, Peter, and Matthew Emerson. "Searching for the Second Adam: Typological Connections between Adam, Joseph, Mordecai, and Daniel." *SBJT* 21 (2017): 123-44.

Lipinski, E. "באחרית הימים dans les textes préexiliques." *VT* 20 (1970): 445-50.

Loewenstamm, Samuel E. *The Evolution of the Exodus Tradition*, translated by Baruch J. Schwartz. Jerusalem: Magnes, 1992.

Lohfink, Norbert. *The Christian Meaning of the Old Testament*, translated by R. A. Wilson. Milwaukee: Bruce, 1968.

Longman, Tremper and Raymond Dillard. *An Introduction to the Old Testament*. 2nd ed. Grand Rapids: Zondervan, 2006.

Louth, Andrew, ed. *Genesis 1–11*. Ancient Christian Commentary on Scripture. Downers Grove, IL: InterVarsity Press, 2001.

Lundbom, Jack. *Deuteronomy: A Commentary*. Grand Rapids: Eerdmans, 2013.

———. *Jeremiah 1–20*. Anchor Bible. New York: Doubleday, 1999.

———. *Jeremiah: Prophet Like Moses*. Eugene, OR: Wipf and Stock, 2015.

Martin, R. A. "The Earliest Messianic Interpretation of Gen 3:15." *JBL* 84 (1965): 425-27.

Mathews, Joshua G. *Melchizedek's Alternative Priestly Order: A Compositional Analysis of Genesis 14:18-20 and Its Echoes Throughout the Tanak*. Bulletin for Biblical Research Supplements. Winona Lake, IN: Eisenbrauns, 2013.

Mathews, Kenneth. *Genesis 1–11:26*. New American Commentary. Nashville: Broadman and Holman, 1996.

Mays, James L. *Psalms*. Interpretation. Louisville: Knox, 1994.

McCarter, P. Kyle, Jr. *II Samuel*. Anchor Bible. Garden City, NY: Doubleday, 1984.

McConville, J. Gordon. *Deuteronomy*. Apollos Old Testament Commentary. Downers Grove, IL: InterVarsity Press, 2002.

Meeks, Russell. "Intertextuality, Inner-Biblical Exegesis, and Inner-Biblical Allusion: The Ethics of a Methodology." *Biblica* 95 (2014): 280-91.

Milgrom, Jacob. *Leviticus 1–16*. Anchor Bible. New York: Doubleday, 1991.

———. *Numbers*. JPS Torah Commentary. Philadelphia: Jewish Publication Society, 1990.

Miscall, Peter. *1 Samuel: A Literary Reading*. Bloomington: Indiana University Press, 1986.

Mitchell, David C. *The Message of the Psalter: An Eschatological Programme in the Book of Psalms*, JSOT Supplement Series. Sheffield: Sheffield Academic, 1997.

Moberly, R. W. L. "The Earliest Commentary on the Akedah," *VT* 38 (1988): 302-23.

Morales, L. Michael. *Who Shall Ascend the Mountain of the Lord? A Biblical Theology of the Book of Leviticus*. Downers Grove, IL: InterVarsity Press, 2015.

Motyer, J. Alec. *The Prophecy of Isaiah*. Downers Grove, IL: InterVarsity Press, 1993.

Mowinckel, Sigmund. *He That Cometh*, translated by G. W. Anderson. New York: Abingdon, 1954.

Nelson, Richard. *Deuteronomy*. Old Testament Library. Louisville: Westminster, 2002.

Niccacci, Alviero. "A Neglected Point of Hebrew Syntax: YIQTOL and Position in the Sentence." *LA* 37 (1987): 7-19.

Noort, Ed and Eibert Tigchelaar, eds. *The Sacrifice of Isaac: The Aqedah (Genesis 22) and Its Interpretations*. Leiden: Brill, 2002.

Noth, Martin. *Exodus*. Old Testament Library. Philadelphia: Westminster, 1962.

O'Brien, Mark. "Deuteronomy 16.18–18.22: Meeting the Challenge of Towns and Nations." *JSOT* 33 (2008): 155-72.

Osborne, Grant. *The Hermeneutical Spiral: A Comprehensive Introduction to Biblical Interpretation*. 2nd ed. Downers Grove, IL: InterVarsity Press, 2006.

Otto, Eckhart. *Deuteronomium*. Herders Theologischer Kommentar zum Alten Testament. 2 vols. Freiburg: Herder, 2016–2017.

Peleg, Yitzhak. *Going Up and Going Down: A Key to Interpreting Jacob's Dream (Gen 28:10–22)*, translated by Betty Rozen. London: Bloomsbury, 2015.

Polak, Frank. "Water, Rock, and Wood: Structure and Thought Pattern in the Exodus Narrative." *JANES* 25 (1997): 19-42.

Postell, Seth. *Adam as Israel: Genesis 1–3 as the Introduction to the Torah and Tanakh*. Eugene, OR: Wipf and Stock, 2011.

———. "Genesis 3:15: The Promised Seed." In *The Moody Handbook of Messianic Prophecy: Studies and Expositions of the Messiah in the Old Testament*, edited by Michael Rydelnik and Edwin Blum, 239-50. Chicago: Moody Publishers, 2019.

———. "Numbers 24:5-9: The Distant Star." In *The Moody Handbook of Messianic Prophecy: Studies and Expositions of the Messiah in the Old Testament*, edited by Michael Rydelnik and Edwin Blum, 285-308. Chicago: Moody Publishers, 2019.

Postell, Seth, Eitan Bar, and Erez Soref. *Reading Moses, Seeing Jesus: How the Torah Fulfills Its Goal in Yeshua*. 2nd ed. Wooster, OH: Weaver, 2017.

Propp, William. *Exodus 1–18*. Anchor Bible. New York: Doubleday, 1999.

Provan, Iain. "The Messiah in the Books of Kings." In *The Lord's Anointed: Interpretation of Old Testament Messianic Texts*, edited by Philip Satterthwaite, Richard Hess, and Gordon Wenham, 67-85. Grand Rapids: Baker, 1995.

Pshenichny, Gennady. "Abraham in the Canonical Hebrew Bible: A Study of the Abrahamic Narrative of Genesis with a View Toward the Reading of That Text by the Later Canonical Authors." Ph.D. diss., Southeastern Baptist Theological Seminary, 2007.

Redford, Donald. *A Study of the Biblical Story of Joseph*. Supplements to Vetus Testamentum. Leiden: Brill, 1970.

Rendsburg, Gary. "Double Polysemy in Gen 49:6 and Job 3:6." *CBQ* 44 (1982): 48-51.

———. "Double Polysemy in Proverbs 31:19." In *Humanism, Culture, and Language in the Near East: Studies in Honor of Georg Krotkoff*, edited by A. Afsaruddin and A. H. Mathias Zahniser, 267-74. Winona Lake, IN: Eisenbrauns, 1997.

———. *How the Bible Is Written*. Peabody, MA: Hendrickson, 2019.

———. "Janus Parallelism in Gen 49:26." *JBL* 99 (1980): 291-93.

———. "Word Play in Biblical Hebrew: An Eclectic Collection." In *Puns and Pundits: Word Play in the Bible and in Near Eastern Literature*, edited by S. B. Noegel. Bethesda, MD: CDL Press, 2000.

Riffaterre, Michael. *Semiotics of Poetry*. Bloomington, IN: Indiana University Press, 1978.

Rösel, Martin. "Die Interpretation von Genesis 49 in der Septuaginta." *Biblische Notizen* 79 (1995): 54-70.

Rosenberg, A. J. *Genesis: A New English Translation / Translation of Text, Rashi, and Other Commentaries*. New York: Judaica, 1993.

Rouillard, Hedwige. *Le Péricope de Balaam (Nombres 22–24): La Prose et les "Oracles."* Paris: J. Gabalda et Cie., 1985.

Ruppert, Lothar. *Die Josephserzählung der Genesis*. Munich: Kösel-Verlag, 1965.

Russell, Brian. *The Song of the Sea: The Date of Composition and Influence of Exodus 15:1-21*. New York: Lang, 2007.

Russell, Vivian. *Monet's Water Lilies*. Boston: Bulfinch Press, 1998.

Rydelnik, Michael. *The Messianic Hope: Is the Hebrew Bible Really Messianic?* Nashville: Broadman and Holman, 2010.

Sabourin, Leopold. "Isaac and Jesus in the Targums and in the New Testament." *RSB* 1, no. 2 (March 1981): 37-45.

Sailhamer, John. Genesis. Expositor's Bible Commentary. Rev. ed. Grand Rapids: Zondervan, 2008.

———. *Genesis Unbound*. Repr., Eugene, OR: Wipf and Stock, 1996.

———. *Introduction to Old Testament Theology: A Canonical Approach*. Grand Rapids: Zondervan, 1995.

———. *The Meaning of the Pentateuch: Revelation, Composition, and Interpretation*. Downers Grove, IL: InterVarsity Press, 2009.

———. "The Messiah and the Hebrew Bible." *JETS* 44 (2001): 5-23.

———. "The Mosaic Law and the Theology of the Pentateuch," *WTJ* 53 (1991): 241-61.

———. *NIV Compact Bible Commentary*. Grand Rapids: Zondervan, 1994.

———. *The Pentateuch as Narrative: A Biblical-Theological Commentary*. Grand Rapids: Zondervan, 1992.

Sarna, Nahum. *Exodus*. JPS Torah Commentary. Philadelphia: Jewish Publication Society, 1991.

———. *Genesis*. JPS Torah Commentary. Philadelphia: JPS, 1989.

Schatz, Werner. *Genesis 14: Eine Untersuchung*. Bern: Lang, 1972.

Schnackenburg, Rudolf. *The Gospel According to St. John*. Vol. 1. Translated by Kevin Smyth. New York: Crossroad, 1987.

———. *The Gospel According to St. John*. Vol. 2. Translated by Cecily Hastings et al. New York: Crossroad, 1982.

Schoenfeld, Devorah. *Isaac on Jewish and Christian Altars: Polemics and Exegesis in Rashi and the Glossa Ordinaria*. New York: Fordham, 2013.

Schmitt, Hans-Christoph. "Redaktion des Pentateuch im Geiste der Prophetie." *VT* 32 (1982): 170-89.

Seitz, Christopher. *Prophecy and Hermeneutics: Toward a New Introduction to the Prophets*. Grand Rapids: Baker, 2007.

Sheridan, Mark, ed. *Genesis 12–50*. Ancient Christian Commentary on Scripture. Downers Grove, IL: InterVarsity Press, 2002.

Smith, Bryan. "The Central Role of Judah in Genesis 37–50." *BSac* 162 (2005): 158-74.

Snearly, Michael. *The Return of the King: Messianic Expectation in Book V of the Psalter*. New York: T&T Clark, 2016.

Sommer, Benjamin. "Exegesis, Allusion, and Intertextuality in the Hebrew Bible: A Response to Lyle Eslinger." *VT* 46 (1996): 483-87.

Staerk, W. "Der Gebrauch der Wendung באחרית הימים im at. Kanon." *ZAW* 11 (1891): 247-53.

Stahl, Nanette, *Law and Liminality in the Bible*. Sheffield: Sheffield Academic, 1995.

Stott, John. *The Message of Acts*. The Bible Speaks Today. Downers Grove, IL: InterVarsity Press, 1994.

Stuckey, Charles, ed. *Monet: A Retrospective*. New York: Hugh Lauter Levin Associates, 1985.

Swenson, Kristin. "Crowned with Blessings: The Riches of Double-Meaning in Gen 49,26b." *ZAW* 120 (2008): 422-25.

Thompson, J. A. *Deuteronomy*. Tyndale Old Testament Commentaries. Downers Grove, IL: InterVarsity Press, 1974.

Tigay, Jeffrey. *Deuteronomy*. JPS Torah Commentary. Philadelphia: Jewish Publication Society, 1996.

Todd, James, III. *Sinai and the Saints: Reading Old Covenant Laws for the New Covenant Community*. Downers Grove, IL: InterVarsity Press, 2017.

Tooman, William. *Gog of Magog: Reuse of Scripture and Compositional Technique in Ezekiel 38–39*. Tübingen: Mohr Siebeck, 2011.

Turner, David. *Matthew*. Baker Exegetical Commentary on the New Testament. Grand Rapids: Baker, 2008.

Van Groningen, Gerard. *Messianic Revelation in the Old Testament*. Grand Rapids: Baker, 1990.

Vischer, Wilhelm. *The Witness of the Old Testament to Christ*. Vol. 1. Translated by A. B. Crabtree. London: Lutterworth, 1949.

Vos, Geerhardus. "The Idea of Biblical Theology as a Science and as a Theological Discipline." In *Redemptive History and Biblical Interpretation: The Shorter Writings of Geerhardus Vos*, edited by Richard Gaffin, 3-24. Phillipsburg, NJ: Presbyterian and Reformed, 1980.

———. *Biblical Theology*. Edinburgh: Banner of Truth, 1948.

Vriezen, T. "Prophecy and Eschatology." In *Congress Volume: Copenhagen, 1953*. Supplements to Vetus Testamentum, edited by G. W. Anderson, 199-229. Leiden: Brill, 1953.

Walters, Stanley. "Wood, Sand, and Stars: Structure and Theology in Gn 22:1-19." *TJT* 3, no. 2 (1987): 301-30.

Walton, John. *Genesis*. NIV Application Commentary. Grand Rapids: Zondervan, 2001.

Watson, W. G. E. *Classical Hebrew Poetry: A Guide to Its Techniques*. Sheffield: JSOT Press, 1986.

Watts, James W. *Psalm and Story: Inset Poems in Hebrew Narrative*. JSOT Supplement Series. Sheffield: JSOT Press, 1992.

Weinfeld, Moshe. *Deuteronomy and the Deuteronomic School*. Oxford: Clarendon, 1972.

Wenham, Gordon. *The Book of Leviticus*. New International Commentary on the Old Testament. Grand Rapids: Eerdmans, 1979.

———. *Genesis 1–15*. Word Biblical Commentary. Waco, TX: Word, 1987.

———. *Genesis 16–50*. Word Biblical Commentary. Dallas: Word, 1994.

———. "Sanctuary Symbolism in the Garden of Eden Story." In *Proceedings of the Ninth World Congress of Jewish Studies, Division A: The Period of the Bible*, 19-25. Jerusalem: World Union of Jewish Studies, 1986.

Wevers, John William. *Notes on the Greek Text of Deuteronomy*. Atlanta: Scholars, 1995.

———. *Notes on the Greek Text of Genesis*. Atlanta: Scholars, 1993.

———. *Notes on the Greek Text of Numbers*. Atlanta: Scholars, 1998.

Williamson, H. G. M. *Ezra, Nehemiah*. Word Biblical Commentary. Waco, TX: Word, 1985.

Wong, Y. C. *Creation, Covenant, and Restoration: An Introduction to the Major Theological Themes of the Torah* [Chinese]. Hong Kong: Tien Dao, 2000.

Würthwein, Ernst. *The Text of the Old Testament*, translated by Erroll Rhodes. 2nd ed. Grand Rapids: Eerdmans, 1995.

Zakovitch, Yair. "Through the Looking Glass: Reflections/Inversions of Genesis Stories in the Bible." *BibInt* 1 (1993): 139-52.

———. *Through the Looking Glass: Reflection Stories in the Bible* [Hebrew]. Tel Aviv: Hakibbutz Hameuhad, 1995.

AUTHOR INDEX

Alexander, T. Desmond, 36, 46, 48, 50, 74, 89, 153, 213
Allison, Dale C., 242
Ambrose, 100, 130
Anderson, Bradford, 122
Ashley, Timothy, 202-3
Auerbach, Erich, 22-23, 30
August, Jared M., 89
Baker, David L., 13-14, 23
Bar, Eitan, 209, 212, 218
Barrett, C. K., 169
Barstad, Hans, 242
Beale, Gregory, 17, 37, 57
Beaugrande, Robert de, 7
Betz, Otto, 129
Blenkinsopp, Joseph, 238
Blomberg, Craig, 31
Bock, Darrell, 2
Borgen, Peder, 169
Braulik, Georg, 261
Brown, Raymond, 15-16, 18
Brueggemann, Walter, 233, 241, 245, 259
Buchanan, George, 113-14
Budd, Philip, 209, 213
Calvin, John, 39-41, 56
Carmichael, Calum, 119, 124, 134, 139
Carson, D. A., 1, 169
Cassuto, Umberto, 92-93, 150, 206
Chan, Alan Kam-Yau, 79, 98
Chen, Kevin, 25, 117, 158, 164-66
Childs, Brevard, 25, 159, 166
Chou, Abner, 15, 20, 177, 200
Christensen, Duane, 226, 241, 255-56, 261-63
Cole, R. Alan, 150
Cole, R. Dennis, 206
Collins, Anthony, 16
Collins, Jack, 43, 50, 72-73
Craigie, Peter, 59, 99, 262
Cross, Frank Moore, 256, 263
Danielou, Jean, 86
Davidson, R. M., 13-14
Day, John, 156
Delitzsch, Franz, 10, 95
Dempster, Stephen, 53, 148-49, 163-65
Dharamraj, Havilah, 243
DiFransico, Lesley, 157, 166-67
Dillard, Raymond, 61
Douglas, Mary, 194-95
Dressler, Wolfgang, 7
Drew, Elizabeth, 61
Driver, S. R., 177, 261-62
Duffy, Kevin, 18
Durham, John, 175
Ebach, Jürgen, 109, 120, 132, 140, 177, 253
Ede, Franziska, 109
Edenburg, Cynthia, 106
Emerson, Matthew, 90
Ernesti, Johann August, 15
Fairbairn, Patrick, 13-14, 16
Fee, Gordon, 170
Fishbane, Michael, 156
Fitzmyer, Joseph, 170
Fohrer, Georg, 25
Fox, R. Michael, 156
France, R. T., 31
Freedman, David Noel, 256, 263-64
Frei, Hans, 16, 23, 39
Fretheim, Terence, 158, 175
Gaffin, Richard B., 21

Gevirtz, Stanley, 253
Glenny, W. Edward, 13
Goldsworthy, Graeme, 15, 17
Good, Edwin, 118-19, 124, 134, 139
Goppelt, Leonhard, 13-14, 22
Groningen, Gerard van, 86
Grypeou, Emmanouela, 129
Gundry, Stanley, 13, 17-18
Gunkel, Hermann, 108, 112
Hagner, Donald, 31, 99
Hamilton, James, 41, 50, 70, 177
Hamilton, Victor, 63, 95, 117-18, 142
Harrison, R. K., 192, 196
Hartley, John, 192-93
Hays, Richard, 7, 22-23
Heck, Joel, 252, 258, 260
Hengstenberg, E. W., 115
Hess, Richard, 82
Hippolytus, 97, 129
Hirsch, E. D., 19
Hoop, Raymond de, 177
Houtman, Cornelius, 105-6, 188-89
Kaiser, Walter, 16, 20
Kalimi, Isaac, 7, 46, 183
Keener, Craig S., 2
Keil, C. F., 95
Kidner, Derek, 41, 253
Kim, Yoon-Hee, 230, 233-34, 236, 243
Kiuchi, Nobuyoshi, 57-58, 203
Klappert, Bertold, 2-3, 21-23
Köstenberger, Andreas, 1, 100, 173, 200, 207
Kraus, H. J., 59
Kugel, James, 100
Lai, Paul, 99
Lampe, G. W. H., 13-15
Lane, William, 170
Leithart, Peter, 7, 177
Leonard, Jeffery M., 7
Levenson, Jon, 99, 124, 128
Levine, Baruch, 203, 212
Levine, Nachman, 266
Link, Peter, 90
Lipinski, E., 110, 112
Loewenstamm, Samuel E., 156, 158
Lohfink, Norbert, 161-63
Longman, Tremper, 61

Lubac, Henri de, 39
Lundbom, Jack, 178, 224-25, 237, 241, 244, 255-56, 261
Martin, R. A., 39
Mathews, Joshua G., 79-81, 83-85, 186
Mathews, Kenneth, 31
Mays, James L., 59
McCarter, P. Kyle, Jr., 99
McConville, J. Gordon, 178, 225, 227-28, 233, 241, 253, 255, 258-59, 261
McKenzie, Tracy, 260
Meeks, Russell, 7
Milgrom, Jacob, 153-54, 190-93, 197, 203, 206
Miscall, Peter, 242
Mitchell, David C., 59
Moberly, R. W. L., 91-92
Morales, L. Michael, 193
Motyer, J. Alec, 151-52
Mowinckel, Sigmund, 112
Nelson, Richard, 228, 233, 237, 241, 255
Niccacci, Alviero, 74
Noort, Ed, 86
Noth, Martin, 154
O'Brien, Mark, 231
Osborne, Grant, 17
Otto, Eckhart, 178, 229, 233, 253, 259
Peleg, Yitzhak, 101-2, 105-6
Polak, Frank, 171-72, 283
Postell, Seth, 37-38, 40, 46, 57-58, 60, 154, 201, 209, 212, 218, 260, 274
Propp, William, 150, 153-54, 171
Provan, Iain, 16, 89-90, 101
Pshenichny, Gennady, 81, 93
Redford, Donald, 109
Rendsburg, Gary, 7, 62
Riffaterre, Michael, 106, 127
Rösel, Martin, 129
Rosenberg, A. J., 40
Rouillard, Hedwige, 210-11, 215, 217
Ruppert, Lothar, 109
Russell, Brian, 158
Russell, Vivian, 287
Rydelnik, Michael, 15, 17
Sabourin, Leopold, 86
Sailhamer, John, 4, 16, 25, 30, 32, 37, 57-58, 73, 76, 90, 108-9, 114, 120-21, 126,

136, 166, 177, 184, 186, 193, 204, 207, 210-11, 217-20, 231, 238-39, 272-73, 290
Sanders, James, 25
Sarna, Nahum, 63, 149, 158
Schatz, Werner, 83
Schmitt, Hans-Christoph, 28
Schnackenburg, Rudolf, 1-3
Schoenfeld, Devorah, 86
Seitz, Christopher, 23
Smith, Bryan, 138
Snearly, Michael, 163
Sommer, Benjamin, 7
Soref, Erez, 209, 212, 218
Spurling, Helen, 129
Staerk, W., 110, 112
Stahl, Nanette, 273, 280
Stott, John, 2
Stuckey, Charles, 11
Swenson, Kristin, 254
Tate, Marvin E., 59, 99
Thompson, J. A., 233, 241

Tigay, Jeffrey, 178, 233, 241, 255-56, 261, 263
Tigchelaar, Eibert, 86
Todd, James, III, 4, 272
Tooman, William, 110
Turner, David, 99
Vischer, Wilhelm, 3, 17, 21, 23, 26
Vos, Geerhardus, 17
Vriezen, T., 113
Walters, Stanley, 86-88
Walton, John, 73-74
Watson, W. G. E., 61
Watts, James W., 33
Weinfeld, Moshe, 244
Wenham, Gordon, 36-38, 42, 53, 62, 81, 87, 91-92, 95, 119, 132, 192, 194, 253-54
Wevers, John William, 129, 217, 256
Williamson, H. G. M., 24
Wong, Y. C., 24
Würthwein, Ernst, 46
Zakovitch, Yair, 101-2

SUBJECT INDEX

Abra(ha)m, 69, 79-80, 85, 93
  father of many nations, 76-77
Adam
  defilement, 57-58
  as historical and representative, 36
  as intentionally foreshadowing a
    king-priest, 35, 55-60, 62
  as Levite or priest, 35, 37-38
  parallels with Israel, 60
  as ruler or king, 35-38, 55-57, 59
  sons of, 49, 68-69, 101
  as type of Christ, 13, 56
  wordplay on, 36, 48, 61, 79
"(a)rouse" vs. "raise" in Gen 49:9 and
  Num 24:9, 125-27, 214, 229
atonement, 251
  Day of. *See* Day of Atonement
author
  OT authors' knowledge of Christ,
    18-20, 26-27, 33, 58-59, 65-66, 111-12,
    132-33, 288
  strategy of Pentateuch's. *See*
    composition and compositional
    strategy
author's intent
  divine, 5-6, 12, 17-19
  dual authorship and, 19
  human, 5-6, 9, 12, 14-19, 21-23, 26, 30,
    33, 41, 59, 289
  in relation to exegesis, 14-17
  sensus plenior and, 17-19, 41. See also
    sensus plenior
Babel/Babylon, 68-69, 79-80, 100-101
Balaam narrative
  Agag/Gog in third oracle, 217

blessing, cursing, and Abrahamic
  covenant, 212-16, 220
comparison of Israel and Messiah to
  lion/lioness, 215-16
context for Messianic prophecies in
  Num 24, 209-10
continuation of nations' opposition to
  Israel, 210
Edenic themes in third oracle, 217
linkage of Messiah and angel of the
  Lord, 212
Messiah/second exodus in third oracle,
  218
parallels to Pharaoh's oppression of
  Israel, 210-11
poetic references to eschatological
  Israel, 213-19, 221
portrayal of Moses as prototype of
  Messiah/prophet like Moses, 211
"proverbs" in, 213, 222
relationship to Deut 13, 226
relationship to Num 21 and to Gen 3,
  210
repetition of Gen 49:9 concerning
  death and resurrection of Messiah,
  219-20
reference to Gen 27:29, 220-21
Spirit's revelation of Messiah to
  Balaam, 216-17, 223
"star of Jacob" prophecy in, 221-22
"three times" in, 212
wordplay of "Pethor" on "interpret,"
  211
Bezalel, 170, 182-90
  as "better Adam," 184-85

called by name, 182-83
Messiah and, 183, 186-87
Moses and, 187, 189
possible priestly overtones concerning, 186-87
successful leadership of Israel, 187
wisdom of, 183-84
wordplay on his and his ancestors' names, 182-83
work on tabernacle as parallel to the Lord and David's seed, 185-86
biblical theology, 289-90
bless(ing), 8, 68-71, 76, 80-81, 83, 85, 93-94, 97, 116, 248, 266
blessing of Judah (Deut 33:7)
consisting of prayer, 255
context in Deut 33 as positive and climactic, 258-59
eschatological context provided by and relation to Deut 32, 249-52, 257-58
as focused on an individual Judahite parallel to Gen 49:8-12, 253-55
intertextual relationships with other Messianic prophecies, 256-57
obscurity of, 247
problems with interpreting as referring to the tribe of Judah, 255-57
relationship of context (Deut 33) to Gen 1, 266-67
relationship of context (Deut 33) to Gen 49, 252-53, 255
bowing down and serving, 95-97, 102, 115
bronze snake, 4
as a sort of "Fall" narrative, 203
as intentionally foreshadowing the Messiah, 205-8
loathing of manna and, 202
possible meaning of "bronze" snake, 206-7
relationship to Num 22-24 through keyword *nakhash* and inclusio referencing Gen 3:15, 201, 210
relationship to preceding literary context, 200-201

seeing bronze snake parallel to Balaam's seeing of Messiah, 205
"the serpent," 201, 203
"serpent" repeated five times parallel to Gen 3, 203-4
"set" as a "banner," 205
wordplay on "snake" and "bronze," 206
wordplay on "snake" and "omen," 201
brother(s), 95, 102, 119, 121, 131
burnt offering, 152-153
Cain, 67
as seed of serpent, 4
Canaan(ites), as seed of serpent, 4
Christology, 53-54, 58, 66, 96-97, 99, 115, 160, 163-64, 185, 212, 229, 251, 264, 267
high, 96-97, 288-89
cleansing (priestly), 58, 66, 154-55, 197
clothes, Messiah's, 136-37, 151
composition and compositional strategy, 9, 14, 16, 24-25, 27-28, 30-32, 55, 57, 66, 77-78, 85, 89, 94-95, 103-4, 113-14, 117, 134, 146, 160-61, 171, 176, 190, 219-20, 229, 267-68. *See also* intertextuality
condemnation, of Messiah by Israel, 206-7
conflicting interpretations of (OT) Scripture
among first-century Jewish people, 1-5
Gentile observation of, 3-4
modern, 4
covenant
Abrahamic, 44-46, 49, 63-64, 75, 80, 83-84, 87, 91-92, 94, 97, 147
Davidic, 44-45, 52, 83
Noahic, 68, 94
curse, 39-40, 69-71, 76, 97, 248
Dan (tribe or place), 80
blessing of (Deut 33:22), 265
Day of Atonement, 170, 190-98
climax of sacrificial system, 192-93
as falling short of the ideal, 197-98
relationship to deaths of Nadab and Abihu, 190-92
relationship to sacrifice of Isaac and Passover, 193-94, 196-97
scapegoat, 194, 196

SUBJECT INDEX

uncleanness and, 191-92, 196
use of two goats, 194-96
Day of the Lord, 222
death, of the Messiah, 55, 58, 66, 77, 89, 91, 107, 130, 134, 136
Decalogue. *See* Ten Commandments
dew, 95, 172-73
disciples' OT-based faith in Christ, 3
divinity of the Messiah, 96-97, 99, 115. *See also* Christology
Eden, Garden of, 36, 95, 132, 198, 217, 259, 269
  humanity's fall in, 38-39, 55-56
  parallels to tabernacle, 36-37
  as sanctuary, 37-38, 56
Edom/Esau/Seir, 46-48, 66
  Edom wordplay on Adam/humanity, 48, 98
  Seir wordplay on "gate," 46
  Seir wordplay on "hairy" and "goat," 195
enemies (enmity, adversaries), 39-40, 46, 51, 70, 87, 115-16, 119, 121, 157, 249-51
  head(s) of, 39, 41, 53-54
  reconciliation of, 122-23, 138
  victory over, 41, 46-47, 51-53, 66, 74-75
eschatology, 3, 64, 163-67
Eve, "building" of, 63-64
event (historical). *See* text and event
exaltation, 68, 103-4
exegesis (grammatical-historical), 12-17, 21, 23, 56, 60, 118, 145
exile, 57, 70, 76
exodus, 146
  death of firstborn and, 147-49
  Pharaoh's oppression leading up to, 147
  second, 70, 156-57, 161-67, 169, 218, 224
Feast of Unleavened Bread
  Passover and, 153-54
  Sabbath and, 153
  yeast, significance of, 153-54
figural interpretation, 22-23. *See also* type/typology
food/bread, 81-83, 85, 131, 171-74. *See also* manna

foreshadowing, 4, 14, 16-17, 23. *See also* intentional foreshadowing; type/typology
Gad, blessing of (Deut 33:20-21)
  gathering of leaders, 264-65
  "lawgiver's portion," 263-64
  part of lion/lioness inclusion, 260
  providing "firstfruits for himself" parallel to provision of lamb and of king, 261-62
  "the one who enlarges," 260-63
gate(s)
  of enemies/haters, 46, 74-75, 104
  of heaven, 102, 104
  wordplay with "Seir," 46
genre (literary), 7
glory, 266, 282, 287, 289
"he" (Hebrew pronoun), strategic use of, 44-45
historical reconstruction, 30
"in the last days," 32, 96, 109-14, 117, 248-49
  juxtaposed with "(in the) beginning," 114
infinitive absolute (in Joseph story), 124-25
inheritance/possession, 45-47, 75-76, 84, 221-222
intentional foreshadowing. *See also* mirror; type/typology
  Adam as, 35, 55-60, 62
  between Gen 49:8-12 and Num 24:7-9, 145
  Bezalel as, 182, 186-87
  bronze snake as. *See* bronze snake
  exegetical basis for, 12, 60
  exodus and, 146, 169, 224
  compared to Messianic prophecy, 10-11
  importance to the Messianic vision of the Pentateuch, 16-17, 288
  intertextual relationship with Messianic prophecy, 12, 86, 145, 288
  Melchizedek as, 78, 86
  as often part of ongoing narrative storyline, 11-12
  Passover lamb as, 150-53
  provision of manna as, 172

as reflection from mirror, 10-11
as relatively indirect, 11, 60
sacrifice of Isaac/ram, 89-91
select themes of, 12, 60
simultaneity with Messianic prophecy, 12, 35, 59, 120-21
two goats on Day of Atonement as, 194
uniqueness of each instance of, 12
intertextuality, 7-10, 12, 41, 44-46, 52-53, 70, 87, 89, 100-104, 130, 132, 136-7, 180-82, 229. *See also* composition and compositional strategy
definition and criteria, 7
Isaac, sacrifice of, 13, 86-93
Ishmael, 90
Israel
chronic failures of, 187, 248
eschatological, 52
Messiah and, 49-50, 71, 76, 97-99, 116, 122, 148, 213, 215-19, 221, 260, 265
salvation of, 169
seed of the woman and, 47-50
wickedness of, 47-49
Jacob
birth of and similarity to serpent, 48
blesses his sons, 118
clothes of, 94-95
ladder of. *See* ladder, Jacob's
as paradigm/representative for Israel and the righteous, 48, 50, 98
perspective on Joseph's dreams, 102-3, 119, 124-25, 127-29, 134
pleasing scent of, 94
steals Esau's blessing, 94
Jesus' belief that the OT is about him, 1-5, 20-21
Joseph
(apparent) death of, 124, 128-29, 134
clothes of, 134-36
dreams of, 102, 119-20, 131
enemies of, 121-23
re-presentation as picture and intentional foreshadowing of the Messiah, 102, 120-25, 128-29, 131, 138, 254-55
reversals concerning, 124-25

resurrection of, 124-28
Joshua, 184
Judah
blessing of as referencing Joseph (Gen 49:8-12), 118-24, 131-32, 134
blessing of as relating to himself (Gen 49:8), 138-44
blessing of in Deut 33:7. *See* blessing of Judah (Deut 33:7)
as leader, 123-24, 139-40, 143
"pledges" of, 140-41
as substitute, 142
transformation of, 139-41, 143
wordplay on "praise," 115, 138
jussive verbs, 74, 115
ladder, Jacob's, 10, 12, 16, 100-106
priestly and kingly overtones regarding, 105
relationship to Joseph's later dreams, 102-3
stone as miniature memorial of, 105
lamb
divinely provided in Isaac's place, 87-88, 90
Passover, 90, 150-55
land
abundance and fruitfulness of, 95, 99, 132-34
Promised, 69, 75-76, 80
law
various meanings of, 27-29
See also Sinai/Deuteronomic law
law-keeping, 5
differing conceptions of, 2, 4
lens, 35, 50-51, 60, 71, 90, 93, 97, 288. *See also* Messianic prophecy
as metaphor for Messianic prophecy, 7-8
interrelated lenses, 8-9, 75, 77
light, 66, 71, 90
Delitzsch's view of Christological development as, 10
dispersed (scattered), 6, 9
reflected, 9-12, 90
spectrum, 6, 8, 50, 55
through a lens as a metaphor for Messianic prophecy, 7-9, 50-51

SUBJECT INDEX 313

through a prism as metaphor for
Messianic prophecies in the
Pentateuch, 5-6
wavelengths of, 6, 50, 60
white, 6
lion(ess), 123-24, 144
identity of lion of Judah, 115
stooping and lying down in Gen 49:9/
Num 24:9, 130
manna, 153, 169, 171
appearance as dew, 172
Messianic blessing and, 172
Melchizedek, 78-86, 105
Messiah's need for divine help, 219, 236, 255-57
Messianic prophecy
central to the Pentateuch, 6, 60-62, 66, 108-9, 219-20, 299
distinct from dual or multiple fulfillment, 17
earlier and later (in the literary context of the Pentateuch), 9
few in proportion to Sinai/ Deuteronomic law, 5-6
importance to the Messianic vision of the Pentateuch, 16-17, 77-78, 199, 288
interrelationship of, 7-9, 41, 44-46, 53, 70-71, 75, 77-78, 87, 89-90, 107, 131-32, 136-37, 219-20, 229
intertextual relationship with intentional foreshadowing, 12, 86, 107, 145
as light through a lens, 7-8
longer and shorter, 8
longest in the Pentateuch, 108, 199
often expressed in poetic form, 11-12
in the Pentateuch as light through a prism, 5-6
in the Pentateuch as complex array of interrelated lenses, 9
in poems in the Pentateuch, 32-33, 61
in relationship to intentional foreshadowing, 11, 199
reticence and skepticism concerning, 15-16, 33
select themes of, 8, 12, 50, 71

simultaneity with intentional foreshadowing, 12, 35, 59, 120-21
Messianic vision of the Pentateuch, 7, 9-10, 12, 14, 16-17, 24, 26, 35, 55, 78, 86, 96-97, 102, 107, 114, 121, 199, 219-20, 223, 229, 232, 267-68, 287
mirror, 35, 60, 90, 93, 288. *See also* intentional foreshadowing
plane (planar), 10-11, 60
reflection from, 10-12, 60
water as (including unique disturbance profile), 11-12
Monet, 11, 287, 290
Moses
as author of the Pentateuch, 25-26
Jewish devotion to, 1-2
parallels to Jesus, 3. *See also* prophet(s), like Moses
wrote about Jesus, 1-4
"my son" (usually favored), 265-66
Benjamin, 131
Isaac, 87, 89
Jacob, 94, 98
Joseph, 131
Messiah, 99, 131, 148
Israel, 99, 148
narrative patterning, 89-90, 101, 198
involving inversions, 101
nations (tribes, families, etc.), 8, 69-70, 76, 79-81, 85, 95-96, 98, 131, 251, 259
new covenant, 155, 187-90, 275-276
Noah, 68
sacrifice of, 68
Noah's ark, 68
oath, 92
Old Testament, intrinsic meaning of, 21, 56
Passover, 147-49
Feast of Unleavened Bread and. *See* Feast of Unleavened Bread
lamb. *See* lamb, Passover
proleptic, 148-49
Shema and, 155
Paul's preaching Christ from the OT, 2, 16, 20-21, 28
Paul's varied use of *nomos* ("law"), 28-29

Pentateuch
  authorship of, 25-26
  distinction between its laws and, 28
  early readers' possible understanding of, 14, 27, 48
  faith-theme in, 28-29, 85, 91
  Galatians and the meaning of, 4
  as instruction/*torah*, 27
  law-focused interpretation of, 1-2, 4-6, 16, 289
  major poetic sections in, 32, 108-9, 160-61, 208-9
  meaning, message, and main point of, 4-6, 24-26, 29, 66, 267, 270-71, 284-85
  Messianic interpretation of, 1-6, 9-10, 12, 32, 53, 66, 276, 288
  misunderstandings of, 1
  more than an accurate historical record, 29-30
  as one book, 1, 23-25
  Second Temple Judaism and, 26
  Sinai/Deuteronomic laws within, 1-2, 4, 171
  structure of, 30-33, 267
  themes within, 4
Pharaoh
  as seed of serpent, 157-58
  wordplay on "locks/leaders," 158
poetry, 127
  compared to narrative, 61
  in the structure of the Pentateuch, 32-33
  as terse and "dense," 60-61
polysemy (and double-entendre), 36, 61-62, 98, 127, 137
possession. *See* inheritance/possession
priest-king, 35, 37-38, 45, 57-58, 60, 62, 66, 78, 80-83, 85, 105, 107, 185-86
priestly work of Messiah, 58-60, 62, 66, 105, 107, 171, 173, 185-86
prism. *See* light, through a prism as metaphor
progressive revelation, 290

prophet like Moses, 4, 70, 146, 211
  as answer to Israel's request, 230-231
  authority of, 227-28, 235
  interpretation of Deut 34:10 and, 237-42
  as leading second exodus, 225, 235, 246
  meaning of designation, 229-30, 245
  as Messianic individual and prophet *par excellence*, 234-37
  non-Messianic individual interpretations of, 242-45
  as prophetic succession, 233, 236-37
  as specifically "raised up" by the Lord, 228-29
prophet(s)
  cessation of, 241
  like Moses. *See* prophet like Moses
  Moses' wish that all Israel would be, 237
  priest and king, 231-32
  testimony about Christ, 3
  tests concerning (including relation to Balaam narrative and *Shema*), 225-27
qatal verbs, 238-40
relationship between the OT and NT, 3, 290
resurrection
  Joseph's. *See* Joseph, resurrection of
  Messiah's, 77, 108, 128-29, 135, 214, 219
rock (or stone)
  anointed, 104
  Lord as, 105, 177-79
  Lord standing upon, 105, 175-76
  Moses standing upon and put in cleft of, 179-80
  ordinary, 100-101, 104
  protection or substitute for Moses, 175, 182
  water from, 174-79, 181
Sabbath, 185
  Jesus' healings on, 1-2
  controversy over its observance, 1-3, 5
sacrifice, Messiah's, 171, 173
sacrificial system, 170-71, 192-93
  contrasted with the divinely provided lamb/ram, 88
  limitations of, 5, 197-98

SUBJECT INDEX 315

Salem, 83
  wordplay on "peace," 82
salvation history, 13
  as framework for typology, 17
sanctuary
  Edenic, 37-38
  eschatological, 166
Second Exodus. See exodus, second
seed
  of Abraham, 8, 70-76, 84, 107
  of David
  of the serpent, 39-41, 47-49, 53, 157-58
  singular or plural, 41-47, 49-50, 71-76, 97, 98, 107
  "son" and, 89, 98
  of the woman, 8, 15-16, 35, 39, 41-53, 75, 89, 107
sensus plenior, 17-18, 41. See also author's intent
  critique of, 18-19
  NT's role in identifying, 18-19
serpent (snake)
  bronze. See bronze snake
  in Eden and identity of, 38-40, 55-57
  poisonous, 40, 54-55
  as unclean animal, 57-58, 62
servant of the Lord in Isaiah, 15. See also Suffering Servant
Shema (Great Commandment), 91, 155, 226-27, 248
signs, 2-3
Sinai/Deuteronomic law, 4-6, 16, 28-29, 38
  association with relational and physical distance from the Lord, 278-81
  association with Moses as permanent mediator, 280-81
  brings wrath, 281
  contrasted with Spirit's work, 187-88
  definition of, 28
  distinction between it and the Pentateuch, 28
  importance of, 4-5
  Israel and humanity's failure to keep, 5, 273-75, 280

Israel's misguided promises to keep, 283-84
  narrative context of, 271-72
  problems on the way to Sinai, 276-78
  purpose of, 29
  relationship between Sinai law and Deuteronomic law, 28-29
  relationship to theme of salvation in exodus, 281-84
  role in the Pentateuch and divine plan of salvation, 4-5, 29, 33, 62, 66, 171, 199, 220, 248, 270-71, 275, 284-85, 289
  temporary, inherently limited, 272-73, 289
son. See "my son"; seed, son and
Song of the Sea, 282
  forgiveness of sin and, 157, 166-67
  generalized and idealized character of, 158-59, 161
  relation to Messianic vision of the Pentateuch, 156, 160
  relation to second exodus, 156-57, 161-65, 167
  uniqueness as major poetic section in the Pentateuch, 156
  relation to well in Num 21:16-18, 208
Spirit, 183-84, 187-88
substitution
  of goat's blood/life for Joseph's, 195
  of Jacob for Esau, 195
  of Judah for Benjamin, 142
  of lamb/ram for Isaac, 87, 90
  of Messiah for sinners, 142-43
  of Passover lamb for Israel, 90
Starry Night (van Gogh), 61
stone. See rock (or stone)
sun (sunrise, moon)
  rule of as parallel to humanity's and Messiah's, 36, 64-66, 266-67
Suffering Servant, 151-52. See also servant of the Lord in Isaiah
synagogue, 2, 4
syntax, 7, 74, 109, 116, 130, 163, 176, 204, 208, 237-40, 261-62, 266
tabernacle, 36-37, 63, 184
  based on a "pattern," 37

temple, 37, 52, 63-64
Ten Commandments (Decalogue), 38, 81, 96-97, 230, 271-73, 279, 281
ten (number), significance of, 81, 89
text and event, 17, 30
themes, 4
    Messianic ("colors"), 7-8
    select, 7
tithe, 80-81, 85
tree of life, 37
tree of the knowledge of good and evil, 38, 55
type/typology, 13-17. *See also* intentional foreshadowing
    Adam as, 13, 56
    allows one to be noncommittal about Messianic prophecy, 15-16, 22
    bronze snake as, 200
    definition of, 13
    distinct from prophecy, intentional foreshadowing, and exegesis, 13-17, 21, 56, 59-60, 78, 86, 90-91, 170, 190
    figural interpretation and, 22
    Isaac as, 13, 18, 78, 86
    Israel as, 13, 18, 170
    hermeneutical weakness of, 21-22
    Melchizedek as, 78
    NT's role in identifying, 18-19, 21-22
    as "pointing to" Christ, 16
    salvation history as framework for, 17
    seed of the woman as, 15
    sensus plenior and, 17-19. See also *sensus plenior*
"ungrammaticality," 106, 203
unity of Scripture, 3. *See also* relationship between the OT and NT
water from the rock. *See* rock (or stone), water from
wayyiqtol verbs, 179, 204, 265
well (in Num 21:16-18), 208-9
    interrelationship with water from the rock and all four major poetic sections in the Pentateuch, 208-9
    wordplay of "gift" on "Mattanah," 209
    wordplay on "Beor," 209
weqatal verbs, 74, 204-5
wisdom, 38-39, 183-84, 188-90
    providing food and drink, 174
women in the salvation plan of God, 51-53
wordplay, 7, 36, 61, 69, 79, 82-85, 98, 106, 115, 127, 137-38, 158, 182-83, 195, 201, 206-7, 209, 211, 254-55
    clause-level, 46, 222
yeast. *See* Feast of Unleavened Bread
yiqtol verbs, 74, 204-5, 240

SCRIPTURE INDEX

OLD TESTAMENT

Genesis
1, 35, 36, 37, 64, 266, 270
1–2, 35, 63, 64
1–3, 37, 56, 59, 60, 63, 65, 66, 70, 78, 154, 186, 201, 267, 274
1–11, 40, 56, 69, 82
1–11:26, 31
1–15, 38, 42, 53, 62, 81
1–50, 146
1:1, 35, 114, 184, 262, 273
1:2, 183, 184
1:3, 35, 267
1:4, 38
1:6, 36
1:9, 36
1:10, 38
1:11, 35, 41, 42
1:14, 36, 267
1:15, 65
1:16, 36, 64, 65, 79, 107
1:17, 65
1:18, 36, 64, 79
1:20, 39
1:21, 203
1:22, 69
1:24, 35
1:26, 35, 36, 49, 55, 56, 57, 64, 65, 67, 79, 82, 133, 183, 184, 186, 222, 267
1:27, 64, 116, 152
1:28, 35, 56, 64, 65, 67, 68, 69, 70, 79, 93, 94, 101, 147, 157, 167, 222, 258, 275
1:29, 35
1:31, 35
2, 37, 58, 63, 166
2–3, 204
2:1, 185
2:2, 185
2:7, 36, 68, 204
2:8, 36, 68, 186
2:9, 36, 37, 38, 204, 277
2:11, 36
2:15, 36, 37, 186
2:16, 36, 38, 40
2:17, 55, 154, 204
2:18, 36
2:20, 36
2:21, 63
2:23, 83
2:24, 204
3, 40, 57, 70, 152, 195, 201, 202, 203, 205, 206, 210, 222, 258, 266, 274
3:1, 38, 52, 55, 56, 152, 201, 203, 207, 274
3:1-6, 51
3:2, 152
3:3, 154, 204
3:4, 152
3:5, 38
3:6, 38, 68
3:7, 58, 68
3:8, 36, 39, 67
3:10, 68
3:13, 51, 152, 207
3:14, 39, 40, 56, 57, 58, 68, 69, 109, 152
3:15, 8, 9, 15, 16, 33, 35, 39, 40, 41, 42, 43, 44, 45, 46, 47, 48, 49, 50, 51, 52, 53, 54, 55, 56, 57, 58, 59, 60, 61, 62, 63, 64, 65, 66, 67, 69, 70, 71, 72, 75, 77, 78, 80, 82, 83, 85, 87, 89, 90, 91, 92, 94, 98, 105, 106, 107, 108, 116, 117, 120, 121, 122, 130, 134, 136, 137, 143, 144, 146, 151, 152, 155, 157, 158, 159, 167, 171, 173, 174, 175, 176, 179, 185, 186, 193, 196, 197, 198, 199, 201, 206, 210, 215, 220, 221, 232, 236, 245, 247, 249, 250, 251, 256, 262, 265, 266, 267, 268, 275, 286, 288, 289
3:16, 38, 64, 67, 79
3:17, 59, 68, 69
3:18, 194
3:19, 40, 47, 59
3:20, 50, 82
3:21, 68, 195
3:22, 36, 39, 47, 70
3:24, 36, 37
4–11, 67, 68
4:1, 49, 82
4:3, 67
4:6, 272
4:7, 47, 59, 64, 67, 79, 167

4:11, *40, 69*
4:23, *67*
4:25, *46, 72, 82*
5:1, *36, 81*
5:2, *69, 94*
5:3, *36*
5:5, *47, 59, 67*
5:8, *67*
5:22, *67*
5:24, *67, 280, 285*
5:29, *68, 69, 82*
6:1, *67, 68*
6:5, *47, 67, 68, 275*
6:6, *68*
6:9, *67, 151, 280, 285*
6:9–11:32, *93*
6:11, *67*
6:13, *67*
6:18, *126*
7:13, *68*
7:17, *68*
7:19, *68*
8:12, *239*
8:19, *69*
8:20, *68, 94, 136, 151, 153*
8:21, *47, 67, 68, 69, 240, 275, 285*
9:1, *68, 69, 94, 147*
9:2, *59, 68*
9:7, *68*
9:9, *68, 73, 94*
9:11, *68*
9:15, *68*
9:17, *68*
9:20, *49, 68*
9:21, *68*
9:22, *68*
9:23, *68*
9:25, *40, 68, 69, 275*
9:26, *40, 69, 261*
10, *70, 79*
10–12, *80*
10–13, *80, 83*
10:5, *70, 79*
10:6, *165*
10:10, *69, 79, 80*
10:18, *70*
10:19, *79*

10:20, *70, 79*
10:21, *69*
10:22, *79*
10:31, *70, 79*
11:1, *69, 79, 100, 101, 102, 103, 107*
11:2, *79*
11:3, *79, 101, 147, 202, 275*
11:4, *68, 69, 100, 101, 103, 106*
11:5, *49, 69, 80, 101, 275*
11:6, *68, 101, 215*
11:7, *101*
11:8, *101*
11:9, *50, 69, 80, 83*
11:11, *81*
11:28, *69*
11:30, *93*
11:31, *69*
11:42, *31*
12, *102*
12–50, *97, 130*
12:1, *25, 69, 70, 71, 76, 78, 80, 85, 91, 93, 210*
12:1-3, *77*
12:2, *44, 45, 69, 71, 76, 80, 85, 93, 94, 116, 147*
12:3, *8, 9, 45, 69, 70, 75, 76, 87, 97, 98, 212, 219, 221, 251, 275, 286*
12:5, *81, 84*
12:7, *44, 45, 49, 64, 70, 71, 72, 75, 76, 77, 92*
12:11, *49*
12:16, *81, 84, 133*
12:20, *81*
13:1, *81, 84*
13:2, *133*
13:15, *80*
13:16, *71, 72, 213*
13:17, *80*
14, *38, 79, 80, 81, 83, 84, 85, 102, 105*
14:1, *79*
14:2, *79*
14:4, *79, 81, 96*
14:5, *79*
14:8, *79, 80*

14:9, *79*
14:10, *79*
14:11, *79, 81, 84*
14:14, *80, 84*
14:15, *84*
14:16, *81, 84*
14:17, *81*
14:18, *78, 79, 80, 81, 82, 85, 105, 107, 116, 171, 174, 186, 225, 251, 265*
14:19, *75, 81, 84, 85, 116, 165*
14:20, *80, 81, 83, 84, 85, 122, 256, 266*
14:22, *75, 84, 165*
14:24, *82*
15, *83, 84, 85*
15:1, *45, 84, 90, 234, 266*
15:2, *44, 81, 84, 93*
15:3, *42, 44, 45, 47, 64, 72, 74, 75, 78, 84, 90, 94, 98, 107, 108, 152, 159, 222, 266, 288*
15:3-4, *43, 77, 85*
15:4, *44, 46, 186*
15:5, *44, 64, 71, 74, 221*
15:6, *28, 85, 174, 204*
15:7, *50, 69*
15:8, *46*
15:9, *88*
15:12, *63*
15:13, *49, 63, 71, 73, 76, 81, 146, 147, 169*
15:14, *147*
15:18, *92, 165*
15:63, *38*
15:80, *53, 62*
15:81, *42*
16–50, *87, 91, 92, 95, 119, 132, 253, 254*
16:10, *72*
16:11, *202*
16:12, *123*
17:1, *67, 151, 280*
17:4, *50, 76, 251*
17:6, *94, 257*
17:7, *45, 71, 73*
17:8, *75*

17:9, *73*
17:12, *152*
17:16, *94, 257*
17:19, *87, 93*
17:20, *90*
18, *95*
18–50, *142*
18:2, *176*
18:10, *215*
18:14, *215*
18:18, *28, 76, 98, 275, 286*
18:19, *91, 143*
20:7, *237*
21, *92*
21:10, *45, 46, 90*
21:12, *90, 91, 92, 93*
21:13, *43, 45, 90*
21:14, *90, 92*
21:15, *90*
21:17, *90*
21:18, *90*
21:19, *90*
21:22, *92*
21:23, *92*
21:27, *92*
21:28, *92*
21:31, *92*
21:32, *92*
22, *18, 86, 88, 93*
22:1, *13, 78, 86, 87, 88, 89, 90, 91, 92, 93, 94, 98, 107, 134, 135, 148, 150, 151, 161, 171, 193, 194, 198, 262*
22:2, *86, 87, 88, 89, 90, 91, 93, 153*
22:3, *87, 88, 90*
22:4, *93*
22:6, *86, 87, 90*
22:7, *87, 90, 151, 152, 193*
22:8, *87, 91, 261, 262*
22:9, *87, 88, 93*
22:10, *90*
22:11, *90*
22:12, *87, 89, 142, 151*
22:13, *87, 90, 142, 143, 151, 193*
22:14, *87, 88, 262*

22:15, *87, 90*
22:16, *85, 89, 91, 92, 93, 98, 216, 250*
22:17, *46, 74, 75, 76, 77, 86, 87, 89, 90, 91, 93, 98, 104, 115, 116, 121, 122, 123, 143, 146, 157, 221, 222, 251, 256*
22:18, *76, 87, 91, 97, 123, 251, 275, 286*
22:19, *87, 92*
23, *75*
23:4, *75*
23:9, *75*
23:18, *75*
23:20, *75*
24:1, *85*
24:7, *92*
24:16, *52*
24:28, *52*
24:35, *85, 133*
24:43, *53*
24:52, *96*
24:55, *52*
24:57, *52*
24:60, *46, 49, 51, 74, 75, 77, 87, 89, 93, 94, 104, 107, 115, 121, 123, 221*
25:10, *75*
25:11, *94*
25:22, *93*
25:29, *94*
26:3, *75, 92, 94, 126*
26:4, *74, 76, 87, 91, 98*
26:5, *91*
26:12, *133*
26:14, *121*
26:22, *75*
26:27, *121*
26:28, *92*
26:34, *99*
27, *195*
27–28, *102*
27:1, *94, 253*
27:4, *94*
27:5, *99*
27:7, *94*
27:9, *195*

27:10, *94*
27:11, *195*
27:12, *94*
27:16, *195*
27:19, *94*
27:21, *195*
27:23, *195*
27:27, *33, 78, 93, 94, 97, 98, 99, 115, 116, 118, 131, 132, 136, 144, 148, 151, 167, 172, 174, 179, 196, 218, 235, 246, 268, 288*
27:28, *95, 104, 105, 172, 174, 198, 254, 267*
27:29, *9, 45, 70, 71, 76, 87, 95, 96, 97, 98, 99, 102, 103, 104, 105, 115, 117, 119, 120, 121, 131, 138, 148, 157, 160, 172, 213, 219, 220, 221, 224, 261, 275*
27:36, *99*
27:39, *172*
27:41, *99, 124*
27:46, *99*
28, *180*
28:1, *100*
28:3, *50, 76, 100, 116*
28:4, *75, 116*
28:5, *100*
28:10, *12, 16, 93, 100, 101, 102, 104, 107, 175, 176, 181, 198*
28:10-22, *10*
28:10–22, *101*
28:11, *63, 100, 101, 104, 175, 180*
28:12, *63, 100, 101, 102, 103, 104, 105, 119, 175, 176, 180, 207, 212, 234*
28:13, *48, 49, 95, 105, 175, 176, 180*
28:14, *98, 101*
28:15, *101*
28:16, *176, 180, 225*
28:17, *104, 165*

28:18, *101, 104, 105, 175, 176, 177, 194*
28:20, *101, 202*
28:21, *83*
28:22, *80, 83, 101, 104, 175, 176, 177*
29:2, *105*
29:4, *95*
29:15, *95*
29:22, *130*
29:30, *138*
29:31, *121, 138*
29:32, *138*
29:33, *121, 138, 202*
29:35, *115, 118, 138, 144*
30:1, *121, 138*
30:2, *143*
30:13, *266*
30:33, *48*
31:10, *102, 234*
31:13, *102, 104, 177*
31:38, *48*
31:44, *92*
31:46, *95*
32:3, *95, 120, 267*
32:4, *195*
32:11, *162*
32:16, *133*
32:28, *98*
32:31, *63*
32:33, *204*
33:1, *122*
33:4, *123*
33:11, *99*
33:18, *75, 83, 177*
33:19, *75*
34, *116*
34:5, *204*
34:27, *250*
35:1, *177*
35:11, *257*
35:14, *104*
35:22, *116, 140*
35:27, *75*
36:8, *267*
37, *102, 125, 195, 257, 279*
37–50, *108, 109, 120, 121, 123, 124, 129, 130, 132,*

138, 140, 177, 206, 218, 253
37:1, *75*
37:2, *119, 142, 143*
37:3, *136, 138*
37:4, *121, 138, 139*
37:5, *95, 96, 100, 102, 104, 107, 119, 121, 176, 212, 232*
37:6, *63, 207*
37:7, *102, 103, 127, 132*
37:8, *64, 121, 125, 206*
37:9, *66, 120, 132*
37:10, *103, 125, 206*
37:11, *103, 116, 119, 121, 128, 138, 140*
37:12, *177*
37:14, *122*
37:17, *140*
37:18, *119, 128, 139, 140*
37:20, *128, 140*
37:21, *53, 139*
37:22, *128, 139*
37:23, *136*
37:24, *128, 140*
37:26, *118, 139, 141, 142*
37:27, *48*
37:28, *119*
37:29, *139*
37:31, *119, 134, 135, 152, 195*
37:32, *124, 131*
37:33, *119, 124, 125, 127, 131, 134, 206*
37:35, *124, 128, 131*
37:36, *119*
38, *118, 119, 139, 140, 141, 257*
38:1, *52*
38:11, *141*
38:14, *141*
38:17, *140*
38:26, *141, 239*
39:1, *128*
39:2, *128*
39:4, *234*
39:7, *135*
39:9, *272*

39:13, *121, 135*
39:15, *135*
39:20, *119, 128, 207*
40–41, *119, 232*
40:5, *211*
40:8, *211*
40:12, *211*
40:15, *125, 128*
40:16, *211*
40:18, *211*
40:22, *211*
40:23, *121*
41:8, *211*
41:11, *211*
41:12, *142*
41:14, *136*
41:25, *183*
41:28, *183*
41:32, *183*
41:33, *120, 183*
41:38, *183, 198*
41:39, *131, 183*
41:40, *82, 96*
41:42, *136, 206*
41:43, *96*
41:45, *82, 206, 232*
41:50, *82, 232*
41:52, *138, 254*
41:54, *131*
41:57, *131*
42:1, *120*
42:5, *48*
42:6, *102, 120*
42:7, *120, 136*
42:9, *120*
42:11, *128*
42:13, *141*
42:19, *128*
42:20, *141*
42:21, *141*
42:23, *206*
42:26, *133*
42:30, *136*
42:31, *128*
42:33, *128, 136*
42:37, *140*
42:37–43:15, *139*
42:38, *131, 142, 151*

43–44, *140, 141*
43:2, *139*
43:3, *125, 136*
43:5, *136*
43:6, *136*
43:7, *124, 125, 136*
43:8, *142*
43:9, *140, 141*
43:13, *136*
43:15, *141*
43:20, *125*
43:26, *120*
43:27, *124*
43:28, *120*
44, *144*
44:1, *141*
44:5, *125, 206*
44:10, *142*
44:13, *141*
44:14, *120, 141*
44:15, *125, 206*
44:16, *141, 142*
44:18, *142*
44:20, *128*
44:22, *142*
44:28, *124, 127, 206*
44:30, *142, 151*
44:32, *140, 142*
44:33, *90, 142, 143, 151*
45:1–47:6, *146*
45:3, *124, 128*
45:5, *128*
45:7, *207*
45:8, *205, 207*
45:9, *131*
45:14, *123*
45:15, *123*
45:26, *124, 129*
45:28, *124, 131*
46:4, *125*
46:20, *82, 232*
46:28, *139, 143, 186*
46:29, *123*
46:30, *124*
47:9, *75*
47:17, *133*
47:29, *146*
48:2, *131*

48:4, *50*
48:5, *254*
48:11, *128*
48:12, *120*
48:15, *48, 105, 177*
48:19, *131*
48:20, *254*
48:21, *146*
49, *109, 119, 129, 160, 168, 169, 177, 185, 199, 209, 229, 236, 247, 249, 251, 252, 253, 254, 255, 258, 260*
49:1, *32, 96, 108, 109, 110, 111, 112, 113, 114, 117, 118, 131, 144, 156, 160, 197, 208, 221, 245, 246, 247, 252, 253, 257, 264, 268*
49:2, *131, 253*
49:2-27, *32*
49:3, *114, 116, 117, 118, 121, 131, 139, 143, 252, 258, 262*
49:5, *252, 258*
49:6, *62*
49:7, *116, 117*
49:8, *40, 45, 47, 52, 63, 66, 95, 96, 97, 99, 100, 102, 103, 104, 106, 107, 108, 109, 110, 113, 114, 115, 116, 118, 119, 120, 121, 122, 123, 124, 129, 130, 131, 134, 135, 137, 138, 139, 140, 141, 143, 144, 146, 148, 151, 156, 157, 159, 160, 174, 175, 176, 179, 183, 185, 197, 198, 199, 210, 215, 218, 219, 220, 223, 232, 235, 246, 250, 252, 253, 254, 255, 256, 257, 258, 268, 288*
49:8-12, *32, 77*
49:9, *9, 99, 119, 123, 124, 125, 126, 127, 129, 130, 131, 132, 134, 135, 137, 138, 148, 152, 167, 174,*

212, 214, 215, 218, 219, 220, 221, 223, 229, 232, 235, 236, 246, 253, 257, 260, 261
49:10, *50, 103, 119, 122, 129, 130, 131, 132, 138, 141, 148, 160, 208, 221, 256, 263, 264*
49:11, *118, 119, 130, 132, 133, 134, 135, 136, 137, 138, 152, 185, 220, 232, 267*
49:12, *137, 215, 220*
49:13, *252, 259*
49:14, *123, 130, 252, 253, 258*
49:15, *258*
49:16, *96, 252*
49:17, *54, 116, 124, 188, 253, 259, 265, 268*
49:18, *54, 116, 160*
49:20, *252*
49:21, *124, 252, 253*
49:22, *116, 118, 254, 255, 260*
49:23, *254, 256*
49:24, *105, 160, 177, 208, 264*
49:25, *254, 255*
49:26, *62, 254, 255*
49:27, *124, 253, 258*
49:28, *96, 116, 122, 252*
49:29, *253*
50:15, *125*
50:18, *120, 143, 147*
50:19, *143*
50:20, *128, 207*
50:23, *263*
50:24, *125, 146, 232*

Exodus
1, *210*
1–2, *211, 212*
1–15, *146, 147, 224, 281, 282, 286*
1–18, *150, 153, 154, 171*
1:1–15:21, *271*
1:6, *147*

1:7, *49, 147, 211*
1:7-9, *77*
1:8, *147, 232*
1:9, *211*
1:10, *211*
1:11, *147, 211, 259*
1:11-22, *211*
1:12, *147, 204, 211*
1:14, *147, 153*
1:15, *211*
1:15-2:10, *147*
1:17, *211*
1:19, *211*
1:22, *211*
2, *211*
2:1, *51*
2:3, *239*
2:11, *259*
2:14, *231*
2:19, *206*
2:23, *147, 157*
2:24, *278*
3-15, *147*
3:1, *244, 277*
3:2, *244*
3:3, *234*
3:6, *147, 234*
3:8, *137, 179, 277*
3:12, *150, 169, 277*
3:14, *230*
3:17, *137*
3:18, *150*
3:19, *147, 159, 282*
3:20, *147, 282*
3:21, *147*
4:1, *227*
4:2, *207*
4:3, *203*
4:5, *227*
4:8, *226, 227*
4:10, *244*
4:12, *277*
4:15, *216, 277*
4:20, *133, 147, 149*
4:21, *147, 282*
4:22, *99, 142, 148, 151, 167, 218*
4:23, *148, 149*

4:24, *148, 149*
4:30, *207*
4:31, *28*
5:1, *150*
5:3, *150*
5:4, *150*
5:5, *153*
6:1, *159*
6:8, *266*
7-12, *147*
7:1, *143*
7:3, *226*
7:4, *123*
7:9, *147, 150, 203*
7:11, *157*
7:14, *211*
7:15, *203*
7:17, *150, 203*
7:20, *175*
7:21, *175*
7:22, *157, 203*
8:2, *203*
8:5, *175*
8:7, *157, 203*
8:15, *211*
8:16, *175*
8:18, *157, 203*
8:24, *211*
8:27, *150*
8:32, *211*
9:3, *211*
9:7, *211*
9:11, *203*
9:15, *282*
9:18, *215*
9:23, *175*
9:29, *240*
10:5, *211*
10:13, *175*
10:15, *211*
11-13, *149*
11:1, *149*
11:5, *149*
11:6, *149*
11:7, *149*
11:8, *150*

12, *90, 145, 146, 147, 150, 151, 171, 197, 198, 235, 246, 262*
12-13, *155*
12:1, *175*
12:2, *150, 196, 273*
12:3, *90, 150, 152, 193, 203*
12:5, *151*
12:6, *151, 154*
12:7, *150, 151, 155*
12:8, *151, 152*
12:9, *153*
12:10, *153*
12:12, *90, 150, 151, 175*
12:13, *150*
12:14, *152, 197*
12:15, *153, 154*
12:16, *197*
12:22, *152, 155*
12:26, *150, 155*
12:30, *156*
12:31, *150*
12:33, *150, 153*
12:40, *28*
12:48, *149*
12:49, *27, 155*
13:2, *151*
13:5, *137*
13:8, *155*
13:9, *155, 159*
13:11, *92*
13:12, *151*
13:16, *155*
13:17, *164, 283*
13:19, *232*
14, *158, 159*
14:2, *156*
14:4, *156*
14:8, *174*
14:9, *133, 250*
14:13, *156, 289*
14:16, *159, 175, 243*
14:17, *156*
14:21, *156, 159*
14:23, *133*
14:26, *159*
14:29, *162*

14:30, *156*
14:31, *3, 28, 159, 203, 245, 277, 282, 283*
15, *160, 185, 209*
15:1, *109, 117, 133, 146, 156, 157, 158, 159, 160, 161, 163, 167, 169, 203, 208, 212, 213, 224, 229, 247, 252, 268, 277, 278, 281, 282*
15:1-18, *32*
15:2, *157, 282*
15:3, *159, 283*
15:4, *158, 162, 167, 250*
15:6, *158, 159, 250*
15:7, *158, 258*
15:8, *161, 162, 163, 188, 217*
15:9, *158, 159, 162, 250*
15:10, *162, 188*
15:11, *162, 250, 266*
15:12, *159, 250*
15:13, *158, 161, 162, 163, 165, 166, 169*
15:14, *159, 160, 161, 162, 163, 164, 165, 167, 168*
15:15, *164, 165, 201*
15:16, *159, 162, 165, 250*
15:17, *25, 117, 158, 159, 165, 166, 185, 186, 215, 250, 264*
15:18, *146, 159, 160, 163, 164, 166, 167*
15:20, *200, 237, 238*
15:22, *171, 277, 283*
15:22-17:7, *200, 277, 281*
15:22-17:16, *171*
15:22-18:27, *271*
15:23, *153, 200*
15:24, *187, 277, 278*
15:25, *231, 277, 278, 283*
15:26, *206, 278, 280, 283*
15:26-17:7, *202*
15:27, *171*
16, *153, 171, 172, 193, 198*
16-17, *278*
16:2, *187, 227, 278*
16:3, *153, 278, 283*

16:4, *171, 172, 202, 278, 283*
16:7, *187, 278*
16:10, *279*
16:13, *172*
16:15, *172*
16:16, *153*
16:19, *153, 278*
16:20, *284*
16:23, *153, 272*
16:27, *284*
17, *204, 205*
17:1, *171, 174, 175, 176, 177, 178, 204, 208, 278, 279, 283*
17:2, *278*
17:4, *175, 181, 278*
17:5, *175, 264, 278*
17:6, *174, 175, 176, 177, 178, 179, 180, 181, 182, 198, 208, 212, 279*
17:7, *176, 180, 278*
17:8, *171, 204, 222*
17:9, *205*
17:11, *205*
17:12, *205, 245*
17:14, *222, 250*
17:15, *205, 208, 283*
18, *171, 227, 231, 279*
18:1, *81*
18:3, *81*
18:4, *81*
18:5, *279*
18:10, *81*
18:13, *231*
18:14, *245*
18:15, *231*
18:16, *231*
18:17, *245*
18:21, *231*
19, *187*
19:1, *171, 271, 273, 279*
19:4, *178, 283*
19:5, *280*
19:6, *82, 265*
19:8, *283*
19:9, *28, 245, 283*
19:10, *279*

19:16, *279*
20, *33, 270, 271*
20:1, *281*
20:2, *150*
20:3, *38, 96, 97*
20:4, *273, 281*
20:5, *96*
20:9, *185*
20:14, *271*
20:17, *38*
20:18, *230, 273, 279, 280*
20:19, *280, 283*
20:20, *280*
20:21, *279, 280*
21:2, *147, 271*
21:6, *155*
22:21, *73*
23:4, *122*
23:5, *130*
23:14, *212*
23:17, *212*
23:18, *154*
23:22, *76*
23:23, *96*
23:25, *96*
23:31, *164*
24:3, *283*
24:7, *283*
24:12, *155*
24:13, *243*
25:7, *36*
25:8, *273*
25:9, *37, 184*
25:11, *36*
25:17, *36*
25:18, *36*
25:31, *36*
25:40, *37, 184*
26:20, *63*
26:26, *63*
26:30, *126*
28:1, *189*
28:2, *189*
28:3, *187, 188*
28:9, *36*
28:38, *194*
28:42, *58*
28:43, *190*

29, *153*
29:1, *151*
29:7, *104, 105*
29:14, *196*
29:17, *152*
29:18, *88, 94*
29:41, *94*
30:18, *37*
30:20, *191*
30:21, *73*
31:1, *170, 185*
31:2, *182, 183, 185, 198, 251*
31:3, *183, 185, 187, 188*
31:4, *184*
31:5, *185*
31:6, *188, 189, 265*
31:7, *184*
31:14, *185*
31:18, *155*
32, *184, 197, 273, 274, 279, 280*
32:1, *180, 187, 188, 231, 274, 281, 283*
32:7, *180*
32:8, *123*
32:10, *5, 280*
32:11, *159, 180, 231, 268, 280*
32:13, *72, 76*
32:14, *180*
32:19, *180*
32:20, *180*
32:26, *228*
32:33, *180*
32:34, *180*
32:35, *180, 281*
33, *182*
33–34, *244*
33:1, *92*
33:2, *180*
33:3, *123*
33:4, *180*
33:7, *180, 181, 204, 244*
33:9, *197*
33:11, *197, 234, 243, 285*
33:13, *180*
33:14, *180, 230*

33:16, *180*
33:17, *182*
33:18, *180, 182, 183*
33:18–34:8, *243*
33:19, *180, 183, 198*
33:20, *180, 181*
33:21, *178, 180, 181, 208, 225*
33:22, *182*
33:23, *180*
34, *6*
34:1, *180*
34:5, *180, 183, 198*
34:8, *225*
34:9, *180*
34:29, *244, 280*
34:30, *280*
34:33, *280, 281*
34:34, *244*
35:5, *189*
35:10, *189*
35:21, *188, 189*
35:22, *189*
35:25, *189*
35:27, *190*
35:30, *182, 183*
35:30–36:1, *183*
35:31, *187, 188*
35:32, *184*
35:34, *143, 186, 188*
36:1, *188*
36:2, *189*
36:3, *190*
36:4, *190*
36:5, *190*
36:6, *240*
36:8, *189*
37:1, *188*
38:22, *183, 188, 189*
39:1, *188, 189*
39:32, *185, 187, 188*
39:33, *189*
39:42, *189*
39:43, *185, 189*
40:1, *187*
40:2, *126*
40:18, *126*

40:33, *185*
40:34, *185*

Leviticus
1–7, *192*
1–16, *153, 154, 191, 192, 193, 197*
1:2, *197*
1:3, *151*
1:8, *152*
1:9, *94*
1:10, *151*
1:13, *94*
2:2, *94*
2:11, *154*
4:3, *152*
4:5, *153*
4:8, *152*
4:12, *196*
4:13, *152*
4:21, *196*
5:2, *154*
5:4, *197*
5:6, *151, 152, 197*
6:3, *197*
6:9, *27*
6:17, *154*
6:25, *153*
7:13, *154*
7:18, *154*
7:20, *154*
8, *153*
8–9, *274*
8:12, *104, 105*
8:17, *196*
8:18, *88*
9:1, *193*
9:2, *193*
9:4, *88, 193*
9:6, *193*
9:8, *193*
9:11, *196*
9:22, *81*
9:23, *193*
10, *191, 274*
10–15, *191, 192*
10:1, *190, 197, 274, 279*
10:3, *191*

10:8, *190*
10:9, *191*
10:10, *57, 191*
10:11, *144, 186*
11, *57, 154, 191*
11–13, *58*
11–15, *57, 191, 196*
11:4, *154*
11:24, *196*
11:29, *203*
11:37, *43*
11:41, *39, 57*
11:42, *57, 58*
11:43, *57*
11:44, *191*
11:46, *39*
11:47, *191*
12:2, *58*
12:4, *196*
13:2, *58, 197*
13:4, *196*
13:6, *58*
13:9, *197*
13:13, *58*
13:45, *196*
13:46, *58*
13:59, *191*
14:2, *194*
14:4, *194*
14:5, *194*
14:6, *194*
14:34, *191*
14:49, *195*
14:54, *191*
14:57, *144, 186*
15:31, *191*
16, *190, 191, 192, 193, 194, 195, 196, 197, 198*
16:1, *190*
16:2, *88, 193, 197, 198*
16:3, *193*
16:5, *193, 194*
16:6, *192*
16:7, *194*
16:8, *194*
16:9, *194*
16:10, *194*
16:11, *192*

16:13, *197*
16:16, *192*
16:17, *192, 197*
16:18, *192*
16:20, *192, 206*
16:21, *194, 195, 245*
16:22, *194, 196, 208*
16:24, *192*
16:26, *194*
16:27, *196*
16:29, *196, 197*
16:30, *192, 197*
16:31, *197*
16:33, *192*
16:34, *192*
17–26, *192*
17:3, *274*
17:7, *187, 194, 240, 274*
18:5, *29, 197, 207*
18:8, *154*
18:27, *154*
19:18, *24*
19:23, *154*
20:2, *88, 89*
20:20, *93*
21:6, *169*
21:8, *169*
21:10, *104*
21:17, *169*
21:23, *191*
23:17, *154*
24:10, *274*
24:11, *188, 265*
24:14, *196*
24:23, *196*
25:55, *97*
26:1, *166*
26:3, *286*
26:12, *36*
26:16, *43*
26:30, *166*
27:30, *43*

Numbers
1:19, *279*
1:54, *279*
2:34, *279*
3:7, *36*

3:38, *36*
3:42, *279*
3:51, *279*
4:49, *279*
5:3, *196*
5:4, *279*
6, *191*
6:23, *81*
9:11, *153*
10, *187*
10:10, *271*
10:11, *171, 271*
11, *172, 193, 200*
11–20, *171, 200*
11:1, *281*
11:3, *202*
11:4, *171, 281*
11:6, *202*
11:9, *172*
11:11, *231, 245*
11:12, *152*
11:17, *184, 188, 242, 243*
11:25, *188, 237, 242, 243*
11:28, *243*
11:29, *237, 242, 275*
11:33, *281*
12:1, *227, 234, 235*
12:2, *202*
12:4, *234*
12:6, *25, 232, 234*
12:7, *234*
12:8, *234*
13:8, *184*
13:16, *184, 243*
14, *200*
14:2, *187*
14:4, *232*
14:9, *156*
14:11, *28, 204, 213, 248, 274*
14:12, *5, 281*
14:13, *231, 268*
14:21, *92, 185, 248*
14:25, *202*
14:28, *92, 216*
14:29, *5*
14:32, *213*
14:37, *281*

14:40, *202*
14:43, *204*
14:45, *202*
15:11, *197*
15:30, *5, 174*
15:35, *196*
16:3, *73, 227*
16:46, *281*
17:10, *277*
18:5, *240*
18:22, *240*
20, *200*
20–21, *200, 204*
20–24, *205*
20:1, *171, 177, 200, 204, 208*
20:2, *174*
20:8, *175, 178, 179, 181, 264*
20:10, *200*
20:11, *37, 174*
20:12, *28, 200, 245*
20:14, *200, 210, 221*
20:17, *208*
20:18, *165*
20:23, *200*
21, *200, 201, 202, 205, 222*
21–24, *201, 202, 210, 222*
21–36, *203, 212*
21:1, *165, 200, 201, 202, 204, 210*
21:3, *202*
21:4, *47, 54, 200, 202, 203, 205, 210*
21:5, *202*
21:6, *201, 202, 203, 207, 249*
21:7, *201, 203, 204, 206, 207, 215*
21:8, *203, 204, 205, 207, 210, 216*
21:9, *201, 203, 204*
21:10, *209*
21:11, *201*
21:12, *208*
21:13, *201*
21:14, *25, 208*
21:15, *201*

21:16, *171, 208, 209, 263, 264*
21:17, *208, 209, 264*
21:18, *132, 208, 209, 263*
21:20, *201*
21:21, *201, 210*
21:22, *208*
21:26, *201*
21:28, *201*
21:33, *178, 201, 210*
22, *212, 226*
22–24, *200, 201, 202, 208, 210, 211, 212, 219, 222*
22:2, *210*
22:3, *42, 165, 202, 211*
22:3-6, *77*
22:4, *165, 211, 215*
22:5, *209, 211*
22:6, *76, 202, 211, 212*
22:7, *226*
22:8, *209, 226*
22:11, *211*
22:12, *49, 76, 202, 213*
22:13, *209, 226*
22:15, *211*
22:17, *209, 211*
22:19, *226*
22:20, *226*
22:22, *133, 210, 211*
22:23, *212, 221*
22:25, *221*
22:26, *211*
22:27, *130, 221*
22:27–23:6, *211*
22:28, *212*
22:31, *212, 216*
22:32, *210, 212*
22:35, *211, 216*
22:37, *211*
22:38, *211, 216*
22:41, *209, 213, 214, 216*
23–24, *160, 178, 209, 224, 249, 267*
23:5, *211, 216*
23:7, *76, 109, 202, 209, 213, 216, 247*
23:7-10, *32*
23:8, *211, 213, 214*

23:9, *178, 213, 214, 215, 217, 221, 258, 261*
23:10, *211, 213, 214, 222, 266*
23:11, *202, 214*
23:12, *211, 216*
23:13, *209, 211, 213, 214, 216*
23:16, *211, 216*
23:18, *209, 214*
23:18-24, *32*
23:19, *211, 214, 229*
23:20, *202*
23:21, *214, 216, 218, 221*
23:22, *161, 215, 218, 224, 259*
23:23, *160, 201, 210, 213, 215, 226, 250, 282*
23:24, *124, 138, 211, 215, 216, 217, 218, 220, 222, 250, 260, 265*
23:25, *202, 216*
23:27, *209, 216*
24, *167, 168, 169, 185, 199, 200, 222, 229, 236, 247, 251, 270, 289*
24:1, *201, 202, 210, 211, 213, 216, 226, 228*
24:2, *223, 261*
24:3, *209, 216, 221*
24:3-9, *32*
24:4, *212, 234*
24:5, *160, 217, 221*
24:5-9, *218*
24:6, *185, 209, 214, 217*
24:7, *109, 145, 156, 160, 199, 205, 211, 214, 215, 217, 218, 219, 220, 221, 224, 235, 268, 286*
24:7-9, *32, 77*
24:8, *53, 138, 160, 161, 163, 168, 211, 215, 218, 220, 223, 224, 226, 229, 235, 244, 246, 250, 251, 254, 256, 257, 258, 261, 265, 268*
24:9, *9, 71, 76, 97, 125, 129, 130, 152, 202,*

209, 212, 213, 214,
215, 218, 219, 220, 221,
223, 229, 236, 260, 261,
275
24:10, *211, 212, 214, 221*
24:11, *211, 221*
24:13, *211*
24:14, *32, 46, 110, 111, 113,
156, 161, 204, 209, 216,
221, 245, 264, 268*
24:15, *209*
24:15-24, *32*
24:16, *212, 234, 251*
24:17, *41, 47, 49, 53, 54,
58, 70, 98, 122, 132,
157, 158, 160, 165, 172,
201, 204, 205, 209, 210,
212, 213, 216, 218, 221,
223, 229, 250, 251, 256,
258, 260, 266, 267*
24:17-19, *32*
24:18, *46, 53, 157, 221,
222*
24:19, *222*
24:20, *114, 204, 209, 222*
24:21, *165, 178, 179*
24:22, *222*
24:23, *160, 222*
24:24, *222*
24:25, *222*
25, *226*
25:11, *5, 281*
26:10, *205*
27:12, *200*
27:14, *245*
27:15, *242, 243*
27:17, *184*
27:18, *184, 188, 242, 243*
27:20, *242, 243*
27:21, *184, 243*
30:14, *126*
31:8, *209*
31:16, *211, 226*
32, *262*
32:2, *263*
32:10, *92*
32:14, *239*
32:25, *263*

33:3, *174*
36:157, *212*

Deuteronomy
1–5, *155*
1–21:9, *226, 241*
1:5, *209*
1:8, *92*
1:15, *227*
1:31, *99*
1:34, *92*
1:39, *38*
1:45, *202*
2–3, *201*
2:14, *162*
2:25, *165*
3:26, *240*
4:1, *227*
4:6, *276*
4:19, *96*
4:20, *203*
4:21, *92*
4:24, *249*
4:25, *57, 249, 274*
4:26, *274*
4:27, *96*
4:29, *19, 208, 244*
4:30, *110, 111, 113, 117*
4:34, *159, 226*
4:37, *73*
5, *230*
5:1, *227*
5:4, *273, 279*
5:5, *230, 280*
5:7, *38, 96*
5:9, *249*
5:15, *153*
5:21, *38*
5:24, *230, 280*
5:27, *230, 280*
5:28, *230, 280*
5:29, *230, 276*
6:4, *91, 227*
6:5, *24, 155, 226, 248*
6:6, *155*
6:7, *30, 155*
6:8, *155*
6:9, *155*

6:10, *92*
6:11, *181*
6:12, *155*
6:13, *96*
6:15, *249*
6:16, *279*
6:20, *155*
6:22, *226*
7:1, *248*
7:9, *173*
7:19, *226*
8, *178*
8:2, *155, 283*
8:3, *171, 172*
8:7, *178*
8:9, *181, 207*
8:10, *249*
8:15, *47, 174, 178, 182,
203, 249*
8:16, *172*
8:19, *96*
9:1, *227*
9:3, *249*
9:5, *126*
9:6, *123*
9:13, *123*
9:19, *202*
9:21, *230*
10:8, *228*
10:9, *228*
10:10, *202*
10:15, *73*
10:16, *240*
11:5, *155*
11:12, *114*
11:13, *155*
11:16, *96*
11:18, *155*
11:20, *155*
12, *73, 225*
12:5, *88, 225*
12:7, *225*
12:11, *88, 225*
12:12, *228*
12:14, *225*
12:18, *225*
12:19, *228*
12:21, *88, 225*

12:26, *225*
13, *227*
13–18, *225*
13:1, *224, 225, 226, 227, 228, 236, 237*
13:2, *225, 227, 236*
13:3, *226, 227, 237*
13:5, *225, 227*
13:6, *227*
13:9, *227*
13:12, *227*
13:14, *227*
13:15, *230*
13:17, *240*
14:22, *43*
14:24, *88*
14:27, *228*
16, *231*
16:3, *153*
16:18, *227, 229*
16:18–18:8, *227*
16:21, *227*
17:2, *227*
17:3, *96*
17:4, *227, 230*
17:6, *249*
17:7, *227*
17:8, *228*
17:9, *228*
17:10, *144*
17:12, *228*
17:13, *240*
17:14, *228, 229, 234, 257*
17:15, *228, 235*
17:18, *30, 65, 83, 228*
17:20, *235*
18, *199, 230, 236, 241, 270, 289*
18:1, *228*
18:5, *228, 230*
18:9, *224, 225, 227, 228*
18:10, *215, 226, 228*
18:13, *151*
18:15, *1, 4, 70, 117, 129, 146, 161, 163, 168, 211, 224, 227, 228, 229, 230, 232, 233, 234, 235,*
236, 237, 241, 242, 243, 245, 246, 247, 251, 286
18:16, *230, 233*
18:17, *230, 231, 280*
18:17-18, *230*
18:18, *117, 129, 146, 161, 168, 211, 216, 224, 227, 228, 229, 230, 234, 235, 236, 241, 242, 243, 244, 245, 246*
18:19, *236*
18:20, *228, 236, 237*
18:22, *225, 236, 237*
19:15, *249*
19:18, *230*
19:20, *240*
20:2, *228*
21:10–34:12, *241, 255, 256, 261, 262, 263*
21:17, *262*
21:23, *29*
22:4, *127*
22:26, *53*
23:3, *24*
23:5, *209, 211*
23:10, *196*
24:7, *48*
25:5, *52*
26:5, *77*
26:7, *202*
27–28, *248*
27:8, *209, 230*
27:9, *228*
27:26, *5, 29, 275*
28, *166, 249, 274*
28:1, *286*
28:9, *92*
28:12, *92*
28:15, *249*
28:17, *249*
28:22, *250*
28:25, *250*
28:45, *250*
28:62, *77*
28:63, *248*
28:64, *165*
28:68, *166, 240*

29:4, *213, 230, 248, 274, 276*
29:25, *96*
30:1, *248, 286*
30:3, *248*
30:6, *117, 248, 276, 285*
30:7, *248*
30:11, *248*
30:14, *155*
30:17, *96*
30:19, *249*
31–32, *248*
31:2, *248*
31:3, *184*
31:14, *253*
31:16, *248, 274*
31:17, *248, 249, 268*
31:19, *216, 248, 249*
31:20, *178, 249, 251*
31:21, *47, 68, 249, 268*
31:22, *249*
31:24, *25*
31:26, *248, 249*
31:27, *249, 274*
31:28, *221, 249, 253, 254, 264*
31:29, *32, 110, 111, 113, 156, 247, 249, 251, 252, 253, 257, 268*
32, *177, 178, 179, 182, 247, 250, 257, 258, 259*
32–33, *113, 158, 160, 172, 209, 247, 249, 257, 267, 268*
32:1, *109, 248, 249, 250, 252, 268*
32:1-43, *32*
32:2, *172, 217*
32:4, *151, 160, 177, 179, 181, 208, 215, 250, 251*
32:6, *266*
32:8, *251*
32:9, *178, 264*
32:10, *177, 178*
32:11, *126, 178*
32:12, *179, 282*
32:13, *177, 178, 179, 182, 208, 251*

32:14, *178*
32:15, *179, 208, 251, 266*
32:18, *179, 182, 251*
32:20, *249, 266*
32:21, *249*
32:22, *249*
32:23, *249, 268*
32:24, *55, 249*
32:25, *152*
32:26, *160, 250, 266, 268*
32:27, *174, 215, 250, 251, 258, 266*
32:29, *276*
32:30, *179, 250*
32:31, *41, 179, 251*
32:32, *153*
32:33, *55*
32:35, *251*
32:36, *250, 268, 269*
32:37, *179, 250*
32:39, *250, 251, 258, 268*
32:40, *92, 250, 251*
32:41, *250, 251, 256*
32:42, *158, 250, 264, 266*
32:43, *20, 58, 197, 220, 250, 251, 252, 256, 258, 259, 268, 269, 275*
33, *199, 247, 252, 253, 255, 257, 258, 259, 260, 263, 264, 266, 267, 268, 270, 286, 289*
33:1, *247, 253, 254, 258*
33:2, *28, 66, 264, 266, 267*
33:2-29, *32*
33:3, *258, 269*
33:4, *263, 264, 266*
33:5, *208, 231, 254, 263, 264, 265, 266*
33:6, *253, 254, 258*
33:7, *32, 109, 132, 156, 160, 202, 236, 247, 251, 253, 254, 255, 256, 257, 265, 266, 268*
33:8, *258, 259*
33:11, *53, 215, 258, 259*
33:12, *254, 258, 259, 261*
33:13, *95, 172, 254, 255, 259*
33:16, *254, 255, 266*

33:17, *254, 255, 259, 260*
33:18, *259, 260*
33:19, *258, 259, 262, 264, 269*
33:20, *260, 261, 262, 263, 264, 265, 268*
33:21, *114, 208, 261, 262, 263, 264, 265*
33:22, *260, 265, 268*
33:23, *254, 265, 266*
33:26, *266*
33:27, *172, 266, 269*
33:28, *95, 172, 213, 258, 261, 267, 269*
33:29, *54, 172, 266, 267, 269*
34, *26, 114, 236, 241, 247, 270*
34:5, *253*
34:8, *161*
34:9, *184, 188, 242, 243*
34:10, *25, 224, 226, 235, 237, 238, 240, 241, 243, 244, 245, 246, 247, 268*
34:11, *235, 243, 244*

Joshua
1:1, *243*
1:2, *76*
1:3, *80*
1:5, *242*
1:7, *25, 27, 243*
1:8, *30, 65, 155, 287*
1:17, *242*
2:9, *158, 164*
2:11, *164, 239*
2:24, *164*
3:1, *164*
4:1, *162*
4:9, *126*
4:14, *242*
4:22, *158*
4:23, *242*
5:1, *164, 239*
5:12, *171, 239*
5:13, *212*
9:1, *239*
9:4, *209*

10:24, *123*
11:6, *215*
11:15, *243*
13:1, *164*
13:2, *164*
13:13, *164*
15:63, *164*
16:10, *164, 258*
17:12, *164*
23:7, *96*

Judges
1:19, *164*
1:34, *188, 265*
2:11, *96*
2:14, *239*
2:16, *126*
3:10, *231*
3:15, *253*
3:31, *164*
4–5, *51, 53*
4:4, *238*
4:8-9, *51*
4:17, *52*
5, *159*
5:2, *159*
5:4, *267*
5:5, *217*
5:9, *263*
5:12, *126*
5:14, *132, 253, 263*
5:25, *52*
5:26, *159*
5:27, *130*
5:31, *159*
6:8, *238*
8:23, *64, 163*
10:2, *231*
10:6, *164*
13:1, *252*
13:5, *255*
13:6, *238*
13:7, *255*
13:8, *238*
13:21, *239*
13:23, *215*
17:6, *231*
20:1, *80*

21:22, *215*
21:25, *231*

Ruth
1:1, *231*
2:5, *52*
4:11, *52, 63*
4:12, *52*
4:17, *52*
4:18, *81*

1 Samuel
1:17, *239*
1:18, *239*
1:23, *126*
2:8, *73*
3:14, *5*
3:20, *80*
7:13, *239*
8:5, *231*
8:7, *163*
8:15, *43*
10–14, *253*
10:1, *104, 105*
12:12, *250*
13:13, *217*
15, *217*
16:1, *262*
17:5, *206*
18:16, *184*
24, *106*
26, *106*
26:12, *63*
27:4, *239*
28:15, *239*
30:8, *257*

2 Samuel
2:28, *239*
3:11, *239*
3:27, *53*
7, *187*
7:8, *98*
7:9, *45, 69*
7:10, *45, 165, 217*
7:11, *52*
7:12, *42, 44, 45, 91, 129, 152, 185, 229*
7:12-14, *43*
7:13, *44, 72, 83, 185, 187*
7:14, *99*
7:16, *83*
7:17, *45*
7:19, *93*
8, *115*
8:18, *186*
11–20, *83*
12:10, *115*
12:16, *127*
14:3, *216*
14:19, *216*
22:41, *123*
22:45, *267*
23:1, *209*
23:3, *65, 83, 267*
23:4, *172*
23:5, *45*

1 Kings
2:27, *16*
3:8, *77*
3:9, *231*
4:25, *80*
5:29, *181*
6:5, *63*
6:9, *264*
6:15, *264*
7:3, *264*
7:7, *264*
8:1, *186*
8:51, *203*
9:5, *217*
9:6, *96*
9:9, *96*
9:19, *64*
9:21, *258*
10, *115*
10:10, *239*
11:11, *115*
12:16, *257*
16:31, *96*
16:34, *16*
17–18, *243*
18:36, *243*
19, *244*
19:8, *243*
22:23, *216*

2 Kings
2:7, *243*
2:8, *164*
2:9, *243*
2:11, *243*
2:12, *239*
2:14, *164*
2:15, *243*
2:16, *243*
5:10, *135*
5:12, *135*
5:13, *135*
5:14, *135*
6:23, *239*
6:24, *239*
9:3, *104, 105*
9:6, *104, 105*
12:13, *181*
17:14, *204*
17:17, *215, 226*
17:20, *73*
17:24, *69*
18:4, *207*
19:15, *257*
19:25, *93*
20:13, *64*
23:25, *241*
24:7, *239*
25:5, *250*

1 Chronicles
17:9, *165*
17:10, *52*
17:11, *42, 44, 45, 129, 152, 164, 229*
17:11-13, *43*
17:12, *45*
17:14, *164*
17:15, *45*
17:17, *93*
19:19, *239*
21:16, *212*
22:2, *181*
22:8, *186*
28:3, *186*

Scripture Index

28:5, *164*
29:12, *64*
29:23, *164*

2 Chronicles
1:10, *184*
2:2, *181*
2:18, *181*
7:3, *115*
8:6, *64*
9:4, *239*
13:14, *257*
13:20, *239*
14:11, *257*
18:22, *216*
20:5, *257*
20:6, *64*
20:33, *238*
25:4, *24*
30:1, *257*

Ezra
1:5, *126*
5:1, *240*
8:17, *216*

Nehemiah
2:12, *42*
8:1, *24*
9:2, *73*
9:7, *69*
9:25, *181*
13:1, *24*

Esther
3, *217*

Job
1–2, *210*
1:1, *280*
2:3, *137*
3:6, *62*
3:8, *126*
4:4, *127*
4:8, *214*
4:13, *63*
5:25, *72*
8:7, *114*

13:26, *153*
14:12, *126*
15:35, *214*
16:12, *123*
19:24, *181*
20:14, *153*
20:16, *55*
21:8, *72*
28:9, *182*
32:15, *239*
33:15, *63*
38–41, *203*
39:3, *130*
41:1, *126*
41:10, *126*
42:12, *114*
42:16, *152*

Psalms
1–2, *163*
1–50, *59, 99*
1–59, *59*
1:2, *27, 277, 287*
2, *99*
2:1, *220*
2:2, *161*
2:6, *83, 163, 185*
2:7, *45, 99, 131, 148*
2:8, *47, 74, 254, 264*
2:9, *207*
3:5, *63*
3:8, *53*
4:5, *259*
4:8, *63*
7:5, *250*
7:7, *126*
7:14, *214*
8, *59*
8:4, *59*
8:5, *59*
8:6, *54, 59, 64*
10:7, *214*
13:3, *63, 138*
14:1, *48*
14:2, *49*
17:8, *183*
18:2, *181*
18:7, *267*

18:16, *162*
18:42, *254*
18:44, *267*
21:6, *59*
21:17, *208*
22:1, *196, 257*
22:29, *96, 97*
22:31, *264*
23:4, *183*
23:5, *250*
27:5, *181*
28:1, *128*
28:7, *266*
30:4, *128*
31:2, *181*
32:8, *277*
32:9, *133*
33:6, *184*
33:11, *184*
33:20, *266*
36:5, *173*
36:8, *183*
37:25, *72*
40:3, *128, 216*
40:10, *173*
44:23, *126*
45:2, *59*
46:5, *37*
49:10, *124*
50:1, *267*
50:2, *59, 99*
51:16, *5*
51:18, *52*
51:19, *259*
53:2, *49*
58:3, *41*
58:4, *55*
59:15, *277*
60:7, *263*
60:9, *132*
60:12, *157*
61:3, *106*
62:2, *181*
66:1, *163*
66:3, *267*
66:5, *158*
66:6, *163*
66:7, *163*

67, 163
68:27, 253
71:3, 181
72, 97, 98
72:11, 97, 98
72:17, 45, 97, 98, 173
72:19, 185
73:20, 126
74:3, 241
74:9, 241
74:12, 241
74:13, 53, 54, 58, 158
74:15, 37
74:20, 242
76:2, 83
77, 162
77:14, 158, 162
77:16, 162
78, 7, 27, 179
78:1, 27
78:13, 162
78:15, 37, 177, 179
78:16, 37
78:20, 37, 179
78:22, 204
78:24, 172
78:32, 204
78:51, 262
81:6, 259
81:15, 267
84:1, 217
88:4, 128
88:5, 239
88:9, 138
88:11, 173
89, 173, 255
89:1, 173
89:13, 174
89:18, 266
89:26, 262
89:27, 148
89:47, 49, 173
89:48, 222
89:52, 45
90, 255
90:2, 49
90:3, 47
90:7, 47

90:10, 214
91:1, 183
91:13, 54
92:2, 173
93–100, 173
93:1, 163
95:3, 163
95:6, 96
96, 282
96:5, 275
96:10, 163, 231
96:13, 231
96:98, 282
96:149, 282
97:1, 163, 231
97:5, 267
97:7, 96
98:3, 173
99:1, 165, 185
99:2, 185
99:9, 185
100:5, 173
102:16, 52, 64
102:28, 72
103:12, 47, 194
103:22, 64
104:22, 130
105:36, 262
105:41, 37, 179
106:9, 158
106:27, 73
107, 246
107:16, 207
108:2, 126
108:8, 263
108:13, 157
110, 83, 85, 187
110:1, 46, 54, 161, 185, 186
110:2, 83
110:4, 45, 58, 78, 83, 155, 187
110:6, 53, 54, 201
112:2, 72
113:7, 127
114:2, 64
114:8, 182
115:9, 266

118, 161
118:14, 157
118:15, 157
118:22, 157, 164
119:18, 33, 287
125:1, 185
127:1, 52
132:1, 202
133:1, 217, 264
133:3, 95, 173
136:8, 64
136:12, 159
136:14, 162
138:1, 115
140:3, 41, 48, 55
144:5, 267
144:7, 162
145:13, 64
146–150, 163
146:10, 163, 166, 185
147:2, 52, 64

Proverbs
1:1, 209
1:7, 38, 189, 262
1:8, 27
1:12, 128
2:6, 38
3:1, 189
3:5, 189
3:7, 280
3:13, 277
3:18, 174
3:19, 184
6:1, 140
7:1, 189
8:22, 184, 262
9:5, 169, 174
10:1, 179, 209
10:8, 189
11:15, 140
11:29, 189
14:12, 38
16:21, 189
16:23, 189
18:10, 106
18:15, 189
19:15, 63

20:5, *73*
21:25, *132*
21:27, *132*
31:17, *183*
32:2, *158*
33:22, *239*
34:23, *129, 229*
35:15, *267*
36:25, *58, 197, 251*
36:26, *184*
37:22, *70*
38–39, *110*
38:16, *111, 113, 217*
38:17, *217*
41:5, *64*
44:21, *191*
47:1, *37, 264*

Daniel
2, *164*
2:28, *111, 113, 164*
2:34, *166*
2:44, *164*
2:45, *166*
4:3, *164*
4:34, *164*
5:4, *166*
5:23, *166*
6:26, *164*
7, *164*
7:7, *81*
7:13, *164*
7:18, *265*
9:2, *19*
9:15, *159*
9:21, *19*
9:24, *194*
9:25, *19*
9:26, *154, 196*
10:14, *111, 113*
11:30, *222*

Hosea
1:10–2:1, *77*
1:11, *70, 76, 225, 245*
2:19, *64*
3:5, *76, 77, 110, 111, 113, 120, 165*

4:9, *265*
6:7, *274*
10:1, *230*
11:1, *142, 218*
11:10, *123*
12:1, *49*
12:13, *225*
13:14, *47*
14:8, *183*

Joel
1:6, *124*
2:1, *165*
2:28, *237, 276*

Amos
2:11, *228*
3:8, *123*
5:2, *127*
5:25, *274*
7:7, *176*
8:14, *188, 265*
9:11, *129, 229*
9:12, *98, 122*
9:13, *137*

Obadiah
1:15, *98*
1:18, *222*
15, *47*
17, *222, 266*
19, *165*
20, *165, 222*

Micah
1:15, *47, 132*
2:13, *165*
3:5, *216*
4:1, *110, 111, 113, 114, 166*
4:8, *64*
5:2, *64*
5:5, *82*
5:8, *54, 265*
5:9, *174*
6:4, *215*
7, *161*
7:3, *230*
7:7, *157, 166, 167*

7:14, *213, 225, 258*
7:17, *39, 249*
7:18, *157, 165, 250*
7:19, *47, 167, 194*

Nahum
2:11, *260*

Habakkuk
1:3, *214*
1:5, *250*
1:6, *126*
2:2, *209*
2:3, *132*
2:14, *185*
3:3, *267*
3:13, *53, 54, 58*

Zephaniah
2:7, *73*

Haggai
1:1, *240*
1:4, *264*
2:7, *81*
2:13, *154*

Zechariah
1:1, *240*
4:6, *186*
6, *45*
6:12, *64, 166, 185, 186*
6:13, *45, 52, 58, 64, 83, 152*
9:6, *165*
9:9, *133*
9:10, *133*
9:13, *126*
10:11, *165*
12:10, *89*
13:7, *175*
14:21, *165*

Malachi
3:2, *222*
4:2, *65, 66, 267*
4:4, *27*
4:5, *222, 241*

Scripture Index

New Testament

Matthew
1–13, *31, 99*
1:1, *45, 186*
1:22, *18*
2:14, *218*
2:15, *18, 99*
2:23, *255*
3:1, *241*
3:3, *19*
3:7, *41*
3:17, *89*
4:3, *60*
4:7, *279*
7:12, *270*
7:28, *31*
11:1, *31*
11:9, *241*
11:14, *241*
12:3, *2, 83*
12:24, *206*
12:34, *41*
13:13, *274*
13:53, *31*
16:18, *63, 166, 190*
19:1, *31*
19:8, *4*
21:2, *133*
22:36, *24*
22:40, *24*
23:33, *41*
23:37, *122*
26:1, *31*
26:2, *145*
26:31, *175*
26:39, *138*
27:29, *194*
28:19, *155*

Mark
1:1, *241*
3:22, *206*
7:13, *4*
11:2, *133*
12:26, *24*
14:1, *145*
14:58, *166*
15:17, *194*

Luke
1:1, *25*
1:72, *242*
2:25, *20*
2:36, *20*
3:7, *41*
4:12, *279*
9:22, *21*
10:18, *40*
10:23, *20*
11:15, *206*
11:18, *206*
13:21, *154*
14:5, *2*
19:30, *133*
20:27, *20*
22:1, *145*
22:3, *40*
23:50, *20*
24:25, *20*
24:44, *21, 27*
24:45, *33, 287*

John
1–10, *100*
1:1, *172*
1:17, *271*
1:29, *145*
1:36, *145*
1:43, *3*
1:45, *3, 20, 26*
1:47, *100*
1:50, *100*
1:51, *100, 102, 104, 200*
2:22, *21*
3:13, *200*
3:14, *4, 200, 205, 207*
4:10, *175*
4:14, *175, 264*
5:5, *1*
5:9, *1*
5:18, *1*
5:24, *50*
5:32, *1*
5:36, *1*
5:37, *1*
5:39, *1, 3*
5:41, *5*
5:45, *1, 3, 5*
5:46, *1, 20, 26, 288*
5:47, *1, 24*
6, *169, 173, 174*
6:5, *173*
6:14, *4*
6:27, *173*
6:32, *169, 173*
6:33, *173, 200*
6:35, *173*
6:38, *200*
6:40, *173*
6:41, *200*
6:47, *173*
6:49, *173*
6:50, *170*
6:51, *173*
6:60, *174*
7:19, *4, 5*
7:23, *2*
7:31, *3*
7:37, *175*
7:40, *3*
7:43, *3*
7:49, *3*
8:44, *49*
8:48, *207*
9:16, *2, 3*
9:22, *2, 4*
9:28, *2*
9:29, *207*
9:31, *2*
9:32, *245*
9:35, *4*
10:11, *173*
10:15, *173*
10:17, *173*
10:18, *173*
10:19, *3*
11:49, *20*
11:51, *20*
12:24, *173*
12:31, *207*
12:32, *136*
12:34, *207*

14:6, *106*
14:12, *189*
15:24, *245*
17:2, *173*
17:3, *3*
18:39, *145*
19:2, *194*
19:5, *194*
19:14, *145*
19:17, *86*
19:34, *175*
19:37, *89*
20:25, *33*
20:26, *33*
20:28, *33*
20:30, *25, 29*
20:31, *1*
21:25, *30*

Acts
2:16, *276*
2:17, *115*
2:24, *129*
2:30, *20*
2:32, *129*
3:15, *129*
3:20, *241*
3:24, *237*
4:10, *129*
5:9, *279*
6:14, *207*
7:38, *271*
7:42, *274*
7:48, *166*
7:53, *28*
9:3, *287*
13:20, *237*
13:34, *129*
13:39, *2*
15:16, *123*
15:21, *2*
16:21, *207*
17:1, *20*
17:2, *2*
17:11, *22*
17:18, *207*
17:28, *49*
17:31, *129*

18:15, *4*
21:21, *207*
23:29, *4*
25:19, *4*
26:8, *129*
26:22, *2, 21, 288*

Romans
1:18, *275*
1:22, *38*
2:15, *28*
2:23, *5*
2:29, *276*
3:9, *5, 48*
3:10, *27, 48*
3:13, *48*
3:19, *5, 27, 28*
3:20, *29*
3:21, *27, 29, 270, 275, 285*
3:25, *136*
3:27, *5*
3:31, *29*
4, *29*
4:13, *75*
4:15, *281*
4:19, *93*
4:24, *129*
5:8, *122*
5:10, *122*
5:12, *56*
5:14, *13, 56, 67*
5:17, *56, 67*
5:20, *29*
5:21, *56, 67*
7:1, *28*
7:6, *188*
7:7, *29*
7:8, *167*
7:13, *281*
8:3, *276*
8:11, *129*
10:2, *5*
10:7, *129*
10:8, *155*
11:7, *274*
11:9, *19*
11:13, *207*
15:2, *190*

16:20, *15, 47, 54, 269*
16:25, *20*
16:26, *20*

1 Corinthians
1:23, *207*
1:24, *174*
1:30, *221*
5, *154*
5–7, *25*
5:1, *154*
5:5, *154*
5:6, *154*
5:7, *145, 152*
6:14, *129*
8:1, *190*
10:1, *13, 170*
10:3, *170*
10:4, *18, 177, 208*
10:11, *93*
13:12, *11*
14:3, *190*
14:12, *63*
15:15, *129*
15:21, *56*

2 Corinthians
1:19, *16*
2:6, *154*
3:6, *188*
4:4, *49*
4:14, *129*
5:1, *166*
11:14, *40*

Galatians
1:1, *129, 130*
2:21, *286*
3:6, *28*
3:8, *28*
3:10, *29*
3:12, *28, 29*
3:17, *28, 271*
3:19, *28, 273*
3:23, *281, 286*
3:24, *285*
4:4, *15, 227*
5:9, *154*
5:18, *188*

Ephesians
1:3, *221*
1:20, *129*
2:1, *49*
2:11, *166*
2:20, *63*
3:3, *19, 20*
3:5, *20*
3:6, *20*
4:29, *190*

Colossians
1:13, *50*
1:21, *122*
1:26, *20*
1:27, *20*
2:11, *166*

1 Thessalonians
5:11, *63, 190*

2 Timothy
2:15, *22*
3:1, *115*
3:16, *26, 30, 65, 238, 247*

Hebrews
1–8, *170*
1:2, *75, 110, 115*
2:1, *279*
2:2, *28*
2:6, *59*
3:2, *187*
3:7, *19*
4:8, *184, 245*
4:9, *185*
7, *78*
7:1, *78*
7:2, *82*
7:4, *80, 81*
7:14, *83*
7:27, *170*
8:5, *190, 289*
9:7, *170, 190*
9:8, *37*
9:11, *166*
9:24, *166*
9:25, *170, 190*
10:1, *170, 171, 190*
10:4, *170*
10:15, *19*
11:8, *95*
11:13, *93*
13:20, *129*

James
1:23, *11*
5:3, *115*

1 Peter
1:10, *20*
2:5, *63*
2:7, *157*

2 Peter
1:20, *12, 19, 26, 29*
2:4, *40*
3:3, *115*
3:16, *22*

1 John
2:2, *136*
2:6, *265*
3:3, *265*
4:18, *285*
5:6, *175*
5:8, *175*

Jude
6, *40*

Revelation
5:6, *136*
5:9, *282*
5:12, *143*
7:9, *190*
7:10, *289*
12:9, *40*
16:13, *203*
17–21, *69*
19:1, *289*

www.ingramcontent.com/pod-product-compliance
Lightning Source LLC
Chambersburg PA
CBHW020109010526
44115CB00008B/760